# Great Truths From Historic Controversies

Edited By Mike Willis

**Truth Magazine Annual Lectures**

**June 22-25, 2009**

ISBN 10: 1-58427-271-6

ISBN 13: 978-158427-271-7

**Guardian of Truth Foundation**
**P.O. Box 9670**
**Bowling Green, Kentucky 42102**
**1-800-428-0121**
**www.truthbooks.net**

# Table of Contents

# Foreword

**Ron Halbrook**

Jesus said, "Ye shall know the truth, and the truth shall make you free" (John 8:32). The truths revealed in God's Word constitute a unified body of truth designed by God for the salvation of the world. There are many threads but the cloth is a seamless whole. At times the whole body of truth has been assailed and rejected by blasphemers, and at times particular truths have been questioned, perverted, or repudiated by men professing to believe the Bible. These lectures on "Great Truths from Historic Controversies" focus mostly on the latter arena, where Satan is perhaps most subtle. In all cases, all the truths constituting the truth of God have emerged from the crucible of controversy intact and undaunted throughout history.

Controversy can be unpleasant and even painful, but it is essential to preserve, protect, and perpetuate truth because Satan is always busy trying to undermine the truth. This is why Jude urgently admonished the brethren "that ye should earnestly contend for the faith which was once delivered unto the saints" (Jude 3).

## The Garden Controversy

Satan initiated the battle over truth in the Garden of Eden by denying God will punish sin and by affirming sin yields great blessings hidden or withheld by God. His first maneuver was simply to question the clarity and definitiveness of the truth revealed by God: "Yea, hath God said, Ye shall not eat of every tree of the garden?" (Gen. 3:2) Then he denied the penalty of sin, claiming, "Ye shall not surely die" (v. 4). Finally, he argued the professed benefits of sin, "For God doth know that in the day ye eat thereof, then your eyes shall be opened, and ye shall be as gods, knowing good and evil" (v. 5).

Eve focused her mind on the seductive lies of Satan rather than on the revealed word of God. She sinned, and Adam sinned with her. They suffered immediate spiritual death in their separation from God, and they suffered gradual physical degeneration and death after their banishment from the Garden (Gen. 3:8, 23).

From that day until this day, the Word of God has been the constant focal point of thousands of historic controversies.

After the historic Garden controversy, Satan initiated a tragic controversy between brothers over how to worship God, resulting in the murder of righteous Abel by Cain. In the process of questioning the truths of God's Word, Satan poisons the minds of people so as to create anger, bitterness, hatred, alienation, character assassination, and, yes, on occasion even murder!

God's people must fight in defense of the truth vigorously but not viciously. We counter false teachers by "speaking the truth in love" (Eph. 4:14-15). John's vigorous defense of the truth was animated by love not malice: "For this is the message that ye heard from the beginning, that we should love one another. Not as Cain, who was of that wicked one, and slew his brother. And wherefore slew he him? Because his own works were evil, and his brother's righteous" (1 John 3:11-12).

### The Master Teacher: Master in Controversy

No truth is sacred to Satan. His mad arrogance drove him to try to seduce even the Son of God. Soon after the baptism of Jesus in water, Satan baptized him in the fiery trial of battle. Jesus did not flinch, not then, not ever. No surrender, no retreat, says the Prince of Peace. "Hence the Prince of Peace never sheathed the sword of the Spirit while he lived. He drew it on the banks of the Jordan and threw the scabbard away" (Alexander Campbell, "Religious Controversy," *Millennial Harbinger* [1830], 41). Thus, he was ready for Satan's onslaught.

Satan met more than his match in Jesus Christ because the Master Teacher was master in controversy. The weapons used by Satan to advance all sins and false doctrines are the lust of the flesh, the lust of the eyes, and the vain pride of life. In a masterful way he combined all three in the temptation of Jesus, but the Master Teacher deflected every blow and destroyed every weapon of Satan one by one. Every blow of Satan was met with the perfectly tempered steel of the sword of truth as Jesus responded simply and confidently to each thrust, "It is written." Having suffered utter and inglorious defeat, "then the devil leaveth him" while "angels came and ministered" unto Jesus (Matt. 4:1-11).

Our King, the Captain of our salvation, leads the armies of God to certain victory under the banner, "It is written." He sends us into battle armed with the loin-girt of truth, the breastplate of righteousness, the footgear of the gospel of peace, the shield of faith, the helmet of salvation, "and the sword of the Spirit, which is the word of God" in order "to stand against the wiles of the devil." Thus armed, we enter and endure the heat of one battle after another—sacrificing blood, toil, sweat, and tears—"and having done all, to stand" victorious with Christ in the end (Eph. 6:10-18).

The Word of God is not some cold academic philosophy, but the truth of God for our salvation which cost the Son of God His very life. As the old covenant was sealed with the blood of animals, how much more is the new covenant, the gospel of Christ, sealed and sanctified by His own precious blood (Heb. 9:13-23). In view of this, those who oppose the truth of His teaching "are the enemies of the cross of Christ" (Phil. 3:18). However unpleasant and painful it may be, we must do battle with those who nullify the truth for which Christ died to save a lost world!

**Historic Controversies of Christ**

Matthew 21-22 records several historic controversies of the Master Teacher involving a wide range of questions and issues.

**1. The Authority Issue (Matt. 21:23-27).** After Jesus accepted praise as the son of David, and after He cleansed the temple, the religious leaders were incensed and demanded to know who gave Him authority to act in such a manner. This really means, "How dare you act without *our* official sanction, and especially how dare you *embarrass us* in the eyes of the people!"

In turn, Jesus asked their assessment of John's baptism, was it "from heaven, or of men?" If they said "from God," Jesus would rebuke their rejection of John. If they said "of men," they would lose respect in the eyes of the people who believed John was sent by God. Knowing that either answer would bring only further embarrassment, they tried to escape the dilemma with the lame response, "We cannot tell." On its very face, this answer only humiliated the proud keepers of official authority. Jesus' point is that He acted on the same authority as John, the authority of God, and the religious leaders could not refute the point.

**2. The Civil Government Issue (Matt. 22:15-22).** Enemies of Jesus who fought each other found common cause in fighting Jesus. The Pharisees and Herodians first flattered Jesus to catch Him off guard, then asked whether it was right to pay taxes to their hated Roman rulers. A "yes" answer could be used by the Pharisees to discredit Jesus to the people, and a "no" answer could be used by the Herodians to have Him arrested for treason. Jesus escaped their trap by teaching that men should give both to God and to Caesar what is due or appropriate. The simple and truthful answer of Jesus exposed His enemies as foolish and inept. They left amazed at His wisdom, frustrated at their own failure, and angry because Jesus had silenced and humiliated them, again (Luke 20:26)!

**3. The Resurrection Issue (Matt. 22:23-33).** The aristocratic Sadducees tried their hand at defeating Jesus by posing what appeared to be a hopelessly tangled hypothetical question about a woman married seven times under the levirate law which perpetuated the family line (Deut. 25:5; Latin *levir*: brother-in-law). They denied the doctrines of the soul and the resurrection. Their question implied these doctrines involve insurmountable obstacles: Whose wife will she be on the resurrection day?

Jesus said the root problem was their ignorance of the Scripture and of God's power. First, there is no marriage in the resurrection. Second, Exodus 3:6 clearly implies the soul survives death to await the resurrection: "I am the God of Abraham, the God of Isaac, and the God of Jacob." God said this to Moses, affirming God's eternal existence and the existence of Abraham, Isaac, and Jacob beyond the grave. What Scripture implies is equivalent to a declaration by God, and these professed teachers of the law should very well have recognized the truth so revealed. Jesus emphatically concluded, "Ye therefore do greatly err" (Mark 12:27).

**4. The Greatest Commandment Issue (Matt. 22:34-40).** Reeling from past defeats and enraged that not even the aristocrats could intimidate Jesus, the Pharisees selected one of their premier lawyers to entangle Jesus. This shrewd fellow queried, "Master, which is the greatest commandment in the law?" Jewish scholars counted 613 separate commandments in the Law of Moses, and it appeared that any answer could provide an opportunity to quibble over other important commands. Jesus went to the foundation of "all the law and the prophets,"citing Deuteronomy 6:4-5 that men should love God first and foremost, and then citing Leviticus 19:18 which teaches "love thy neighbor as thyself." The lawyer could not quibble with these clear and well-known passages. In fact, he was so impressed with this answer that he openly acknowledged its truth, and Jesus pronounced him near to the kingdom of God (Mark 12:34).

**5. The Messianic Issue (Matt. 22:41-46).** In this series of encounters, Jesus had answered all questions, silenced all enemies, and nearly converted a prominent protagonist. With His enemies still at hand and the crowds listening with delight, the Master Teacher went on the offensive by posing a simple question about the Messiah from Scripture, "What think ye of Christ? Whose son is he?" They answered, "The son of David." Citing Psalm 110:1 ("The Lord said unto my lord. . ."), Jesus asked, "If David then call him Lord, how is he his son?" His astute enemies were put to total silence and to humiliating flight.

Did these battles accomplish any lasting good? At the conclusion of this series of controversies, Mark observes, "And the common people heard him gladly" (Mark 12:37). The enemies of Jesus could not destroy the truth he taught, and they would not accept it, and so they devised a plan to murder the messenger. Yet, these historic controversies helped prepare the people for the coming day of Pentecost when 3,000 souls were saved! Yes, controversies conducted in the right spirit with the right focus on truth are essential to the work of saving souls.

### Great Truths from Historic Controversies

The present series of lectures calls attention to great truths which were clarified, defended, and preserved for future generations as a result of historic controversies. A survey of the titles will show that Christ Himself is the central figure in this lectureship, for He is indeed the source of all truth as deity, and the various lectures focus on particular truths He revealed which have been assailed by Satan through the centuries.

Steven Deaton ably traces the controversy surrounding Jesus in the first century as He proved Himself to be the Messiah or Christ of Old Testament promise and hope ("Jesus Is the Christ: Conflict with the Jews"). As the centuries unfolded Satan concentrated his attack on the divine Sonship or deity of Jesus Christ, a crucial battle illuminated by Steven J. Wallace ("Jesus Is the Son of God: The Controversies Over Jesus"). The issues of authority, unity, and creeds are examined in the light of the teaching of Christ and of subsequent history by Ray Warfel, Scott Finley, and Mark Dunigan respectively ("By What Authority?", "That Ye All May Be One: The Efforts to Find a Basis for Unity," and "No Creed But Christ").

The first-century church was plagued with controversies involving stern Judaizers and libertine Gnostics, as we are reminded by Jim Deason and Dan King ("I Came Not to Destroy But to Fulfill: Conflict with the Judaizers" and "Walking in the Light: Conflict with the Gnostics"). In the centuries which followed, apostasies multiplied as the New Testament prophesied, giving rise to arguments over the relationship between faith and works, and to power struggles as papal pretensions developed, each of which is analyzed by Alan Piner and by Greg Litmer ("Faith Without Works Is Dead: The Augustinian Controversy" and "Was Peter the First Pope? Conflict Over Catholicism"). Some recurring errors have developed into theological systems such as premillennialism, Calvinism, and the charismatic movement, and these developments are chronicled and dissected by Keith Greer, Ethan Longhenry, and Danny McKibben respectively ("My Kingdom Is Not of This World: Conflicts over Premillennialism," "Whosoever Will: Conflict over Calvinism," and "We Cannot Deny It: Miracles and the Charismatic Movement").

Joe Price presents an incisive study of a burning question which never grows old and which never ceases to generate controversy: "What Must I Do to be Saved?" Other issues which draw fire century after century are "The All-Sufficiency of Scripture," studied by John Gibson, and the one true church, examined by Justin Monts ("There Is One Body: Conflicts over the Oneness of the Church"). For the last two hundred years brethren pleading for a restoration of New Testament Christianity have been divided over the use of instrumental music in worship and various institutional and centralized programs among the churches, issues reviewed by Charles Willis and Tom Roberts ("In Vain Ye Do Worship Me: Conflicts over Instrumental Music" and "The Pillar and Ground of the Truth: Conflict over Institutionalism").

The concluding lecture brings us back to sit again at the feet of Jesus Christ, the Master Teacher in all situations, with a stirring exhortation by Johnie Edwards entitled "Building on a Rock."

While controversy is essential to the life of truth in a world of sin and error, God's people must not become obsessed with fighting as if we had no other duties in life. Like the Jews rebuilding the wall of Jerusalem in Nehemiah's time, we are building while we are also guarding (Neh. 4:16-18). Like those who carried materials for the wall, we labor with one hand and hold a sword ready in the other. Like those who did the actual building, we wear a sword at our side while we work. As the Jews were ready any moment to respond to the trumpet's call, we too are ready to answer the call to arms when false doctrines and false teachers rise to trouble God's people. All the while, the work of spreading the gospel to the lost and of edifying the saved demands our time, attention, energy, and efforts.

The Guardian of Truth Foundation publishes this presentation of "Great Truths from Historic Controversies" in the hope that it will inform, inspire, warn, equip, and encourage all who read it both now and for many years to come.

February 6, 2009

# Part One
# The Evening Lectures

# Jesus Is The Christ

**Steven Deaton**

The controversy over Jesus started when He was a young boy and will only end when time is no more. Herod, misunderstanding the nature of Jesus' Kingship, sought to put Him to death when He was a baby (Matt. 2:1-18). Early in His public teaching, people were debating the nature of this Man and His doctrine (Mark 1:21-28). He was even rejected by the people of His home town (Luke 4:16-30). Such controversy followed Jesus wherever He went, even into the grave (Matt. 27:62-66). Some sixty years later the storm was still raging as the Roman Empire sought to crush the movement animated and motivated by one simple truth, Jesus is the Christ (Rev. 2:8-11).

There continues to be intense disputation over whether or not Jesus is the Christ. This should not shock or discourage believers. As we will see, Jesus faced sharp opposition to His claims to be the long-awaited Messiah. His apostles took the message into the world and were treated with contempt. Christians of the first century were embroiled in controversy continually as they declared their faith and urged others to believe. It is no different

---

**Steven Deaton** spent four years in the United States Air Force before beginning full-time work as a preacher, passing fourteen years last January. He has labored in Texas and Kentucky in located work and several other states in gospel meetings. Steven writes for *Truth Magazine* and has his own personal web site, *www.PlainFaith.com.* He and his wife, Ashlie, recently celebrated their eighteenth anniversary. They have two children, Hannah and Elijah. He is currently living in Shepherdsville, KY, working with the Hebron Lane church of Christ in a two-preacher arrangement with Ron Halbrook. Steven holds a Bachelor of Arts degree in Speech Communication, has an interest in the internet and new media, and enjoys reading a wide variety of materials.

today. The world has not changed. The truth has not changed. Therefore the controversy has not changed.

We will examine the clash concerning the Messiahship of Jesus, looking at prophecies, what Jesus personally faced, and the resulting consequences. While the religious and secular leaders of the first century rejected Him, the truth was established with certainty (Luke 1:1-4). Certainty, that is, to the opened minded and honest of heart (John 1:46-51; 7:17). And, no matter what men say or do, this truth will not change.

The truth of Jesus is the Christ was hammered out in the midst of extreme contention. The struggle of those who first proclaimed it was great indeed. They sacrificed home and heart; life and limb. If we do not appreciate this great truth and the hard-fought contest from which it was born, we will end up fighting for it again—in the church.

### The Jews As They Were

First century Jews, at least in Jerusalem and especially among the ruling class and religious leaders, were hide-bound to tradition. They had perverted the Law of Moses by adding their regulations and opinions. For instance, when Jesus and His disciples walked through a grain field one Sabbath plucking heads to eat, the Pharisees were beside themselves (Matt. 12:1-8). They believed the disciples were doing something unlawful on the holy day. They were also angered when Jesus healed on the Sabbath (Matt. 12:9-14).

On another occasion, Jesus' disciples did not wash their hands before eating, drawing a rebuke from the Pharisees in the form of a question. "Why do Your disciples transgress the tradition of the elders? For they do not wash their hands when they eat bread?" (Matt. 15:2). To them, it was unacceptable to go against the traditions passed down through the generations. Their standard was a mixture of the Law of Moses along with human wisdom and practices. They simply could not see the purity, goodness, and righteousness of Jesus and His disciples because of their beloved traditions.

The Pharisees, who held great influence among the Jews, were nationalistic. They despised Roman rule and greatly desired to rid themselves of it. This feeling was so deep they demanded a known insurrectionist, murderer, and thief to be released by Pilate (Mark 15:6-11; Luke 23:18, 19; John 18:40). The reason his actions were excused by the Jews, besides wanting Jesus to die, was because his actions were against the Romans.

Ironically, the Pharisees agreed with the less nationalistic Sadducees on getting rid of Jesus because they feared losing power (John 11:47-53). The love of personal power trumped love of nation. The rulers wanted to keep ruling. The set up was nice for them and they did not want to lose it.

Priests, in the sect of the Sadducees, and Pharisees were arrogant snobs for the most part. They looked down on common people as lower class. This is quite evident when officers sent to arrest Jesus returned empty handed, saying, “No man ever spoke like this Man” (John 7:46). The Pharisees replied, “Are you also deceived? Have any of the rulers of the Pharisees believed in Him? But this crowd that does not know the law is accursed” (John 7:47-49). In other words, “The people are too stupid to know any better; we of the Sadducees and Pharisees are more intelligent and informed and reject Him, so should everyone else.”

Jesus did not fit into the mold of the Jewish sects. He did not fit their preconceived idea of a nationalistic Messiah. His refusal to go along with their traditions angered them. His condemnation of their behavior and beliefs infuriated them. And, finally, His direct claim to be God’s Son caused them to snap. Controversy was stirred pretty much whenever Jesus and these Jews met each other. He was unrelenting; they were immovable.

## What Really Stirred The Controversy

There were many different occasions when the Jews were angered by the actions and words of Jesus. On more than one occasion they wanted to dispose of Him, but were either hindered by Him or their fear of the people. In an attempt to counter Jesus’ teaching and influence, the Jews attacked the message, Messenger, and miracles.

In Capernaum Jesus declared a man’s sins forgiven (Mark 2:1-12). The Jews immediately complained to themselves about this stunning declaration, rightly believing only God can forgive sins. The point they missed was Immanuel was with them. He proved, though, by His subsequent actions that He had the power to do the unseen by doing what was seen and readily judged by the eyes of men.

The people of Jesus’ home town of Nazareth did not receive Him. Rather, when He read from the Law and made application of it, they were enraged (Luke 4:16-30). It is interesting that the people gathered in the synagogue “marveled at the gracious words which proceeded out of His mouth,” then just a few moments later “were filled with wrath, and rose up and thrust Him out of the city; and they led Him to the brow of the hill on which their city was built, that they might throw Him down over the cliff." Controversy rose among those who should have known Him best.

Jesus really stirred things up in Jerusalem on the two occasions when He cleansed the temple (John 2:13-22; Matt. 21:12-17). He was appalled by the blatant irreverence of the Jews who turned the temple into a common market. It was their "tradition," something with which neither the common people nor the priests had a problem. Yet, this outsider flinched not at making a mess of things to make a point; they were in sin. We can only imagine how many weeks or months people talked of these incidents.

Amazingly, even the miracles of the Lord were controversial. He healed a demon-possessed, blind, mute man (Matt. 12:22-30). When the crowd began to speculate that this was the son of David, the Pharisees said, "This fellow does not cast out demons except by the power of Beelzebub, the ruler of demons." Jesus, of course, masterfully refuted this absurd claim. Later, the scribes and Pharisees demanded a sign from Him (Matt. 12:38). In other words, the signs He already performed and they already witnessed, were not good enough. They essentially wanted Jesus to pass their test; maybe by opening a rift between the physical and spiritual worlds, bringing heaven down to earth (or at least getting a peak at it).

Jesus made it clear in His teaching that He did not oppose Moses (Matt. 5:17, 18). His respect for and observance of the Law was unparalleled. He even taught the disciples to keep the Law while it was in effect (Matt. 23:1-3). Still, the Jews believed Him to be in rebellion against the Law. This is seen when they accused the formerly blind man with being Jesus' disciple while they insisted they were Moses' disciples (John 9:28, 29). They drew a distinction between the two, instead of rightly discerning that Jesus was the fulfillment of the Law and Prophets.

## Controversy in John

Perhaps there is no better way to examine the controversy surrounding Jesus and His assertion to be the Savior, than to go through the book of John. As mentioned above, He cleansed the temple in John 2. Before that, Nathanael considered the idea of a Man of God from Nazareth to be highly debatable (John 1:45-51). The rest of the book, at least from one perspective, is a series of controversies encircling Jesus. He made claims, and proved them by His miracles, that the Jews just could not tolerate.

The Lord healed a man on the Sabbath and told him to take up his bed and walk (John 5:1-9). The Jews were angered over this and confronted

Jesus (John 5:10-15). During the exchange, Jesus made several unacceptable claims with regard to equality with God (5:16-18): action (5:19, 20); power (5:21); judgment (5:22); honor (5:23); source of spiritual life (5:24); source of physical life (5:28, 29); will (5:30). To back His incredible statements, Jesus offered four proofs (John 5:31-47). John testified Jesus was the Lamb of God who takes away the sins of the world (John 1:29). The miracles He performed were evidence of His truthfulness. The Father testified of Him (Matt. 3:13-17; cf. John 1:6, 31-34). The Scriptures pointed to Jesus as the Christ (more on this later). Still, the controversy went on.

After Jesus fed the five thousand, they wanted more, but He refused (John 6:1-27). He proceeded to teach them a lesson on that for which they should seek, true Bread from heaven. He taught them He was the true Bread from heaven and anyone coming to Him would never hunger or thirst. This gave rise to complaints (John 6:35-42). He went on to say, "Whoever eats My flesh and drinks My blood has eternal life" (John 6:54). Many of the people could not bear with this, believing it to be a scandalous saying (John 6:60). Because He pressed the point, the text says, "From that time many of His disciples went back and walked with Him no more" (John 6:61-66). Note, these were disciples who turned away. Do you suppose Jesus knew the Jews would be offended by stating they must eat His flesh and drink His blood? Controversial to say the least!

In the next chapter, John 7, Jesus was back in Jerusalem during the Feast of Tabernacles. He went to teach in the temple and surprised the people with His knowledge (John 7:10-15). When the people began to speculate about Him being the Christ, the Pharisees became upset and sent officers to arrest Him (John 7:31, 32). After they heard Him, they returned without Him, saying, "No man ever spoke like this Man" (John 7:46). This caused a heated rebuke and a bitter discussion among the leaders (John 7:47-52). In the mean time, the people were debating the nature of Jesus to the point that "there was a division among the people because of Him" (John 7:43).

Again, Jesus was not passive in agitating. As He was teaching those who believed in Him, He told them they were not of Abraham or God, but of the devil and liars (John 8:31, 32, 39, 42, 44, 55). To cap it off, He made the bold statement that He was the "I AM" (John 8:58). He had earlier stated the same thing, twice, but they evidently did not quite get it (John 8:24, 28). This third time, however, they got it and attempted to stone Him (John 8:59).

Jesus transgressed the Pharisees' traditions when He healed a blind man on the Sabbath (John 9). And, again, there was a division, but it was among the Pharisees (John 9:13-17). As they investigated the incident, the parents of the man refused to take a stand. Their son, however, did not. He was prodded and pushed back (John 9:24-33). For his conviction that Jesus was a Man of God—because being blind from birth Jesus gave him sight—the man was kicked out of the synagogue (John 9:34). The evidence was obvious and overwhelming, yet the Pharisees refused to accept it. Jesus' words and actions continued to cause controversy.

The Man from Nazareth told the people He was the "good shepherd" (John 10:1-18). "Therefore, there was a division again among the Jews because of these sayings" (John 10:19). Some claimed He was demon possessed, while others said His words could not be from one who has a demon (John 10:20, 21). The Jews surrounded Him in Solomon's porch and pushed Him to state plainly whether or not He was the Christ (John 10:22-24). He had and reiterated the point by saying, "I and My Father are one" (John 10:30). This antagonized the Jews so much they "took up stones again to stone Him" understanding that He was claiming equality with God (John 10:31, 33).

In John 11 Jesus raised Lazarus from the dead. Since this was a great testimony to the power of the Son of God, giving proof to His Messiahship, the Jews were troubled and nervous (John 11:45-53). Because the evidence was so apparent, the leaders decided to get rid of it, that is, they intended to kill Lazarus so the claim that he was raised from the dead would be blunted (John 12:9-11).

## Proof in the Prophecy

As mentioned above, Jesus laid down prophecy in the Scripture as one proof that He was the Christ. Specific descriptions of the Messiah were given in the Old Testament in order for the Jews, and others, to recognize Him when He came. This significant piece of evidence cannot be over estimated. The Old Testament revelation came to an end about 400 years before Jesus was born of Mary. The books were collected and translated into Greek about 200 years before His birth. The one-volume work was copied and disseminated throughout the ancient world. Jews in many areas had copies of the Law in their synagogues. Hence, when Jesus and His disciples came along, it was impossible for them to go back and rewrite the Scriptures to fit His life. It is incontrovertible proof that Jesus is the Christ.

The Old Testament foretold of the birth, life, and death of the Messiah. Isaiah, the most messianic of the prophets, covered all three. He said one sign of the Savior was the virgin birth (Isa. 7:14). This One would be known as Immanuel. When the angel spoke to Joseph, he applied this prophecy to the child to be born of Mary (Matt. 1:23). Isaiah spoke of the nature of the King's rule and kingdom (Isa. 2:1-4; 9:6, 7; 11:1-9). In various places he also described the life and death of Jesus. In chapter 53, Isaiah told of the hard life and rejection of Christ (vv. 1-7). He specifically said He would be "cut off from the land of the living," an obvious reference to Jesus' death (Isa. 53:8). The prophet detailed the place and circumstances of His burial with the wicked and the rich which was fulfilled when Jesus' body was placed in Joseph's (a rich man) grave among men—the wicked (Isa. 53:9; Matt. 27:57-61). Isaiah said Jesus would prolong His days, speaking of His resurrection (Isa. 53:10). Finally, in chapter 53, it was prophesied that the Savior would be "numbered with the transgressors" which was fulfilled when He was hung between two thieves (Isa. 53:12; Matt. 27:38).

Micah nailed down the birthplace of Jesus as Bethlehem Ephrathah (Mic. 5:2). He did not simply give the location as Israel or even Judah. Rather, he tied it to a specific town. To foretell the place of the Christ's birth 700 years before it occurred is an impossibility from a human point of view, but the prophet foretold the birthplace of Jesus.

Jesus used prophecies as one of His tools to establish His credentials as the Savior. At the synagogue in Nazareth He applied Isaiah 61:1, 2 to Himself (Lk. 4:16-21). When John's disciples asked Jesus if He was the One of whom the prophets foretold, He referenced Isaiah 35:5, 6:

> Go and tell John the things which you hear and see: The blind see and the lame walk; the lepers are cleansed and the deaf hear; the dead are raised up and the poor have the gospel preached to them. And blessed is he who is not offended because of Me (Matt. 11:4-6).

While Jesus was hanging on the cross He quoted Psalm 22:1, "My God, My God, why have You forsaken Me" (Matt. 27:46). He clearly understood that the prophecies applied to Him.

As with their Lord, the ambassadors of Christ made prophecy a key in establishing His Messiahship. In the first gospel sermon, Peter applied Psalm 16:8-11 to Jesus. He used Deuteronomy 18:15-19 and Psalm 118:22 to prove Jesus was the Christ (Acts 3:21-23; 4:11). Paul applied Psalm 2:7, Isaiah 55:3, and Psalm 16:10 to the Lord in one sermon (Acts 13:33-35).

In spite of the fact that Jesus and the apostles utilized the Scriptures, in which the Jews believed, and applied the prophecies to Him, He was rejected; and so was His religion.

### The Last Straw

When we read the accounts of the trials of Jesus, it is beyond question that controversy surrounded them. He was put on trial by the Jews for perceived blasphemy. The false witnesses did not agree in their testimony (Mark 14:53-56). Finally, they found those who twisted His words about destroying this temple, implying the degradation of the sacred temple, but they did not agree (Mark 14:57-59; cf. John 2:18-22). The high priest pressed Jesus to answer and put Him under oath to say once and for all whether or not He was "the Christ, the Son of the Blessed" (Mark 14:60, 61; Matt. 26:63). Jesus said, "I am" (Mark 14:61). With this, the high priest exploded and all condemned Him to death (Mark 14:63, 64; Matt. 26:65, 66).

The Jews then led Jesus to Pilate, who sent Him to Herod, who sent Him back to Pilate (Matt. 27:1-31; Mark 15:1-20; Luke 23:1-25; John 18:28-19:16). During these trials, there was great debate. Pilate could not see anything wrong with Jesus, but the Jews kept insisting He must be executed. The thing that pushed the governor over the edge was a false claim. The Jews said, "If you let this Man go, you are not Caesar's friend. Whoever makes himself a king speaks against Caesar" (John 19:12). What the Jews were saying was this: "Pilate if you do not put Jesus to death, we are going to tell Caesar that you let a rival to his throne go." They surely would have done it and Pilate would have been killed. So, Pilate moved quickly and gave sentence (John 19:13-16).

### The Controversy Settled Once And For All

The enemies of Jesus thought He was shown to be a fraud and all debate settled when His body was put in the grave. Pilate confirmed Jesus was dead (John 19:31-37). The Jews had Pilate set a guard to ensure that nothing "fishy" happened (Matt. 27:62-66). They were confident. However, as with all enemies of God, their confidence was false.

Somewhat understandably, the disciples also thought all hope was lost. They had hope in Jesus, but lost it when He was killed.

Early on Sunday Jesus came forth from the grave and appeared to multitudes over the next forty days (Matt. 28:1-20; Mark 16:1-20; Luke 24:1-53; John 20:1-21:25; 1 Cor. 15:1-6). All His claims were affirmed. Every word He taught was established beyond doubt. He was justified in all that He ever said or did. This proof, beyond any, settled the controversy once and for all of whether or not Jesus was and is the Christ.

From the beginning, God declared His Son would be killed and raised from the dead. The thread begins with Moses' writing and continues through the teaching of the apostles, as they expound and explain Old Testament passages. Moses recorded God's declaration that the Seed of woman would bruise the head of the serpent, while the serpent would bruise His heel (Gen. 3:15). David foretold of one whose soul was not left in *Sheol* and whose body was not corrupted (Psa. 16:10). Philip taught the eunuch from Isaiah 53 where it states the suffering Servant would be cut off from the land of the living, but also have His days prolonged (Acts 8:32-35).

Jesus made many statements about His death, burial, and resurrection giving evidence to His nature. When challenged for a sign for His authority, He said, "Destroy this temple, and in three days I will raise it up" (John 2:18-22). He told Nicodemus "And as Moses lifted up the serpent in the wilderness, even so must the Son of man be lifted up, that whoever believes in Him should not perish, but have eternal life" (John 3:14, 15). Jesus declared that, if He was "lifted up from the earth," He would draw all men unto Himself (John 12:32). Over and over He staked His Messiahship on His resurrection. It proved He is the Christ.

To sum it up, Paul said Jesus was "declared to be the Son of God with power according to the spirit of holiness, by the resurrection from the dead" (Rom. 1:4).

### The Unfolding Consequences

After the resurrection and ascension, the apostles and others taught men that Jesus is the Christ. From the outset, though, trouble was stirred. As Peter and John preached the resurrection of Jesus, the Sadducees arrested them—twice (Acts 4, 5). The Jewish leadership was not going to tolerate the truth being taught.

As the faithful continued to press the truth, the intensity of the conflict increased. Stephen delivered a blistering sermon to the council and paid for it with his life (Acts 7). The disciples were then scattered abroad (Acts 8:1-4). The pattern was developing that wherever the Jews had control, the religion of Christ and those who practiced it were not welcome.

Paul's practice was to enter the synagogues of the towns where he journeyed. Some would listen to him for a while, but there came a point when the "honeymoon" was over. The opposition either drove him from the synagogue or from the town altogether. He experienced this in Antioch (Acts 13:13-52), Iconium (Acts 14:1-7), Lystra (Acts 14:8-20), Thessalonica (Acts 17:1-10), Berea (Acts 17:11-15), Corinth (Acts 18:1-8), and Ephesus (Acts 19:1-10). The Jewish community simply would not endure fellowship with those who believed Jesus to be the Christ.

The conviction in Jesus as the Son of God brought a separation. Not only was there a general division from the Jews, but also divisions within households. Jesus foretold this and cautioned His disciples to make the right choice (Matt. 10:34-39). And, it did not stop with the Jews, but Christians were also separated from the Gentile community (cf. 1 Pet. 4:3, 4).

### Relevance to Today

The controversy over whether or not Jesus is the Christ is the greatest controversy of all time. While it began in the first century, it continues to this very day. And though some may think it is not as heated now as then, the truth is, nothing has changed. If the Lord were to come back to earth, walk on it, teach what He taught, and perform the miracles again, He would still be violently opposed.

It is true His presence would be controversial among the Muslims, Jews, Buddhists, Hindus, and Atheists. However, the greatest controversy might just be from "Christendom." Modernism in the church rejects the idea that Jesus is the Christ, just as it rejects everything associated with the life of Christ that implies His deity and the miraculous. But modernists are not the only ones who might stumble over Christ. When you look back at the Savior's life in the first century, you realize that those who should have been most likely to accept Him were the very ones who put Him to death. Do you think it is any different today?

Take a closer look.

The Jews expected a nationalistic, earthly Messiah, but His kingdom is not of this world (John 18:38). What do most denominations expect? An earthly kingdom. If it is not the Jehovah's Witness view of an eternal life on a regenerated earth, it is the Premillennial view of a 1,000-year kingdom on earth. They reject outright that the Church and Kingdom are one and the same, though each has the same leader and subjects (Eph. 1:22, 23; Rom. 12:5; Col. 1:13, 18, 24).

Tradition hobbled the Jews in their expectation and view of Christ. They thought the Son of David would uphold their traditions and justify their practices; that He would agree with them. Yet, we know Jesus vigorously assaulted their error (Matt. 15:1-14; 231-39). The religions of men today have the same reaction. They despise and demean anyone who brings the truth to their attention. If you point out that there is only one true church, nearly all of them get angry. When you tell a Roman Catholic that the pope is an apostate and rival to the true Head of the Church, they get livid.

In the first century there was elitism among the Jewish religious leaders, as we noted previously. If a man was not trained by the rabbis, he was nothing; he had no right, let alone skill and knowledge, to teach. In our time, the churches of men almost universally require a man (or woman) to have a degree from the right seminary and/or be credentialed and properly ordained. Their view is that only certain individuals are qualified to teach the word. This is contrary to what we see with Jesus, the apostles, the prophets, evangelists, and saints of the first century (Acts 8:4). As far we know, Paul was the only apostle to have received a formal religious education. He used it where he could, but did not depend on it for his right or ability to preach the gospel (Phil. 3:1-8; 1 Cor. 1:18-2:16).

Controversy is also stirred today when we follow the example of the Christ in condemning men in sin. On more than one occasion He agitated people by accusing them of sin. When we do this, with pure hearts and motives, with the best interest of their soul in mind, many get hostile. If you do not believe this, the next time you see your Baptist friend, point out that Billy Graham is a false teacher who is headed to hell and leading others there as well. You only need bring up one point to show he is a false teacher: salvation. He teaches faith-only salvation, the Bible teaches faith plus baptism equals salvation (Mark 16:16; Acts 2:38; 22:16; 1 Pet. 3:21). In spite of the fact you can show them in the Bible that Graham is wrong, they will most likely reject you and the word.

Another controversial area in the life of Jesus, one we did not touch on earlier, is His association with publicans and sinners. The Jews nearly had a heart attack when Jesus sat down with them (Mark 2:15, 16). They considered it beneath a good Jew, let alone a prophet or the Christ, to have any contact with such people. While an association with sinners, for the sake of saving their souls, would not draw much attention today, there is a wide-spread feeling that some things are beneath a believer. For instance, a sharp rebuke, especially publicly, draws a sharp disapproval from denominationalists. If you employ sarcasm or biting comments, like Elijah or Jesus or Paul, you are accused of being unchristian (1 Kings 18:27; Matt. 23:15, 24, 33; 1 Cor. 4:6-10).

People who truly believe in Jesus as the Christ adhere to His will. Such conviction and action draws a sharp rebuke from the world, including the religious world. If believers compromise their faith, the next generation will be at a disadvantage. The battle will have to be fought yet again, with many casualties along the way.

**Why Is The Truth "Jesus Is The Christ" Controversial?**

We know the Jews objected to claims of Jesus as Christ for various reasons, but why? It comes down to basically one point that Jesus made more than once. They simply did not believe God.

The Jews rejected the commandment of God to keep their traditions—traditions which Jesus condemned (Mark 7:1-13). He told them if they believed Moses they would have believed Him (John 5:46, 47). Moses was one they supposedly believed was a great prophet of God. However, they not only altered his Law by ignoring the commands, but they also did not believe what he wrote about Christ.

Their disbelief in God is the reason they refused to answer Jesus' question in Matthew 21:23-27. When they challenged Jesus for His authority, He turned it around on them. He said, "I also will ask you one thing, which if you tell Me, I likewise will tell you by what authority I do these things: The baptism of John—where was it from? From heaven or men?" Notice their reasoning. "If we say, 'From heaven,' He will say to us, 'Why then did you not believe him?' But if we say, 'From men,' we fear the multitude, for all count John as a prophet." You see, either way they answered they were rejecting God. If they admitted John was a prophet, but did not listen to him, they did not believe God. If they denied John as a prophet, which he was, they did not believe God.

Jesus said that those who receive the apostles, receive Him and receive the Father (Matt. 10:40). John said that those who did not receive his writing (teaching) did not receive him (3 John 9). This means anyone who rejects the apostles does not receive the Lord. To put it another way, it is not possible to receive Jesus as the Christ and reject the teaching of the inspired men of the New Testament.

There are two categories of those who reject Jesus among those who claim to believe in Him. One consists of those who affirm something that is untrue. The other is those who deny something that is true. By the way, these usually go together.

In the first group are people who believe in things not taught in the Bible: inherited sin (Eze. 18:20); once saved always saved (Phil. 2:12); premillennialism (John 18:38); denominationalism (Eph. 4:4); faith-only salvation (Jas. 2:14-26); and many such things.

In the latter category people deny what is taught in God's word: one man for one woman for life, with one exception (Matt. 19:9); modest dress (1 Tim. 2:9, 10); male leadership (1 Tim. 2:11, 12; 3:1-13); existence and marking of false teachers (Rom. 16:17, 18); deity of Christ on earth (John 1:1-14); and many such things.

People can pretend all they want, but if they reject the teaching of the New Testament, in doctrine or morality, then they reject Jesus. And, whether or not they believe He is the Christ is irrelevant in such a situation.

### What Does It Mean to Believe Jesus is the Christ?

You probably realize this from the above section. Still, for the sake of clarity and thoroughness, we will examine this idea further.

If we believe Jesus is the Christ, then there are certain unavoidable truths that follow. These are not popular among men. Hence, they resist the fact that Jesus is the Christ; for them it is controversial.

Whenever you are truly convicted that Jesus is the Christ, then you must necessarily submit to Him as Master (cf. Luke 8:24). You are no longer your own master. The ruling authority has shifted from you to Jesus. Let us put it this way, when you truly believe, you will be baptized into Christ (Mark 16:16; Rom. 6:3, 4). When this is done, Paul said, "you are not your own. . . . For you were bought at a price; therefore glorify God in your body and your spirit, which are God's" (1 Cor. 6:19, 20). The Christian does not have the freedom to do as he or she pleases. All things are subject to the Lord's approval.

The funny thing about people who want to resist Jesus as the Christ because they do not want to lose their freedom is that they are already slaves (Rom. 6:16-18; 2 Pet. 2:18-22). There is no such thing as absolute freedom. We are either subject to sin and Satan or to righteousness and Christ.

Since Jesus is the Master, we are obligated to follow His will. For some people this is extremely controversial. People do not want to change their lives. Yet, that is exactly what the Christ calls on them to do. Paul wrote, "And do not be conformed to this world, but be transformed by the renewing of your mind, that you may prove what is that good and acceptable and perfect will of God" (Rom. 12:2). Believers in Christ are required to offer their bodies as a living sacrifice (Rom. 12:1). Many are unwilling to do this.

Additionally, another extremely controversial point with numerous people is something the Hebrew writer stated, "Therefore we also, since we are surrounded by so great a cloud of witnesses, let us lay aside every weight, and the sin which so easily ensnares us, and let us run with endurance the race that is set before us" (Heb. 12:1). People generally agree with setting aside sin, but have a hard time accepting putting off the "weight." The weight is not something that is sinful in-and-of itself. Rather, it would be what the Lord described as "cares of this world." There are many things that can steal our attention and sap us of time and energy to do God's will, to truly grow in the grace and knowledge of the Lord.

Finally, a truth that is inescapable by the fact that Jesus is the Christ is judgment. All men will be judged by the Lord (John 5:28, 29). However, those who deny He is the Savior can carry on blissfully in sin because they do not believe they will be held accountable. The one who acknowledges Jesus as the Christ is obligated that he will face Him in the judgment. It is an unavoidable event when our lives in the body will be judged, whether good or bad (2 Cor. 5:10). There are those who simply do not want to think about this, let alone accept it. So, for them, Jesus being the Christ is a controversial statement.

### Final Exhortation

This great truth, Jesus is the Christ, was not settled in a calm and dispassionate environment. Rather, it was hashed out in a volatile milieu. The truth was manifest because of the unrelenting, unapologetic declaration by Jesus (and his apostles). He did not cower from the conflict of controversy. He was wise as a serpent and harmless as a dove. He maintained His purity and integrity, yet pressed the point of His Messiahship.

Our duty today is to carry on in proclaiming the divisive truth of Jesus is the Christ. And, instead of shrinking from the intensity of the conflict, we need to stoke the fire. If we live godly in Christ Jesus, we will suffer persecution (2 Tim. 3:12). We will face opposition and controversy will surround us. This is nothing of which to be ashamed. Rather, we need to be overjoyed at being counted worthy to suffer shame for His name (Acts 5:41).

We need to be thankful for the establishment of the truth that Jesus is the Christ. Men and women shed blood in the battle. The perfect, pure Son of God was killed for it. If we do not appreciate this truth and the struggle that brought it to us, then there will be controversy among the children of God. Our children and grandchildren will be faced with infidelity and a terrific fight just to confirm a basic truth. Thus, we must continually remind ourselves from the word that Jesus is the Christ.

# "That Ye All May Be One"

**Scott Finley**

## Introduction: The Tragedy of Division

In 2 Corinthians 2:11, Paul warned that God's people should exercise caution as Satan is always trying to get an advantage on us, ". . . for we are not ignorant of his schemes." Satan has many tools in his arsenal: worldliness, persecution, prejudice, and false teaching, to name a few. But, perhaps one of his most prolific devices is "divide and conquer."

The cause of Christ has always been plagued with division. In Acts 15, Judaizers arrived in Antioch from Jerusalem saying, "Unless you are circumcised according to the custom of Moses, you cannot be saved" *(v. 1). Their error resulted in "great dissension and debate"* (v. 2) in Antioch, Jerusalem, and Galatia. John battled the divisive evils of Gnosticism (or, "antichrist") which said that Jesus had not come in the flesh (2 John 7); the error also became to them a license to gratify the flesh. These were responsible for atrocities such as the, "Gospel of Judas," which portrayed Judas as a hero for betraying the Lord.

Division raised its ugly head among the Corinthians. Notice that of all

**Scott Finley** was born in Port Arthur, Texas on November 7, 1960 to Robert and Sue Finley. After attending Florida College, he married Vicki (Hewgley) of Houston in 1981. The Finleys have two children: Brandon (age 23) and Shannon (age 19). Scott has preached the gospel for twenty-eight years, working with churches in Houston, Texas (Kleinwood 1980-1982), Jacksonville, Texas (1982-1985), Greenwood, Arkansas (1985-1987), Freeport, Texas (1987-1991), Henderson, Texas (1991-1994), and Kilgore, Texas (1994-2000). Scott is currently serving as an evangelist and elder with the University Oaks Church of Christ (formerly known as West Avenue) in San Antonio, Texas (2000–Present). Scott has written articles for a number of periodicals, and conducts several gospel meetings each year.

the problems the Corinthian church had (carnality, immorality, lawsuits, abuses of spiritual gifts and of the Lord's Supper, etc.), the first issue Paul addressed was the internal strife that existed within their ranks. "Now I exhort you, brethren, by the name of our Lord Jesus Christ, that you all agree and that there be no divisions among you, but that you be made complete in the same mind and in the same judgment. For I have been informed concerning you, my brethren, by Chloe's people, that there are quarrels among you" (1 Cor. 1:10-11).

Back in the nineteenth century noble, God-fearing men of the restoration movement recognized the necessity of oneness, and that it could only be achieved by a return to the word of God. Slogans such as, "No creed but the Bible," and "Where the Bible speaks, we speak; where the Bible is silent, we are silent," served to remind truth-loving people that the only valid basis for unity is the inspired word of God. In those days, erroneous views on issues like the plan of salvation, premillennialism, and instrumental music threatened the peace, and did much damage to the cause of Christ.

During the middle decades of the twentieth century, unity was threatened again. Issues that divided brethren during the 1940s, 1950s, and 1960s included institutionalism, the sponsoring church arrangement, and church sponsored recreation and entertainment. Some who fought on the front lines of those battles remain to this day, and possess vivid memories of the conflict, tears, and dissension. In more recent years, errors on marriage and divorce, fellowship, the deity of Jesus, and creation, as well as compromises on moral issues such as dancing, the use of alcohol, and immodest clothing have divided brethren.

Over the past half century, the American religious climate has been dominated by the ecumenical message of "unity in diversity." The movement claims to promote "better understanding and cooperation" among differing faiths in the name of love and unity. Unfortunately, some of our own brethren have been drinking this Kool-Aid. While it is certainly true that the Bible teaches love and unity, the sophistry involved contains two fundamental errors: it is based on a false, manmade standard for unity, and the acceptance of error. To demonstrate where ecumenical thinking leads, in 1995 Max Lucado said, "Whenever I hear a man call God Father, and Jesus Savior, I see a brother." He said that in the same year that he swapped pulpits with Buckner Fanning, a well-known Baptist preacher in San Antonio. Clearly, as far as Lucado is concerned, issues such as the necessity of baptism, Calvinism, the use of instruments of music in worship, etc., no longer matter. But, when the teachings of the Bible are viewed objectively, it is easy to see that the Lord's plea for unity was not unqualified. He doesn't want unity at just any price.

### The Lord's Prayer for Unity

The night before His death, somewhere between the upper room and Gethsemane, the Savior uttered what is believed by some to be the most beautiful prayer ever prayed. After informing the twelve of His departure, revealing Judas as the betrayer, comforting their heavy hearts, promising them the Holy Spirit, teaching them the Lord's Supper, and washing the feet of His disciples, Jesus worded the eloquent appeal found in John chapter 17.

After praying for Himself, then on behalf of the Twelve, the Lord uttered these words:

> I do not ask on behalf of these alone, but for those also who believe in Me through their word; that they may all be one; even as You, Father, are in Me and I in You, that they also may be in Us, so that the world may believe that You sent Me. The glory which You have given Me I have given to them, that they may be one, just as We are one; I in them and You in Me, that they may be perfected in unity, so that the world may know that You sent Me, and loved them, even as You have loved Me. Father, I desire that they also, whom You have given Me, be with Me where I am, so that they may see My glory which You have given Me, for You loved Me before the foundation of the world. O righteous Father, although the world has not known You, yet I have known You; and these have known that You sent Me; and I have made Your name known to them, and will make it known, so that the love with which You loved Me may be in them, and I in them.

### What God Has Done To Make Unity Possible

Though the root cause of discord and estrangement is our sins, in His infinite wisdom, love, and mercy, God has provided a path by which there can be unity again, both with Himself and among men. Our Lord's prayer was that those who claim to be His disciples be as one. In a manner of speaking, the whole message of the Bible is one of unity (the reconciliation of man to God).

**A Perfect Sacrifice.** The pathway to unification led to a little hillside called Calvary, just outside the city of Jerusalem about two thousand years ago. After He was betrayed, arrested, falsely accused, and illegally tried in the early morning hours, Jesus was condemned on the charge of blasphemy, and was delivered over to the Gentiles. And, though Pilate repeatedly acknowledged His innocence, our Lord was smitten, spat upon, and mocked. They dressed Him in a purple robe, put a reed in His hand, pressed a crown of thorns into the flesh of His precious brow, and mockingly bowed before Him in worship saying, "Hail, King of the Jews." After scourging Jesus, and pardoning Barabbas, they led Jesus, bearing His own cross, to "the place of a skull." With hateful nails viciously driven through His innocent hands and feet, His body was "lifted up from the earth" that all men might be drawn to and united in Him (John 12:32). After commending His Spirit into the hands of His loving Father, He died.

**Reconciliation with God.** The Lord's blood provides atonement for our sins, and reunion with God, when we believe and obey the gospel. The saved possess a "common salvation" (Jude 3), and are the "partakers of a heavenly calling" (Heb. 3:1) on which men can unite. Reconciled to God, the redeemed no longer live in fear and doubt, but in confidence, "standing on the promises of God."

**Abrogation of Moses' Law.** But, the death of our Lord also did something else that unity might exist. It fulfilled and removed the old covenant, which stood as a barrier between Jews and Gentiles. In Ephesians 2:13-16, Paul wrote:

> But now in Christ Jesus you who formerly were far off have been brought near by the blood of Christ. For He Himself is our peace, who made both groups into one and broke down the barrier of the dividing wall, by abolishing in His flesh the enmity, which is the Law of commandments contained in ordinances, so that in Himself He might make the two into one new man, thus establishing peace, and might reconcile them both in one body to God through the cross, by it having put to death the enmity (cf. Col. 2:14-16; Gal. 3:23-25).

**Inauguration of the New Covenant.** When Jesus died, His blood ushered in a new covenant, the gospel of Jesus Christ, a "common faith" (Tit. 1:4). The author of the Hebrew letter emphasizes that Jesus' blood brought the new covenant into effect,

> For this reason He is the mediator of a new covenant, so that, since a death has taken place for the redemption of the transgressions that were committed under the first covenant, those who have been called may receive the promise of the eternal inheritance. For where a covenant is, there must of necessity be the death of the one who made it. For a covenant is valid only when men are dead, for it is never in force while the one who made

> it lives. Therefore even the first covenant was not inaugurated without blood. For when every commandment had been spoken by Moses to all the people according to the Law, he took the blood of the calves and the goats, with water and scarlet wool and hyssop, and sprinkled both the book itself and all the people (Heb. 9:15-19).

It was God's intent from the beginning that men unite on the gospel message. The Bible is the complete and final revelation of the mind of God to mankind. God's will for people of this age is the New Testament. In correcting the division among the Corinthians, Paul demanded, "by the name of our Lord Jesus Christ, that you all agree and that there be no divisions among you, but that you be made complete in the same mind and in the same judgment" (1 Cor. 1:10). How is this kind of unity achieved? By loving, believing, respecting, and practicing God word.

The Bible is replete with warnings against tampering with its contents. Moses wrote, "You shall not add to the word which I am commanding you, nor take away from it, that you may keep the commandments of the Lord your God which I command you" (Deut. 4:2). And, "Do not add to His words or He will reprove you, and you will be proved a liar" (Prov. 30:6).

Similar warnings are found in the New Testament. When Judaizers attempted to impose Mosaic requirements on Gentile converts, Paul addressed those who had listened to them,

> I am amazed that you are so quickly deserting Him who called you by the grace of Christ, for a different gospel; which is really not another; only there are some who are disturbing you and want to distort the gospel of Christ. But even if we, or an angel from heaven, should preach to you a gospel contrary to what we have preached to you, he is to be accursed! As we have said before, so I say again now, if any man is preaching to you a gospel contrary to what you received, he is to be accursed! (Gal. 1:6-9).

The gravity of this matter is also emphasized by John who wrote, "Anyone who goes too far and does not abide in the teaching of Christ, does not have God; the one who abides in the teaching, he has both the Father and the Son. If anyone comes to you and does not bring this teaching, do not receive him into your house, and do not give him a greeting; for the one who gives him a greeting participates in his evil deeds" (2 John 9-11). And, as the Bible comes to its grand conclusion we find these words of promise and warning, "I testify to everyone who hears the words of the prophecy of this book: if anyone adds to them, God will add to him the plagues which are written in this book; and if anyone takes away from the words of the book of this prophecy, God will take away his part from the tree of life and from the holy city, which are written in this book" (Rev. 22:18-19). Some may attempt to water down these words by saying, "they only apply to the book of Revelation." Do we not understand that the underlying principle of these verses apply to the whole of God's word?

**A Platform for Unity.** In Ephesians 4, the New Testament provides a foundation upon which Christians can unite. This chapter emphasizes the need for Christians to be united in order to reflect the glory of God (3:21), provide an atmosphere for spiritual growth and development, and to allow the body of Christ to function in keeping with heaven's objectives. When Jesus returned to heaven, He provided His people with apostles, prophets, evangelists, pastors, and teachers. Their purpose was "for the equipping of the saints for the work of service, to the building up of the body of Christ; until we all attain to the unity of the faith, and of the knowledge of the Son of God, to a mature man, to the measure of the stature which belongs to the fullness of Christ" (Eph. 4:12-13). The critical path to these results is laid down in verses four through six. After accentuating the need to preserve unity (v. 3), Paul provides a list of seven (the number is not without significance) things which serve as a solid foundation for oneness among God's people.

There is *"one body,"* the church for which Christ died, which He saved, and of which He is the Head. "For the husband is the head of the wife, as Christ also is the head of the church, He Himself being the Savior of the body" (Eph. 5:23). "And He put all things in subjection under His feet, and gave Him as head over all things to the church, which is His body, the fullness of Him who fills all in all" (Eph. 1:22-23). While there are many local churches, Paul speaks here of the church universal—all obedient believers in the world. The fact of *"one body"* denotes that there is unity of relationship; the redeemed are all children of God, and brethren one of another.

There is *"one Spirit,"* the Holy Spirit. The letter to the Ephesians shows that the Father planned our redemption from eternity past, that the Son executed the Father's plan, and that the Holy Spirit revealed it for the benefit of all mankind. This revelation is found in the Scriptures. Paul wrote, ". . . when you read you can understand my insight into the mystery of Christ, which in other generations was not made known to the sons of men, as it has now been revealed to His holy apostles and prophets in the Spirit" (Eph. 3:4-5). The unveiling of God's will is not found today through dreams, visions, still voices, and signs. The Spirit's work of inspiration provides all instruction, for all men, for all time, "so that the man of God may be adequate, equipped for every good work" (2 Tim. 3:17). Thus, there is unity of revelation.

There is *"one hope."* God's people live in hope of eternal life—unity of reward. The aspiration of being raised from the dead to dwell in the presence of God for all eternity is a "sure and steadfast" anchor to our souls (Heb. 6:19) in the midst of life's storms, and gives life joy and assurance as we live in harmony with His Word. Hebrews 3:6 identifies us as the household of Christ, "if we hold fast the confidence and the rejoicing of the hope firm to the end" (NKJV).

There is *"one Lord"*—unity of authority. All authority, in heaven and on earth, belongs to the Son of God (Matt. 28:18). He created all, sustains all, and rules over all. And, upon His return, He will be the Judge of all. Perhaps no passage extols His greatness more than Colossians 1:15-19,

> He is the image of the invisible God, the firstborn of all creation. For by Him all things were created, both in the heavens and on earth, visible and invisible, whether thrones or dominions or rulers or authorities — all things have been created through Him and for Him. He is before all things, and in Him all things hold together. He is also head of the body, the church; and He is the beginning, the firstborn from the dead, so that He Himself will come to have first place in everything. For it was the Father's good pleasure for all the fullness to dwell in Him.

Paul further declared there to be *"one faith,"* thus unity of doctrine, or teaching. Simply stated, the one faith is the gospel, or the New Testament message. Christians are expected to "contend earnestly for the faith which was once for all handed down to the saints" (Jude 3). No one has the right to alter the gospel message, and those who do so fall under God's curse (Gal. 1:6-9). There isn't a more arrogant man than the one who takes it upon himself to change God's word. Some contend that the gospel, as it is, is outdated, and that we need a modern message for modern man. This was the contention of Edward T. Hiscox in his *Standard Manual for Baptist Churches*. On page 22, in the chapter on "Church Membership," Hiscox wrote,

> . . . it is most likely that in the Apostolic age when there was but "one Lord, one faith, and one baptism," and no differing denominations existed, the baptism of a convert by that very act, constituted him a member of the church, and at once endowed him with all the rights and privileges of full membership. In that sense, "baptism was the door into the church." Now, it is different. . . ."

Mr. Hiscox was right about one thing: baptism was the "door into the church" in the New Testament age. God Himself made baptism "the door into the church" (cf. 1 Cor. 12:12-13). We ask, "Who made it different?"

The reasoning employed by Mr. Hiscox, along with that of Cain, Nadab and Abihu, Judaizers, and Gnostics is the very cause of religious denominationalism today. Just as God gave one Lord, not many, He also gave one faith. Some have argued, "But, we can't all understand the Bible alike." The fact is that if we can understand it at all, we will understand it alike; Paul says we can and must (cf. Eph. 3:2-4; 1 Cor. 1:10).

There is *"one baptism"* (Eph. 4:5). Predicated on faith and repentance, the entryway into Christ and His church is water baptism. "For all of you who were baptized into Christ have clothed yourselves with Christ" (Gal. 3:27; cf. 1 Cor. 12:13). All who enter into Christ and His church do so in precisely the same way; therefore there is unity of access. John introduced the practice of water baptism but was limited in where he could baptize because it required "much water" (John 3:23)—obviously more than he could carry around, eliminating sprinkling or pouring as a possibility. In both Romans 6:4 and Colossians 2:12 Paul refers to baptism as a burial. Jesus Himself was baptized in water (Matt.3:13ff), and taught others to do the same (John 3:5, Mark 16:16, Matt.28:18-20). The *"one baptism"* is not baptism with the Holy Spirit, fire, or suffering, but water. It was clearly God's intent that baptism symbolize the death, burial, and resurrection of Jesus. After baptism, we are raised from our watery grave to walk in newness of life, our sins having been washed away (Acts 22:16).

The final point in this list of seven is the *"one God and Father of all who is over all and through all and in all"* (Eph. 4:6). Paul taught the Athenians of God,

> Who made the world and all things in it, . . . is Lord of heaven and earth, . . . gives to all people life and breath and all things; and He made from one man every nation of mankind to live on all the face of the earth, having determined their appointed times and the boundaries of their habitation, . . . He is not far from each one of us; for in Him we live and move and exist (Acts 17:24-28).

He alone is to be worshipped and served, thus there is unity of worship. Jesus rebuked Satan when He was tempted, and said, "You shall worship the Lord your God, and serve Him only'" (Matt. 4:10).

In a passage in which the central point is the unity of God's people, these seven fundamental truths are presented as the foundation rock on which we can unite. We must have the will, courage, and fortitude to stand and defend them.

**Made Us Equals**. One final point to be made regarding what God has done to make unity possible, is that He has made us all equal in His eyes. We are all brethren, with the same benefits and blessings in Christ.

> For you are all sons of God through faith in Christ Jesus. For all of you who were baptized into Christ have clothed yourselves with Christ. There is neither Jew nor Greek, there is neither slave nor free man, there is neither male nor female; for you are all one in Christ Jesus. And if you belong to Christ, then you are Abraham's descendants, heirs according to promise (Gal. 3:26-29).

No one due to his money, social status, race, or sex is better than another. There are no "great ones" in the kingdom of God; all are fellow-servants with Christ. In the upper room, during Jesus final meeting with the Twelve the disciples began to contend among themselves as to who would be the greatest (Luke 22:24). Note the Lord's answer,

> The kings of the Gentiles lord it over them; and those who have authority over them are called "Benefactors." But it is not this way with you, but the one who is the greatest among you must become like the youngest, and the leader like the servant. For who is greater, the one who reclines at the table or the one who serves? Is it not the one who reclines at the table? But I am among you as the one who serves (Luke 22:25-27).

The point was powerfully reinforced by the Lord as He laid aside His garments, girded Himself with a towel (as a servant), and washed the feet of His disciples.

The Almighty has done much to make oneness possible. By offering His Son on the cross, He reconciled the obedient to Himself, annulled the Law of Moses in favor of a new covenant in which, "There is one body and one Spirit, just as also you were called in one hope of your calling; one Lord, one faith, one baptism, one God and Father of all who is over all and through all and in all" (Eph. 4:4-6). He has made all believers equals, "For you are all sons of God through faith in Christ Jesus" (Gal. 3:26). We "are all fellow heirs and fellow members of the body, and fellow partakers of the promise in Christ Jesus through the gospel" (Eph. 3:6).

### What We Must Do to Make Unity Happen

Just as there is both a divine and human role in God's plan for human redemption, so it is in the matter of achieving unity. Man must take an active role.

**Love for God.** When Jesus was asked which of God's commands is the greatest He said, "You shall love the Lord your God with all your heart, and with all your soul, and with all your mind" (Matt. 22:37). It is the greatest command because it is the most fundamental. Supreme love for Almighty God above self, family, or material things will motivate us to make the sacrifices essential for unity. Given all He has done for us, how can we refuse Him? "We love him, because he first loved us" (1 John 4:19, KJV).

**Love for God's Word.** Loving God means loving His word. Jesus said, "If you love Me, you will keep My commandments" (John 14:15). Love isn't any good unless it is expressed, and love has no higher expression than when we chose His will over our own. The word of God is our connection to Him; it is the means by which He dwells within us. The unity of God's people absolutely depends on our love for God's word, and the will to obey it.

In addition, those who love God and His word will militantly defend it. As a loving father protects his children and as a good soldier defends the land he loves, so those who love God's word take a stand against those who practice and propagate error. Jude wrote urging God's people to "contend earnestly for the faith which was once for all handed down to the saints" (Jude 3). Many today don't seem to have "the stomach" for controversy, or the will to fight. But, when the errors of Calvinism, premillennialism, institutionalism, error on marriage and divorce, creation, or anything else are taught, souls are in the balance and unity is at stake. Who will take a stand?

Does it seem inconsistent to say that we must fight in order to have peace? Paul wrote to Timothy, "This command I entrust to you, Timothy, my son, in accordance with the prophecies previously made concerning you, that by them you fight the good fight, keeping faith and a good conscience, which some have rejected and suffered shipwreck in regard to their faith" (1 Tim. 1:18-19). Paul defended the truth against Judaizers, "But it was because of the false brethren secretly brought in, who had sneaked in to spy out our liberty which we have in Christ Jesus, in order to bring us into bondage. But we did not yield in subjection to them for even an hour, so that the truth of the gospel would remain with you" (Gal. 2:4-5).

**Love for the Lost.** While the greatest command is loving God with all our heart, soul, strength, and mind, "The second is like it, 'You shall love your neighbor as yourself'" (Matt. 22:39). How much do we really care about those who are lost? Enough to swallow our pride? Enough to "go the extra mile"? Enough to make a special effort to get along with others for the greater good, and for the sake of peace? That is precisely what Jesus expects, "I do not ask on behalf of these alone, but for those also who believe in Me through their word; that they may all be one; even as You, Father, are in Me and I in You, that they also may be in Us, so that the world may believe that You sent Me" (John 17:20-21). Error divides and truth unites—common sense tells us that, and when people who are outside of Christ look at the body of Christ and see uniformity of belief and practice, it has a powerful drawing effect.

**Love for the Brethren.** One of the most obvious points to be made on what is required of us for the sake of unity is that we are to love our brethren. God's people are to love and be as dedicated to one another as Christ was to His disciples. "This is My commandment, that you love one another, just as I have loved you. Greater love has no one than this, that one lay down his life for his friends" (John 15:12-13). John wrote, "We know that we have passed out of death into life, because we love the brethren. He who does not love abides in death" (1 John 3:14). "If someone says, 'I love God,' and hates his brother, he is a liar; for the one who does not love his brother whom he has seen, cannot love God whom he has not seen. And this commandment we have from Him, that the one who loves God should love his brother also" (1 John 4:20-21). The badge we wear identifying ourselves as true disciples of the Lord is the deep, abiding affection we have for our brothers and sisters in Christ.

Loving our brethren is paramount to unity because it determines how we treat them. Active goodwill promotes unity, while the demonic spirit of selfishness causes division and strife. James wrote,

> Who among you is wise and understanding? Let him show by his good behavior his deeds in the gentleness of wisdom. But if you have bitter jealousy and selfish ambition in your heart, do not be arrogant and so lie against the truth. This wisdom is not that which comes down from above, but is earthly, natural, demonic. For where jealousy and selfish ambition exist, there is disorder and every evil thing. But the wisdom from above is first pure, then peaceable, gentle, reasonable, full of mercy and good fruits, unwavering, without hypocrisy. And the seed whose fruit is righteousness is sown in peace by those who make peace (James 3:13-18).

**Attitudes Essential to Unity.** "Therefore I, the prisoner of the Lord, implore you to walk in a manner worthy of the calling with which you have been called, with all humility and gentleness, with patience, showing tolerance for one another in love, being diligent to preserve the unity of the Spirit in the bond of peace" (Eph. 4:1-3).

**Walking Worthy of the Calling.** In the verses above, Paul speaks of the attitudes and behavior essential to oneness. In verse one, he reminds his readers of the responsibility they accepted upon their conversion, "to walk in a manner worthy of the calling with which you have been called," (v. 1). The call is that of the gospel (2 Thess. 2:14) which calls us out of sin, rebellion, and the world into the glorious kingdom of heaven. We are called to be "saints" (1 Cor. 1:2). A saint is a "holy one," one who is "separated" from the ordinary, common, or unclean, "sanctified," or "set apart" for divine service. The simple point is that the gospel "raises the bar," calling Christians to lead lives that are dramatically different from those of the world. Paul urged the Philippians to attain these higher standards, "Finally, brethren, whatever is true, whatever is honorable, whatever is right, whatever is pure, whatever is lovely, whatever is of good repute, if there is any excellence and if anything worthy of praise, dwell on these things. The things you have learned and received and heard and seen in me, practice these things, and the God of peace will be with you" (Phil. 4:8-9). In short, for the sake of unity we must live in a manner consistent with the gospel's high standards.

**Humility.** Ironically, the gospel's high standards are achieved through lowliness, or "humility." Paul urged the Philippians on to unity with these words, ". . . make my joy complete by being of the same mind, maintaining the same love, united in spirit, intent on one purpose" (Phil. 2:2). By what means?

Paul continues, "Do nothing from selfishness or empty conceit, but with humility of mind regard one another as more important than yourselves; do not merely look out for your own personal interests, but also for the interests of others. Have this attitude in yourselves which was also in Christ Jesus" (Phil. 2:3-5). The "my way or the highway" spirit will destroy a man's influence now, and his soul in eternity. He may also destroy local churches along the way. Realizing that we are all sinners with weaknesses, ignorance, and vulnerability, and that no one has all the answers, should keep us humble, make us open and attentive to what others have to say, and willing to defer and cooperate with others in matters of judgment.

**Gentleness.** A child of God wouldn't hurt a fly. A natural outgrowth of humility is "gentleness" or "meekness" (Eph. 4:2). Moses, in his day was said to be "very meek, above all the men that were upon the face of the earth" (Num. 12:3, ASV). Jesus spoke of His own nature saying, "Take My yoke upon you and learn from Me, for I am gentle and humble in heart, and you will find rest for your souls. For My yoke is easy and My burden is light" (Matt. 11:29-30). Weldon Warnock wrote,

> A meek man is one who has equanimity of spirit, an inner-control of the mind that reacts properly under all circumstances. In relationship to God, it is a temper that accepts His dealings with us as good, and, therefore, without disputing (cf. James 1:21). In regard to man, it is an inward virtue that shows no resentment when wronged, nor seeks revenge when threatened. It is the opposite of bitterness, violence and vehemence (*Searching the Scriptures*, Vol. XXIX, No. 5 [May 1988], 18).

**Patience.** Humility also leads to the "patience" or "longsuffering" (ASV) that is conducive to unity. "Longsuffering is that quality of self-restraint in the face of provocation which does not hastily retaliate or promptly punish; it is the opposite of anger, and is associated with mercy. . ." (W.E. Vine). The "kindness, and tolerance, and patience" of God toward us is very effective is gaining our cooperation with Him (cf. Rom. 2:4). God expects us to exercise the same virtue toward our brethren; it too is an expression of goodwill.

**Tolerance.** "Showing tolerance for one another in love" (Eph. 4:3). The word translated "tolerance" literally means to "hold up, sustain, bear with, or endure." Local churches consist of people with different backgrounds, educational levels, mindsets, and social classes, and thus where "two or three are gathered" there will also be conflicts, misunderstandings, and hurt feelings. Genuine love for one another demands that we demonstrate forbearance. "A gentle answer turns away wrath; But a harsh word stirs up anger" (Prov. 15:1).

**Diligence.** "Being diligent to preserve the unity of the Spirit in the bond of peace" (Eph. 4:3). According to Joseph Henry Thayer, the word "diligent" means "to hasten, to make haste," and to "exert oneself, endeavor." The idea here is that we comprehend the seriousness of preserving unity, and exhaust every effort to make it a reality. It is to be done with a sense of urgency—souls are at stake! The "unity of the Spirit" (v. 3) is equivalent to "unity of the faith" in verse 13, the Spirit having revealed the faith. God's people must unite on the gospel message which the Spirit has provided.

## Incentives to Unity

The word of God provides every incentive for us to put aside the selfish behavior of division, and work hard to seek the unity of God's people.

**God's Love.** While it is true that God loves all men, and gave His Son for all (John 3:16), God loves His obedient, unified children in a special way, in a familial sense. In His prayer for unity (John 17) Jesus speaks of this love of God as an incentive for us—that the Father would have the same affection for us that He has for Jesus. "The glory which You have given Me I have given to them, that they may be one, just as We are one; I in them and You in Me, that they may be perfected in unity, so that the world may know that You sent Me, and loved them, even as You have loved Me" (John 17:22-23).

**Salvation.** "Being diligent to preserve the unity of the Spirit in the bond of peace" (Eph. 4:3), is not presented to God's people as an option; it is commanded. Hebrews 5:9 states that Jesus is the source of eternal salvation "to all those who obey Him." Those who disobey and become the source of trouble and division "will not inherit the kingdom of God" (Gal. 5:21). Paul urged the Romans to "keep your eye on those who cause dissensions and hindrances contrary to the teaching which you learned, and turn away from them" (16:17). He ordered Titus to "reject a factious man after a first and second warning, knowing that such a man is perverted and is sinning, being self-condemned" (3:10-11). On the other hand, God will richly reward those who work for oneness. "Finally, brethren, rejoice, be made complete, be comforted, be like-minded, live in peace; and the God of love and peace will be with you" (2 Cor. 13:11).

As stated earlier, winning over those who are outside of Christ depends, in part, on our being one. "I do not ask on behalf of these alone, but for those also who believe in Me through their word; that they may all be one; even as You, Father, are in Me and I in You, that they also may be in Us, so that the world may believe that You sent Me" (John 17:20-21). Wouldn't it be tragic to know that someone rejected the gospel because he witnessed discord among believers?

**Peace.** One can find trouble just about anywhere; the world is a place of conflict, tribulation, hostility, and estrangement. But, it ought to be that among God's people we can take refuge from such things. Jesus Christ is the Prince of Peace (Isa. 9:6); His message is the "gospel of peace" (Eph. 6:15) and His blood is the means by which men can have peace with God, self, and others (Col. 1:20). It was His prayer that His church be a peaceful refuge from a world of trouble (John 17).

> Who among you is wise and understanding? Let him show by his good behavior his deeds in the gentleness of wisdom. But if you have bitter jealousy and selfish ambition in your heart, do not be arrogant and so lie against the truth. This wisdom is not that which comes down from above, but is earthly, natural, demonic. For where jealousy and selfish ambition exist, there is disorder and every evil thing. But the wisdom from above is first pure, then peaceable, gentle, reasonable, full of mercy and good fruits, unwavering, without hypocrisy. And the seed whose fruit is righteousness is sown in peace by those who make peace (James 3:13-18).

**Growth.** While Paul urges saints to adopt the attitudes and conduct essential for unity (Eph. 4:1-3), and to recognize the doctrinal basis for it (Eph. 4:4-6), the main point of his appeal for unity is that it is needed to promote spiritual growth and development among the saints. Growing up to spiritual maturity, we will no longer "be children, tossed here and there by waves and carried about by every wind of doctrine, by the trickery of men, by craftiness in deceitful scheming" (Eph. 4:14). In addition, the growing saint is able to contribute his part toward "the growth of the body for the building up of itself in love" (Eph. 4:16). A congregation that is unified and at peace is like a fertile garden, for branches firmly connected to the Vine to glorify the Father, bear much fruit, and prove to be true disciples of the Lord (cf. John 15:8).

**Reflect Divine Unity.** The Father, Son, and Holy Spirit live and function in perfect harmony. This is demonstrated both in creation (Gen. 1:1-2, 26; John 1:1-3), and in human redemption (Matt. 28:19). It is God's intent that we reflect that harmony in the body of Christ.

> I do not ask on behalf of these alone, but for those also who believe in Me through their word; that they may all be one; even as You, Father, are in Me and I in You, that they also may be in Us, so that the world may believe that You sent Me. The glory which You have given Me I have given to them, that they may be one, just as We are one; I in them and You in Me, that they may be perfected in unity, so that the world may know that You sent Me, and loved them, even as You have loved Me (John 17:20-23).

**Glory To God.** Ultimately, our incentive in seeking unity should be to glorify Almighty God. He is our Creator, Sustainer, Protector, Savior, and King. To attempt an exhaustive list of all He has done on our behalf would be futile; it would be as John said about the works of Jesus, ". . . if they were written in detail, I suppose that even the world itself would not contain the books that would be written" (John 21:25).

In keeping with His eternal purpose, God gave His only begotten Son as our Savior. Through Him the church was brought into being. By its existence today, and place in God's plan from eternity past, the church shows the manifold wisdom of God to the universe. Thus, "to Him be the glory in the church and in Christ Jesus to all generations forever and ever. Amen" (Eph. 3:21).

### Conclusion

On the darkest night in all human history, our loving Savior offered prayer to the Heavenly Father. Among the last words that fell from His lips were these: "I do not ask on behalf of these alone, but for those also who believe in Me through their word; that they may all be one" (John 17:20-21). For as long as God's grace allows us to live on earth, may we never permit ourselves to forget that His parting words were on our behalf—that we might be one, and that we might have glory.

Through His word, God summons us to love Him with our whole heart, and our neighbor as ourselves. He calls on us to put aside our pride, selfishness, opinions, and personal preferences to do what is right: to stand together as one— hand in hand, and arm in arm, on the firm foundation of His revealed word—that's the critical path to unity. "Now may the God who gives perseverance and encouragement grant you to be of the same mind with one another according to Christ Jesus, so that with one accord you may with one voice glorify the God and Father of our Lord Jesus Christ" (Rom. 15:5-6).

"Behold, how good and how pleasant it is
For brothers to dwell together in unity!
It is like the precious oil upon the head,
Coming down upon the beard,
Even Aaron's beard,
Coming down upon the edge of his robes.
It is like the dew of Hermon
Coming down upon the mountains of Zion;
For there the Lord commanded the blessing—life forever" (Psa. 133).

# Building On A Rock

**Johnie Edwards**

My assignment is *"prepare a lecture on, 'Building On A Rock and tie the whole series together and wrap it up!'"* This is what I want to do. The word *rock* is found in 118 verses in the Bible. The word for rock is *petra,* which denotes a mass of rock, as distinct from *petros,* referring to a detached stone or boulder, as a stone that might be easily thrown or moved.

## The Text

The mountain message contains the basic text for this study, as Jesus draws a conclusion from what He has been teaching:

> Therefore whosoever heareth these sayings of mine, and doeth them, I will liken him to a wise man, which built his house upon a ***roc***k. And the rain descended, and the floods came, and the winds blew, and beat upon that house; and it fell not; for it was founded upon ***a roc***k. And every one that heareth these sayings of mine, and doeth them not, shall be likened unto a foolish man, which built his house upon the sand: And the rain descended, and the floods came, and the winds blew, and beat upon that

---

**Johnie Edwards** was born in Dixon, Kentucky and married Loretta Crowley. They have three sons. Johnie is a part of three generations of gospel preachers. He has worked with the Church of Christ in Ellettsville, Indiana for forty years and has been a staff-writer for *Truth Magazine* since 1977. John Isaac and Johnie Edwards share the work with the Ellettsville Church of Christ. He and his son, Johnie Paul and grandson, John Isaac Edwards own Edwards Publishers, which is committed to producing sound Bible materials. Johnie preaches in a number of gospel meetings each year, and has made two preacher training trips to the Philippines, along with Johnie Paul and John Isaac. Johnie, Johnie Paul and John Isaac have conducted a two-week preacher training for the Church of Christ in Ellettsville, the last two weeks in July for several years. A number of men, ranging from age 12-83, have attended.

> house; and it fell: and great was the fall of it. And it came to pass, when Jesus had ended these sayings, the people were astonished at his doctrine (Matt. 7:24-28).

Luke put it this way: "Whosoever cometh to me, and heareth my sayings, and doeth them, I will shew you to whom he is like: He is like a man which built an house, and digged deep, and laid the foundation on a *rock*: and when the flood arose, the stream beat vehemently upon that house, and could not shake it: for it was founded upon a *roc*k" (Luke 6:47-49).

### An Unshakeable Foundation

Every builder knows the importance of building on a foundation that cannot be shaken. To have a well built house, the foundation must be sure. The Bible says, as Paul told the Ephesians Christians: "Now therefore ye are no more strangers and foreigners, but fellow citizens with the saints, and of the household of God; And are built upon the foundation of the apostles and prophets, Jesus Christ being the chief corner stone; In whom all the building fitly framed together growth unto an holy temple in the Lord; In whom ye also are built together for an habitation of God through the Spirit" (Eph. 2:19-22). That sure foundation on whom we must build is Christ. Looking beyond his time, Isaiah penned: "Therefore thus saith the Lord God, Behold I lay in Zion for a foundation stone, a tried stone, a precious corner stone, a sure foundation: he that believeth shall not make haste" (Isa. 28:16). This prophecy of a "foundation stone, a tried stone and precious" is applied to our Lord as Matthew quotes this Isaiah prophecy: "Jesus saith unto them, Did ye never read in the scriptures, The stone which the builders rejected, the same is become the head of the corner: this is the Lord's doing, and it is marvellous in our eyes" (Matt. 21:42). The Holy Spirit guided the apostle Peter to write about this sure foundation: "To whom coming, as unto a lively stone, disallowed indeed of men, but chosen of God and precious" (1 Pet. 2:4). Peter then quotes Isaiah 28:16 as it is applied to Christ (1 Pet. 2:6-8). As Paul warned the Corinthians to ". . . take heed how he buildeth" (1 Cor. 3:10); he then added: "For other foundation can no man lay than that is laid, which is Christ Jesus" (1 Cor. 3:11). What a great foundation on which to build! May all of us take the command of Paul to heart: ". . . let every man take heed how he buildeth there upon" (1 Cor. 3:10).

### Let Us Rise Up And Build

Building, as in the days of Nehemiah, should capture a builder's attention. The Lord's people had the task to "build up the wall of Jerusalem," as "Jerusalem lieth waste. . ." (Neh. 2:17). The attitude of these building-people is worth emulating. They said: ". . . come, and let us build up the wall of Jerusalem" (Neh. 2:17). Then, " they said, Let us rise up and build. So they strengthened their hands for this good work" (Neh. 2:18). Even though they were "laughed to scorn" (Neh. 2:19); "mocked" (Neh. 4:1); "Tobiah said, even that which they build, if a fox go up, he shall even break down their stone wall" (Neh. 4:3); had to work "with one of his hands, and with the other hand held a weapon" (Neh. 4:17); working "from the rising of the morning till the stars appeared" (Neh. 4:21); "none of us put off our clothes, saving that every one put them off for washing" (Neh. 4:23); they said, "The work is great and large" (Neh. 4:19); they possessed an uncompromising disposition when Sanballat and Geshem said: "Come, let us meet together in some of the villages in the plain of Ono" (Neh. 6:2). They responded: ". . . I am doing a great work, so that I cannot come down; why should the work cease, whilst I leave it, and come down to you?" (Neh. 6:3). The Jerusalem wall was built in fifty-two days (Neh. 6:15); because "they perceived that this work was wrought of our God" (Neh. 6:16). The main reason they were successful in building is stated in Nehemiah 4:6: " So built we the wall; and all the wall was joined together unto the half thereof: for the people had a mind to work" ( Neh. 4:6). We would do well to maintain their disposition in *"Building On A Ro*ck."

### Except The Lord Build

As we are thinking about *"Building On A Rock,"* we must not forget biblical warnings. The Psalmist warned: "Except the Lord build the house, they labour in vain that build it" (Psa. 127:1). The New Testament house is the Lord's church as Paul wrote Timothy: "But if I tarry long, that thou mayest know how thou oughtest to behave thyself in the house of God, which is the church of the living God, the pillar and ground of the truth" (1 Tim. 3:15). The words of Jesus must not be overlooked as He said, "Every plant which my heavenly Father hath not planted, shall be rooted up" (Matt. 15:13). The bottom line of this teaching means, we must always build as the Lord directs, lest our building be in vain!

### Building According to the Pattern

God has never told man to build without first giving him a pattern by which to build. When God was ready for Noah to build the ark, He said: "Make thee an ark of gopher wood. . . . And this is the fashion which thou shalt make it of . . ." (Gen. 6:14-15). The word "fashion" means this is the way to build the ark. Spiritual building requires that a patten or blueprint be followed in building. "The Lord spake to Moses, saying . . . according to all that I shew thee, after the pattern of the tabernacle, and the pattern of all the instruments thereof, even so shall ye make it" (Exod. 25:1, 9). God wanted Moses to be sure to follow His exact instructions, as he built the tabernacle. So, He further said, "And look that thou make them after their pattern, which was shewed thee in the mount" (Exod. 25:40). As the Hebrew writer wrote of the priesthood of Jesus, he said of the pattern: "Who serve unto the example and shadow of heavenly things, as Moses was admonished of God when he was about to make the tabernacle: for, See, saith he, that thou make all things according to the pattern shewed to thee in the mount. . ." (Heb. 8:1-5). We need to know that whatever the Bible says on any subject, that constitutes the pattern for that subject. So, whatever is to be built, it must be built "according to the pattern"!

### The Rock-Built Church

One time when the disciples came in from preaching, Jesus asked them, "Whom do men say that I the Son of man am? And they said, Some say that thou are John the Baptist: some, Elias; and others, Jeremias, or one of the prophets. He saith unto them, But whom say ye that I am? And Simon Peter answered and said, Thou art the Christ, the Son of the living God. . . . And Jesus answered and said unto him. . . . And I say also unto thee, That thou art Peter, and upon this *Rock* I will build my church; and the gates of hell shall not prevail against it" (Matt. 16:13-18). The church of Christ is built on the deity of Christ, that He is the Son of God! The church of Christ is not built on the apostle Peter or any other man, but on the grand ledged truth confessed by Peter, that Jesus Christ is the Son of living God!

### Some Requirements of Rock-Building

1. Requirements concerning the relationship Christ has with the church:

- *The head of the church* (Eph. 1:22-23; Col. 1:18; Eph. 5:23).
- *The church must be subject to Christ* (Eph. 5: *24).*
- *The saviour of the b*ody (Eph. 5:23).
- *Its foundation* (1 Cor. 3:11).
- *Inseparable from the church* (Eph. 5:32).
- *Deliverer* (1 Cor. 15:23-28).

2. Requirements as to the worship of the church:

- *Directed to God, the Father* (Matt. 4:10; John 4:24; Rev. 20:8-9).
- *In spirit and in truth* (John 4:24; 17:17).
- *Proper channels* (Acts 2:42; Acts 20:7; 1 Cor. 16:1-2; Acts 12:5; Eph. 5:19; Heb. 2:12).

3. Requirements of the work of the church:

- *Evangelism* (Eph. 4:11-12; 1 Thess. 1:8; Phil. 4:15-16).
- *Benevolence* (Acts 6; Rom. 15:26; 1 Tim. 5:16; Acts 11:27-30).
- *Edification* (Eph. 4:12,16).

4. Requirements of the organization of the church:

- *Elders, Deacons and Saints* (Acts 14:23; Phil. 1:1).

**"Rock" Songs**

There are a number of songs which emphasize the need for building on a rock. We take a look at a few:

- *There Stands A Rock.* This song comes from Psalm 71:3 where the Psalmist said: "Thou art my Rock and my fortress." The chorus says it well: "Some build their hopes on the ever drifting sand, Some on their fame or their treasure or their land; Mine's on the Rock that forever shall stand, Jesus the 'Rock of Ages.'"
- *The Rock That Is Higher Than I.* "When my heart is overwhelmed: lead me to the Rock that is higher than I" (Psa. 61:2).
- *Rock Of Ages.* Who among us has not relished the times when we have blended our voices with this great song? It stems from the words of the Psalmist: "And it shall come to pass, while my glory passeth by, that I will put thee in a cleft of the rock, and will cover thee with my hand while I pass by" (Exod. 33:22).
- *The Solid Rock.* To keep us from being ignorant of how God has dealt with His people, Paul reminded the Corinthians that Israel of old "did drink the same spiritual drink: for they drank of that spiritual Rock that followed them: and that Rock was Christ. . ." (1 Cor. 10:1-11). May we never forget: *On Christ, the solid Rock, I stand; All other ground is sinking sand.*
- *Hide Me, Rock Of Ages.* When the storms of life rage, there is no better place than hiding in the rock of ages. "But the Lord is my defense; and my God is the rock of my refuge" (Psa. 94:22).

**A Quick Reminder of the Whole Truth Lecture Series**

- Even there are those who deny that Jesus is the Christ and when all the conflicts are passed, the Bible still says, ". . .for if ye believe not that I am he, ye shall die in your sins" (John 8:24).

- As we build on a rock, may we remember, as Peter confessed, "Thou art the Christ, the Son of the living God. . ." (Matt. 16:16).
- Since the first covenant has been "fulfilled" (Matt. 5:17-18); we build according to the "law of Christ" (Gal. 6:2).
- Though the Gnostics thought of themselves as being highly knowledgeable; we can "know the truth (John 8:32); as we have "the light" to walk in (I John 1:7). This walking brings about "fellowship one with another," as the "blood of Jesus Christ . . . cleanseth us from all sin."
- The doctrine of salvation by faith only has to give way to "faith without works is dead. . ." (Jas. 2:24, 26); as we build on complete obedience.
- While Catholicism teaches that the apostle Peter was a pope; the Bible teaches no such thing. It does teach that the church was built on the truth that Jesus Christ is the Son of the living God (Matt. 16:16-18).
- Having studied that the Bible is our only authority (2 Tim. 3:16-17); with Christ having "all authority" (Matt. 28:18), we continue to build on "For what saith the scripture. . ." (Rom. 4:3).
- Real Bible miracles are not to be compared with the charismatic movement we have encountered.
- We heard it emphasized that: "All scripture is given by the inspiration of God, and is profitable for doctrine, for reproof, for correction for instruction in righteousness: That the man of God may be perfect, throughly furnished unto all good works" (2 Tim. 3:16-17).
- The Lord's invitation can be seen from "come unto me, all ye that labour and are heavy laden, and I will give you rest" (Matt. 11:28) to "and the Spirit and the bride say, Come. And let him that heareth say, Come. And let him that is athrist come. And whosoever will, let him take the water of life freely" (Rev. 22:17).
- The Lord's kingdom "is not of this world" (John 18:36). It has already been set up (Col. 1:13; Rev. 1:9); and will be "delivered up" at "Christ's coming" (1 Cor. 15:23-28).
- Too many are shy to teach what the Bible says about the one body.

Paul said, "there is one body" (Eph. 4:4). The one body is identified as "the church" (Col. 1:24). We must teach every generation this truth, or they may never know.

- It must be emphasized that there is no creed but Christ. Having learned that the word creed has to do with what is believed. It is as Luke reported: "Forasmuch as many have taken in hand to set forth in order a declaration of those things which are most surely believed among us" (Luke. 1:1).
- One question everyone must ask is: "What must I do to be saved," as asked by the jailor (Acts 16:30). Then study to find the answer to that great question (Acts 16:31-34) which includes hearing the gospel, believing, repenting of sins, confessing faith in Christ and being baptized to be saved (Matt. 17:5; Heb. 11:6; Acts 17:30; Matt. 10:32; Mark 16:16).
- Even though mechanical instrumental music is the music of most religious bodies, and some churches of Christ, the Bible still teaches: "Speaking to yourselves in psalms and hymns and spiritual songs, singing and making melody in your heart to the Lord" (Eph. 5:19; Col. 3:16; Heb. 2:12). To avoid our worship becoming vain, we must not submit to the "doctrines and commandments of men" (Matt. 15:9). We need to heed the teaching of Jesus at the well (John 4:24).
- The church being "the pillar and ground of the truth" (1 Tim. 3:15), we must not add layers of human organizations to do the work God has assigned the New Testament church.
- To assist in answering the prayer of Jesus, "That they all may be one; as thou, Father, art in me, and I in thee, that they also may be one in us: that the world may believe that thou hast sent me" (John 17:20-21), we must be found "endeavouring to keep the unity of the Spirit in the bond of peace" (Eph. 4:3).

It is our hope and prayer that all of us have been benefitted by studying these great truths! As we look into the "perfect law of liberty" (Jas. 1:22-25), may we be determined to build according to the pattern, on the Rock of Ages.

# Part Two
# The Day Lectures

# "I Did Not Come to Abolish, But to Fulfill"

**Jim Deason**

Solomon said, "Iron sharpens iron, So one man sharpens another" (Prov. 27:17). Men are molded and shaped by their interaction. In the crucible of controversy, particularly honorable controversy, lives can be shaped and molded for the better as ideas are tested, arguments honed, and an accurate view of truth is formed. In debate, one can soon find out whether his arguments are convincing. This is perhaps what led Alexander Campbell to say, "A week's debating is worth a year's preaching" (Earl Irvin West, *Search for the Ancient Order*, Vol. I: 66).

The early church was no stranger to controversy. Within the ranks of our first brethren, a wide variety of issues were debated. Could a Christian eat meat sacrificed to idols (Rom. 8; 1 Cor. 9-10)? Can one brother take another to civil court to settle issues that should be decided within the church (1 Cor. 6)? Questions concerning marriage and divorce plagued the first century

---

**Jim Deason** was born on June 30, 1953 in Jasper, AL. In his formative years he fell under the influence of gospel preachers like Jackie Richardson, Dwight Edwards, Art Thomas, and Hiram Hutto. These men helped to place within him a passion to preach. On May 4, 1973 Jim married the former Paige Adams, daughter of J. Wiley Adams, and they have three children: Melissa Gipson (Bell Buckle, TN), David Deason (Athens, AL), and Wiley Deason (Memphis, TN). Six grandchildren (Hannah, Emily, Julia, Joshua, Emma Grace, and James David) light up his life. Jim has preached locally in Georgia, South Carolina, Alabama, and Tennessee and holds seven to eight gospel meetings each year. He has done foreign work in Almaty, Kazakhstan and Mariupol, Ukraine and was instrumental in getting Bob and Sandra Waldron's *History and Geography of the Bible* translated and printed in the Russian language. Jim is a regular contributor to *Biblical Insights.*

church (1 Cor. 7) and were, no doubt, hotly contested. So much was this so that the church at Corinth wrote Paul to ask about it. The role of women was a major issue in the first century church: Whether or under what conditions women might speak in the assembly (1 Cor. 11, 14; 1 Tim. 2)? Paul had a spiritual tussle with Hymenaeus and Philetus over whether the resurrection had already taken place (2 Tim. 2:16-18; cf. 1 Cor. 15). This issue was significant because it had "upset the faith of some." Pre-gnostic philosophies like asceticism (Col. 2:20-23) had to be confronted in the church at Colossae. Paul said that these have "the appearance of wisdom in self-made religion . . . but are of no value against fleshly indulgence" (Col. 2:23). These are just a few of several issues that I mention merely to demonstrate that controversy existed in the early church. Truth was revealed, discussion took place, and arguments were formed in order to influence people in the way of right and strengthen them in the practice of faith.

## The Law, the Christian, and Conflict

In my judgment, the most significant controversy faced by the early church centered around the Christian's (particularly the Gentile's) relation to the Law of Moses. As one makes a quick survey of the book of Acts, little of significance is seen of this issue in chapters 1-9, but the battle lines were drawn when Peter went to Caesarea and preached the gospel to Cornelius and his family (Acts 10).

Indications are that God knew preaching the gospel to the Gentiles would be a problem, even for Peter. God sent him a vision, not once but three times (Acts 10:9-16), to impress upon his heart "that God is not one to show partiality, but in every nation the man who fears Him and does what is right is welcome to Him" (Acts 10:34-35). Furthermore, Peter understood that his preaching to the Gentiles would be a problem for his Jewish brethren. He told Cornelius, "You yourselves know how unlawful it is for a man who is a Jew to associate with a foreigner or to visit with him" (Acts 10:28). Peter, therefore, wasn't surprised when "those who were circumcised took issue with him" (Acts 11:2) and he was called upon to defend his actions.

With this event, the controversy over the Christian's relationship to the Law of Moses came front and center. There were two specific questions: (1) Is the gospel to be preached to the Gentiles? (2) Must a Gentile be circumcised to be saved? Approximately, two-thirds of the book of Acts is devoted to the historical narrative surrounding the inclusion of the Gentiles and the controversy that ensued.

On his first missionary journey and in Pisidian Antioch, Paul entered the synagogue and, after the reading of the Law and the prophets (Acts 13:15), was permitted to speak. His message was that "God has brought to Israel a Savior, Jesus" (Acts 13:23) and "through Him forgiveness of sins is proclaimed to you, and through Him everyone who believes is freed from all things, from which you could not be freed through the Law of Moses" (Acts 13:38-39). Preaching Jesus as Savior and the limitation of the Law stoked the fires of controversy. Rejection in the synagogue turned Paul and Barnabas to the Gentiles (Acts 13:46) and jealous Jews instigated a persecution that followed Paul and Barnabas into Iconium and Lystra (Acts 14).

After Paul returned to Antioch of Syria, men came from Judea teaching, "Unless you are circumcised according to the custom of Moses, you cannot be saved" (Acts 15:1). Paul and Barnabas went to Jerusalem and met with other apostles, the elders, and the church in Jerusalem about the matter. Certain of the Pharisees who had believed stood up, saying, "It is necessary to circumcise them and to direct them to observe the Law of Moses" (Acts 15:5). There was much debate over the issue (Acts 15:7). Peter related the conversion of the Gentiles in Cornelius' household (Acts 15:7-11) and affirmed that they were saved on the basis of faith, not by the yoke of the Law. In affirmation of Peter's words, Paul and Barnabas related their work among the Gentiles (Acts 15:12). Finally, James quoted from Amos, the prophet (Acts 15:13-19), whose words were words of inclusion. God had spoken on the matter. In the words of James, "Therefore it is my judgment that we do not trouble those who are turning to God from among the Gentiles" (Acts 15:19). Yet, the Jerusalem conference did not entirely abate the controversy.

Upon deciding to take a second journey, Paul persuaded Silas to join him in visiting the churches of Asia Minor (Acts 15:36, 40-41). In Lystra, Paul found a young man named Timothy whom he recruited as a traveling companion. Needing to move freely among the synagogues, Paul "took him and circumcised him because of the Jews who were in those parts, for they all knew that his father was a Greek" (Acts 16:3). Avoiding the emotional issue of circumcision seems to have been the fundamental motive.

Paul's arrest in Jerusalem was based upon the false charge that he had defiled the Temple by bringing a Greek into its sacred places (Acts 21:26-30). His enemies said, "This is the man who preaches to all men everywhere against our people and the Law and this place . . ." (Acts 21:28).

The Christian and his relationship to the Law, therefore, was one of the most significant controversies of the first century. The content of the epistles give testimony to this fact. Following the book of Acts in our English Bibles are twenty-two letters written by five or six authors (depending upon how you view the authorship of Hebrews). Of these twenty-two books, at least six contain significant sections dealing with this controversy: Romans, Galatians, Ephesians, Colossians, Hebrews, and Revelation. Paul pointedly wrote to the Galatians saying,

> Behold I, Paul, say to you that if you receive circumcision, Christ will be of no benefit to you. And I testify again to every man who receives circumcision, that he is under obligation to keep the whole Law. You have been severed from Christ, you who are seeking to be justified by law; you have fallen from grace (Gal. 5:2-4).

Controversy over the relationship between Jew and Gentile, Christ and the Law, was a significant part of the first century Christian experience.

What relationship did Christ and His followers sustain with the Law of Moses? Was the gospel of Christ intended for all people and, if it was, are we also under obligation to keep the Law of Moses? Can we turn to the Law and the prophets to authorize present day religious practices? These are questions that troubled the first century church and they have been debated in almost every generation since.

### The Law of Moses Foretold of Christ and the Gospel

Since the introduction of sin into the world by Adam, the promise of God has been to redeem man from the bondage of sin. The story of redemption and a coming Redeemer is the theme of the Old Testament. Perhaps Genesis 3:15 is a veiled reference to the ultimate victory over sin when God promised that the seed of woman would bruise the head of the serpent. The promise came into clearer focus when God promised Abraham, ". . . in you all the families of the earth will be blessed" (Gen. 12:3). That promise was renewed through Isaac and Jacob; and of Judah it was prophesied, "The scepter shall not depart from Judah, Nor the ruler's staff from between his feet, Until Shiloh comes, And to him shall be the obedience of the peoples" (Gen. 49:10).

Through the eye of prophetic blessing Balaam said, "I see him, but not now; I behold him, but not near; A star shall come forth from Jacob, A scepter shall rise from Israel, And shall crush through the forehead of Moab, And tear down all the sons of Sheth" (Num 24:17).

God said to David, "When your days are complete and you lie down with your fathers, I will raise up your descendant after you, who will come forth from you, and I will establish his kingdom. He shall build a house for My name, and I will establish the throne of his kingdom forever" (2 Sam. 7:12-13). Peter said that God was speaking of Jesus (Acts 2:29-31).

Isaiah prophesied that Jesus would be born of a virgin (Isa. 7:14; cf. Matt. 1:23) and that the "government will rest on his shoulders" (Isa. 9:6; cf. Luke 1:31-33). He prophesied that Jesus, the suffering servant, would bear our griefs, carry our sorrows, and that He would be pierced for our transgressions (Isa. 53).

This wonderful Messiah would establish a new covenant that would be for all the people. Moses said, "The Lord your God will raise up for you a prophet like me from among you, from your countrymen, you shall listen to him" (Deut. 18:15; cf. Acts 3:23; 7:37). Moses and Elijah appeared with Jesus on the Mount of Transfiguration but it was of the Savior that God spoke to Peter, James, and John. He proclaimed, "This is My beloved Son, with whom I am well-pleased; listen to Him!" (Matt. 17:5).

Prophesying of the Messiah's kingdom, Isaiah said that "all the nations will stream into it" (Isa. 2:2) and herein the Lord will "teach us concerning His ways and that we may walk in His paths" (Isa. 2:3).

To Jeremiah God said, "Behold, days are coming, declares the Lord, "when I will make a new covenant with the house of Israel and with the house of Judah. . . .I will put My law within them and on their heart I will write it; and I will be their God, and they shall be My people" (Jer. 31:31, 33). The writer of Hebrews, after affirming that Jesus is a mediator of a better covenant and quoting the promise of Jeremiah 31:31-34, said, "When He said, 'A new covenant,' He has made the first obsolete. But whatever is becoming obsolete and growing old is ready to disappear" (Heb. 8:13).

Jesus rebuked the Jews of His day for not receiving Him. Pointing out their inconsistencies He said, "You search the Scriptures because you think that in them you have eternal life; it is these that testify about Me" (John 5:39).

## The Nature of the Law of Moses

I think it is important at this juncture to look at the nature of the first covenant, the Law of Moses.

*First, the Law of Moses was given only to the children of Israel.* The book we know today as Deuteronomy was given this title by the translators of the Septuagint in the third century before Christ. The name Deuteronomy means "second law" referring to the fact that Moses was repeating to a new generation what had originally been given at Mount Sinai (Horeb). Hear Moses when he says, "Now this is the law which Moses set before the sons of Israel" (Deut. 4:44) and "The Lord our God made a covenant with us at Horeb" (Deut. 5:2). The Law of Moses was never intended as a universal law. Paul reaffirms this fact in the New Testament when he said ". . . to whom (the Israelites, jhd) belongs the adoption as sons, and the glory and the covenants and the giving of the Law and the temple service and the promises" (Rom. 9:4).

*Second, the Law of Moses, including the Ten Commandments, was not given to nor observed by previous generations*. Moses said, "The Lord our God made a covenant with us at Horeb. The Lord did not make this covenant with our fathers, but with us, with all those of us alive here today" (Deut. 5:2-3).

*Third, the Law of Moses was not intended for other nations.* Moses, in speaking of the nations around them, asked, "For what great nation is there that has a god so near to it as is the Lord our God whenever we call on Him? Or what great nation is there that has statutes and judgments as righteous as this whole law which I am setting before you today?" (Deut. 4:7-8).

*Fourth, specifically, the Law of Moses was not given to the Gentiles.* Paul said that, "when Gentiles who do not have the Law do instinctively the things of the Law, these, not having the Law, are a law to themselves" (Rom. 2:14). This same apostle reminded the Gentile Ephesians that formerly they were "separate from Christ, excluded from the commonwealth of Israel, and strangers to the covenants of promise, having no hope and without God in the world" (Eph. 2:12), but now, in the blood of Jesus Christ, they were brought near (Eph. 2:13).

*Fifth, the Law of Moses was designed to point out sin and to point men to the Savior.* The Hebrew writer affirmed that the Law "has only a shadow of the good things to come" (Heb. 10:1) and, by its animal sacrifices, could never "take away sins" (Heb. 10:4). However, "through the offering of the body of Jesus Christ" (Heb. 10:10), full pardon for sin is found. The insufficiency of animal sacrifices compared with the all-sufficient sacrifice of Jesus Christ is the reason why Paul told the Jews of Antioch in Pisidia that "through Him everyone who believes is freed from all things, from which you could not be freed through the Law of Moses" (Acts 13:39).

*Sixth, the Law was given to point out sin.* Paul explained: "Why the Law then? It was added because of transgressions, having been ordained through angels by the agency of a mediator, until the seed would come to whom the promise had been made" (Gal. 3:19). The law "taught that certain acts were sinful, it gave names to those actions, and showed that they were offensive to God, hurtful to men, and deserving of death" (Dan Petty, *"Alexander Campbell's 'Sermon on the Law,"* www.lessons.online.info/churchhistory.htm). No one could be justified by the Law but, "through the Law comes the knowledge of sin" (Rom. 3:20). Paul said, "I would not have come to know sin except through the Law; for I would not have known about coveting if the Law had not said, "You shall not covet" (Rom. 7:7).

*Seventh, the Law of Moses was given to bring us to Jesus Christ.* "But before faith came, we were kept in custody under the law, being shut up to the faith which was later to be revealed. Therefore the Law has become our tutor to lead us to Christ, so that we may be justified by faith. But now that faith has come, we are no longer under a tutor" (Gal. 3:23-25). Mike Willis described the role of a tutor in his commentary on Galatians. The tutor "was a slave who was charged with attending an upper-class boy during his years before reaching maturity. He had the duty of conducting the boy to and from school, although he had no responsibilities as the teacher; rather, his job was to take the boy to the teacher" (*Truth Commentaries: Galatians*, 163). The Law of Moses, therefore, served God's purpose to bring history to the fulness of time when He sent forth His Son to redeem mankind from sin (Gal. 4:4-6).

### Jesus and the Law

This brings us to the specific point of this lecture. What relationship did Jesus sustain to the Law of Moses? What did Jesus mean when He said, "Do not think that I came to abolish the Law or the Prophets; I did not come to abolish but to fulfill" (Matt. 5:17)? When considering the role of the Law in our lives today, understanding Jesus' statement becomes a critical issue.

*First, Jesus recognized the authority of the Law.* Even at the tender age of twelve, Jesus possessed an above average knowledge of the Law of Moses. He amazed the Jewish rabbis with His understanding and application of the Scriptures (Luke 2:46-47). Later, in the wilderness, His first response to Satan's temptations was to quote Scripture (Luke 4:4, 8, 12). Take a quick look sometime through any of the gospels, particularly Matthew because it was written primarily for Jewish readers, and observe how often Jesus quoted from Scripture. In responding to the Sadducees,

Jesus made His argument for the resurrection on the tense of a single verb (Matt. 22:29-33). When Jesus entered into a discussion with anyone about the Law of Moses, He knew what He was talking about. It strikes me that, if Jesus believed it was important to possess such a detailed knowledge of the Scriptures, shouldn't we (cf. Eph. 1:15-17; 3:3-4; 4:11-13; Phil. 1:9; Col. 1:9-10; 2 Tim. 2:15)?

Jesus urged, "For truly I say to you, until heaven and earth pass away, not the smallest letter or stroke shall pass from the Law until all is accomplished. Whoever then annuls one of the least of these commandments, and teaches others to do the same, shall be called least in the kingdom of heaven . . ." (Matt. 5:18-19). The commands of the Law were not to be annulled, at least until "all was accomplished" (Matt. 5:18-19). Vine defines the word *annul* in this way: "'to loosen,' especially by way of deliverance, sometimes has the meaning of 'breaking, destructively,' *e.g.*, of 'breaking' commandments, not only infringing them, but loosing the force of them, rendering them not binding, Matt. 5:19" (W. E. Vine, M. F. Unger, & W. White, *Vine's Complete Expository Dictionary of Old and New Testament Words* [2:78]). Even in view of the fact that He would one day fulfill its prophecies, complete its purposes, and replace it with His own Law, Jesus taught that the Law of Moses was to be respected. To Jesus, a statement from the Law settled any religious question.

*Second, Jesus affirmed that the Law must be kept until such time as it was fulfilled.* Not only is this seen in Jesus' statement in Matthew 5:19 but He demonstrated this numerous times in His ministry. A lawyer once came to Jesus asking Him the question, "Teacher, what shall I do to inherit eternal life?" (Luke 10:25). Jesus pointed the man to Moses by asking, "What is written in the Law?" (Luke 10:26). After the lawyer answered correctly, Jesus told him, "Do this and you will live" (Luke 10:28). When the rich young ruler came to Jesus asking essentially the same question, Jesus pointed him to the Ten Commandments and told him to keep them (Matt. 19:16-21). He knew that the young man had already violated the first and last of the Commandments. To the ten lepers whom He was about to cleanse Jesus said, "Go and show yourselves to the priests" (Luke 17:14). This was an ordinance of the Law (cf. Lev. 14:2) and required for every leper to be pronounced clean and readmitted into society.

Jesus spoke to His disciples and said, "The scribes and the Pharisees have seated themselves in the chair of Moses; therefore all that they tell you, do and observe, but do not do according to their deeds; for they say things and do not do them" (Matt. 23:2-3). The tension between Jesus and the Pharisees was not created because they taught men to keep the Law of Moses. It was because of their hypocrisy and their manmade traditions. As they taught the Law, Jesus told His disciples to listen, learn, and obey.

*Third, Jesus affirmed that He came to fulfill the Law.* "Do not think that I came to abolish the Law or the Prophets; I did not come to abolish but to fulfill" (Matt. 5:17). Speaking to His disciples just prior to His ascension, Jesus reminded them, "These are My words which I spoke to you while I was still with you, that all things which are written about Me in the Law of Moses and the Prophets and the Psalms must be fulfilled" (Luke 24:44).

Jesus fulfilled the Law in at least two ways. First, He kept its precepts perfectly. Pointing us to Jesus as a perfect example, Peter encouraged us to follow in His steps because He "committed no sin, nor was any deceit found in His mouth" (1 Pet. 2:21-22; cf. Isa. 53:9). We are told by the writer of Hebrews that He "has been tempted in all things as we are, yet without sin" (Heb. 4:15). Wouldn't it be nice to know someone who kept God's laws perfectly? Actually, we can — and His name is Jesus. Secondly, Jesus fulfilled the Law by fulfilling all that had been prophesied about Him. Most scholars list over 300 specific prophecies (and many more allusions) in the Old Testament that refer to and were fulfilled by Jesus of Nazareth. These prophecies include the following:

- He would miraculously be born of a virgin (Isa. 7:14).
- He would be born in the city of Bethlehem (Mic. 5:2).
- He would be a prophet (Deut. 18:15).
- He would descend through the family of Abraham and David (Gen. 12:3; 2 Sam. 7:12-14).
- He would die for the sins of the world (Isa. 53).
- He would be buried in a rich man's grave (Isa. 53:9).
- He would be raised from the dead (Psa. 16:9-11).

There are many, many more prophecies which Jesus fulfilled. He fulfilled all that the prophets said about Him. Not a single prophecy failed.

Some see an apparent contradiction between Jesus' statement, "Do not think that I came to abolish the Law" (Matt. 5:17) and Paul's claim that Jesus did that very thing, *i.e.*, "abolishing in his flesh the enmity, which is the Law of commandments..." (Eph. 2:15). The word *abolish* in Matthew 5:17 means "to invalidate" and is set in contrast to the word *fulfill*, i.e., "I did not come to abolish, but to fulfill." Contrary to the opinion of the Pharisees, Jesus did not come as an opponent to Moses and the Law nor to prevent its fulfillment. Rather, He brought its promises and prophecies to fruition.

Jesus also added a time element when He said, ". . . not the smallest letter or stroke shall pass from the Law until all is accomplished" (Matt. 5:18). The implication is that, once the Law was fulfilled and all was accomplished, the Law would pass away.

This is the very point that Paul is making in Ephesians 2:15. If Jesus accomplished His purpose and fulfilled the Law, then, there is no contradiction. The word *abolish* in Ephesians 2:15 means, "to take out of the sphere of activity." By keeping its precepts and fulfilling its prophecies, Jesus removed or abolished the Law in order that all men might be one in Christ Jesus (Eph. 2:11-16)

As Jesus hung on the cross, His final words were, "It is finished!" (John 19:30). The significance of these three words is likely far greater than any of us can imagine. His purpose for coming to earth was consummated. The supreme act of redemption was done. He had completed all that had been planned from before the foundation of the world for Him to accomplish by robing Himself in human flesh. Everything Jesus meant when He said, "I did not come to abolish but to fulfill" (Matt. 5:17), was finished and the Law of Moses was nailed to the cross and taken out of the way (Col. 2:14).

### Christ Is The End of the Law

"For Christ is the end of the law for righteousness to everyone who believes" (Rom 10:4). The Hebrew writer said that Jesus is the "mediator of a new covenant" (Heb. 9:15). This covenant is new in nature and, by implication, better. The Law of Moses, being only a shadow and insufficient to remove sin, was replaced by the supreme sacrifice of Jesus and this new covenant. The Hebrew writer said of Jesus, "He takes away the first in order to establish the second. By this will we have been sanctified through the offering of the body of Jesus Christ once for all" (Heb. 10:9-10).

Today we are under this new covenant, the "Law of Christ" (Gal. 6:2; 1 Cor. 9:20-21). It is not Moses to whom we turn for religious authority but Jesus. He possesses "all authority . . . in heaven and on earth" (Matt. 28:18). He is the "blessed and only Sovereign, the King of kings and Lord of lords" (1 Tim. 6:15). "All things are in subjection under His feet" and He is "head over all things to the church" (Eph. 1:22).

### Applying The Principles

Most of the religious world does not recognize a distinction between the Law of Moses and the gospel. Few feel they need divine authority for religious practices and those who do might go to the book of Leviticus as quickly as they do the book of Acts to find it. Yet, we have shown that the Law of Moses is not our standard of faith and rule of practice today. If it is true, and it is, that we are not under the Law of Moses but subject to Christ and His will in all things, some important and relevant applications follow.

*1. Christians today are not subject to the Ten Commandments.* This does not mean that we are free to steal, murder, and commit adultery, etc. These things are wrong today, however, not because they are forbidden by the Ten Commandments, but because they are condemned by the gospel of Christ.

*2. The practice of tithing is not to be bound in New Testament churches.* The practice of tithing is common among denominations today. Sectarian preachers offer as their biblical authority the words of Malachi, "'Bring the whole tithe into the storehouse, so that there may be food in My house, and test Me now in this,' says the Lord of hosts, 'if I will not open for you the windows of heaven and pour out for you a blessing until it overflows'" (Mal. 3:10). Yet this is an Old Covenant passage and, as such, is not to be bound upon New Covenant people. While the New Testament is silent on tithing, we are commanded to give bountifully as we are prospered upon the first day of the week (2 Cor. 9:6-7; 1 Cor. 16:2).

*3. Christians cannot go to the Old Testament to find authority for mechanical instruments of music in worship.* King David certainly worshiped with trumpets and stringed instruments (Ps. 33:1-3; 150:3-5), because God commanded their use (2 Chron. 29:25). Does that mean we can use musical instruments in worship today? If it does, then what about "dancing before the Lord" (Ps. 150:4), burning incense, and offering animal sacrifices? David did those things also. If we are to turn to the Old Covenant for authority for one religious practice, what are we to do with the others?

*4. The Sabbath day is no longer to be observed.* God gave Israel the Sabbath law at Mt. Sinai to remind them that He made the world in six days and rested on the seventh. The seventh day, to ancient Israel, was to be a day of complete rest. Sabbatarians argue for a distinction between ceremonial law and moral law claiming that, although the ceremonial is no longer applicable, we must observe the moral. They maintain that the Sabbath is a part of the moral law and, therefore, binding today. Yet, Moses made no such distinction. He viewed all of God's statutes and judgments as a single entity, the "whole law" (Exod. 4:1-8), and commanded the people that they should not add to it nor subtract from it. Jesus died to take the Old Law out of the way (Col. 2:14) and replace it with the New (Heb. 10:9). The apostles, in the New Covenant, specifically ordered that, "no one is to act as your judge in regard to . . . a Sabbath day— things which are a mere shadow of what is to come; but the substance belongs to Christ" (Col. 2:16-17). Hence, there is no divine authority for Sabbath observance today.

### Conclusion

In view of these few observations, I think it is appropriate for me to ask the same question posed by the apostle Peter, "Why do you put God to the test by placing upon the neck of the disciples a yoke (the Law of Moses, jhd) which neither our fathers nor we have been able to bear?" (Acts 15:10). New Testament writers saw the "Law of commandments" as a barrier, a dividing wall, that was broken down by the death of Jesus on the cross that all men might be one in Christ (Eph. 2:11-16). The man who seeks to be justified by the Law, or who attempts to find authority for modern practices from within the Law, has fallen from the grace which is in Christ Jesus (Gal. 5:2-4).

# Walking in the Light: Gnosticism and John's Letters

**Daniel H. King, Sr.**

It has long been understood that John's writings intentionally address themselves to certain Gnostic beliefs in order to refute those notions, even if they do so in a way that is often subtle and restrained. Certainly John does not go about his work the way that the later "heresy hunters" did, but then again he was only dealing with a system that was more or less in its infancy, perhaps only a new and dangerous way of thinking rather than an organized movement or a fully developed system of thought.

These later orthodox Christian writers on the other hand who worked one hundred and more years afterward were treating several distinct and

---

**Daniel H. King, Sr.** was born August 1, 1948 in Union City, TN. He and his wife Donna have two children: Dan Jr. and Jennifer. Dan has preached for churches in Downers Grove, IL and Lakeland, FL, but most of his local work has been in Tennessee. He lives in Nashville, TN and is associated with the church of Christ in Kingston Springs, TN, where he serves as local preacher and elder. He has written extensively in many religious journals, both popular and professional. Dan attended Wayne State University, David Lipscomb College (B.A.), Harding Graduate School of Religion (M.A.), and Vanderbilt University (Ph.D.). He served as an adjunct professor at Tennessee State University in 1976 and at Florida College during 1984-88. He has authored several tracts and a number of books: *Hebrew and Hellenistic Thought in the Book of Wisdom*, *We Have a Right* (with Mike Willis), *Responsibility and Authority in the Spiritual Realm* (with Leon Boyd), *At the Feet of the Master Teacher*, *Commentary on the Gospel of John*, *Commentary on the Epistles of John*, *Commentary on the Book of Hebrews*, *The Days of Creation*, *Searching for Happiness?*, and *Ezekiel* and *Hebrews* in the Bible Text Book series. Currently he is engaged in writing a commentary on the Old Testament book of Daniel.

full-blown Gnostic sects operating on the basis of well thought out doctrinal positions. John saw only early trends toward an eventual apostasy, while Justin Martyr, Irenaeus, Hippolytus, and others observed the smoldering wreckage that decades of this twisted ideology had wrought upon the body of Christ: divided churches, alienated relationships, broken fellowship, strange sounding doctrines, Scripture reinterpreted and uprooted from its historical moorings, libertinism on the one hand and prudish asceticism on the other, and spiritual villains like Cain and Judas turned into the splendid heroes of the new Gnosis.

It is our plan to address in this essay John's most obvious points of attack against this insidious and threatening way of viewing religion and in particular the religion of Jesus Christ. In order to do so, we would like to approach our subject generally, and then specifically. The first aspect of our study will address some fundamental principles of Gnostic thinking in order to assure that we appreciate some of the intricacies of that sophisticated theological network which John was crossing swords with. Gnosticism was extraordinarily complex as it developed over time. The *Refutatio* of Hippolytus (written about A.D. 222), a kind of encyclopedia of heresies, listed some thirty-three distinctly different Gnostic systems of belief. Groups like the Sethians, Ophites, Cainites, Carpocratians, Borborites, Bogomils, Paulicans, Archonites, Cathars, Thomasines, Valentinian, Basilidian, Cerinthian, Marcionites, followers of Simon Magus, along with many others, are mentioned by the early Christian writers and represented in the surviving literature.

On the other hand, there are a few things which almost all Gnostics had in common. We shall attempt to draw together some of these principles before we proceed to our analysis of John's rejoinder. Next, we will attempt to isolate several texts from John's writings and look more closely at them in the context of the Gnostic menace.

### Gnostic Basics

Only half a century ago investigation into the nature and beliefs of the Gnostics was limited to only two basic sources. The first was comprised principally of the very few remarks found in the New Testament regarding this heresy in its earliest developmental stages in the epistle to the Colossians, in the epistles of John, especially 1 John, and a few other simple but sometimes arguable references. The second was the rather extensive assortment of treatments and quotations from the so-called "heresiologists," the orthodox Christian scholars who in the early centuries of the church wrote refutations of these heretics and their literary works. They are many in number and their literature is quite extensive: Justin Martyr (*First Apology*), Irenaeus of Lyons (*Against Heresies*), Hippolytus of Rome (*Refutation of All Heresies*), Tertullian (*Prescription Against The Heretics*), Clement of Alexandria (*Paedagogus*, and *Stromata*), Origen (Eight books of exposition on the Gospel of John deal with Gnostic exegesis of that work; *Against Celsus*), Eusebius of Caesarea (*Church History*), Epiphanius of Salamis (*Anchoratus*, "the firmly anchored"; *Panarion*, "the Medicine Chest"), Ephraem of Edessa (*Madrashe)*, Theodoret of Cyrus (*History of Heresy,* 5 vols.), Augustine (*De haeresibus*, "catalogue of heresies" listing 88 heresies), and John of Damascus (*Source of Knowledge*). The major problem with this wide body of source material is the second-hand nature of it. It did not proceed from the Gnostics themselves but from their avowed enemies. So, many scholars were uncertain about whether or not to trust some aspects of the material, considering it fanciful and perhaps even at times a misrepresentation of these groups and of their actual views.

The discoveries at Nag Hammadi on the west bank of the Nile in Upper Egypt near the ancient monastic settlement of Chenoboskion, in 1945 and afterward, changed the entire dynamic in terms of the study of this old but already well-known heresy. Ancient receipts found with the manuscripts firmly dated their burial to the era immediately preceding A.D. 350. It seems that they represented manuscripts from a library (a Father Pachom is mentioned, along with presbyters and monks) which may have been hidden in a large pottery jar after Athanasius of Alexandria issued his Thirty-Ninth Festal Letter condemning the writings of the heretics. At any rate, scholars now had available to them many of the original documents of this prolific movement, whereas previously they were limited to descriptions by the "heresiologists" in their anti-Gnostic diatribes.

Thirteen major volumes were contained in the entirety of this extensive and well preserved collection, containing some fifty-one separate writings, with 1153 pages out of an original total of 1257 pages. Six of the documents were already known from other sources. Ten tractates were preserved only in fragmentary condition, but the other thirty-one were in good or even excellent condition. They have become the best examples of the literature of the Gnostic sects which have come down to us. Names like the *Gospel of Truth*, the *Apocryphon of John*, the *Gospel of Thomas* and the *Gospel of Philip*, as well as the *Gospel of the Egyptians*, the *Apocalypse of Paul*, the *Apocalypse of James*, the *Apocalypse of Adam,* and many other titles saw the light of day for the first time in many hundreds of years. This intrigued scholars and a vast body of investigational and analytical literature has resulted from the discoveries associated with Nag Hammadi.

These mysterious new documents came from several different Gnostic sects and movements and therefore reflected more than just one stream of Gnostic thought. This is one of the truly valuable aspects of the literature. Consequently, Coptic scholars were finally able to read the writings of these Gnostic thinkers directly, rather than through the prism of orthodox theologians wishing to refute their arguments and cast their views in the worst possible light. It shortly became clear that most of what the heresy hunters said about them was absolutely true. Their thinking and writing were quite unconventional and certainly unorthodox! Scholarship has learned much more besides. Orthodox theologians like Irenaeus and Hippolytus were justly upset at the many outrageous views and claims of these heterodox claimants to *gnosis*. Now after some fifty years of close investigation of their primary source materials, several facts are crystal clear to all of those who read after them:

*1. Gnostics laid claim to a higher "knowledge" above and beyond that which was revealed through Jesus Christ and His apostles and prophets.* What has been called the "central myth" of Gnosticism is the idea of the presence in man of a divine "spark" which has proceeded from the divine world and has fallen into this world of destiny, birth, and death, and which must be reawakened through its own divine counterpart in order to be finally restored. Gnostic revelation of knowledge was vastly different from the biblical concept of revelation. In the *Book of Thomas* (The Contender) Christ says to His (supposed) twin brother Judas Thomas, "Examine yourself and know who you are and how you were and how you shall be. . . .You have already come to knowledge, and you will be called, 'The one who knows himself,' for he who has not known himself has known nothing. But he who has known himself has already come to knowledge concerning the depth of the All." In essence, therefore, Gnostic knowledge is to be identified with "knowledge of self" in the sense of a rediscovery of the primordial divine spark within the human soul.

*2. The "knowledge" about which Gnostics spoke was esoteric and elitist in nature.* It was not ordinary data or information which could be learned by ordinary people. This knowledge was exclusive to those who were visited with it. Only certain *pneumatikoi* or "spiritual ones" claimed to possess this special knowledge of truth and of spiritual realities. Ordinary

Christians did not and could not grasp this secret knowledge. The content of this knowledge or understanding was primarily religious, in so far as it relates to the background of man, the world, and God, but also because it rested not upon one's own investigation of truth, but on heavenly mediation. It was knowledge provided through divine revelation which was made available only to those who were elect and chosen to be able to receive it. Valentinus, for example, believed that only certain people have the spiritual spark and the chance for salvation, and so only they could be taught these doctrines and benefit from them.

The arcane nature of the material is obvious from its essential style and the character of the writing. It is not easy to read, nor does it seem that was it intended to be:

> And there is scarcely any religious literature written in any language at any time that can be more perplexing and deliberately obscure than some of the Gnostic writings of Christian antiquity. To be sure, these are all available in good English translation. But even as translators try to present these texts in terms comprehensible to modern readers, they remain obtuse in places, as, for example, they detail the complex relations of incalculable divine beings described in the subtle nuances of highly symbolic language. Sometimes you may suspect the translation is bad, but in fact, most of the time the English translation is clearer than the Coptic of the texts themselves [Bart D. Ehrman, *Lost Christianities: The Battles for Scripture and the Faiths We Never Knew* (New York: Oxford University Press, 2003), 115].

So, it was genuinely esoteric in character, and calculated to be that way. The breadth of this "knowledge" was almost unlimited. It could pertain to a basic insight into the nature of man, his origin or his destiny, but it could also extend far beyond any of this to include the entirety of a doctrinal system. The New Testament, before its close, voiced stern warnings regarding the gathering storm surrounding these views, calling them "the *gnosis* falsely so called" (1 Tim. 6:20, 21).

*3. Gnostic "knowledge" was opposed to faith as the means of salvation; Gnostics believed that reception of the gnosis was the only route to salvation.* Faith, which is considered in the New Testament as one of the most rudimentary elements of the salvation process, was looked upon by the Gnostic as a form of pitiful ignorance. The Gnostic was not concerned with faith but with his own special brand of "knowledge." In the *Gospel of Philip* the following pronouncement appears: "He who has the *gnosis* of the truth is free. Ignorance is a slave." But not only ignorance stands in contrast to the knowledge of the Gnostic, so also does faith, since it knows almost nothing concerning itself and remains attached to what is immediately in the foreground. Paul wrote, "By grace are you saved through faith, and that not of yourselves, it is the gift of God" (Eph. 2:8); and, "Therefore, being justified by faith we have peace with God through our Lord Jesus Christ" (Rom. 5:1).

In the New Testament documents emphasis is placed on the importance of faith. In the Gnostic documents emphasis is placed on the importance of knowledge. The Christian believer trusts God in the absence of knowledge. It is precisely, therefore, this opposition of "faith" and "knowledge" which was one of the central themes in the strenuous and hard-hitting debates of the early church heresy hunters with the Gnostic doctrinal system. The Gnostic "Christ" was not a suffering savior. He did not suffer and could not suffer. He was above all that sort of thing. He was an Illuminator or Revelator. Man is "redeemed" in the language of *gnosis* only in the sense that the divine spark is released by illumination through increased knowledge, resulting in self-awareness and a high level of spiritual insight.

*4. Gnostics were dualistic in their thinking: they believed in two principles of good and evil, diametrically opposed to one another.* This dualism was made concrete in two great divisions of reality – the physical and the spiritual. The physical world was evil, and the spiritual world was good. These philosophical notions were foreign to the Bible; they were patently borrowed from both Zoroastrianism and Platonism, although in the process of this borrowing the Gnostics put their own unique twist on the dualism which resulted. Iranian Zoroastrianism sets a good god and an evil god at the beginning of world history and views this history as dominated by the conflict between the two, until the good god with help from his adherents at the end of time carries off the victory. Platonic thought knew two levels of existence: the spiritual eternal ideas and their transitory material (spatial) counterparts, which form the cosmos. Neither of these notions was followed precisely in Gnosticism. Gnostics ignored the moral aspects of Zoroastrianism and played down the beauty inherent in the Platonist's material world. In fact, the late Neoplatonist Plotinus (third century A.D.) in his treatise *On Providence* wrote in opposition to the Gnostic perception of matter and spirit [cf. Kurt Rudolf, *Gnosis: The Nature and History of Gnosticism*, trans. by R. M. Wilson (Edinburgh: T. & T. Clark, 1983), 60-61].

These concepts as they were applied in Gnostic thought entailed a number of distinctive doctrines. First, they needed to explain how such an evil world came to exist. They posited that the good God could not have created it, so some Gnostics believed in a lesser god, an ignorant or evil one, whom they described as the *Demiurge* or "creator god" who fashioned the physical world. Some systems instituted an elaborate mythology with a pantheon of lesser deities in order to explain all of this. Valentinus, for example, believed that the spiritual world contained thirty-one deities, arranged in a hierarchy from the highest God of all, "Bythos" or "Depth," ranging down to "Sophia" or "Wisdom." Sophia rebelled, dissatisfied with her position at the bottom of the divine scale; she was restored, but her "Passion" was purged from her and cast out. Out of this Passion emerged matter and the Demiurge, who, unaware of the spiritual world, believed himself to be God, and made the physical world. This ignorant Creator was the "God" of the Old Testament, a different being from the loving Father of the New Testament [cf. J. Hill, *Zondervan Handbook to the History of Christianity* (Grand Rapids: Zondervan, 2006), 65].

*5. Gnostic dualism led to radical views of Jesus Christ.* On account of their guiding conviction that the material realm and thus all matter should be viewed as inherently evil, two major factions arose to deal with the complex idea of God becoming man in the person of Jesus of Nazareth. The Docetic Gnostics denied the humanity of the heavenly Christ. The word "docetic" comes from the word *dokeo*, "to seem." According to this Gnostic system it was impossible for the true God, who was spirit and good in his nature, to become flesh, which was material and therefore evil. So the orthodox view of Jesus had to be rejected. They believed that the man Jesus was a mere phantom; he did not possess real flesh and blood. He only "seemed" to have a body. The Cerinthian Gnostics, named after Cerinthus a contemporary of the apostle John in Asia Minor, dealt with this issue differently. They surmised that the man Jesus was different from the spiritual *aeon*, the power of Christ. Cerinthians believed that when the dove descended upon the man Jesus at His baptism, the power of the Christ rested upon Him and remained with Him until the crucifixion. Immediately before His death on the cross the Christ departed from the man Jesus. So, it was simply the man Jesus who suffered and died on the cross, not Jesus Christ, God in the flesh, as the orthodox Christians believed. Both of these theories in their assorted variations negated the unique Christian doctrine of the incarnation in order to pay homage to their dualistic view of flesh and spirit.

*6. Gnosticism was a non-Christian religion having roots outside of*

*Christianity.* One of the results of the Nag Hammadi finds has been the recognition of the already suspected origin of Gnostic speculation outside of Christianity. In other words, Gnosticism per se was not a uniquely Christian doctrinal system. It was borrowed from pre-existing currents of thought circulating in the Greco-Roman world at the time that Christianity had its origin. As Kurt Rudolph candidly observed regarding the Nag Hammadi documentary evidence,

> The discovery contains both strongly Christian and also less Christian and non-Christian documents; it therefore shows on the one hand the interrelationship of Gnosis and Christianity, but on the other hand also their independence from one another. Since analyses so far undertaken on some specific Christian gnostic texts were able to show that they have been secondarily Christianized, this provided confirmation for the theory of the non-Christian origin of gnosis, which was advocated in particular by the so-called "Religionsgeschichtliche Schule" (Bousset, Reitzenstein) (*Gnosis*, 51).

*7. Gnosticism was not a single belief system but represented many different religious schemes and structures.* This is a fact which makes it very difficult to understand and appreciate in its ancient context. In some cases they believed things which were polar opposites of one another. For example, some Gnostic leaders taught that they could begin the process of returning the spiritual spark to the divine realm in the here and now. This they could accomplish by living ascetic, austere lives, involving themselves with matter as little as possible. Others reasoned the other way around. They thought that if the material world is evil, it does not really matter what one does within this realm, so they lived as virtual libertines, enjoining and living by no moral rules at all. Gnostic communities evidently did not lay any claim to exclusiveness against one another, and there was no Gnostic canon of Scripture. It used the "holy scriptures" of other religions, like the Bible or Homer, which were employed and interpreted in very creative ways for the purpose of authorizing their own religious views.

*8. Gnosticism was an alien, parasitic belief system which attached itself to Christianity and fed off its life-force.* Almost nothing associated with Gnostic belief was original. It borrowed much from ancient philosophical systems and from the so-called "mystery" religions popular during the apostolic period and beyond; it used the language and figures of both Old and New Testament history and gave them entirely new meanings; it twisted the doctrinal and theological concepts from Christian tractates and books and used them in extraordinarily imaginative ways. At the end of the process only some of the language and names from Judaism and Christianity appeared similar. Their original context and significance were altered entirely. Almost nothing was left of their earlier meanings.

### John's Assault on Incipient Gnostic Leanings

As surprising as it may seem, this weird amalgam of bizarre ideas combined itself with Christianity and a substantial number of people eventually came to embrace it. So much so, in fact, that it worried orthodox religious leaders incessantly over several hundred years and called forth a substantial body of literature to combat it. All of this reminds one of the apocryphal anecdote told in evangelical circles about a theology student who was a follower of both the high sounding theologian Paul Tillich and the country evangelist Billy Graham. According to the story this fellow was asked to pronounce the benediction at a certain important event. He did so, and this is what he said: "And now may the Ground of All Being bless you real good!" Genuine Christianity and Gnostic speculation did not mix well together either!

In the time of the apostle John this threatening combination was being blended together into a poisonous witch's brew for the first time and the toxic mixture was gaining sympathy among some Christians in the various churches of Asia Minor where the aged soldier of the cross spent his final years after Patmos. As he wrote the three epistles, first a larger general one and then two smaller ones to individuals, he made six solid references to Gnostic beliefs. Five of them are in 1 John and one of them is in 2 John. Even though there is no direct allusion made to Gnosticism as a doctrinal system or to a particular sect or faction, or even to any of the leading lights of that movement, it is nevertheless abundantly clear from his verbal parries against their assumptions that he is referring to the ideology which later came formally to be called Gnosticism. John also made several allusions to their thinking in his Gospel, but that is a matter for discussion at another time. In the lines that follow we shall give some consideration to each of John's several responses to their destructive dogmas.

#### A. 1 John 1:1: Our Hands Handled Him

> That which was from the beginning, which we have heard, which we have seen with our eyes, which we looked upon *and have touched with our hands*, concerning the word of life. . . (1 John 1:1, ESV).
>
> I will tell you another glory, brothers, sometimes when I meant to touch

> him I encountered a material, solid body; but at other times again when I felt him, his substance was immaterial and incorporeal . . . as if it did not exist at all (*Acts of John* 93).
>
> He appeared as a man in semblance. (The Gnostic teacher Saturninus described the body of Jesus thus.)
>
> In the system of Valentinus, Jesus Christ descended to reveal God for the purpose of restoring the fallen souls to him self. The *Monogenes* existed from primal times in the fullness of the *pleroma*: "Unbegotten, incorporeal, and without form" [Quoted in John G. Harris, *Gnosticism: Beliefs and Practices* (Portland: Sussex Academic Press, 1999), 96].
>
> If the flesh came into being because of the spirit, it is a wonder. But if spirit came into being because of the body, it is a wonder of wonders. Indeed, I am amazed at how this great wealth has made its home in this poverty (*The Gospel of Thomas*).

John's opening salvo against those who were disturbing the churches appears almost in the first line of the First Epistle. The heretics claimed that the heavenly Christ had no real human body, no true physical reality, only a psychic and spiritual reality. John on the other hand argues from his own personal experience rather than from the perspective of mere ideas. He had touched Jesus with his own hands. It was impossible for those who opposed him to argue with his real life encounters with the man Jesus whom John affirmed to be one and the same with the Christ. Yet somehow they did.

There was a radical difference in their approach, however, forced upon them by the brutal realities of history. These speculators were arguing from theoretical postulates. The Gnostics were approaching the matter from the perspective of their *a priori* views of matter and spirit. Matter was inherently evil to them, so the heavenly Christ could not have in any way participated in it. John though was unencumbered with their philosophical assumptions, describing only what he heard with his own ears, saw with his own eyes, and touched with his own two hands. He was saying, "What we saw and heard, and the man whom we put our hands upon, was not a phantom. He had real human form and substance. He was like us, he had flesh and blood." Human hands cannot handle a spirit (cf. Luke 24:39 "feel me and see"; and John 20:27). Yet John's hands had handled Jesus. So Jesus Christ was a real human being with skin and bones and a genuine physical anatomy, despite the Gnostics claims to the contrary.

The audacity of such folk in opposing a living apostle of Jesus Christ and denying his perception of what he had seen, heard, and felt with his own two hands is almost incomprehensible. Elbert Hubbard once said that, "Logic is an instrument used for bolstering a prejudice." In this case, at least, that pathetic definition is fully justified.

### B. 1 John 1:5-7: Walking in the Light Means Living a Christ-Like Life

> This is the message we have heard from him and proclaim to you, that God is light, and in him is no darkness at all. *If we say we have fellowship with him while we walk in darkness, we lie and do not practice the truth.* But if we walk in the light, as he is in the light, we have fellowship with one another, and the blood of Jesus his Son cleanses us from all sin (1 John 1:5-7. ESV).

> Moreover, that this Marcus compounds philters and love-potions, in order to insult the persons of some of these women, if not of all, those of them who have returned to the Church of God— a thing which frequently occurs—have acknowledged, confessing, too, that they have been defiled by him, and that they were filled with a burning passion towards him. A sad example of this occurred in the case of a certain Asiatic, one of our deacons, who had received him (Marcus) into his house. His wife, a woman of remarkable beauty, fell a victim both in mind and body to this magician, and, for a long time, travelled about with him. At last, when, with no small difficulty, the brethren had converted her, she spent her whole time in the exercise of public confession, weeping over and lamenting the defilement which she had received from this magician. Some of his disciples, too, addicting themselves to the same practices, have deceived many silly women, and defiled them (Irenaeus, *Against Heresies* 1.13.5, 6).

> If ethics and morals are taken to refer to a system of rules, the Gnostic is not likely to regard them very highly. Rules without the consciousness that reveals the reason behind the rules are little better than useless. Thus many Gnostics say that rules and laws in themselves are not salvific, for salvation comes only by gnosis. On the other hand, if morality is defined as an inner integrity arising from the illumination stemming from the indwelling supernal spark, it is likely to be enthusiastically embraced by followers of the Gnostic tradition.

> The Gnostic worldview holds a perennial appeal because it has always been in accord with the "knowledge of the heart" that is gnosis. Some feel that Gnosticism is especially timely at the beginning of the third millennium. The end of the second millennium saw the radical deterioration of many ideologies that could not stand up to the questions of the times; these questions, however, are addressed by the sages of Gnosticism. The clarity, frankness, authenticity, and frequently the contemporary relevance

> of Gnostic answers to questions of the human predicament cannot fail to impress, and, in time, to convince [Stephan A. Hoeller, *Gnosticism: New Light on the Ancient Tradition of Inner Knowing* (Wheaton: Quest Books, 2002), 22, 24].

The larger section represented here in 1 John (1:5-2:11) is primarily directed against the Gnostic doctrine that to the man of enlightenment all conduct is morally indifferent. The immorality of some of the Gnostic practitioners was legendary; Irenaeus went so far as to describe one particular band of them as "a vile company of revelers" (*Against Heresies* 1.13.4). Against every form of the doctrine, which incessantly gnawed away at the very foundation of Christian ethics, the apostle John never wearies of inveighing. So far from its being true that all conduct is alike to the enlightened man, to John's mind it is the character of his conduct that will show whether one is enlightened or not.

If a person is truly walking in the light, John says that several things will naturally follow. They will be found in rich abundance in his life and exhibited in his conduct:

1. The faithful Christian must maintain continual fellowship with God and with the holy brethren (1:5-7).

2. Consciousness of sin and confession of the same must be persistently practiced, in the confident assurance that forgiveness waits for him in God, through our holy Advocate who is the Propitiation for our sins. Salvation does not come through the revelation of knowledge which these heretics promote so vociferously, but through the shed blood of Jesus in His sacrificial death (1:8-2:2).

3. Walking in the light involves living as Christ lived and so obeying the commandments of God; those who ignore the commandments of God cannot be walking in the light of God (2:3-6); some of the Gnostics claimed sinless perfection: "They proclaim themselves as being 'perfect,' so that no one can be compared to them with respect to the immensity of their knowledge, nor even were you to mention Paul or Peter, or any other of the apostles. They assert that they themselves know more than all others, and that they alone have imbibed the greatness of the knowledge of that power which is unspeakable" (Irenaeus, *Against Heresies* 1.13.6).

4. Love the brethren. The darkness is passing, it is on the wane, the true light is showing more and more of its power; therefore, I bid you walk as children of light, that is in love for one another. The darkness is not yet

past, far from it; shadows remain here, there and everywhere, but it is passing, for the light is certain to conquer it ultimately. Christianity is the true light as opposed to these heresies circulating everywhere. They destroy the fellowship and hence, brotherly love. So even though they talk much and often about the light, in reality they walk in darkness. Do not be tempted to walk there with them (2:7-11).

The quotation from Stephan Hoeller given above is remarkable in that it captures a modicum of the thinking of the modern-day writers who retain an eccentric fascination with this ancient heresy. The argument set forth by Hoeller and others like him is that the rediscovery of the documents at Nag Hammadi haa proven how truly diverse the Christian culture was in the second century A.D. This is only partially true. Certainly these materials are important for historical reasons. But they say nothing at all about the richness of the Christian tradition at the time. Gnosticism was a loose agglomeration of bizarre philosophical and theological speculations among a host of small sects which almost completely died out and their sacred documents almost entirely disappeared. That is a far cry from saying that they were any part of the genuine Christian tradition. They comprised a heterodox departure from primitive Christianity, not a constituent element of the apostolic Christian continuum. John himself declared that they had "gone out from us" and that they "were not part of us" or else "they would not have left us" (1 John 2:19).

Why are the Gnostics *really* making such an astonishing comeback in the modern imagination? The most obvious reason, to our way of thinking at least, is the rejection of historical Christianity by modern scholarship. The views of the Gnostics were decidedly different and certainly far more liberal than those of the orthodox Christian writers. The same thing applies to most modern scholarship, even in the universe of so-called "Christian" scholars. Gnosticism was a different faith than historic Christianity. So is the faith of the majority of religious scholars today. Their views very often are as virulently anti-Christian as were those of the ancient Gnostics.

Darrell L. Bock, on the back cover of his book, *The Missing Gospels: Unearthing the truth Behind Alternative Christianities* (Nashville: Thomas Nelson, 2006), alluded to the Nag Hammadi finds and said, "Now revolutionary questions about Christian faith are being raised as a result of these findings: Is Jesus truly a divine Savior or just a teacher of wisdom? Is orthodoxy a by-product of third-century or fourth-century theologians? Did Judas betray Jesus because of evil intent or a request by Jesus? Does salvation include the physical body or just the soul?" Bock writes convincingly against this new approach promoted in the headlines and news media and fostered by secularist university professors. These scholars are conspicuously motivated by their anti-Christian agenda when they tell us that "history is written by the winners" in order to argue that orthodox Christianity merely subverted the views of the otherwise altogether legitimate positions held by some early Christians, *i.e.* the Gnostics. Bart D. Ehrman of the University of North Carolina illustrates this new thinking:

> The early Christian church was a chaos of contending beliefs. Some groups of Christians claimed there was not one God but two or twelve or thirty. Some believed that the world had not been created by God but by a lesser, ignorant deity. Certain sects maintained that Jesus was human but not divine, while others said he was divine but not human. . . . Modern archaeological work has recovered a number of key texts . . . these spectacular discoveries reveal religious diversity that says much about the ways in which history gets written by the winners (*Lost Christianities*, inside jacket).

The final chapter in Ehrman's book is titled, "Winners, Losers, and the Question of Tolerance." It is not even necessary to read the section to get the drift regarding where he wishes to take the reader! Elaine Pagels is also among those who utilize the original works of these heretics to set forth an agenda in opposition to historic Christianity and on behalf of pluralism. She writes:

> The concerns of Gnostic Christians survived only as a suppressed current, like a river driven underground. . . . Now that the Nag Hammadi discoveries give us a new perspective on this process. . . . All the old questions – the original questions, sharply debated at the beginning of Christianity – are being reopened. . . . Today we read them (the Gnostic texts) with different eyes, not merely as 'madness or blasphemy' but as Christians in the first century experienced them – a powerful alternative to what we know as orthodox Christian tradition [*Beyond Belief: The Secret Gospel of Thomas* (New York: Random House, 2003), 86-88].

Clearly there is an agenda here, and just as clearly it may be observed that it is one which is both sympathetic to heresy and antithetical to orthodoxy. Pagels along with others who write in this new tradition oppose the notion that true Christianity ought to possess a unified set of core beliefs based upon the New Testament documents. They are wed to religious pluralism and they see the Gnostics as a suppressed minority, abused by the orthodox writers and "heresy hunters." In point of fact it is quite impossible to see both of these groups as equally Christian and equally legitimate even though this new breed of scholars would long to have us look at them this way.

In point of fact, even the ancient Gnostics would not have agreed to this naïve approach. Tertullian (*Against Marcion* 4:4) said pointedly, "I say that my Gospel is the true one; Marcion, that his is. I affirm that Marcion's Gospel is adulterated; Marcion that mine is. . . ." He was correct in this simple observation. These two very different views of God and the world, of man, of Jesus, of the crucifixion, of redemption, of true knowledge, of spirituality, of morals – of all these things and far more besides are diametrically opposite to one another. Both cannot be equally legitimate at the same time. The Gnostics with whom Tertullian had dealings would not even have affirmed that. Marcion denied the legitimacy of the Gospel preached by Tertullian just as vociferously as Tertullian opposed Marcionite Gnosticism. Both had the good sense to agree that the two very different views could not be true at one and the same time. Unfortunately, the same cannot be said of the modern pluralist.

Even though the early Gnostics were very open to the sometimes fantastic speculations of other Gnostics, they knew that Gnosticism and Christian orthodoxy had almost nothing in common. Only a modern pluralist could believe that! Writers of this pluralistic mold are anxious to cast the orthodox in the worst possible light and so are quick to recall that Irenaeus labeled the Gnostic heresy as "an abyss of madness, and blasphemy against Christ!" But when we read their writings first-hand we are motivated to agree that Irenaeus had a fair appreciation of the poisonous and destructive nature of their beliefs and practices. Gnosticism was heresy, not an alternative route to truth and so ultimately to God.

### C. 1 John 2:18-23: Shun the Anti-Christian Influences Who Deny Jesus is the True Christ of God

> Children, it is the last hour, and as you have heard that antichrist is coming, so now many antichrists have come. Therefore we know that it is the last hour. They went out from us, but they were not of us; for if they had been of us, they would have continued with us. But they went out, that it might become plain that they all are not of us. But you have been anointed by the Holy One, and you all have knowledge. I write to you, not because you do not know the truth, but because you know it, and because no lie is of the truth. *Who is the liar but he who denies that Jesus is the Christ?* This is the antichrist, he who denies the Father and the Son. No one who

> denies the Son has the Father. Whoever confesses the Son has the Father also (1 John 2:18-23, ESV).

> For he suffered all these things for our sakes, in order that we might be saved; and he truly suffered, just as he truly raised himself – not, as certain unbelievers say, that he suffered in appearance only (it is they who exist in appearance only!). Indeed, their fate will be determined by what they think: they will become disembodied and demonic (Ignatius, *Letter to the Smyrneans* 2:1).

Seven times in this epistle John has spoken of heretics as liars *(pseustes)*, but this particular instance is the most forceful and biting, because it is the only case where he uses the direct article, "the liar." It seems that these words were spoken to respond to the nasty criticism directed at John and others who were telling the truth but being called liars for doing so. "Who really is the one telling lies?" is his rhetorical question fired back into the faces of those accusing him and the other faithful. The *Apocalypse of Peter* (79:30) declared of orthodoxy that its representatives were only "empty channels" devoid of substance, not flowing with the "water of life" as they claimed. The author of the *Testimony of Truth* (34:26) alleged of the traditionalists that, "They do not have the Word which gives life." So their insulting rhetoric was regularly directed at faithful Christians, John no doubt included.

The arrogance of these agitators became legendary. Irenaeus in his *Against Heresies* spoke of the Valentinian Gnostics, asking the question, "Where did all of this come from?" His answer was that the system derived not from the Scriptures or from apostolic tradition. None of the great churches of the Empire had ever taught these doctrines. Valentinus himself (born about A.D. 110 in Egypt) had been a man of brilliance, eloquence, and personal magnetism. In the fifth century Jerome wrote of him: "No one can bring an influential heresy into being unless he is possessed by nature of an outstanding intellect and has gifts provided by God. Such a man was Valentinus." Yet all of these gifts led to a pompous pride and a typical loathing of those who did not agree with his doctrines. The Valentinians, according to Irenaeus, "maintain that they have attained to a height beyond every power, and that therefore they are free in every respect to act as they please, having no one to fear in anything. For they claim that because of the *redemption* . . . they cannot be apprehended, or even perceived by the judge." He further alleged that the Gnostics he encountered were characteristically "unchristian" in their attitudes: "If anyone yields himself to them like a little sheep and follows their practice and their *redemption*, such a person becomes so puffed up that . . . he walks with a strutting gait and a supercilious countenance, possessing the pompous air of a cock!" [quoted in Tobias Churton, *The Gnostics* (New York: Barnes & Noble, 1987), 55].

Their self-designations show their arrogance; they are called in their literature, the "chosen," "children of the Light," "spiritual ones," "perfect," "truthful," "holy," "alien," and "free." They saw themselves as "the children of the unbegotten father," "the generation of the perfect eternal men of light," "having their origin in an unchanging aeon," and the "cultivated, perfect, homogeneous generation."

The Gnostic disseminators of error with whom John had dealings in Asia Minor have denied that Jesus is the Christ in the divine sense of being the Son of God. It must be remembered that promoters of this heresy made a distinction between the man Jesus and the divine Christ. The man Jesus suffered on the cross. The divine Christ stood and watched the whole episode from the sidelines. The two were not one in their Christology. So, John argues that they deny that Jesus is the Christ and are therefore antichristian in their approach to Jesus. Being so, they separate themselves not only from the fellowship of faithful Christians (as they have already done by their pulling away) but they alienate themselves from God the Son and so from the Father also.

### D. 1 John 4:1-3: Those Who Deny That Jesus Christ Became Flesh Are Not of God

> Beloved, do not believe every spirit, but test the spirits to see whether they are from God, for many false prophets have gone out into the world. By this you know the Spirit of God: *every spirit that confesses that Jesus Christ has come in the flesh is from God*, and every spirit that does not confess Jesus is not from God. This is the spirit of the antichrist, which you heard was coming and now is in the world already (1 John 4:1-3, ESV).

> I saw him apparently being seized by them. And I said, "What am I seeing, O Lord? Is it really you whom they take? And are you holding on to me? And are they hammering the feet and hands of another? Who is this one above the cross, who is glad and laughing?" The Savior said to me, "He whom you saw being glad and laughing above the cross is the Living Jesus. But he into whose hands and feet they are driving the nails is his fleshly part, which is the substitute. They put to shame that which remained in his likeness. And look at him, and look at me!" (*Apocalypse of Peter* 81:4-24).

> It was another . . . who drank the gall and the vinegar; it was not I. They

> struck me with the reed; it was another, Simon, who bore the cross on his shoulder. It was another upon whom they placed the crown of thorns. But I was rejoicing in the height . . . over their error. . . . And I was laughing at their ignorance (*Second Treatise of the Great Seth* 56:6-19).

Unlike some in our own time, who are far too "nice" to ask one who is involved in the promotion of erroneous doctrine what he believes and teaches on a certain matter, John was not so inclined. Rather he was quick to slice through to the heart of the most fundamental issue and urge that they be forced to make a "confession" of sorts. His solution to the problem of recognizing who is telling the truth and who is promoting falsehood is simple: ask them! Ask them what they believe on this issue. He says, "By this you know the Spirit of God: every spirit that confesses that Jesus Christ has come in the flesh is from God, and every spirit that does not confess Jesus is not from God."

The word "confesses" *(ho homologei)* is from *homologeo*, "to acknowledge, affirm, or confess." Somehow such a person must be pressed to acknowledge what he believes about the Lord's incarnation. That is certainly the conclusion which must be drawn from John's selection of this word to communicate the idea. It should also be thoughtfully noted that John chooses his language carefully with regard to precisely what he meant by Jesus coming in the flesh. Apparently the Gnostics were skilful in their usage of the nuances of language so as to confuse certain unwary souls. John is acutely aware of this and words his description so that there would be no misunderstanding. He does not say "come *into* the flesh," but "*in* the flesh" *(en sarki).*

His point is that Christ did not descend into an already existing man, as Cerinthus and his followers were teaching throughout Asia Minor, but that he came in human nature; he became flesh (John 1:14). In the spurious *Gospel of Peter* the words of Christ on the cross are perverted to read, "My Power, my Power, why hast thou forsaken me?" (1.5.15). The Gnostic Christ was never really a participant in human flesh, but only a visitor to it. John is forceful in his judgment on this critical matter; there can be no misunderstanding of his position: "every spirit that does not confess Jesus is not from God. This is the spirit of the antichrist, which you heard was coming and now is in the world already." When he speaks of confessing Jesus, he means the one who "came in flesh" *(en sarki)*, not the one whom the Cerinthians and other Gnostics were confessing.

Greatly encouraged by the forceful words of John and other New Testament writers who fought tenaciously against the Gnostic attempt at reshaping Jesus into a mere teacher of wisdom separate from the Divine Christ, Melito of Sardis (*circa* 160) brilliantly affirmed the humanity and divinity of Jesus side by side as follows:

> On these accounts he came to us; on these accounts, though he was incorporeal, he formed for himself a body after our fashion – appearing as a sheep, yet still remaining the Shepherd; being esteemed a servant, yet not renouncing the Sonship; being carried in the womb of Mary, yet arrayed in the nature of his Father; treading upon the earth, yet filling heaven; appearing as an infant, yet not discarding the eternity of his nature; being invested with a body, yet not circumscribing the unmixed simplicity of his Godhead; being esteemed poor, yet not divested of his riches; needing sustenance inasmuch as he was man, yet not ceasing to feed the entire world inasmuch as he is God; putting on the likeness of a servant, yet not impairing the likeness of his Father. He sustained every character belonging to him in an immutable nature: he was standing before Pilate, and at the same time was sitting with his Father; he was nailed upon the tree, and yet was the Lord of all things (*Discourse on the Cross*).

### E. 1 John 5:6-8: Three Witnesses to the Incarnation

> This is he who came by *water and blood* – Jesus Christ; *not by the water only but by the water and the blood.* And the Spirit is the one who testifies, because the Spirit is the truth. For there are three that testify: the Spirit and the water and the blood; and these three agree (1 John 5:6-8, ESV).

> What makes us free is the gnosis
> of who we were
> of what we have become
> of where we were
> of wherein we have been cast
> of whereto we are hastening
> of what we are being freed
> of what birth really is
> of what rebirth really is (*Excerpta de Theodoto*)

> If you bring forth what is within you, what you bring forth will save you. If you do not bring forth what is within you, what you do not bring forth will destroy you. . . . For whoever has not known himself has known nothing, but whoever has known himself has simultaneously achieved knowledge about the depth of all things (*Gospel of Thomas* 45:30ff.).

> But Jesus said, "Look, Father, upon this being (*i.e.* the human) pursued by evils, which on the earth wanders about, far from your breath. It seeks

> to escape from the bitter chaos and knows not how it shall win through. For its sake send me, Father! Possessing the seals I will descend, all the aeons will I pass through, all secrets will I reveal, the forms of the gods will I disclose, and the hidden things of the holy way, which I have called 'knowledge' *(gnosis)* will I impart (regarding the Naassene Gnostics; Hippolytus, *Refutation of All Heresies* 5.10.2).

John affirms that, "This is he who came by water and blood." This passage has been variously read by different Bible scholars because it seems to be intentionally vague. Perhaps this is so because John meant more than just one thing by his words. This would certainly fit in well with his style and method elsewhere. At any rate, some interpreters have argued that the expression "water and blood" refer to that which flowed from the Savior's side at the cross (cf. John 19:34). Others have concluded that the "water" refers to the Spirit of God and that the "blood" refers to the Lord's blood shed on Calvary. A third position states that it is a reference to natural birth, where "water and blood" are present. A fourth view says that it is a cryptic reference to baptism, wherein one is immersed in water and the blood of Christ is applied to the soul for the forgiveness of sins. Another interpretation takes particular account of the Gnostic heresy which the apostle has been seeking to expose and combat in his Epistle. It is this view which we would like to explore for the present.

As we mentioned previously, many Gnostics believed that the heavenly Christ came upon Jesus at His baptism in the Jordan River and left Him before His passion, in the Garden of Gethsemane. The logical conclusion which must be drawn if this view is correct is that the death of the man Jesus on the cross did not possess any atoning power for the sins of others. If the writer is using "water" as the emblem of Jesus' baptism and "blood" as a symbol of His atoning death then he is drawing attention to these two terminals of the public ministry and redeeming work of Christ [cf. William MacDonald, *Believer's Bible Commentary*, ed. by A. L. Farstad (Nashville: Thomas Nelson, 1995), 1192ff].

If this approach is followed, the apostle would then be setting forth the proposition that Jesus was just as much the Christ when He died on the cross as when He was baptized in the Jordan. "This is He who came by water and by blood – not only by water" (which Gnostics would readily concede), "but by water and by blood" (the latter they were not willing to concede). John would deny the Gnostics their Christ who did not suffer and shed His blood.

"It is the Spirit who bears witness, because the Spirit is truth" (v. 7). The "apostle of love" allows no room for a Gnostic Christ. God's Holy Spirit has testified otherwise, namely that Jesus was God in the flesh and that as such He suffered and shed real, red, liquid blood. This is God's truth, testified to by the Holy Spirit. If Gnostics claim otherwise, then they are denying the testimony of God's Holy Spirit. Jesus came by water and by blood, not by water only!

### F. 2 John 7: Many Deceivers Have Gone Forth, Those Who Deny the Incarnation Are Among Their Infamous Number

> For many deceivers have gone out into the world, *those who do not confess the coming of Jesus Christ in the flesh*. Such a one is the deceiver and the antichrist (2 John 7, ESV).

> (Mary, speaking to Jesus) When you were little, before the spirit had come upon you, while you were in the vineyard with Joseph, the spirit came out of the height and came to me in my house, like you; and I had not known him, but I thought that you were him. And the spirit said to me: 'Where is Jesus my brother that I may meet with him?' And when he had said this to me I was at a loss and thought that it was a phantom to try me. So I seized him and bound him to the foot of the bed in my house, until I went forth to you, to you and Joseph in the field, and I found you on the vineyard, Joseph leaning back in the vineyard. It came to pass, therefore, when you heard me speak the word, that you were joyful and said: 'Where is he, that I may see him; else I await him in this place.' And it came to pass when Joseph had heard you say these words, that he was startled. And we went down together, entered the house and found the spirit bound to the bed. And we looked on you and him and found you to be like him. And he who was bound to the bed was unloosed; he took you in his arms and kissed you, and you also did kiss him. You then became one (*Pistis Sophia* 61:120-121).

> This then is the word and its solution. 'Grace' is the spirit which came down out of the height through the First Mystery, for it had mercy on the race of men and sent its spirit that he should forgive the sins of the whole world, and they should receive the mysteries and inherit the Light-kingdom. 'Truth' on the other hand is the power which has sojourned with me. When it had come forth out of Barbelo, it became material body for you, and has made proclamation concerning the region of Truth. 'Righteousness' is your spirit, who has brought the mysteries out of the height to give them to the race of men. 'Peace' on the other hand is the power which has sojourned in your material body according to the world, which has baptized the race of men, until it should make it a stranger to sin and make it at peace with

> your spirit, so that they may be at peace with the emanations of the Light; that is, 'Grace and truth kissed each other.' As it said, 'Truth sprouted forth out of the earth,' – 'truth' is your material body which sprouted out of me according to the world of men, and has made proclamation concerning the region of Truth (*Pistis Sophia* 61:121-122).

Already by the time John penned his second epistle, these "deceivers" had proliferated to such an extent that he could say that "many deceivers have gone out into the world." They were not few, they were many. What makes this most interesting is the fact that this had occurred while living apostles still walked the earth – or at least *one* living apostle! These esoteric doctrines seem to us today to be altogether strange and obscure, mysterious and abstruse. But for those who were intrigued by the cryptic and arcane nature of such things, it must have been electrifying and exhilarating. They must have seen the facts and doctrines of orthodox Christianity as mundane, unremarkable, and even rather boring. The two readings from the *Pistis Sophia* (dated around A.D. 250-300) cited above illustrate the point rather well. Hidden deep within all of this apocryphal speculation and high sounding jargon is the matter which lies at the heart of the issue between the Gnostics and John. Both quotes involve complicated conjecture regarding how the heavenly Christ came to be joined with the earthly body of Jesus of Nazareth, confirming that John has touched an important nerve with the purveyors of *gnosis*.

John is rather pointed in his estimation of such teachers: (1) He declares that they are *deceivers* because what they teach is not the truth but a fabrication; (2) He affirms they are *antichrist*, meaning that they oppose the Christ of orthodoxy who was perfectly God and perfectly man in the same embodiment or incarnation; (3) He says that they *confess not that Jesus Christ came in the flesh*; their view holds that Jesus was a man of flesh and that a heavenly spirit descended upon Him which was the divine Christ. Some Gnostics maintained that the Christ descended upon Jesus at His baptism in the Jordan (apparently this was so in the case of those whom John opposed, cf. 1 John 5:6-8), but those who composed the *Pistis Sophia* believed it occurred sometime during His youth. So they deny the historic view of Jesus Christ as set forth in the New Testament documents and taught by all of the apostles and prophets.

Apparently this sort of thing did not concern them at all, but it concerned the apostle John greatly. He considered their limitless speculations about such things as constituting damnable heresy. Furthermore, he believed that the only cure for this insufferable disease was to defeat it and excise it from the body of Christ. Therefore, he warned "the elect lady and her children" to avoid these people and to have no fellowship with them at all (2 John 9-11), lest thereby they unwittingly collaborate with them in their destructive and evil works.

## Conclusion

In deference to the theme of the present lectureship, let us now attempt to draw together some of the "Great Truths" that John set forth in the course of his polemical response to the Gnostic error and to those who were so passionately promoting it in the churches of Asia Minor. Taking the broadest possible view of what we have learned from those texts from the Johannine corpus which we have analyzed, the following points should be considered:

*(1) The argument from apostolic authority is understated but always present in John's interactions with his opponents.* Jesus had said, "He who receives you receives me, and he who receives me receives him that sent me" (Matt. 10:40); and again, "Truly, truly, I say to you, he who receives whomsoever I send receives me; and he who receives me receives him that sent me" (John 13:20). John did not enter into lengthy or overly complex arguments with the Gnostic sympathizers. He operated on the assumption that if they were not willing to hear the authoritative word of one of the Lord's apostles, then they were guilty of rejecting the Christ and thus of rebellion against the God of heaven. That is a not-too-subtle assumption present throughout his treatment of their heresy. When we today encounter opponents who "argue with the Bible" and deny the authenticity of Holy Scripture generally, there is not much that we can do for them. Jesus said, "Give not that which is holy unto the dogs, neither cast your pearls before the swine, lest haply they trample them under their feet, and turn and rend you" (Matt. 7:6). John did little to try to "convert" these divisive Gnostic sectarians, he spent his time and effort attempting to salvage those who might yet be reached through loving concern, some gentle persuasion, and exercise of his genuine claim to apostolic authority. Our principal efforts under similar circumstances ought to mimic those of John.

*(2) Gnostic "enlightenment" constituted nothing less than an attack upon the sufficiency of the divine revelation through Jesus Christ, the apostles and all of the holy prophets.* John pointed out to the faithful disciples of the Lord that they did not need the supposed "illumination" boasted of by these conceited protagonists. They were already beneficiaries of the highest

form of divine revelation: "You have been anointed by the Holy One, and you have all knowledge. I write to you, not because you do not know the truth, but because you know it, and because no lie is of the truth" (1 John 2:20-21). The Gnostics may have even used the language which John, in that case, commandeers. John employed the word *chrisma*, "unction," repeatedly (2:20, 27; 3:6f.; and 4:7) to describe the divine "anointing" which they had received to prepare them for the challenges which they were currently facing. Gnostics may have alleged possession of their own special "unction" of a totally different type, something comparable to what is claimed by many today who say that they are "led by the Lord" when in reality they are only guided by their own inner leadings. Obviously the apostle has in mind for true disciples the consecration to divine service, attended by the indwelling word of God, the sincere study of which provided them with perfect knowledge of all divine things [cf. D. H. King, *Truth Commentaries: The Three Epistles of John* (Bowling Green: GOTF, 2004), 73, 74). The revelation supplied to them already by the Holy Spirit's guidance of the apostles was sufficient to give them all that they needed (John 16:13; 2 Pet. 1:3; Jude 3). That identical revelation today supplies us also with all the "anointing" we shall ever need.

*(3) The controversy over the nature of the Lord's humanity allowed John to underscore important aspects of this doctrine and at the same time label as heretical any alternative to the truth.* While "every rose has its thorns," it is also true that "every storm cloud has a silver lining." Were it not for the doctrinal missteps of the Gnostics in their struggles with these issues, some facets of the nature of Jesus Christ would be far less clear to us, so in the end we have all benefited by their unfortunate mistakes. Our orthodox understanding of the perfect humanity and divinity of Jesus Christ is greatly enlarged upon because both aspects of his character are painstakingly emphasized in John's writings. It was imperative for him further to explain these important concepts on account of the challenges to the truth about both which were the unseemly product of runaway Gnostic speculation. Hence, John labels as "antichrist" (or "unchristian") any theory which denies the true humanity of Jesus Christ (1 John 4:1-3). We must not be eager to describe other people with names that are unkind or overly harsh, but John teaches us also that there is a time and a place when it is appropriate to "label" those who have crossed over the line into heresy as the heretics that they have become by the nefarious doctrines they have embraced and are actively promoting among the people of God (Rom. 16:17, 18; 2 Pet. 2:1). It is neither truly loving nor genuinely considerate to allow error free

access to the hearts and minds of God's faithful people. Heresy must be actively opposed and called by its name!

*(4) John did not allow himself to be drawn into the unique and confusing thought world of Gnosticism, nor did he permit his opponents to "shape the battlefield" by the sophisticated nature of the error with which he wrestled.* Instead, he set forth simple truths and kept his discussion on the level of the ordinary reader. Paul rightly warned the Corinthians, "I fear, lest by any means, as the serpent beguiled Eve through his subtlety, so your minds should be corrupted from the simplicity that is in Christ" (2 Cor. 11:3). It would be well for us to take a lesson from John's example. Not many wise after the flesh are called by the gospel (1 Cor. 1:26). This was true when Paul reminded the faltering Corinthians of this axiom, and it is just as true today. We must defend the truth of God against intellectual assaults upon it with all the force of our being and at the highest level of our ability, but we must not be fooled into thinking that great numbers of university professors and other elites will be moved by our arguments and attracted to the simplicity of the gospel message. More than one aspiring young Christian intellectual, motivated by this foolhardy delusion, has had his faith destroyed in the process of seeking to impress the intelligentsia. John had no desire to impress these elitists with his superior brain power or rhetorical skills. He labored only to protect vulnerable sheep from ravenous wolves (Acts 20:29). Knowing that the Gnostics were drawn to a more elaborate and sensational message, and that the Christ of the traditional Gospels held little appeal for them, John therefore kept his message unpretentious and plain. We ought to follow his lead.

*(5) The Gnostics whose teaching and influence John was attempting to suppress were men who claimed to walk in the light of special divine revelation, but their lives frequently were associated with the darkness of sin.* John branded their religion a "lie" (1 John 1:6). It was false on the very surface of it. The apostle declared that a life lived inconsistent with God's commands was one lived in darkness and not in the light. Somehow these religious con men had convinced themselves and others that one could practice sin and yet have an ongoing relationship with the Holy God. They could not have been further from the truth. This is an eternal lesson, a "Great Truth" which every succeeding generation should learn. Persistent disobedience leads to spiritual death and separation from the fellowship of Christ and God. Ongoing consciousness of sin and repentance with respect to the same, on the other hand, creates an abiding relationship with God

through the forgiveness made possible by the blood of Jesus (1 John 1:7). Those men today who promote the idea that divine forgiveness of sins is somehow mysteriously "automatic" and that the sinner ought not be overly concerned with repentance and prayer, not only ignore the specific requirement set forth by John in this context, but they follow in the footsteps of the old Gnostics, oblivious to how uncannily their own error equates with that of this ancient heresy. This is certainly a "Great Truth" which we cannot fail to learn.

Gnosticism was a multifaceted religious system, characterized by many strange twists and odd turns of reason and logic. There is little wonder that it did not have widespread appeal among the masses. At the same time, there is little wonder that it had a special appeal to certain kinds of people. Those who were looking for something complicated and esoteric were assuredly drawn to its complex mythology and its profound philosophical leanings. The simplicity of the Gospel of Christ did not appeal to such folk. Those who needed to feel "different" and "out of the mainstream" found a home in its strangeness. Biblical Christianity was far too "traditional" and ordinary for their peculiar tastes. The solid geographical and historical footing of the Christian message about Jesus Christ, His atoning death, burial, resurrection and ascension in the land of Palestine was far too mundane for them. Those who sought to know obscure "secrets" and "mysteries" found plenty of this sort of thing in Gnosticism, but none of it in orthodox Christianity.

To our mind there is little wonder then that Gnosticism ultimately died out, and if it had not been for the copious writings of the "heresiologists" the Gnostics might have been almost completely forgotten until the Nag Hammadi finds. The writings of the "heresy hunters" were the best sources for understanding these heretical movements and the speculations of their leaders for nearly two millennia! Gnosticism's secrecy and abstruseness were its ultimate undoing. Orthodox Christianity's simplicity, historical grounding and wide appeal to the common man were its strengths. They guaranteed its persistence throughout the passing centuries while Gnosticism's secret knowledge was lost in the mists of antiquity.

Finally, we would like to add a simple footnote to our narrative, for whatever it is worth. We have always thought it imminently strange that the apostle John, who was an avowed enemy of Gnosticism, and who dealt with their errors more directly and powerfully than any other New Testament writer, ultimately became the favorite author among the various purveyors of gnosis. John's style, frequently accentuated by double entendre and other skillful special techniques, apparently intrigued them immensely, and thus his writings made perfect tender for the fires of their fertile imaginations. Their own skill at twisting the meaning of his symbols and elaborating his portrait of Jesus far beyond John's own masterful description of him knew no boundaries. His works were therefore used and abused by them more often than any other apostolic writer. What an amazing historical and theological paradox!

# Faith Without Works Is Dead (James 2:26)

**Alan Piner**

## The Augustinian Controversy

What doth it profit, my brethren, though a man say he hath faith, and have not works? Can faith save him? If a brother or sister be naked, and destitute of daily food, and one of you say unto them, Depart in peace, be ye warmed and filled; notwithstanding ye give them not those things which are needful to the body; what doth it profit? Even so faith, if it hath not works, is dead, being alone. Yea, a man may say, Thou hast faith, and I have works: shew me thy faith without thy works, and I will shew thee

---

**Alan Piner** was born on December 19, 1967 in Kingsport, Tennessee. He is the third child of Clifton L. and Jackolyn Piner. All three of their children are faithful to the Lord. Clifton has served as an elder for a number of years with his devoted wife at his side. In 1989 Alan married his wonderful wife, Julie Ann Kilgo. Their marriage has been blessed with five children: Britney Ann (17), Ethan Lee (15), Cameron Grey (12), Logan Alan (9), Olivia Javonne (4). Alan began part-time preaching at the age of sixteen in various country churches in eastern Tennessee. He spent a summer in England in 1983 working with Matt Qualls. The summers of 1987, 1988 were spent preaching in Crossville, Alabama and in Vanduzer, Missouri. He received his A.A. at Florida College with a major in communications (1988) and went on to the University of South Florida where he received his B.A. in Elementary Education (1992). He began preaching full time in 1989 in Merritt Island, Florida. After a short time teaching elementary school, he returned to full time preaching and has continued to work for the Lord in this way. Through the years he has devoted full time work to congregations in Richlands, Virginia; Granite Falls, North Carolina; Winnetka, California; and Hemet, California. He is currently preaching for the Southport church of Christ in Indianapolis, Indiana. Alan has made five trips to China in the work of evangelism between the years of 1997 and 2000. Besides sharing time with his family, Alan enjoys gardening, fishing, camping, and hiking. Most of all he enjoys teaching interested souls the Gospel of Christ.

> my faith by my works. Thou believest that there is one God; thou doest well: the devils also believe, and tremble. But wilt thou know, O vain man, that faith without works is dead? Was not Abraham our father justified by works, when he had offered Isaac his son upon the altar? Seest thou how faith wrought with his works, and by works was faith made perfect? And the scripture was fulfilled which saith, Abraham believed God, and it was imputed unto him for righteousness: and he was called the Friend of God. Ye see then how that by works a man is justified, and not by faith only. Likewise also was not Rahab the harlot justified by works, when she had received the messengers, and had sent them out another way? **For as the body without the spirit is dead, so faith without works is dead also** (Jas. 2:14-26).

The question, "How am I saved?" is an age old question which has occupied the minds and writings of men through many centuries.

- Augustine said, "I was brought by the works of God."
- Pelagius said, "I came by myself."
- "I started to come and God helped me," said semi-Pelagians.
- "God started to bring me and I cooperated," said Arminians.
- "God brought me," said Calvinists.

### The Augustinian Controversy

The seriousness and extent of Augustinian thinking has been a point of contention at times. It is not unusual to have comments about Augustinianism met with blank stares, a degree of indifference, or even a degree of hostility. Augustinian teachings became a source of contention throughout the centuries and are still to our present day. There are several of his teachings which could be covered in a presentation on Calvinism. It is the purpose of this presentation to examine his teachings regarding meritorious works for salvation. He taught against the teaching of the young Catholic church regarding a man's works causing one to deserve and achieve salvation or continue to merit it in some way. He wrote, "If those things delight us which serve our advancement towards God, that is due not to our own whim or industry or meritorious works, but to the inspiration of God and to the grace which he bestows" (*To Simplician*, II. 21, as quoted by T. Kermit Scott, *Augustine*, 203).

Aurelius Augustinus (A.D. 354-430) was born in the Roman town of Thagaste in North Africa (now Ahras, in Algeria). He was the son of Patricius and Monica (later to be known as Saint Monica for whom the suburb city of Los Angeles is named, Santa Monica). He was nine years old when the last pagan Roman emperor, Julian, died and fifty-seven years old when Alaric and the Goths sacked Rome. Augustine would eventually emerge as the preeminent architect of the new Rome. He would refer to it as the spiritual city, *The City of God* in his book by the same name. He also became the most influential leader of the Roman Catholic Church of his time. His greatest achievement, and the source of his profound influence, was a doctrinal system which shaped and dominated Roman Catholic theology throughout the Middle Ages and also heavily permeated Protestant theology. Robert Meagher quoted William Barrett who wrote of Augustine saying,

> Indeed, in the matter of intellectual influence he has to be reckoned as one of the three major thinkers, along with Plato and Aristotle, that the west has produced; and in point of his actual and direct influence on historical matters he is perhaps the greater than the other two. Thus virtually single-handed, he created Catholic Christianity for the Latin West and so shaped the intellectual and spiritual of a thousand years of the middle ages that followed. He was the dominate authority invoked in the explosive theological controversies of the Protestant reformation in the sixteenth and seventeenth centuries (Meagher, xiii).

The Roman Catholic Church taught for many centuries that Christians are saved by meritorious works (beginning with baptism) and that salvation is maintained by good works (receiving the sacraments, confession of sin to a priest, the worship of Mary and saints and relics, as well as other meritorious works that could achieve salvation, etc.). Augustine thought this theology not only unappealing, but cumbersome and unfounded.

In taking up the role of interpreting scriptures Augustine and many others (even today) have argued that the Bible states Christians are saved by grace through faith, totally apart from works (Tit. 3:5; Eph. 2:8-9; Gal. 3:10-11; Rom. 3:19-24). Their basic argument is, if in fact the Bible says it is "apart from works that we are saved" and "we are not saved by works lest anyone boast," then why is it still taught that we have to "do" things for God? They also say, the God who made the world and everything in it is the Lord of heaven and earth and does not live in temples built by hands. He is not served by human hands, as if he needed anything. Our works do not help Him, He does not *need* us. Rather, they believe, He wants us to believe in His Son, and what His Son did for us. He wants a relationship with us and for us to love Him. He gives us free will because love comes from free will, not wanting mindless puppets who have to work for Him night and day. They turn to statements in the Bible that say that Christians are saved by grace through faith, totally apart from works (Tit. 3:5; Eph. 2:8-9; Gal. 3:10-11; Rom. 3:19-24).

Those opposing Augustine debate the above arguments emphasizing James 2. They focus on the following verses: "So also faith of itself, if it does not have works, is dead" (v. 17). Do you want proof, that faith without works is useless? "Was not Abraham our father justified by works when he offered his son Isaac upon the altar? You see that faith was active with his works, and faith was completed by his works" (vv. 20-22). "See how a person is justified by works and not by faith alone" (v. 24). "For just as a body without a spirit is dead, so also faith without works is dead" (v. 26).

There is a deeply rooted feeling in the heart of man that he ought to contribute something of his own to his salvation. This contribution in various teachings has taken a number of different forms. First, they may seek to secure one's salvation directly by some kind of overbalance against his sins. Secondly, they may predispose God to favor man and grant him salvation as a gift otherwise unattainable. Third, they may add works to the weight of merit with the sacrifice of Jesus Christ, which by itself is not sufficient. In most cases, salvation is viewed as a cooperative effort. Yet it has always been felt by theologians that the idea of cooperation is not a worthy one. Therefore the effort is made to introduce cooperation without letting it appear as such.

The developing controversy and debate of the concept of faith without works has shaped religious history through the years. Three time periods easily traced from Augustine through today are: Early Church – Augustinianism versus Pelagianism; The Reformation – Calvinism versus Arminianism; Modern Church – Reformed (Calvinism) versus Evangelical Restoration. Let us examine each period and consider the contrasting teachings of these times.

### Early Church: Augustinianism Versus Pelagianism

Augustine's views were greatly affected by his background. Augustine wrote an autobiography of his life called, *The Confessions*. According to Sheen, "No other Latin book with the exception of Virgil has been translated into so many languages and read over such a long period of time as *The Confessions* of Saint Augustine. Modern best sellers, aided by the artificial respiration of advertising, hold first place no longer than a few months and yet St. Augustine has been at the top of best-seller lists since the year 400" (Sheen, vii).

He was born in North Africa to a pagan father and a Catholic mother. The differences in the religious beliefs of his parents typify, and perhaps led to, the prolonged conflict he experienced between his ideals and his actual conduct. He felt two natures at work in himself; one earthly and base, and the other spiritual and idealistic. The lower of his two natures held sway during the earlier part of his life, though he was never really happy to have it so. Pursuing an academic education and career, he finally wound up as a teacher of rhetoric in Milan, Italy in 384. During his early years he was influenced, but never wholly captivated, by various philosophies. After his return to North Africa, Augustine's inner struggle finally culminated in his "conversion" in 386, though he was not baptized until the next year. In his autobiography he gave credit for his conversion to his mother, Monica, and the theologian, Ambrose, at Milan. Ambrose was so powerful at the time that he ordered the emperor Theodosius to do penance. Augustine spake of his mother that she loved Ambrose for Augustine's salvation saying, "she loved most entirely; and he her again, for her most religious conversation, whereby in good works, so fervent in spirit, she was constant at church; so that when he saw me, he often burst forth in her praises; congratulating me that I had such a mother." Of Ambrose he reflected, "And Ambrose himself, as the world counts happy, I esteemed a happy man, whose personage I held in such honor." He credits Ambrose with providing him the example of a love for the Scriptures saying, "When he was reading, his eye glided over the pages, and his heart searched out the sense. . . . I heard him indeed every Lord's day, rightly expounding the word of truth among the people; and I was more and more convinced that all the knots of those crafty calumnies, which those our deceivers had knit against the Divine Book could be unraveled" (*Confessions*, 98, 99).

Ambrose baptized Augustine in 387. Augustine then applied himself diligently and wrote numerous works. Brown said that he quoted the Bible 42,816 times in his writings. Soon after his baptism he rose through the hierarchy to become bishop of Hippo, where he died during a siege by the Vandals on August 28, 430 at the age of 75 (Cairnes, 139-142). Quincy Howe, Jr. said of Augustine, "He is supremely confident in the truth of his beliefs and the depth of his learning"(Howe, vii, viii). To summarize, Howe described the attitude of Augustine as one of complete confidence in himself and his teaching. His teachings represented an irrefutable and logical system of beliefs that left no question unanswered.

Perhaps the most prominent of Augustine's teachings were those relating to sin and salvation. He believed that the whole human race, even infants suffered under the curse of Adamic depravity—that in Adam all sinned and fell into a hopelessly wicked state. God arbitrarily predestined individuals, whose number was definitely fixed, to be saved. Augustine's conception of the grace by which these individuals were saved left no room for an exercise of free will on their part. According to Augustine, "God's grace is irresistible. This grace infuses faith, love, and enabling power into the heart and life of the individual. Faith, then, is a direct gift of God" (Lombardo, *Ancient Christian Writers,* 47, 99, as quoted by Howe).

These concepts were closely tied to the background of Augustine, who felt that he had been saved from the enslaving power of sin by the irresistible grace of God. He stated, "The soul takes its life from God when it lives holily, for the reason that it cannot live holily unless God is the cause of its good works" (*City of God*, 270-273). Augustine made the statement, "For I not only judge it healthful to believe before using reason (since one is unfitted to comprehend reason), and, with faith itself, to prepare the ground to receive the seeds of truth, but I believe that such is the way, generally, by which safety can alone return to sick souls" (*Advantage of Believing* 14:31). The point is made in Augustinianism that mankind is saved not by reason or right conduct, but only by making a fundamental choice regarding the object of love. Merit lies not in works but in the will of man. "Therefore, if we should love and embrace with our will the good will, and place it before all other things that we cannot keep even if we will to do so, then those virtues . . . will dwell in our spirit, and to possess them is to live rightly and honorably" (*Free Choice*, I 13.97).

The central emphasis of Augustinianism is on the absolute supremacy of God and the resulting helplessness and dependency of man on the grace of God alone. It rejects meritorious works for salvation. Augustine's words already noted in the introduction highlight this, "If those things delight us which serve our advancement towards God, that is due not to our own whim or industry or meritorious works, but to the inspiration of God and to the grace which he bestows" (Scott, 203.)

We have here one of Augustine's most firmly held philosophical beliefs. Largely on the basis of his own introspective experience, he is convinced that human action is always motivated by self-love in the final analysis. Even the most selfless acts, if they are human acts, are ones that one finds most gratifying. The very struggle of "good" people to overcome self-will ends only in strengthening self-will and is finally an exercise in "pride." While using this thinking in his book, he ridicules the stoics who pretend to be able to attain the highest good through living a virtuous life of self-control *(City of God*, 115). The very idea that they can set themselves free by practicing virtues, reduces the virtues themselves to mere servants of human pride. Human striving ends always in pride and pretension. Happiness is a gift of God, and only by ceasing human striving can happiness be found.

The argument Augustine makes is basically that Christianity, unlike other religions, rests not at all on propitiation of its God by ritual practices or even moral conduct. The heart of Christianity he believed is the atonement, by which humans are saved only when recognizing their sinful condition and surrendering their creature will wholly to God. Augustinianism concludes that humans are not free to "*work out* their own salvation." As he wrote in his work, *Spirit and Letter* (XVI),

> Must then the unrighteous man, in order that he may be justified – that is, become a righteous man – lawfully use the law, to lead him, as by the schoolmaster's hand, to that grace by which alone he can fulfill what the law commands? Now it is freely that he is justified thereby – that is, on account of no antecedent merits of his own works. It is not because we have done good works, but that we may be able to do them – in other words, not because we have fulfilled law, but in order that we may be able to fulfill the law (Kermit, 205).

Augustine, and many who would follow his teachings through the centuries, used the following verses to support faith without works.

> **Romans 9:11-13:** "(For the children being not yet born, neither having done any good or evil, that the purpose of God according to election might stand, **not of works**, but of him that calleth;) It was said unto her, the elder shall serve the younger. As it is written, Jacob have I loved, but Esau have I hated." As Augustine saw it there was no work the twins could do to merit their destiny.
>
> **Ephesians 2:8-9.** He also believed, if we have the faith in God that will save us, that very faith is said to depend completely on the will of God. Ephesians 2:8-9 "For by grace are ye saved through faith; and that not of yourselves: it is the gift of God: **Not of works**, lest any man should boast."
>
> **Philippians 2:13:** "For it is **God which worketh** in you both to will and to do of his good pleasure." Augustine and his followers use this to say that it is God that does the work and yet they ignore verse 12, "Wherefore, my beloved, as ye have always obeyed, not as in my presence only, but

now much more in my absence, **work out your own salvation** with fear and trembling."

**Romans 11:5-7:** Augustine concluded, if humans are not hopelessly damned, if some few are preserved, only the will and mercy of God can be found as the reason. Romans 11:5-6 "Even so then at this present time also there is a remnant according to the election of grace. And if by grace, then is it **no more of works**: otherwise grace is no more grace. But if it be of works, then is it no more grace: otherwise work is no more work."

Augustine also used these verses to write much about what is now known as the doctrine of predestination. This doctrine has been left to be covered in the lecture on Calvinism, however, these verses have noticed here for their connection to the assigned verse James 2:26, "faith without works is dead."

Augustine's concepts were seriously challenged by a Welch monk named Morgan (this name came from the Gaelic for "sailor," which translated into Latin as *Pelagius*). He came to Rome in 400 and North Africa in 410 with his disciple, Celestius, where his doctrines came into conflict with the teaching of Augustine. Pelagius and his followers, saw some of Augustine's doctrines as a threat to human freedom and moral responsibility. Pelagius had been a popular man as a spiritual counselor in high society, but things were about to change as he moved on to Rome. According to Strathern,

> When Brother Morgan arrived in Rome, his upright Welsh spirit was appalled by the moral laxity of the priesthood, which tended to take a rather more easy-going, Mediterranean view of its vows. But Morgan soon detected the cause of the trouble. One day he heard a sermon in which a bishop referred to a passage in Augustine's *Confessions* (whose dwelling on unspecific salaciousness had soon stimulated sales and imaginations throughout Christendom). The passage quoted by the bishop explained Augustine's view that goodness is not possible without the intervention of divine grace, a doctrine verging on predestination. Morgan realized that many were using this doctrine as an excuse for moral lassitude. There was no point in making an effort to be good if this depended upon the intervention of divine grace. Morgan opposed this view with a doctrine of his own. This stated that there was no such thing as original sin, and that people were capable of earning a place in heaven without intervention from God's grace (Strathern, 32).

This was immediately seen as heresy and raised a storm of protest, not the least from Augustine, who at once set about defending his teachings.

Pelagius held to the idea of free will in men. "If I ought, I can," well expresses his thinking. Men did not inherit any original sin from Adam. Adam merely set a bad example for men to follow. Thus, men had the power not to sin, though they failed to use this power. Pelagius did not rule out grace, but felt that it consisted of the remission of sins through baptism and obedience to divine teaching. Pelagius taught that man is spiritually sick, and as such he does need the help of God's grace in order to get better. However, it is up to man to take the spiritual medicine which God offers. God must have man's cooperation.

In theological terms this was called "synergism." A Synergist believes in God and man working together. Pelagius taught self-help religion. He was positive about human nature. He feared both the despair of human power to do what God commands and cheap grace. He felt it must be unthinkable that God would ever command the impossible. If man so chose, he had the power to keep the commandments, even that "awkward one forbidding adultery." Augustine led a vigorous battle against the views of Pelagius by introducing his doctrine that no person could do anything to save himself, but God must do it all (Brumback, 59). Pelagius, although not without his strong and influential supporters, was condemned by various synods, councils, emperors, and popes. The Catholic Church and, later, the Protestant Churches embraced Augustine's views on sin and salvation. Pelagius' followers went farther than their teacher and removed justification through faith, setting up the morality and works based salvation now known as Pelagianism (Pawson, 89).

Augustine wrote two treatises: the first was entitled, *On the Predestination of the Saints* (*http://www.newadvent.org/fathers/15121.htm*) and the second, *On the Gift of Perseverance* (*http://www.newadvent.org/fathers/15122.htm*). In the second treatise Augustine showed that the perseverance of the saints, by which he meant the eternal security of the believer, is not dependent upon the good works of the individual believer which would result from his conversion, but entirely upon the constancy and unchangeableness of God's elective choice. Both these replies clearly downgraded the importance of good works or holiness of life in so far as these were regarded as contributing to a man's salvation. According to Augustine, good works were not relevant to salvation.

There was a short period of time when the Catholic church was under the influence of semi-Pelagianism, during this time individuals appeared here and there on the scene who recaptured something of the theology of Augustine. However, some of these over emphasized one aspect of this theology and some another, and the wholeness was distorted into a new error. One of these was Gottschalk of Orbais (c. 805-869). What was very clear to Gottschalk was that little or no importance could be attached to the natural goodness of man or to any supposed works of merit performed before conversion. Gottschalk was accused of heresy, tried, and condemned. He was allowed no opportunity to defend himself or present his own case in a reasoned form. He was flogged mercilessly and imprisoned under cruel conditions until his death. Even some of his foes protested at the unchristian character of his treatment. Yet he died without recanting and apparently with great peace of mind, holding firmly to his Augustinian theology.

**The Reformation: Calvinism verses Arminianism**

For those who came after him, Augustine entered both the Catholic Church and the religious world as an unfortunate revolutionary force. He not merely created an unwanted place in the history of the church, but determined the course of its history in the west up through the reformation and into the present day. Studying Augustine's theology of grace is particularly appropriate because it was Augustine who gave us the Reformation. This is so, not only because Calvin quoted Augustine more than any other theologian, but also because the Reformation witnessed the ultimate and unfortunate triumph of Augustine's doctrine of grace over the legacy of the Pelagian view of man.

As we head into the next period of time it is interesting to note that the Reformation found its mainspring in criticizing medieval Catholic piety as resting more on human effort than on divine grace. The Counter-Reformation replied that one can affirm the sovereignty of God's grace without also denying the freedom of the will and the moral value or merit of good conduct. Both sides in the controversy appealed on a huge scale to texts of Augustine.

Ever since Augustine's battle with the Pelagians in the fifth century, there has been dispute, particularly in the western church, about theological cornerstones of soteriology—including depravity, predestination, and atonement. The Calvinist-Arminian debate was a dispute between Protestants in the early seventeenth century where they generally deemphasized concerns about human salvation.

The Medieval Catholic Church touched and dominated every thread of the fabric of life during the Middle Ages. The Catholic Church was everything, and those not a part of "The Church" were nothing. It was this kind of dominance that contributed to the power and the abuse of power against which serious religionists began to rebel. A number of men in the Roman Catholic Church began seeing faults which they protested, thus paving the way for Martin Luther and other later reformers.

The system of grace taught by the Catholic church was a large problem, including its assertion of a treasury of merit which consisted of works that were more than needed. This system said that the treasury of merit was supplied by Christ's meritorious work and the meritorious deeds of the saints. Grace was dispensed from this treasury in three areas: (a) First dispensed by means of the seven sacraments (baptism, confirmation, holy Eucharist, penance, matrimony, holy orders, extreme unction); (b) Secondly, by means of sacramentals (actions or objects used in conjunction with the sacraments) like holy water, blessed ashes, sign of the cross, priestly blessing, rosary, and candles; and (c) finally dispensed by means of the grant of indulgences (remission of temporal punishment due for sins, which was granted after the guilt of sin and its eternal punishment were remitted by sacramental absolution or by perfect contrition), which were sold during the Middle Ages (Notes from Bobby Graham).

In January of 1530, King Charles called upon the estates of the empire to meet at Augsburg to settle the controversies between Luther and the Roman Catholic Church. Luther stayed at home but sent a summary of his beliefs with Melancthon. Melancthon thought there could be unity between the Catholic Church and Luther, but Luther knew it would never happen. According to Brumback, "Luther was the first to teach justification by 'faith only.' He did a wonderful work in calling attention to the abuses of the church in Rome when they were teaching justification by works only, yet he went to the opposite extreme when he taught justification by faith only" (Brumback, 159). Luther was so intent on justification for his beliefs that he changed Romans 3:28 to read, "Therefore, we conclude that man is justified by **faith only** without the works of the Law." This was an obvious contradiction of James' statement, "Ye see then how that by works a man is justified and not by faith only" (Jas. 2:24).

Augustine's teaching on grace was considered the touchstone of orthodoxy within the western church throughout the Middle Ages. Nevertheless, within an Augustinian context, theologians continued to debate the precise nature of God and man's participation in salvation, as well as attempting to work out a place for the emerging system of sacraments in the overall scheme of salvation.

Thomas Aquinas, the most influential Catholic theologian of the Middle Ages, taught that, from man's fallen state, there were three steps to salvation:

1. *Infusio gratiae*—God infuses grace into the human soul—the Christian now has faith and, with it, the ability to do good—this step is entirely God's work and is not done by man, and once a man has faith, he can never entirely lose it—however, faith alone is not enough for salvation;
2. *Fides caritate formata*—with man's free will restored, man must now do his best to do good works in order to have a faith formed by charity"; and then
3. *Meritum de condigno*—God then judges and awards eternal life on the basis of these good works which Aquinas called man's "condign merit" (Pawson, 91).

Aquinas believed that by this system, he had managed to reconcile Ephesians 2:8 ("By grace are ye saved through faith, and that not of yourselves: it is the gift of God") and James 2:20 ("faith without works is dead") and 2:24 ("by works a man is justified and not by faith only"). He also believed that he had provided an exposition of the Bible's teaching on salvation compatible with Augustine's teachings.

There was a second stream of medieval thought, commonly referred to as the Ockhamists after William of Ockham.

> This second stream of thought rejected Aquinas' system as destroying man's free will. The Ockhamists argued that if a man loved God simply because of "infused grace", then man did not love God freely. They argued that before a man received an *infusio gratiae*, man must do his best in a state of nature (*i.e.* based on man's reason and inborn moral sense). They argued that just as God awards eternal life on the basis of man's condign merit for doing his best to do good works after receiving faith as a gift from God, so too, the original *infusio gratiae* was given to man on the basis of *meritum de congruo* "congruent merit", a reward for man's doing his best in a state of nature. (Unlike "condign merit", which is fully deserved by man, "congruent merit" is not fully deserved, and includes a measure of grace on God's part. Congruent merit is therefore also sometimes called "semimerit". According to the Ockhamists, a gracious God awards an individual with congruent merit when he or she does the best that he or she is able to do [*facere quod in se est*].)

> Aquinas' followers, commonly referred to as the Thomists, accused the Ockhamists of Pelagianism for basing the *infusio gratiae* on man's works. The Ockhamists defended themselves from charges of Pelagianism by arguing that, in the Ockhamist system, God was not bound to award the *infusio gratiae* on the basis of congruent merit; rather, God's decision to award the *infusio gratiae* on the basis of congruent merit was *ex liberalitate Dei*, an entirely gracious act on God's part. Martin Luther's condemnation of "justification by works" also clearly condemned Ockhamism.
>
> Many Protestants believe that Thomism's requirement of man doing his best in a state of grace in order to earn condign merit is a form of "justification by works" and is therefore semi-Pelagian. They therefore believe that all Catholic salvation theology is semi-Pelagian, and, as such heretical, or at least semi-heretical (*http://en.wikipedia.org/wiki/History_of_Calvinist-Arminian_debate#ref_4-Wynkoop*).

Monergists following Augustine's path, such as Luther and Calvin, believe in grace alone. Luther, and especially Calvin, taught that, if a person is to be saved, salvation must come from something outside of the person. Man is purely passive in his salvation. Spiritual salvation is a spiritual resurrection. The spiritually dead person is no better positioned to save himself than a physically dead person is positioned to restore life to his body.

Calvin taught that salvation comes by grace. Grace, by definition, is a gift. He thought this grace comes not from anything man does or can do. The prompting cause of grace is the love of God. The Greek word used to refer to the love of God is *agape*. This type of love is a love that comes solely from the one loving. The one loved does nothing to merit love. "This is love: not that we loved God, but that he loved us and sent his Son as an atoning sacrifice for our sins" (1 John 4:10). Calvin taught that the prompting cause of God's grace is His love. The meritorious cause of God's grace is the perfect life, innocent death, and resurrection of Jesus Christ.

This grace then, Calvin said, is received through faith. To him faith is a work of God. Paul tells us, in his letter to the Christians at Ephesus, "For it is by grace you have been saved, through faith, and this not of yourselves: it is a gift from God, not by works, so that no one can boast" (Eph 2:8). He reasons therefore, faith is a work of God and an act of man. It is man who does the believing. However, the Holy Spirit works faith in the heart of man enabling him to believe.

Calvin's ideas, however, had opposition in Holland from James Arminius (1560-1609). Arminius was the father of Arminian theology. He was a pastor first. Later he became a professor at the University of Leyden. He and his followers were trying to liberalize the state church of Holland (Cairns, 317).

James Arminius stressed that "repentance" is not a meritorious work" and that "the same is true of faith" (Bangs, 351). He wrote, "We give the name of 'believers' not to those who would be such by their own merits or strength, but to those who by the gratuitous and peculiar kindness of God would believe in Christ" (Bangs, 351). In emphasizing that faith is not a meritorious work, he points out that "no one except a sinner can know or acknowledge Christ for his Savior, for he is the Savior of sinners" (Bangs, 342).

Arminius died in 1609. The Remonstrants were the Dutch protestants who maintained the views associated with his name after his death. The following are summaries of their beliefs which were points of departure from the stricter Calvinism:

- that the decree of predestination is conditional, upon obedience in works
- that the atonement is offered to all seeking it
- that though the grace of God is a necessary condition of human effort, it does not act irresistibly in man
- that believers are able to resist sin but are not beyond the possibility of falling from grace

Arminianism is quite divided. It is sometimes referred to as semi-Pelagianism which taught that man works with God in salvation. To use a common phrase from their altar calls, "If you take one step, God will take two." Or another misleading analogy, "Faith is one row, works are the other row that leads to heaven." In some circles, salvation is by grace through faith (Eph. 2:8-9; Tit. 3:5-7) but then they stress the works of man to keep oneself saved, often pointing to James 2:14-26. Arminianism, however, also has some similarities to Augustinianism, which teaches that from first to last, salvation is a work of God by His Spirit (John 6:44). No good works can obtain the righteousness necessary for eternal life in heaven (Isa. 64:6). It further teaches that because of our depraved state, we can only find salvation in the Lord Jesus Christ and His work on the cross (Rom. 10:4). Without Jesus' blood, we have no salvation (Heb. 9:22). Thus it concludes we are saved by faith in Jesus alone and not our goodness or good works (Phil. 3:7-10).

## Modern Church: Reformed Augustinianism Versus Evangelical Restoration

In the modern church age, Arminianism stretches through much of mainstream evangelical Protestantism. Due to the influence of Anglican priest and evangelist John Wesley, Arminianism is perhaps most prominent in the Methodist movement.

Remember, Arminianism is most accurately used to define those who affirm the original beliefs of Jacobus Arminius himself, but the term can also be understood as an umbrella for a larger grouping of ideas including those of Hugo Grotius, John and Charles Wesley, as well as others.

As found in the modern church age, there are two primary perspectives on how the system is applied in detail. Classical Arminianism sees Arminius as its figurehead. Wesleyan Arminianism sees John Wesley as its figurehead. Wesleyan Arminianism is sometimes used synonymously with Methodism. In addition, Arminianism is understood by some of its critics to also include semi-Pelagianism or even Pelagianism, each of which opposed Augustinianism.

In fact some Arminianism seemed to be a reincarnation of semi-Pelagianism with its emphasis on man's freedom. This explains why so many churches acted resolutely with respect to Arminianism. They saw it as a serious threat to the gospel and condemned it "as being in principle a return to Rome (because in effect it turned faith into a meritorious work) and a betrayal of the Reformation (because it denied the sovereignty of God in saving sinners, which was the deepest religious and theological principle of the Reformer's thought). Arminianism was, indeed, in Reformed eyes a renunciation of New Testament Christianity in favor of New Testament Judaism; for to rely on oneself for faith is no different in principle from relying on oneself for works, and the one is as un-Christian and anti-Christian as the other" (Packer, 59).

The Arminian theory of free will was far from dead. Among the liberal clergy of England, the theory of free will was very popular. In the 1700s, a man by the name of John Wesley, a strong believer in the Arminian doctrine of free will, formed the Methodist denomination. It was through Methodism that Arminian doctrine would come to America. Rowe in his book, *History of Reformation Movements*, wrote of John Wesley's experience in America.

> He talked much with some of the Moravian brethren after his arrival in Savannah; but it was not until after his return to England in 1738, that

> Peter Bohler, a Moravian preacher in London, after much conversation, aided by the testimonies of several living witnesses, convinced him that to gain peace of mind he must renounce that dependence upon his own works which had hitherto been the bane of his experience, and replace it with a full reliance on the blood of Christ shed for him. To gain this faith he strove with all possible earnestness. And at a Moravian Society meeting in Aldersgate Street, while one was reading Luther's statement of the change which God works in the heart through faith, Wesley says: "I felt my heart strangely warmed. I felt I did trust in Christ, Christ alone, for salvation; and an assurance was given me that he had taken away my sins, even mine, and saved me from the laws of sin and death." – Rev. D. Wise (Rowe, 111).

In America, Charles Grandison Finney would embrace Arminianism in matters of salvation and begin what today is common practice in most Protestant churches in America. Most of today's churches teach the free will doctrine of Arminius. Like Finney, they do not consider revival a miracle as much as they consider it the natural result of applying appropriate methods. The primary duty of the preacher is to induce the free will to give in to the emotionally charged presentation of the Gospel. In short, the preacher convinces the intellect into agreement with what is preached and then attempts to move the emotions to support that reasoning. Finney introduced the modern day concept of altar calls. Altar calls were designed for sinners, who have been moved by the preaching, to come forward and pray and give themselves over to God. This practice is widespread and is in use in most Protestant churches here in America today.

Many Roman Catholic theologians took the position that man must prepare himself to merit the grace of God without which he cannot be saved. Arminian theologians have modified this somewhat and now take the position that while man cannot by good works merit the grace of God, he can prepare himself to receive it by declaring his willingness to do so. The end result is much the same; the one is as much a cooperative process as the other, and Roman Catholics have as easily adopted the non-resistance alternative as they adopt the preparatory works alternative.

There was great hostility toward Augustinianism during the eighteenth-century. For that hostility there were reasons. The bitter wrangles of the Reformation and Counter-Reformation, producing long wars that inflicted vast damage, had largely been disputes between different interpretations of Augustine's doctrine of the church and of grace. The sixteenth century controversy about justification by grace alone on condition of faith alone was conducted within an Augustinian and medieval framework of ideas, and was a further chapter in the dispute about the relation between nature and grace. In the sixteenth century both sides made great appeal to Augustine. "The Council of Trent's decree on justification (1547) was a mosaic of Augustinian phrases, so anti-Pelagian that the Protestants could not bring themselves to believe in its sincerity" (Chadwick, 119)

## Current Landscape

When one considers the current landscape of American churches there is evidence of many of these previous teachings and controversies throughout all denominations.

Advocates of both Arminianism and Augustinianism find a home in many Protestant denominations, and sometimes both exist within the same denomination as with the Anglican Communion. Denominations leaning in the Arminian direction include Methodists, Free Will Baptists, General Baptists, Church of the Nazarene, Seventh-day Adventists, Pentecostals, and Charismatics. Denominations leaning in the Augustinianism direction are grouped as the Reformed churches and include Particular Baptists, Reformed Baptists, Presbyterians, and Congregationalists. The majority of Southern Baptists, including Billy Graham, accept Arminianism with an exception (allowing for a doctrine of eternal security). Many see Augustinianism as growing in acceptance, and some well-known Southern Baptists such as Albert Mohler and Mark Dever have been trying to lead the Southern Baptist Convention to a Reformed view of faith. The majority of Lutherans hold to a third view of salvation and election that was taught by Philip Melanchthon" (notes from *http://en.wikipedia.org/wiki/Arminianism*).

It is not surprising then to find today modern arguments stemming from Augustine's teachings. This is further evidence of the grip his doctrines have had down through the years. As we approach Bible study today we need to be sure we are going back to the word and never hesitate to question a man's thought no matter what his name. It would be good to heed the caution that Charles Hodge gave in his third volume of *Systematic Theology* (section "Soteriology" under the heading "Works Not the Ground of Justification") in which he stated,

> In reference to men since the fall the assertion is so explicit and so often repeated, that justification is not of works, that that proposition has never been called in question by anyone professing to receive the Scriptures as the word of God (Hodge, 134).

In each generation of the modern church age, there have been people who are willing to get into the word and debate against false teaching. A summary study of these debates gives us an understanding of the current landscape of the "faith without works is dead" controversy started so long ago with Augustine.

It is evident in a number of sources and debates that there are those who explain works, such as baptism, to be nonessential to salvation. They teach that the works mentioned in James are works to be done after one's salvation and have nothing to do with their salvation. For as they say, "Salvation is by faith alone and without works that man can do."

In the *Folk-McQuiddy Discussion*, published in 1907, on the plan of Salvation, Folk takes the position regarding works that,

> . . . if we could save ourselves by our own works, we should have occasion to be proud and boastful. We could stand in the very presence of God in heaven and brag about how we have saved ourselves, and say to him: "I do not owe any honor or any glory to you for my salvation, but all the honor and all the glory belong to me."

Folk goes on to explain his understanding of the relationship between faith and works.

> Faith is the substance and works the shadow, faith the cause and works the effect, faith the antecedent and works the consequent, faith the engine and works the train of cars, faith the root and works the fruit, faith the essential element in salvation and works the outcome, the evidence of faith (Folk, 35, 41).

In 1946 when Cogdill and Jackson debated, Jackson made the affirmative statement that,

> We are created or made anew in Christ Jesus unto good works. We are saved before baptism and baptism is a good work. Eph. 2:8-10 "Not by works of righteousness that we have done but according to his mercy he saved us, by the washing of regeneration and renewing of the Holy Spirit." That's Titus 3:5. Now notice, you connect that with Eph. 2:8-10 "For by grace are ye saved through faith; and that not of yourselves, it is the gift of God: Not of works, lest any man should boast. We are his workmanship, created in Christ Jesus unto good works." Notice that we are in Christ Jesus, created in Christ Jesus, unto good works. And so in Romans 11:6 Paul says it can't be by works and by faith combined, and if so, which one must be eliminated? And so Titus 3:5 eliminates the one. Which one is that? "Not by works of righteousness that we have done, but according to

> his mercy hath saved us by the washing of regeneration and the renewing of the Holy Spirit." So it is, we are created in Christ Jesus, not by our good works, we believe in good works, but good works to come after we have been created in Christ Jesus our Lord (Jackson, 7, 8.)

In Cogdill's comments on the works of faith he said,

> Paul talked about the work of faith and the labor of love. Does faith work? Why James says in chapter 2 in three different verses, 14, 17, and 20, that "faith without works is dead, being alone." In James 2 we hear faith only—faith without works, described as "dead", "barren", "vain", "imperfect" and in verse 24 – the only passage in the Bible that mentions justification by faith only, James declares "you see how a man is justified by works and not by faith only." Faith must work in order to be alive. And if faith does not work it is dead, and there are works that belong to faith, that grow out of faith, that are identified with faith, and in that same second chapter of James, James says that the faith of Abraham worked with his works. There are the works of faith (Cogdill, 44, 45).

In the *Harding-Nichols Debate* in 1947 the proposition was "A sinner is justified from past sins by faith only." One of Mr. Nichols arguments was:

> I understand that this unreserved committal of all to God through Christ is the faith by which a sinner is justified from past sins. Here let me make a plain statement of what I mean when I say that a sinner is justified from past sins by faith only: I mean that degree of faith which commits all to God—which does not trust in any kind or amount of good works for pardon, but comes to God trusting alone in the merit of Christ for justification—that faith is the only immediate instrumental cause of justification (Nichols, 4).

He further argued:

> Take Romans 4:5, "But to him that worketh not, but believeth on him that justifieth the ungodly, his faith is counted for righteousness." Here the apostle cuts off all works as a condition of justification from past sins. How can anybody urge upon a sinner to work for justification from past sins, when Paul plainly says, "to him that WORKETH NOT, but believeth"?

In his response, Harding paired John 12:42,43 with James 2:19 to express that faith alone is not enough.

> John 12:42,43 "Nevertheless, among the chief rulers also, many believed on him; but because of the Pharisees they did not confess him, lest they should be put out of the synagogue. For they loved the praise of men more

> than the praise of God." Then James 2:19 "But wilt thou know, O vain man, that faith without works is dead?" "The rulers believed," Harding says, "But their faith was altogether an internal affair; it did not express itself in action. The devils believed, but their faith, like that for which Mr. Nichols is contending, was "faith only." In both cases the faith was dead. It bore no fruit, reached no blessing, accomplished no good. It did no work, and James says, "'As the body without the spirit is dead, so faith without works is dead also." James 2:26.

Harding argued the conclusion that faith only is dead faith:

> Dead faith is as different from faith, as a dead man is from a man, or a dead horse from a horse. And I would just as soon try to ride home on a dead horse, as to reach justification by a dead faith (Harding, 19).

When Fuqua debated Reynolds in 1948, in one of his affirmatives, he stated:

> I believe with the New Testament, that "as the body without the spirit is dead, so faith without works is dead also." (James 2:26.) Hence when the New Testament speaks of justification "by faith," I know it is talking about a LIVE, not a DEAD faith. I believe in justification by a LIVING faith. Mr. Reynolds believes in justification by a DEAD faith. And that is the principle difference between us: I stand for the LIVING principle of faith. He stands for the DEAD thing he calls "faith." The "faith" Mr. Reynolds says we are justified by is exactly AS DEAD as a body WITHOUT THE SPIRIT. Since he bases all his religion upon "Faith," his religion IS DEAD because his "faith" IS DEAD. That is the type of religionists I am debating with. And it is the only difference between us, on the ground of faith. I am saved by a LIVING faith; he is saved (?) by a DEAD faith (Fuqua, 31, 32).

In another debate, the Reeves-Cook debate, which was published in 2006 by the Guardian of Truth Foundation, the first proposition was: "The Scriptures teach that the alien sinner receives the forgiveness of his past sins by faith only, before and without water baptism." According to Keith Sharp in his introduction for the book, the debate was based mostly on the passages of Romans 4 and James 2. Sharp pointed out that the debate was not about salvation by grace through faith because both men strongly believed the passages regarding that. The point that Reeves was trying to make throughout the debate was that salvation is conditional and that men are not saved by faith only. One of the issues in the debate was the nature of saving faith (*i.e.*, the faith that submits to God's sovereign will by obeying him). He showed from the classic Old Testament examples of Noah,

Jericho, and Naaman that salvation by grace includes the obedience of faith (Cook, Reeves, viii).

As Sharp noted,

> Bruce [Reeves] pointed out that Cook ignored the fact that the word "works" is used in different ways in the Scriptures. It can be used to denote works of merit (Eph. 2:8; Titus 3:5), to name a system that demands sinless perfection for justification (Romans 3:27, 4:2-8; 11:6), and to denote works of faith (1 Thess. 1:3; Jas. 2:14-26). This third use reveals the kind of faith that saves and is the way it is properly used to include repentance, confession, and baptism (Cook, Reeves, ix).

In summarizing a few of the debates not quoted here, many proponents of Augustine who taught that we cannot be saved by any works point to Ephesians 2:4ff. Augustine and his followers would say that we are introduced to the wonderful grace of God, which comes about not because of anything good in us, but "because of the great love with which he loved us." They point to the text which says, God works salvation in us even "when we were dead in our trespasses," thus showing his tremendous grace (his unmerited kindness to those who do not deserve it). In fact they go on to say, as the text reads, the display of God's wondrous grace is the reason for our salvation: "so that in the coming ages he might show the immeasurable riches of his grace in kindness toward us in Christ Jesus." In their minds, Paul then explains how our salvation displays the grace of God: "For by grace you have been saved through faith; and that not of yourselves, it is the gift of God, not a result of works, so that no one may boast."

This writer's response would direct the Bible student with the thought, yes, salvation is by grace, through faith, and it is not of works. But what is meant when it is said salvation is not of works? Simply, that it is not in reward for our work; we do not pay for it by our works. There is no merit in what we do upon which we can demand salvation. Certainly without the help of grace, the sinner could not do all that he ought, and his duty is the imitation of Christ's example. Grace is assisting, not all controlling. God built the stairway to His grace which is accessible to every man. He gives us the blessings of that grace. The doctrine that everything is the gift of grace, including will itself is debilitating to the point of catastrophe.

## Faith Without Works Is Dead

The doctrine is commonly taught in the world that a person is saved the very moment he believes in Jesus Christ, that he is saved without any further acts of obedience. James has much to say on the subject of faith and works. For example: "Even so faith, if it hath not works, is dead, being alone" (Jas. 2:17).

Possibly misunderstood as much as any other part of the Bible doctrine is the essentiality of good works to salvation. People confuse the good works of the gospel which the Bible clearly defines as essential, with the works of the law of Moses or the meritorious works of men in an effort to earn salvation.

The Bible does not teach that people are saved by works of the Old Testament law of Moses, for we read in Romans 3:20, that "by the deeds of the law shall no flesh be justified in his sight." From Colossians 2:14, we learn that the law of Moses was nailed to the cross of Christ and is no longer bound upon anyone. We know today that the only hope of salvation for lost humanity is through the gospel of Christ. We do not propose to be saved by the works of the law, but through the works of faith and the labor of love in obedience to Christ. We come to God only on His terms, in the way He has established, which demonstrates our faith in Him and His word.

While the Bible says: "By the deeds of the law shall no flesh be justified," it also says in James 2:24: "Ye see then how that by works a man is justified and not by faith only." These works mentioned in James must not then be the works of the law, but are the works of faith revealed in the gospel of Christ. The Law of Moses is dead and its works mean nothing today, yet the works of the gospel mean much.

A person is saved by the blood of Christ, through the grace of God. He is not saved by faith alone, but through obedience to the commandments of Christ. Jesus became "the author of eternal salvation unto all them that obey him" (Heb. 5:9). This does not mean that the obedient soul earns, merits, or deserves salvation, but that he conditionally receives the mercy and the grace of the Lord, who according to His mercy saves us "by the washing of regeneration and the renewing of the Holy Ghost" (Tit. 3:5). The Bible makes it clear in that same passage that, while we are being saved through the washing of regeneration (or baptism) and the renewing of the Holy Ghost, it is not by works done in righteousness which we have done ourselves. By putting the knowledge of these scriptures together, we see that, if we do not submit ourselves to the righteousness of God in obedience to His word, we cannot be saved.

There are many Bible passages which show the essentiality of faith, that we are saved by faith, justified by it, and so on. Every one of these passages is to be believed and accepted. There is one similar thing about all these passages on faith, not one single passage ever says we are saved by faith only. There are no such passages in the Bible.

Here is a great point to remember: Never in any age or dispensation in human history has God saved man by faith alone. God has always required faith and obedience. No other formula for salvation has ever worked. None ever will. Jesus said, "'He that believeth and is baptized shall be saved" (Mark 16:16). It is faith plus obedience. This is the embodiment of the principle under which God has always worked in saving man. It is utter folly to expect him to make an exception to the rule now and save anyone by faith only and without obedience.

The proponents of this faith only opinion appeal especially to the Scriptures in support of their argument, first to Paul in Romans 3:28, where it says, "Therefore we conclude that a man is justified by faith without the deeds of the law," and Romans 5:20, "Moreover the law entered, that the offence might abound. But where sin abounded, grace did much more abound." They appeal to the Gospels where Christ praises the faith of the Canaanite woman. Matthew 15:28, "Then Jesus answered and said unto her, O woman, great is thy faith: be it unto thee even as thou wilt. And her daughter was made whole from that very hour."

The scripture in James clearly and emphatically states that faith without works in dead and cannot save. People will endanger the salvation of their souls if they act on the false assurance proposed by Augustine and others that faith alone is sufficient for salvation, or that they need not perform good works in order to be saved. James 2:14, 21, "What doth it profit, my brethren, though a man say he hath faith, and have not works? Can faith save him? . . . Was not Abraham our father justified by works, when he had offered Isaac his son upon the altar?"

There are numerous texts in Scripture, both from the epistles of the apostles and from the Gospels, that prove good works must be joined to faith if one hopes to be saved. It is evident that those whom Christ will place on His left hand at the last judgment (Matt. 25:41) and whom He rebukes, are so placed not because they did not believe in Him, but because they did not perform good works. In fact, this is why He said that He will separate all who were united together by the same faith, in order that no one might think that faith alone, or a dead faith (that is, a faith without works) is sufficient for eternal life. "Likewise also was not Rahab the harlot justified by works, when she had received the messengers, and had sent them out another way?" (Jas. 2:25).

This is the teaching of both Paul and James. Paul says that the law entered in that sin might abound. "And where sin abounded, grace did more abound" (Rom. 5:20). He does not mean to say, as some have thought, that man should do evil that there may come good (Rom. 3:8), but rather that it was necessary that God give man grace to forgive his transgressions of the law. Likewise, when he says that man is justified by faith and not by the observance of the law (Rom. 3:28), he is speaking here of works of the law by which one would try to earn justification, not of works of faith as conditions for justification. Moreover, Paul does not say that just any faith in God is good but that faith is good which results in works of love. As for that faith which is dead, he says that it profits nothing: "If I should have all faith, so that I could remove mountains, and have not charity, I am nothing" (1 Cor. 13:2). Clearly it can be concluded from Paul's writing the necessity of good works. James is so opposed to those who think that faith can save without good works that he compares them to devils in James 2:19. "Thou believest that there is one God; thou doest well: the devils also believe, and tremble."

The apostles Peter, John, James, and Jude insisted very strongly in their epistles on the necessity of good works because there were some, even at that time, who misinterpreted the teachings of Paul in this matter. In his second epistle (3:11-18), Peter warns the faithful that, although there are in Paul some things hard to understand, nevertheless he has the same mind on the questions of eternal salvation as have all the other apostles. There is no opposition between Paul and James and the other apostles, but there is also no contradiction in Paul himself. To those who place their trust in faith alone, James recommends the works of Abraham, whose faith Paul praised. Thus, faith and works must be joined to one another. Abraham was justified by faith, not by works, but good works certainly followed his faith.

If anyone objects that Paul does not teach this, then let him consider well Galatians 5:6, 14 and Romans 13:10. It is not necessary to contrast James with Paul, but Paul with Paul himself. The Apostle emphasizes justification by faith without works of the law in order to deprive man of self-praise and of the thought that faith is obtained by works. The faith that is deserving of praise is that faith by which the just man lives (Rom. 1:17), the faith by which we believe in him who justifies the sinful (Rom. 4:5), that faith which excludes boasting (Rom. 3:27), and finally it is that faith which is made effective by love (Gal. 5:6). Faith is not from works, but works come from faith. Faith is the first work through which all other works are obtained. Faith cannot be merited by works, otherwise justification (of which faith is the beginning) would depend upon good works. We are not justified by the law or by our own wills, but through the grace of God as we receive the forgiveness of sins upon meeting the conditions he has required. Wherever you find the word "death," whether it be used literally or figuratively, you find a separation. Therefore, when James says, "faith without works is dead," he simply means that it is separated from all effectiveness – it reaches no blessing, accomplishes no good.

Augustinianism has been so dominant because it rested on a conception of God that was so satisfying to the public of the time. Once it was established as a possible conception, it was almost impossible to reject. Like the children's story of the Emperor's New Clothes, few wanted to say, "The king is naked!" or "The theology was flawed!" A second reason for the success of Augustinianism, and one that cannot be adequately discussed in this presentation, was the scope and depth of all his works. In his works one finds both truth and error, and many controversies.

> No part of Christian doctrine or practice escaped Augustine's notice, and the sheer volume of his work and his almost incredible attention to detail marked him as undoubtedly the most comprehensive intellect in western history. Reviewing the enormous body of his works, the correspondence, the many sermons, the books, which this author only read a very small percentage, it is hard not to agree with Isidore of Seville, who inscribed above the cabinet containing Augustine's works: "He who claims to have read all this is a liar (Scott, 153).

The pull towards Augustinianism is to a religious man, what the pull of gravity is to the material world. It is a subtle ever-acting downward pull that is never absent and that, once yielded to, causes an increasingly rapid descent. Such descent spiritually leads to the debasement of the truth of the Gospel. To fight this pull, the believer's intelligence has constantly to be brought into subjection to the revealed Word of God so as to monitor his thoughts and works.

## Sources

Augustine, Aurelius. *The Advantage of Believing.* Translated by L. Meagher. Included in *Augustine: His Thought in Context*, T. Kermit Scott. New York: Paulist Press, 1995.

_____. *City of God*. An abridged version from the translation by Gerald G. Walsh, S.J., Demetrius B. Zema, S.J. Grace Monahan, O.S.U. and Daniel J. Honan. New York: Image Books Doubleday, 1958.

_____. *The Confessions of Saint Augustine*. Translated by Edward B. Pusey, D.D. Random House, Inc. 1949.

_____. *On Free Choice of the Will*. Translated by A.S. Benjamin and L. H. Hackstaff. New York 1964, included in *Augustine: His Thought in Context*, T. Kermit Scott. New York: Paulist Press, 1995.

Bangs, Carl. *Arminius: A Study in the Dutch Reformation*. Nashville: Abingdon, 1971.

Brents, T.W. *The Gospel Plan of Salvation*. Nashville: Gospel Advocate Company, 1950.

Brumback, Robert H. *History of the Church through the Ages*. Lufkin (TX): Select Books, 1957.

Cairnes, Earle E. *Christianity Through The Centuries, A History of the Christian Church*. Grand Rapids: Zondervan, 1996.

Calvin, John. *Institutes of the Christian Religion*, Volumes 1, 2. Edited by John T. McNeill. Translated and Indexed by Ford Lewis Battle. The Westminster Press, 1960.

Chadwick, Henry. *Augustine*. New York: Oxford University Press, 1986.

Cook, Gene and Bruce Reeves. *The Reeves-Cook Debate on Baptism*. Bowling Green: The Guardian of Truth Foundation, 2006.

Cogdill, Roy E. and D. N. Jackson. The Cogdill-Jackson Debate. Marion (IN): Cogdill Foundation Publications, 1977.

Folk, Edgar E. and J.C. McQuiddy. *Folk-McQuiddy Discussion on the Plan of Salvation*. Nashville: Gospel Advocate, 1907.

Fuqua, E. C. and G. R. Reynolds. *The Fuqua-Reynolds Debate*. Fort Worth: The Vindicator Press, 1948.

Graham, Bobby. Notes on Catholic Church and meritorious works.

Houchen, Hoyt H. and Ray Tatum. *The Houchen-Tatum Debate*. Amarillo (TX): Hoyt H. Houchen, 1951.

Howe, Quincy, Jr. *Selected Sermons of Augustine*. New York: Holt, Rinehart, Winston Inc., 1966.

Neander, Augustus. *General History of the Christian Religion and Church*, Translated by Joseph Torrey, Volume 3, 4. London: Henry G. Bohn, 1851.

Nichols, James and W. R. Bagnall. *The Writings of James Arminius*, Volume 1. Grand Rapids: Baker Book House, 1977.

Meagher, Robert E. *An Introduction to Augustine*. New York: New York University Press, 1978.

McGregor Wright, R.K. *No Place for Sovereignty: What's Wrong with Freewill Theism*. Downers Grove: InterVarsity Press, 1996.

Mott, L.A. Jr., *Faith in the Book of Romans*. Gainesville (FL): Mott Books, 1977.

Pawson, David. *Once Saved, Always Saved?* London: Hodder & Stoughton, 1996.

Piper, John. *The Legacy of Sovereign Joy*. Crossway, 2000.

Porter, Curtis, W. and Glenn V. Tingley. *The Porter-Tingley Debate*. Bowling Green: Guardian of Truth Foundation, 1947.

Rowe, John F., *History of Reformatory Movements*. Indianapolis: Faith and Facts Press, 1993.

Scott, Kermit T. *Augustine: His Thought in Context*. New York: Paulist Press, 1995.

Shepherd, J. W. *The Church The Falling Away, and the Restoration*. Nashville: Gospel Advocate Company, 1977.

Strathern, Paul. *St. Augustine in 90 minutes*. Ivan R. Dee, Chicago, 1997.

**Web Sites consulted:**

*http://en.wikipedia.org*
*http://en.wikipedia.org/wiki/Arminianism*
*http://arminiantoday.blogspot.com/2007/10/mistaking-arminianism.html*
*http://en.wikipedia.org/wiki/History_of_Calvinist-Arminian_debate#ref_4-Wynkoop*
*http://www.gfcto.com/2007/03/gods_grace.php#sdfootnote21sym#sdfootnote21sym*

# Upon This Rock . . . Was Peter The First Pope?

**Greg Litmer**

Without question the single most visible symbol of Roman Catholicism to the world is the pope. His position is set forth in the following manner:

> The Pope, Bishop of Rome and Peter's successor, "is the perpetual and visible source and foundation of the unity both of the bishops and of the whole company of the faithful." "For the Roman Pontiff, by reason of his office as Vicar of Christ, and as pastor of the entire Church has full, su-

---

**Greg Litmer** was born in Cincinnati, Ohio on September 27, 1954. He married his best friend, Vicky (Brown), in 1976. The Litmers have two children: Adam Joseph (currently working with the Evendale congregation in Cincinnati as an evangelist) and Rachel Elizabeth, who lives in Northern Kentucky. On October 5, 2007, Adam and his wife Jackie presented Greg and Vicky with their first grandchild, Alexander Delos Litmer. Greg received his formal education at the University of Cincinnati, majoring in theater. He began preaching in Covington, Kentucky (1976-77). He worked with Wayne Chappell and the Lockland church in Cincinnati, Ohio (1977-1980); the Northside church in Hillsboro, Ohio (1980-82); the Southport church in Indianapolis, Indiana (1982-1985); the Fairfax church in Cincinnati, Ohio (1985-91); the Expressway church in Louisville, Kentucky (1991-2001); and the Northern Kentucky church in Florence, Kentucky (2001-present). He has conducted gospel meetings in several states and has preached in Canada and Ireland. In Louisville and Cincinnati, Greg participated in daily call-in radio programs for many years. His articles have appeared in a number of periodicals. He co-edited *Catholicism Examined*, a monthly publication which has been compiled into a book by the same title. He also wrote *That Ye May Grow Thereby* and *Messianic Prophecy.* Greg is currently working on two fiction novels, *Just Another Sunday* and *So It Begins and So It Ends.*

> preme, and universal power over the whole Church, a power which he can always exercise unhindered" (*Catechism of the Catholic Church, 234*).

Perhaps only events involving the royal family of Britain are characterized by such pageantry and ceremony as are the public appearances of the Roman Pontiff. The extent of his influence is seen in his "full, supreme, and universal power over the whole company of the faithful" and the Roman Catholic Church is by far the largest body of people on earth who claim to worship Christ.

Roman Catholics are taught that the papacy began with Peter, the apostle. Roman Catholics teach the following: "The Lord made Simon alone, whom he named Peter, the 'rock' of his Church. He gave him the keys of his Church and instituted him shepherd of the whole flock" (*Catechism of the Catholic Church, 233*).

### The Historical Evidence

In *A Catechism of Christian Doctrine, Revised Edition of the Baltimore Catechism* (111), the following question and answer appears.

> **Did Christ give special power in His Church to any of the apostles?** Christ gave special power in His Church to Saint Peter by making him the head of the apostles and the chief teacher and ruler of the entire church. (a) The power of the keys was promised to Saint Peter and was actually conferred on him. (b) Saint Peter was recognized by the early Christians from the beginning as the head of the church.

The primary passage of Scripture given to support these statements is found in Matthew 16:13-19. The passage reads as follows,

> When Jesus came into the coasts of Caesarea Philippi, he asked his disciples, saying, Whom do men say that I the Son of man am? And they said, Some say that thou art John the Baptist; some, Elias; and others, Jeremias, or one of the prophets. He saith unto them, But whom say ye that I am? And Simon Peter answered and said, Thou art the Christ, the Son of the living God. And Jesus answered and said unto him, Blessed art thou, Simon Barjona: for flesh and blood hath not revealed it unto thee, but my Father which is in heaven. And I say also unto thee, That thou art Peter, and upon this rock I will build my church; and the gates of hell shall not prevail against it. And I will give unto thee the keys of the kingdom of heaven: and whatsoever thou shalt bind on earth shall be bound in heaven: and whatsoever thou shalt loose on earth shall be loosed in heaven.

If we move just one page further in *A Catechism of Christian Doctrine* (112), we find this question and answer,

> **Did Christ intend that the special power of chief teacher and ruler of the entire church should be exercised by Saint Peter alone?** Christ did not intend that the special power of chief teacher and ruler of the entire church should be exercised by Saint Peter alone, but intended that this power should be passed down to his successor, the Pope, the Bishop of Rome, who is the Vicar of Christ on earth and the visible head of the Church. (a) A successor to Saint Peter, the first bishop of Rome, was required as chief teacher and ruler for the same reason that successors were required for the other apostles. From the very beginning it was acknowledged by the Church that the successor of Saint Peter as Bishop of Rome was at the same time the head of the entire Church. This successor of Saint Peter is called the Pope.

As a product of the parochial school system, this is what I was taught. It is what all Roman Catholics are taught. However, it is simply not true and history, from both secular sources and sources claimed by the Roman Catholic Church itself, conclusively prove that it is not.

I find it fascinating, and more than a bit revealing, that there is no absolute, unquestioned biblical evidence to support the idea that Peter ever resided in Rome. When Paul wrote his letter to the Romans in late 57 or early 58 A.D., there is no mention of Peter. Twenty-six members of the church in Rome are mentioned by name, but not Peter. When Paul was a prisoner in Rome, there is no indication that Peter was there. "Only Luke is with me" is what Paul wrote in 2 Timothy 4:11. While this does not prove that Peter was absent from Rome at that time, it does make one wonder why, if he was there, he had deserted the imprisoned Paul. Also, in Peter's letters, he makes no mention of Rome. In his salutation of 1 Peter 5:13, he wrote, "The church that is at Babylon, elected together with you, saluteth you; and so doth Marcus my son." There is no reason to assume that Babylon is symbolically referring to Rome at this time. There was a Babylon in both Egypt and Assyria when Peter wrote this letter. Even the noted scholar, Philip Schaff wrote, "Of a residence of Peter in Rome the New Testament contains no trace, unless, as the church fathers and many modern expositors think, Rome is intended by the mystic 'Babylon' mentioned in 1 Pet. 5:13 (as in the Apocalypse), but others think of Babylon on the Euphrates, and still others of Babylon on the Nile (near the present Cairo, according to the Coptic tradition)" (*History of the Christian Church*, I: 250).

Even informed Roman Catholic scholars admit that any biblical evidence of Peter actually being in Rome is extremely weak. Karl Keating, president and founder of Catholic Answers and the author of the best selling book *Catholicism And Fundamentalism* (201) wrote, "In any event, let us be generous and admit that it is easy for an opponent of Catholicism to think, in good faith, that Peter was never in Rome, at least if he bases his conclusion on the Bible alone. But restricting his inquiry to the Bible is something he should not do, external evidence has to be considered, too." The external evidence to which Keating refers is not nearly as strong as I would personally like it to be if I were going to base such an important doctrine as Peter being the first Pope, Vicar of Christ on earth and Bishop of the universal Church upon it.

For more than the first five hundred years of the church there was no such thing as one man presiding in Rome as the universal bishop of the Church. To be sure, there were bishops in Rome over those years who sought supremacy for themselves and Rome, the most notable of which would be Leo I (440-461). He succeeded in getting Emperor Valentinian III to issue an edict declaring the Roman See as the supreme court of appeal for all bishops (*Encyclopedia Britannica*). However, when one considers the fact that such an edict was even necessary it becomes readily apparent that the Roman bishop (which is in itself a departure from the biblical pattern) was not recognized as the universal bishop as late as the fifth century A.D.

The Roman Catholic Church places a great deal of importance upon the writings of what they called the "Early Church Fathers." The writings of the Ante-Nicene Fathers, many of whom are regarded as having been Catholics by the Roman Church, are filled with statements indicating that no one man, including Peter, was at any time viewed as the Vicar of Christ on earth and the universal bishop of the church.

Tertullian, who admittedly held some heretical views in the latter years of his life, wrote in the early part of the third century, "Just, for example, as if Peter too had censured Paul, because whilst forbidding circumcision, he actually circumcised Timothy himself. Never mind those who pass sentence on apostles. It is a happy fact that Peter is on the same level with Paul . . ." (*On Prescription Against Heretics*, XXIV).

Origen, another third century writer who is called by *The Catholic Encyclopedia*, "a priest" and an instructor of many Roman Catholic "saints" wrote,

> And perhaps that which Simon Peter answered and said, "Thou art the Christ, the Son of the living God," if we say it as Peter, not by flesh and blood revealing it unto us, but by the light from the Father in heaven shin-

> ing in our heart, we too become as Peter, being pronounced blessed as he was, because that the grounds on which he was pronounced blessed apply also to us, by reason of the fact that flesh and blood have not revealed to us with regard to Jesus that He is Christ, the Son of the living God, but the Father in heaven, . . . And if we too have said like Peter, "Thou art the Christ, the Son of the living God," not as if flesh and blood had revealed it unto us, but by light from the Father in heaven having shone in our heart, we become a Peter, and to us there might be said by the Word, "Thou art Peter," etc. For a rock is every disciple of Christ of whom those drank who drank of the spiritual rock which followed them, and upon every such rock is built every word of the church (*Commentary on Matthew*, 10).

In the same commentary (11), Origen wrote,

> But if you suppose that upon that one Peter only the whole church is built by God, what would you say about John the son of thunder or each one of the Apostles? Shall we otherwise dare to say, that against Peter in particular the gates of Hades shall not prevail, but that they shall prevail against the other Apostles and the perfect? Does not the saying previously made, "The gates of Hades shall not prevail against it," hold in regard to all and in the case of each of them? And also the saying, "Upon this rock I will build my church"? . . . For in this place these words seem to be addressed as to Peter only, "Whatsoever thou shall bind on earth shall be bound in heaven," etc; but in the Gospel of John the Saviour having given the Holy Spirit unto the disciples by breathing upon them said, "Receive ye the Holy Spirit."

In the mid-third century, Cyprian wrote,

> For neither did Peter, whom first the Lord chose, and upon whom He built His Church, when Paul disputed with him afterwards about circumcision, claim anything to himself insolently, nor arrogantly assume anything; so as to say that he held the primacy, and that he ought rather to be obeyed by novices and those lately come (Epistle LXX, 3).

Truly, on and on we could go with quote after quote from the Ante-Nicene Fathers that clearly indicate that the idea of one universal bishop, Vicar of Christ on earth, presiding in Rome as the Father of the Faithful, was unknown to the early Church. The earliest usage of the word "pope," *papa* in Latin, that can be found was by Dionysius of Alexandria, some time between 200-265 A.D., in his "Epistle VII – To Philemon, a Presbyter," in which he refers to "our Blessed *Father* Heraclus," who was his predecessor at Alexandria. It is apparent that this term came to be applied to all bishops, and signified no pre-eminence in those who bore it.

The first person to assume the title of "Pope" as universal bishop, was not even in Rome. It was John, bishop of Constantinople, in 588 A.D. In response to this, Gregory I, bishop of Rome and later called Gregory the Great and recognized by Rome as one of the greatest of Popes, wrote to him,

> You know it, my brother; hath not the venerable council of Chalcedon conferred the honorary title of universal upon the bishops of this apostolic See, whereof I am, by God's Will, the servant? And yet none of us hath permitted this title to be given him; none has assumed this bold title, lest by assuming a special episcopate, we should seem to refuse it to all the brethren. . . . But far from Christians be this blasphemous name by which all honor is taken from all other priests, while it is foolishly arrogated by one.

Gregory the Great was not done. To the emperor, Mauritius, he wrote, "I am bold to say, that whosoever adopts or affects the title of universal bishop has the pride and character of anti-Christ, and is in some manner his forerunner in this haughty quality of elevating himself above the rest of his order" (*The Bible vs. Romanism*, 67-68). These are words from the man recognized by most Roman Catholic scholars as a primary architect of the modern papacy.

Later, the title of Pope as universal bishop was applied to this same Gregory in 604 A.D. by the extremely wicked Emperor Phocas. This was a man who had "beheaded each of his predecessor's five sons, then put out Mauritius' eyes (this was his predecessor), and after torture, disemboweled him" (*The Decline and Fall of the Roman Church*, 80). Malachi Martin was a former Jesuit professor who served in Rome with Cardinal Augustine Bea and Pope John XXIII. Gregory refused the title, but it was later assumed by Boniface III in 607 A.D. Even then it was a mere "court title" and certainly not recognized universally by the Roman Church, even as it passed down to his successors, until the days of Charlemagne and the Holy Roman Empire.

I have presented all of this simply to demonstrate that the Papacy did not spring from the mind of God and it did not start with Peter. Such statements as we saw earlier, "From the very beginning it was acknowledged by the Church that the successor of Saint Peter as Bishop of Rome was at the same time head of the entire Church," are just not true. They are blatantly false. History shows that the Papacy grew in the minds of ambitious men and bears no resemblance to what Jesus promised to build, His Church.

### The Scriptural Evidence

Our attention now turns to the scriptures. Whenever Roman Catholic authorities speak of the Papacy, the passage most often used by them in its defense is Matthew 16:18. Those twenty-nine words have been used as the starting point for what has grown to be the massive organization of the Roman Catholic Church. Due to the importance placed upon this particular verse by the Roman Catholics, it is important, for Catholics and non-Catholics alike, to know exactly what it says and the use made of it by those who believe in the primacy of Peter.

Let us notice, once again, Matthew 16:18, "And I say also unto thee, That thou art Peter, and upon this rock I will build my church; and the gates of hell shall not prevail against it."

As we begin our examination of Matthew 16:18, the source that I will be using to present the Roman Catholic teaching concerning it will be *The Question Box*. It bears the *Nihil Obstat*, meaning "Nothing stands in the way" and the *Imprimatur* meaning "Let it be printed."

On page 148, this question is asked, "Does not the rock mean Christ? (Matt. 16:18) we read in the Bible 'and that rock was Christ' (1 Cor. 10:4)?"

Conway begins his answer by saying, "In Matt. 16:18 the word 'rock' refers to Saint Peter as many fair-minded Protestant commentators admit. . . ."

On page 150, this question is asked, "Does not the use of the two words, *Petros* and *Petra* (Matt. 16:18) prove a clear difference in meaning?"

Conway's answer was, "Not at all. Our Lord did not speak Greek, but Aramaic, which uses the same word, *Kepha*, in both places. Saint John tells us Peter's name, Cephas, was equivalent to *Petros* (John 1:42)."

It is important to realize that in Matthew 16:18, *petros* is the word used for Peter, while *petra* is the word translated "rock." Do these two words prove a clear difference in meaning as the question asked, or do they support the Catholic position that the two words refer to the same thing?

According to *Vine's Complete Expository Dictionary of Old And New Testament Words* (537), the comments concerning *petra* are as follows: "Denotes a massive rock, as distinct from *petros*, a detached stone or boulder, or a stone that might be thrown or easily moved. . . . In Matt.

16:18, metaphorically, of Christ and the testimony concerning him; here the distinction between *petra* concerning the Lord himself, and *petros*, the apostle, is clear."

Conway, as is consistent with all Roman Catholic scholars, makes a major point out of the fact that Jesus spoke Aramaic, a language that would use the same word in both instances. However, Matthew, writing under the inspiration of the Holy Spirit, wrote in Greek, a language that does allow for the distinction between the two. Evidently the Holy Spirit saw fit for Matthew to make the distinction clear. *Petra* and *petros* do not refer to the same thing.

At this point we should mention that Roman Catholic scholars persist in the claim that Matthew originally wrote his gospel in Aramaic and that the Greek gospel of Matthew was simply a translation. They base this assertion upon a questionable quotation of Papias in *Eusebius' Ecclesiastical History*, 3, 39, 14, in which he was alleged to have written, "Matthew composed his history in the Hebrew dialect (probably Syro-Chaldaic, sometimes called Hebrew, g.l.), and every one translated it as he was able."

Roman Catholic authorities continue to make this assertion in spite of considerable evidence to the contrary.

> One thing which seems certain is that whatever this Heb. (Aram) document may have been it was not an original form from which the present Gr. Gospel of Mt. was translated, either by the apostle himself, or by somebody else. . . .Indeed, the Greek Matthew throughout bears the impress of being not a translation at all, but as having been originally written in the Greek. . . . (*The International Standard Bible Encyclopedia*, III: 2010).

> "It must be admitted, however, that no fragment of an Aram. Matthew has ever been found and a Greek edition is more plausible than a Greek translation. Matthew's gospel does not give evidence of being a translation, which is one of the weak evidences for the Aram. theory" (*The Zondervan Pictorial Encyclopedia of the Bible*, IV: 124).

Conway also mentioned that John tells us that Peter's name, Cephas, was equivalent to *petros* in John 1:42. He is absolutely correct and that just serves to prove our point. *Thayer's Greek-English Lexicon of the New Testament* (676) tells us that *petros* means "stone." So *petra* (the rock) denotes a great, immovable mass of rock; while *petros* denotes a detached stone or boulder. These are two completely different things.

As is typical of so much of the Roman Catholic reasoning, Conway launches into a bit of circular logic. We have already noted that he wrote, "The word rock refers to Saint Peter." However, we find this question, "Do not the early Fathers speak of Peter's faith as the rock? Does not Saint Augustine state that the rock is the confession Peter made? Do not others declare that the rock is Christ?" Here is Conway's answer.

> None of these interpretations deny that Peter is the rock foundation of the Church, as we have explained. Taken together they make the true meaning all the more clear. Christ is the original Rock on which Peter rests; Peter is the Rock or foundation of the Church. Faith is the Rock of the Church, i.e., Peter's faith is that which makes him the foundation of the Church. Peter's confession is the rock inasmuch as his profession of Christ's divinity merited him the honor of being made the foundation of the Church (*The Question Box*, 150).

Despite the fact that Peter and his confession cannot both be the rock, and grammatically they do not refer to the same thing, this reasoning adds yet another foundation. The truth is, the rock is the fact that Jesus is the Christ, "the son of the living God." Simply adhering to what the Bible says removes all question. "For other foundation can no man lay than that is laid, which is Jesus Christ" (1 Cor. 3:11). "And are built upon the foundation of the apostles and prophets, Jesus Christ himself being the chief corner stone" (Eph. 2:20).

Even though it is a relatively simple thing to disprove the Catholic claims concerning the papacy, including their assertion that Peter was the first pope to be followed by successors, all of whom were to be recognized as the universal bishop of Christ's church and vicar of Christ on earth, it is obvious that these claims have continued to be made and have grown to this present time. Through the centuries, courageous men have stood in the crucible of controversy, often at great personal cost, to combat these claims. While many of us may take the truth for granted, it is important to remember that men such as Martin Luther and John Calvin of the Reformation, and many others whose names we will never know, have fought the battle before us. Honorable men who are determined to stand on God's Word as the sole authority in religious matters must never fear the white-hot heat of controversy.

## Works Cited

*A Catechism of Christian Doctrine (Revised Edition, Baltimore Catechism #3)*. Cincinnati, Ohio: Christian Investigation Center Press, 1949.

*Catechism of the Catholic Church.* Liguori, Missouri: Liguori Publications, 1994.

Conway, Bertrand L. *The Question Box, New Edition.* New York: Paulist Press, 1929.

*Encyclopedia Britannica,* Vol. 19.

Herbermann, Charles G., Edward A. Pace, Conde B. Pallen, Thomas J. Shahan, and John J. Wynne, Editors. *The Catholic Encyclopedia.* New York: Robert Appleton Company, 1907.

Keating, Karl. *Catholicism And Fundamentalism.* San Francisco: Ignatius Press, 1988.

Martin, Malachi. *The Decline and Fall of the Roman Church.* New York, New York: G. P. Putnam's Sons.

Orr, James, General Editor. *The International Standard Bible Encyclopedia.* Grand Rapids: Wm. B. Eerdmans Publishing Co., 1976.

Pamphilus, Eusebius. *Eusebius' Ecclesiastical History.* Grand Rapids: Baker House, 1990.

Roberts, Alexander and James Donaldson, Editors. *The Ante-Nicene Fathers, Vol. III, V, VI, X.* Grand Rapids: Wm. B. Eerdmans Publishing Co., 1986.

Schaff, Philip. *History of the Christian Church.* Grand Rapids: Wm. B. Eerdmans Publishing Co., 1995.

Tenny, Merrill. *The Zondervan Pictorial Encyclopedia of the Bible.* Grand Rapids: Zondervan Publishing House, 1975.

Thayer, Joseph Henry. *Thayer's Greek-English Lexicon of the New Testament.* Grand Rapids: Zondervan Publishing House, 1975.

Trice, A.N. *The Bible Vs. Romanism.* Out of print.

Vine. W.E., Merrill F. Unger, and William White, Jr. *Vine's Complete Expository Dictionary of Old and New Testament Words.* Nashville: Thomas Nelson Inc., 1985.

# What Must I Do To Be Saved?

**Joe R. Price**

The Prince of Peace who preached the gospel of peace brought great conflict into the world. Jesus said, "Do not think that I came to bring peace on earth. I did not come to bring peace but a sword" (Matt. 10:34). Thus, the Savior focuses our attention on a spiritual struggle; the great battle between God and Satan, between righteousness and sin, between truth and error, between redemption and condemnation, between the saved and the lost (Matt. 10:35-39).

History records one of the most basic conflicts in this epic battle: the controversy over "What must I do to be saved?" The stakes in this dispute could not be higher: the salvation of lost souls. More particularly, what is at stake is the salvation of *your* soul. "What must I do to be saved?" is the most important question anyone can ever ask. God's answer to this question

---

**Joe R. Price** was born in Paris, Texas on October 16, 1957, and grew up in nearby Delta County. In July of 1974 he obeyed the gospel at Cooper, Texas, having grown up in the Methodist Church. He and his wife, Debbie, were married on January 5, 1979. They have four children (Philip, Jeremy, Ethan, and Alyssa). Joe began full-time preaching during the summer of 1978. From 1978 to 1983 he worked with churches in Denver, Colorado; Lufkin, Texas; and Dumas, Texas. In 1983 he moved west to work with the church in Kaysville, Utah, where he remained until 1996. That year he moved to Bellingham, Washington, where he continues to work with the Mt. Baker church. He serves as an elder of the Mt. Baker church, holds several gospel meetings each year, publishes a weekly bulletin, *The Spirit's Sword*, and maintains the Bible Answers website (http://www.bibleanswer.com). Since 2006 Joe has made annual preaching trips to India where he helps teach preacher training classes. These classes are equipping men to abandon the liberalism that infects many churches of Christ and to hold fast the pattern of sound words.

is a great light to all who are lost in sin (Acts 26:18). The battle lines are drawn and the centuries old controversy shows no sign of letting up.

We live in an age of ecumenism where doctrine is minimized and compromise with error is virtuous. Not a few brethren say we must develop a more positive approach if we are to reach the lost with the gospel. Some view as too harsh the old Jerusalem gospel that identifies sin, presents the Savior as the only answer to sin, and calls sinners to immediate faith, obedience, and salvation.

We do not advocate rudeness and callous disregard for others when teaching them what to do to be saved (2 Tim. 2:24-26; Col. 4:4-6). On the contrary, we advocate "great plainness of speech" when teaching people how to be saved (2 Cor. 3:12, KJV). Giving the Bible answer to "What must I do to be saved?" demands clarity—words that cannot be mistaken. Unambiguous language is needed to identify sin and its solution. Our words must convey faith in the power of the gospel to save sinners (Rom. 1:16). The answer that God's word gives to this timeless question is as clear as ever. Our responsibility is to hold fast to that word and sound forth the Bible answer.

When first century Christians believed and advanced the wrong answer to "What must I do to be saved?" they were severed from Christ (Gal. 5:4; 3:26-27). Even so today; we cannot teach and approve the wrong answer and yet be saved. Some Christians who once stood firmly upon the Bible answer to "What must I do to be saved?" now reject the gospel plan of salvation. They are now in fellowship with false teachers and false churches who oppose the Bible plan of salvation. Let us not say it cannot happen to us (1 Cor. 10:12; Heb. 3:12). Every generation must be firmly grounded in the word of truth. Our answer to "What must I do to be saved?" must conform to the apostolic answer (Col. 2:6-7; 2 Tim. 2:2). We must all "stand fast and hold the traditions which you were taught, whether by word or our epistle" (2 Thess. 2:15).

### The Nature of the Question

James said to be "doers of the word, and not hearers only, deceiving yourselves" (Jas. 1:22). Let us then take a moment to examine each part of the question and by so doing appreciate the individual responsibility of being doers of the word (Jas. 1:25).

***What.*** There is an identifiable answer to the question. Furthermore, the answer can be understood and followed. Jesus said, "You shall know the truth, and the truth shall make you free" (John 8:32). A careful study of God's word will tell us *what* to know and to do to be saved. The question implies the use of free will – I must choose to do "what" God says in order to be saved.

***Must.*** The answer is imperative, necessary, and essential. The answer is not suggested, recommended, or merely proposed; it is mandatory for salvation to be obtained.

***I.*** Me, myself, and every other morally responsible person. This person is presently outside of Christ, "having no hope and without God"; he is lost in his sin and under the wrath of God (Rom. 3:23; Eph. 2:1-3, 12).

***Do.*** There is action to perform, a duty of obedience to the Master's will. The Lord has given commandments that *I* must do (obey) in order to be saved (Heb. 5:8-9; Matt. 7:21). Whatever the Lord has commanded, *I* have the ability to do it.

***To be.*** There is an expectation, a result is in view. When one does the Lord's will, the Lord will give him the promised blessing.

***Saved.*** This is the blessing of salvation, deliverance, and freedom from the bondage of sin (John 8:34-36).

A general answer is given to "What must I do to be saved?" in Romans 6:17-18: "But God be thanked that though you were slaves of sin, yet you obeyed from the heart that form of doctrine to which you were delivered. And having been set free from sin, you became slaves of righteousness." Please notice that . . .

- The Romans had been lost in sin ("slaves of sin");
- The Romans did something ("obeyed from the heart" the gospel that was preached to them);
- The Romans were saved from their past sins ("And having been set free from sin");
- The Romans then had a new relationship with Christ ("you became servants of righteousness").

The New Testament reveals the "form of doctrine" which the Romans "obeyed from the heart." In just a moment we will allow the Scriptures to identify the teaching to be obeyed to be set free from sin.

But first, please note that our question implies knowledge that one needs to be rescued from his lost spiritual condition. He knows he is lost – he just does not know what to do to be saved. To ask "What must I do to be saved?" one must be convinced he is lost! The Pentecostians, Saul of Tarsus, and even the Philippian jailer were all acutely aware of their need to be saved from their present circumstance before they asked what they must do (Acts 2:37; 9:6; 16:27-30).

We should not expect the lost person to ask what to do to be saved before he has been convinced he is lost (cf. Acts 17:23, 30-31). Our task is to teach sinners they are lost and that Jesus Christ is the only one who can save them (Acts 4:12). Unbelievers must first be convicted of "sin, and of righteousness, and of judgment" by the word of truth (John 16:13). Then they can ask, "What must I do to be saved?" and we can give them the Bible answer.

**The Bible Answer to the Bible Question**

Lost people asked "What must I do to be saved?" (or its variation) three times in the New Testament. They were not told there was nothing for them to do. They were not told they could do nothing to affect their salvation. Instead, each one who asked the question was given a specific answer that reflected where he was on the way to salvation.

*1. The Philippian Jailer (Acts 16).* "What must I do to be saved?" was asked by the jailer of Paul and Silas in Acts 16:30 after he witnessed the miraculous effects of God's power. A great earthquake had opened the doors to the prison and loosed the prisoners' restraints (Acts 16:25-26). The jailer was prepared to take his own life (supposing his prisoners had escaped) when Paul's reassuring voice stayed his hand (vv. 27-28). Fearfully, this **unbeliever** humbly asked the all important question, "Sirs, what must I do to be saved?" (v. 30). Paul and Silas answered with the most general of statements, "Believe on the Lord Jesus Christ, and you will be saved, you and your household" (v. 31). Some have taken this as final proof that the only thing necessary in order to be saved is to believe in Christ (the "faith only" doctrine of salvation). These fail to define correctly the nature of saving faith (Matt. 7:21-23; Jas. 2:14-26). Faith was the first step for the jailer (there is no evidence he even knew who Jesus was), otherwise, "how then shall they call on him in whom they have not believed?" (Rom. 10:14). The jailer and his household needed to hear the gospel and believe it in order to be saved.

The command to believe on the Lord Jesus Christ necessarily includes all the other commands one must obey to be saved (Rom. 6:17-18). An examination of the events that followed convinces us the jailer and his household purified their souls by "obeying the truth" and not by faith only (1 Pet. 1:22).

Following his question and their answer, Paul and Silas "spoke the word of the Lord to him and to all who were in his house" (v. 32). This is understandable, since they had to *hear* the gospel before they could believe it: "faith comes by hearing, and hearing by the word of God" (Rom. 10:17). Having heard the gospel, it is evident that the jailer *believed* the gospel since it caused a change in his heart and his conduct: "he took them the same hour of the night and washed their stripes" (v. 33). This was a clear action of *repentance* since he had previously "put them into the inner prison and fastened their feet in the stocks" (v. 24). Now, having heard the gospel, believed it, and repented, "immediately he and all his family were *baptized"* (v. 33). What a joyful occasion! Please observe when the man and his house rejoiced in their newly obtained salvation; not at the point of initial faith, nor even when they repented of their past sins, but after they were baptized (v. 34).

The reason for joy is given in verse 34: "he rejoiced, having believed in God with all his household." The faith that saved him included obedience to the commands of the gospel just as certainly as it included believing that Jesus is the Christ. The jailer was saved by faith when he had the faith to obey the gospel he heard (Matt. 7:21; 1 Pet. 1:22). The faith that saves is the faith that obeys.

When an **unbeliever** asks "What must I do to be saved?" he is told to *believe* on the Lord Jesus Christ. He must *hear* the gospel and *believe* it (Rom. 10:17) in order to *confess* his faith (Rom. 10:9-10), to *repent* of his sins and then to *be baptized* for the remission of his sins (Rom. 10:17; Heb. 11:6; Acts 17:30; Mark 16:16). Then he is saved by the Lord from his sins.

*2. The Day of Pentecost (Acts 2).* "What shall we do?" was asked by the murderers of Jesus when they were convicted of their sin against Jesus. The apostolic gospel produced faith in their hearts, convincing them of their crime against the Son of God: "Now when they heard this, they were cut to the heart, and said to Peter and the rest of the apostles, "'Men and brethren, what shall we do?'" These **believers** were told to "*Repent*, and let every one of you *be baptized* in the name of Jesus Christ for the remission of sins; and you shall receive the gift of the Holy Spirit" (vv. 37-38). When a **believer** asks what to do to be saved, the gospel answer is to *repent* and *be baptized.*

The different answers given in Acts 2:38 and Acts 16:31 indicate a difference in the people asking the question. The men of Acts 2 were already believers, having just been convicted of their sins by hearing and believing that Jesus is "Lord and Christ." On the other hand, the jailer was an unbeliever when he asked the question. The first were told to repent and be baptized to be saved. The latter were told to believe to be saved. If you are a believer in Jesus Christ, you must repent and be baptized to be saved (Acts 2:38). But, if you are not a believer in Jesus, you must first believe on the Lord to be saved (Acts 16:31) – then you are also commanded to repent and be baptized.

*3. Saul of Tarsus (Acts 9, 22).* The question is found a third time in Acts 9:6 when Saul was on his way to Damascus to persecute Christians. Jesus appeared to him, giving him undeniable proof that He is the Christ (vv. 2, 4-5). Saul asked, "Lord, what do you want me to do?" (v. 6). Jesus told him to go into Damascus "and you will be told what you must do." Blinded for the next three days, Saul prayed but did not eat or drink. The former unbeliever was now a **repentant believer** (Acts 9:9-11). What was Saul told he must do when he got to Damascus? Would it lead to his salvation, or was he saved on the road? Many believe Saul was saved when Jesus appeared to him. However, the preacher Ananias, whom Jesus sent to Saul, appealed to him saying, "And now why are you waiting? Arise and be baptized, and wash away your sins, calling on the name of the Lord" (Acts 22:16). Saul was not saved from his sins on the road to Damascus. A vision of Jesus did not wash away his sins. Faith only did not wash away his sins. Fasting and prayer did not wash away his sins. Saul was saved from his sins three days later in Damascus when he obeyed the Lord's command and was baptized (see Mark 16:16).

In summary, the Bible answer to "What must I do to be saved?" is (1) to *hear* the gospel message of sin and a Savior (John 5:24-25; 6:45); (2) to *believe* in God and in Jesus as the Christ, the Son of God (John 8:23-24; Heb. 11:6); (3) to *confess* one's faith that Jesus is the Christ (Rom. 10:9-10); (4) to *repent* of personal sin against God (Acts 2:38; 11:30); and (5) to *be baptized* into Christ for the remission of sins (Matt. 28:19; Mark 16:15-16; Acts 2:38, 41; 22:16).

These conditions of salvation remain in effect today. No sinner can be saved from his past sins unless and until he obeys these God-given conditions from a willing and humble heart. When the lost person obeys these gospel commands he is saved by grace, through faith (Eph. 2:8).

## Truth Clarified through Historical Controversy

Opponents of the truth did not remain silent as the apostles preached the saving gospel "in Jerusalem, and in all Judea and Samaria, and to the ends of the earth" (Acts 1:8). The gospel plan of salvation has faced resistance from the first century to the present. Consider some of the most prominent resistance to the gospel plan of salvation.

*1. Controversy over adding circumcision and keeping the Law of Moses.* The God-revealed conditions of salvation were challenged as the gospel spread from the environs of Jerusalem into Gentile regions. Jewish Christians from Jerusalem came to Antioch teaching Gentiles that "unless you are circumcised according to the custom of Moses, you cannot be saved" (Acts 15:1). The doctrine that "it is necessary to circumcise them, and to command them to keep the law of Moses" caused "no small dissension and dispute" between them, Paul and Barnabas. This led to a meeting in Jerusalem to determine what was being taught by the apostles on this matter (Acts 15:2-5; Gal. 2:1-2). In this meeting it was sufficiently documented that compelling Gentiles to keep the Law of Moses in order to be saved was not a part of the gospel. Teaching such a doctrine was without divine authority (Acts 15:6-21). This false doctrine was being advanced by the will of men, not the will of God (Acts 15:22-29).

Much of the conflict faced by the advance of the gospel in the first decades after Calvary came from false teachers who tried to bind circumcision and the traditions of Moses as conditions of salvation. The very nature of the gospel was at stake, and so the saints earnestly contended for the faith against this error (Rom. 1:16-17; Gal. 1:6-10; Jude 3).

The epistles of Galatians, Romans, and Hebrews thoroughly refuted this false teaching. The apostles of Christ preached the sufficiency of the gospel of Christ to save without any vestiges of the old covenant being added to supplement and complete the new covenant. They emphasized that God's plan of salvation is not "by the works of the law" but "by faith in Jesus Christ" (Gal. 2:16). With clarity of truth they taught that "the law was our tutor to bring us to Christ, that we might be justified by faith. But now that faith has come, we are no longer under a tutor" (Gal. 3:24-25). Any attempt to be justified by the Law of Moses caused one to be "estranged from Christ" and "fallen from grace" (Gal. 5:4). Only "righteousness by faith," obtained by "obeying the truth," frees sinners from their sin (Gal. 5:5-7, 1).

We thus conclude that "What must I do to be saved" is fully answered in the New Testament of Christ without adding anything to it from the Old Testament Law of Moses.

*2. Controversy over taking away man's free will to choose to be saved.* As time advanced controversy erupted over man's free will—the sinner's ability to choose to be believe and to obey in order to be saved. Dispute arose over whether men possess the ability to choose to believe, obey, and be saved. Did man even have the ability to ask, "What must I do to be saved?", much less the ability to meet any stipulated conditions of salvation?

The corruption of the soul by sin came to be regarded as so severe and the expanse between the holy and sovereign God and sinful man so great that it was thought man (corrupted by sin and completely given to evil) could do nothing to affect his salvation. It was said that free will to choose what is good is destroyed by man's total depravity in sin. Based on such an analysis, only through a sovereign election by God would anyone be saved. Augustine (354-430) concluded man is a "mess of sin" and totally incapable of moving toward God ("Augustine and Pelagius," R. C. Sproul, www.leaderu.com/theology/augpelagius.html). Augustine viewed man as completely controlled by evil impulses and thus unable to make choices for salvation. God must do the choosing (electing) of those who would be saved; man could not act to save himself (cf. Acts 2:40; Phil. 2:12-13).

Over one thousand years later the Protestant Reformers agreed that because of the total corruption of original sin man cannot choose right and wrong. Luther reasserted the Augustinian view that man could do nothing that removes him from the bondage of sin; all depended on the sovereign act of God working on reprobate man to accomplish salvation.

The *Westminster Confession of Faith* (1646) would codify the Augustinian view. It states that men are "wholly inclined to all evil" ("The Westminster Confession of Faith," VI:IV; *Creeds of the Churches*, Third Edition, John H. Leith, ed., 201). Accordingly, salvation depends upon the sovereignty of God to elect (choose) those who would be eternally saved and those who would be eternally lost (reprobate):

> By the decree of God, for the manifestation of his glory, some men and angels are predestined unto everlasting life, and others foreordained to everlasting death. These angels and men, thus predestinated and foreordained, are particularly and unchangeably designed; and their number

> is so certain and definite that it cannot be either increased or diminished (*Ibid.,* III: III-IV; 198).

Thus, a basic Reformation doctrine is that salvation was not really open to everyone. Only the elect of God – those God immutably chose to be saved – were said to actually be called to salvation. All others are eternally lost – reprobate and damned – regardless of their desire and actions. Like Augustine long before, free will to choose to be saved was abandoned; all was left to the predestination of God to both save and destroy.

As one author astutely observed, the Protestant Reformation

> . . . taught that the predestined are saved by grace alone and the rest of mankind are eternally damned. It's a popular myth that John Calvin introduced the doctrine of predestination, but Calvin was simply repeating established Reformation theology. So today, those who say that the offer of salvation is open to everyone contradict a basic Reformation doctrine (*Will the Real Heretics Please Stand Up,* David W. Bercot, 70).

In answer to this error, the Bible definitively declares that God offers salvation to all sinners and that every sinner possesses the free will to choose or reject the salvation God's grace offers in His Son:

- "For God so loved the world that He gave His only begotten Son, that *whoever* believes in Him should not perish but have everlasting life" (John 3:16).
- "Then Peter opened his mouth and said: 'In truth I perceive that *God shows no partiality*. But in every nation *whoever* fears Him and works righteousness is accepted by Him'" (Acts 10:34-35).
- "And it shall come to pass that *whoever* calls on the name of the Lord shall be saved" (Acts 2:21; Rom. 10:13).
- "For this is good and acceptable in the sight of God our Savior, who *desires all men to be saved* and to come to the knowledge of the truth" (1 Tim. 2:3-4).
- "The Lord is not slack concerning His promise, as some count slackness, but is longsuffering toward us, *not willing that any should perish* but that *all* should come to repentance" (2 Pet. 3:9).
- "And the Spirit and the bride say, 'Come!' And let him who hears say, 'Come!' And let him who thirsts come. *Whoever desires,* let him take the water of life freely" (Rev. 22:17).

The election God made is that sinners will obtain redemption "in Christ" (Eph. 1:3-12). God's election is that those who believe and obey the gospel of Christ will be saved (John 3:16; Matt. 7:21-23; 2 Thess. 2:13-14). Each sinner is called by the gospel to choose to believe and obey *"the word of truth, the gospel of your salvation"* (Eph. 1:13). Each person must choose whether or not to fear and obey God (Acts 10:34-35). Some will choose to reject the word of salvation and others will choose to believe it (Acts 13:45-49).

We thus conclude that "What must I do to be saved" can be asked and obeyed by every sinner, because Jesus Christ is the Savior of all men. Those who believe in Him will be saved (1 Tim. 4:10). Salvation in the Son is obtained by all who do the will of the Father (Matt. 7:21).

[In the nineteenth and twentieth centuries religious debate proved to greatly benefit those intent on examining the Scriptures to know and teach God's word on the subject of God's election and man's free will. Such debates helped many brethren clarify their thinking and solidify their teaching on the topic of Calvinism. As a result of these debates, a great many lost souls came to know, believe and obey the truth. Honorable debate continues to be capable of meeting these worthy objectives. Representative debates include: *A Theological Debate between T. W. Brents and E. D. Herod* on the conditional nature of salvation, 1887, Franklin, KY; *F. B. Srygley-C. H. Cayce* (1915); the *Cogdill-Jackson Debate* on the plan of salvation, Lufkin, TX, 1946; and the *Nichols-Holder Debates* on the conditions and availability of salvation, 1944 in Tallassee, Alabama, and 1950 in Medina, Tennessee. An important study of the doctrines of Calvinism and their impact on brethren is *Neo-Calvinism in the Church of Christ*, Tom Roberts, editor.]

*3. Controversy over salvation by faith only: Corrupting the nature of saving faith.* Protestant Reformers corrupted the nature of saving faith in their reaction to the Roman Catholic Church's abuse of grace and works. Concluding that salvation is by faith only, they objected to any act of obedience in order to be saved as "earning" or meriting salvation. The following statements from Protestant creeds and confessions reflect this false view of "what must I do to be saved?"

> We are accounted righteous before God only for the merit of our Lord and Saviour Jesus Christ, by faith, and not for our own works or deservings. Wherefore, that we are justified by faith, only, is a most wholesome doctrine, and very full of comfort ("The Articles of Religion," Art. IX, *The Book of Discipline of the United Methodist Church, 1980,* 57).

> We believe that the great gospel blessing which Christ secures to such as believe in him is justification; that justification . . . is bestowed, not in consideration of any works of righteousness which we have done, but solely through faith in the Redeemer's blood . . . ("The New Hampshire Confession," V; *Baptist Church Manual, Revised*, J. M. Pendleton, 48).

It is true that sinners cannot earn or merit salvation. Our "own works" cannot save us because we are sinners (2 Tim. 1:9). The only way one could "earn" his salvation is never to sin. Then, God's grace would be a debt owed to him because of his sinless life. Having never sinned (violated God's law), the sinless person's justification would be merited by his sinless works (Rom. 4:1-4; cf. Gal. 3:12). But, since "all have sinned," salvation by "works" (of law, sinlessness) is forever off the table (Rom. 3:21-23; 4:5; Eph. 2:8-9). We need God's grace in order to be saved. God's grace is accessed "by faith" – by meeting the conditions of salvation (Rom. 4:5-8; 5:1-2).

The nature of saving faith is active and obedient. Faith that is "unto the saving of the soul" obeys the word of God, fully trusting in the salvation God assures the faithful (Heb. 10:36-39). Hebrews 11 repeatedly shows the obedient nature of saving faith. Consider just three examples stated there:

- Abel. By faith Abel "offered to God a more excellent sacrifice than Cain" and "obtained witness that he was righteous" (Heb. 11:4). Abel's faith was obedient to God and he was counted righteous, not because he earned his righteousness, but because God approves of faith that obeys his word.

- Noah. By faith Noah "prepared an ark for the saving of his household" and he "became an heir of the righteousness which is according to faith" (Heb. 11:7). Did Noah's obedience nullify God's grace (Gen. 6:8)? No, his obedience in building the ark was a full expression of his faith that God would save him and his family.

- Abraham. By faith Abraham "offered up Isaac" (Heb. 11:17). Abraham was "justified by works when he offered Isaac his son on the altar" (Jas. 2:21). When by faith he obeyed, God said, "Now I know that you fear God" (Gen. 22:12). "And the Scripture was fulfilled which says, 'Abraham believed God, and it was accounted to him for righteousness'" (Jas. 2:23). Undeniably, faith that is counted for righteousness is faith that obeys the commands of God.

Faith that does not act (work, obey) is not saving faith. Such inactive faith is described in James 2:14-20 as profitless, dead, unseen, demonic, and useless. James declared that "a man is justified by works, and not by faith only," and that "faith without works is dead" (Jas. 2:24, 26). The "works" that justify are the *works of faith*, the obedience of one who believes in God, who takes God at His word and does everything He says. Abel obeyed by faith, and God saved him. Noah obeyed by faith, and God saved him. Abraham obeyed by faith, and God saved him. A sinner obeys by faith, and God saves him.

One has not earned his salvation when the conditions of salvation are obeyed any more than Noah earned his salvation from the flood by building the ark. The sinner who is saved by grace through faith cannot boast in himself; his salvation is a gift of God (Eph. 2:8). The humble, obedient believer is an unprofitable servant who has simply done his duty (Luke 17:10).

[The religious debates of the nineteenth and twentieth centuries on the nature of saving faith profited many as they gave opportunities for brethren to solidify their faith and teaching on this vital subject as they reached out to those under the sway of false doctrine. Such debates continue to be useful in reaching lost souls with the truth as they confirm sound doctrine. Representative debates on faith include: *Campbell-Jennings*, Nashville, TN, 1830; *A Theological Debate between T. W. Brents and E. D. Herod*, 1887, Franklin, KY; *Porter-Tingley* on the plan of salvation, Birmingham, AL, 1947; *Warren-Ballard* debate on when the alien sinner is saved, Fort Worth, TX, 1952.]

*4. Controvery over the essential nature of water baptism for salvation.* The controversy over the nature of works and faith naturally formed a battleground over the necessity of water baptism for salvation. In the early and mid-1800s as men in this country and others began to abandon the creeds and confessions of Protestant denominations in favor of the New Testament plan of salvation, the necessity of water baptism for salvation began to be fervently preached and vigorously opposed. The meaning, purpose, mode, subjects, and figures of water baptism were widely studied, discussed and debated. (See *The Gospel Plan of Salvation,* T. W. Brents, 210-454 for a thorough study of water baptism.) Through the refining process of controversy the essential nature of water baptism in God's plan of salvation was plainly set forth. Many souls left the denominations in favor of God's plan of salvation, being baptized into Christ for the remission of their sins (Mark 16:15-16; Acts 2:38).

Protestant denominations have generally rejected the baptism of a believer as essential for salvation from sins, and that rejection continues today. Here are just a few examples of this rejection:

> **The Presbyterian Church:** "Although it be a great sin to contemn or neglect this ordinance (baptism, jrp), yet grace and salvation are not so inseparably annexed unto it as that no person can be regenerated or saved without it, or that all that are baptized are undoubtedly regenerated" ("The Westminster Confession of Faith," XXVIII:V; *Creeds of the Churches*, 224).
>
> **The Baptist Church:** "The spiritual change of the new birth constitutes Christian fellowship; but to secure church fellowship, that change must be confessed in baptism" (*The Hiscox Guide for Baptist Churches*, Edward T. Hiscox, 39). And again, "Baptism may not be essential to salvation, but it is essential to obedience" (*Ibid.,* 87).
>
> **The Methodist Church:** "Baptism is not only a sign of profession and mark of difference whereby Christians are distinguished from others that are not baptized; but it is also a sign of regeneration or the new birth. The baptism of young children is to be retained in the church" ("The Articles of Religion," Art. XVII, *The Book of Discipline,* 59).

The New Testament pattern of the necessity of water baptism is distinctly different from the creeds of men. Jesus commanded baptism in order to be "saved" (Mark 16:16). The apostles commanded baptism for the "remission of sins" (Acts 2:38). Ananias emphatically urged Saul to "arise and be baptized, and wash away your sins" (Acts 22:16). Baptism is said to be "into Christ" and "into His death," as well as "into death" to sin (Rom. 6:3-4). Therefore, without water baptism one is not in Christ, he does not have the saving benefits of his death, and he is still dead in his sins.

The New Testament continues its emphasis on the necessity of baptism for salvation by noting that every person who is "baptized into Christ" has "put on Christ" (Gal. 3:27). Without baptism one is not in a saved relationship with the Father, the Son, and the Holy Spirit (Matt. 28:19). Sinners are buried with Christ in baptism and raised from their spiritual death by the power of God (Col. 2:12; Rom. 6:4-5). Baptism "saves us" like water saved Noah, by delivering us out of the corrupt world of sin into a new life with God (1 Pet. 3:20-21).

When asked "What must I do to be saved?" we must hold fast the pattern of sound words and include the necessity of water baptism in our answer (2 Tim. 1:13). Like belief, confession, and repentance, water baptism is an essential condition for salvation.

[Many religious debates have been held over the past two hundred years on the nature, purpose, subjects and mode of water baptism. As previously noted, such debates magnified the truth and its simple power to save the lost as they provided occasions for sinners to believe and obey the gospel in order to be saved. Such debates continue to be useful today to achieve the same godly results (1 Pet. 3:15; Jude 3). Representative debates on water baptism include: *Campbell-Walker*, Mount Pleasant, Ohio, 1820, *Campbell-McCalla*, Washington, KY, 1823; *Oliphant-Rice*, Dallas, TX, 1935; *Houchen-Tatum*, Amarillo, TX, 1950; *Reeves-Cook*, Conway, AR, 2005.]

*5. Controversy over personal salvation experiences.* Many people do not rely on the Spirit-given word of God to confirm their salvation (Rom. 8:16). Instead, they rely on a personal experience to convince them they have been saved. There are as many different experiences offered as proof of salvation as there are people who experience them. Some believe God spoke directly to them. Others insist the Holy Spirit fell upon them and sanctified them through a miraculous experience such as speaking in tongues. Still others believe that through prayer God revealed Himself to them and assured them they are saved. Some claim to have seen visions while others attest to having dreamed dreams. And so it goes.

A common thread running through all these personal salvation experiences is the absence of objective truth to support the claim. Where is the supporting evidence from the Scriptures that the Lord saves through such personal experiences? Whenever an experience is held up to document or "prove" one's salvation, the word of God is no longer regarded as the final word on the matter (Heb. 1:1-2). Instead of the Scriptures, one's emotions and feelings during an experience are accepted as sufficient proof of what "must" be right. We are inclined to ask the person who rests his salvation upon a personal salvation experience how he is able to know that experience was from God and not a lying wonder of Satan? To believe that personal experiences give assurance of salvation is to believe a lie. To cling tightly to an experience that has no support in the Scriptures while denying the gospel plan of salvation is to be deceived by strong delusions from the devil (2 Thess. 2:10-12).

By examining the Scriptures one can know whether an experience is really from God (Acts 17:11). The Scriptures say, "There is a way that seems right to a man, but its end is the way of death" (Prov. 14:12). For example, Saul of Tarsus thought his opposition to Jesus of Nazareth was proof he pleased God (Acts 26:9-11; Gal. 1:13). But, even his clean conscience did not approve him before God (Acts 23:1). Even after Saul had experienced seeing Jesus followed by three days of fasting and praying, he still was not saved through his experiences. He was told to "arise and be baptized, and wash away your sins" (Acts 22:16). Whose personal experience today is greater than Saul's? Yet he was not saved by his personal experience with Jesus. Nor should anyone today think he has had a personal experience with Christ that frees him from meeting the conditions of salvation. "What must I do to be saved?" still applies.

The truth is, one experiences (obtains) salvation when he obeys the gospel in faith by repenting, confessing his faith, and being baptized for the remission of his sins (cf. Acts 8:34-39). So-called personal salvation experiences that deny the gospel conditions of salvation will never give a correct answer to "What must I do to be saved?"

### Present-day Concerns

The historical controversy over "What must I do to be saved?" teaches us that without constant instruction, continued vigilance, and careful obedience any of us can fall from our own steadfastness (2 Pet. 3:17-18).

Just as Israel was "destroyed for lack of knowledge," we are concerned today that Christians are being destroyed by not having a clear knowledge of God's plan of salvation (Hos. 4:6). The answer to "What must I do to be saved?' is being influenced by false doctrines and by false brethren. The faith of elders, deacons, preachers, and saints is being shaken and overthrown. Uncertain sounds can be heard in Israel concerning the accuracy and the necessity of the gospel plan of salvation. Some are tired of hearing the plan of salvation and want to go in a different direction away from a "thus saith the Lord" in all things. Others have already cast off restraint and abandoned the gospel plan of salvation. We must vigilantly continue to preach the conditions of salvation and make them known to the next generation; souls are at stake (1 Tim. 4:16).

*1. The emotional experience plan of salvation: "What must I feel to be saved?"* Many people look for a direct operation of God upon them to validate their salvation. Some seek a direct experience with the Holy Spirit, expecting him to fall upon them as he did on the house of Cornelius. (The Holy Spirit did not fall on Cornelius and his house to save them, but to bear witness that Gentiles could hear the word of the gospel, believe it, and be saved by faith [Acts 15:7-9; 11:17-18].) Others look for a "better felt than told" experience to persuade them they are saved. (Remember,

Saul felt he was saved but the Lord told him he was not [Acts 26:9-11, 14; 22:10, 16]!)

There is no doubt that great joy attends one's conversion to Christ, and we shall not minimize the joy of being saved (cf. Acts 8:39; 16:34). Yet, some Christians are being made to question and doubt their conversion because they did not have some great and grand emotional experience when they obeyed the gospel. They hear their religious friends – sometimes New Testament Christians – talk about their experience of being saved and wonder if they were really saved when they believed and were baptized. They begin to doubt their faith and the correctness of their confession since they did not "feel" the Spirit of God moving on them like so many have claimed for themselves. Such considerations and concerns do not arise from the Scriptures but from the false doctrines of men that equate emotion with spirituality.

When Peter exhorted the murderers of Jesus he said, "Save yourselves from this untoward (corrupt) generation" (Acts 2:40, KJV). He did not tell them to wait for an emotionally overwhelming experience or for a direct operation of the Holy Spirit to save them; he said, "save yourselves."

There is abundant joy in heaven and on earth that attends the salvation of every soul (Luke 15:7). Salvation does not depend on an emotional experience, but on a faith experience. Every sinner who believes and obeys the gospel plan of salvation will experience salvation and its attendant joy (Acts 8:39; 16:34).

*2. The ecumenical plan of salvation: "There are saved people in the denominations even though they have not obeyed the gospel plan of salvation."* Men who once believed and preached the gospel plan of salvation now reject it as legalistic and narrow-minded. With men like Max Lucado writing books that pervert and deny the gospel plan of salvation, and with brethren drinking from such broken cisterns, we should not be surprised when brethren begin to question and doubt the Bible teaching on salvation.

Lucado recently wrote: "The heart of the human problem is the heart of the human. And God's treatment is prescribed in John 3:16. He loves. He gave. We believe. We live" (*The 3:16 Promise*, 2). He goes on to deny the gospel plan of salvation by encouraging a prayer to satisfy the belief that leads to life (57). The false doctrine of the "sinner's prayer" contradicts the truth revealed in Hebrews 11 and James 2:14-26 that defines and describes faith that saves the soul. The "heart of the problem" is sin! The way out of sin is the Savior and His plan of salvation (not the "sinner's prayer"). Yet, like Israel in the wilderness who lusted for "the cucumbers, the melons, the leeks, the onions and the garlic" of Egypt while loathing the manna, some Christians lust for the sectarian notions of men while loathing the truth of the gospel that feeds us from heaven (Num. 11:5-6; 21:5; John 6:48-58; 1 Pet. 2:2).

Some brethren have suggested there are Christians in the denominations and that it is our duty to get them out. People in the denominations are lost; the Bible tells me so (2 John 9; Gal. 1:6-10). But, are there Christians in the denominations? No, that is not Bible teaching.

If there are Christians in the denominations, how did they get there? The denominations do not teach the gospel truth about how to be saved. Since the doctrines of the denominations do not save the lost, it follows that the saved are not in the churches of the lost (Matt. 15:7-9).

If there are Christians in the denominations, then who added them to these denominations? The churches of men are not the church of Christ (Matt. 16:18; Eph. 1:22). Jesus adds the saved to His church, not the churches of men (Acts 2:47; Eph. 1:23). And, since Jesus saves His church, He does not add saved souls to the churches of the lost (Eph. 5:23). Yet, that is what He must be doing if there are Christians in the denominations.

There are good moral people in the denominations. But just as surely as a good, moral man named Cornelius was lost in his sin and needed to hear words that would save him, the good moral people in the denominations are also lost in their sins and must "hear the word of the gospel," believe it, and obey it to be saved (Acts 10:1-2, 22; 11:14; 15:7). The good moral people in the denominations are not Christians until they believe and obey the gospel plan of salvation (Acts 2:41). Furthermore, when they do that they will leave the denominations of men and be added by the Lord to the church that belongs to Him – the church of Christ (Acts 2:47).

Such thinking belies a misunderstanding of the Lord's church as well as His plan of salvation.

*3. The positive plan of salvation: "We love you too much to say you are lost."* The so-called positive approach to gospel preaching has borne the fruit of ambiguity and fear when teaching the lost. Not wanting to "run anybody off," some brethren will not tell sinners what they need to hear so they can repent and be saved.

Gospel preaching must be a balance of reproof, rebuke, and exhortation (2 Tim. 4:2). This must be done out of love for the truth and love for the lost. If we fail to reprove and rebuke we may feel better, but sinners will remain lost in their sins!

As predicted, some brethren are not enduring sound doctrine and are gathering to themselves teachers who scratch their itching ears (2 Tim. 4:3-4). The result is brethren who are either unwilling or unable to convict sinners of sin and call them to repentance. Those who oppose such preaching should go again to Acts 24:24-25 and learn how Paul preached the faith in Christ and called the sinners Felix and Drusilla to repentance. May they go again to Matthew 14:3-12 and remember the preacher who lost his head because he dared to rebuke the sin of a king. May they carefully study Acts 20:17-38 and learn – perhaps for the first time – how the apostle preached the whole counsel of God in an effort to save the lost and protect the saved.

Those who would "eliminate the negative" from preaching have unwittingly conditioned a generation of Christians to have no stomach for the hard work of rebuking and reproving sin. Let us be balanced in our preaching, but let us also realize it is far better momentarily to hurt a person's feelings with the truth and lead him to salvation, than it is to shield his feelings, fail to teach him the truth, and see him lost forever! The gospel will "cut to the heart" – it will hurt – but it will save those who receive its reproof and rebuke (Acts 2:37, 41). If we do not understand this about the gospel then we will not urgently and plainly tell the lost what they must do to be saved.

*4. The personal plan of salvation: "My relationship is more important than my salvation."* We all have family and friends whom we dearly love, and most have some family member who are lost; they are not Christians. Sometimes out of misplaced love for earthly relations people reject the gospel plan of salvation and cling to the flesh. Jesus warned, "He who loves father or mother more than Me is not worthy of Me. And he who loves son or daughter more than Me is not worthy of Me" (Matt. 10:37). The priority of truth and Christ above all else must be complete and constantly remembered. When a generation grows up lacking the fundamental ingredient of self-denial and love for Christ and for His truth above everyone else, brethren begin to question the eternal condition of the dearly departed loved one who "was such a good person" but who never obeyed the gospel plan of salvation. Exceptions are made where the Scriptures make none. This leads to less trust in the Bible to save and more trust in human relationships. We must continually teach and recall that close relationships on earth do not change the truth of the gospel. Let us instill in our hearts an overriding love for the lost that tries to reach them with the saving gospel. To do otherwise is not showing love for the lost.

*5. The silent plan of salvation: "No gospel invitation preaching."* More and more reports are heard of sermons being preached without gospel invitations being offered. Brethren, this ought not to be! For, "'whoever calls on the name of the Lord shall be saved.' How then shall they call on Him in whom they have not believed? And how shall they believe in Him of whom they have not heard? And how shall they hear without a preacher?" (Rom. 10:13-14) When people do not hear the gospel plan of salvation they cannot believe and obey the gospel call to be saved. Consequently, they remain lost in their sins. We must be preaching the conditions of salvation and inviting the lost to believe and obey the gospel to be saved!

Some preach and never invite the lost to do anything! This is not how the apostles preached. For example, Peter exhorted the lost to save themselves; surely we must do no less today (Acts 2:40).

When an invitation to the lost consists of "If we can help you in any way, please come forward while we stand and sing," then be sure you have told them from God's word how you can help them (or better yet, how God can help them). Have you told them that you can help them by hearing their confession of faith? Have you told them you can rejoice with them over their repentance from sins? Have you told them you can baptize them into Christ for the remission of their sins?

When an invitation to the lost consists of "if you have a need, come forward and let it be known while we stand and sing," then be sure you have told them from God's word what it is they need. If there are lost ones in the audience they certainly do have a need – they need salvation in Christ! Tell them of their need of salvation. Tell them the plan of salvation. Urge them to come to Jesus and be saved by faithfully obeying Him (Heb. 5:9).

The "if you have a need" invitation makes many assumptions. Among them are the assumptions that . . .

- The lost person knows he has a need.
- The lost person knows what it is he needs.
- The lost person knows he needs to do something in order to meet his need.
- The lost person knows what he needs to do in order to meet his need.

- The lost person does not need to be told he has a need or what to do about his need.
- The lost person does not need to be persuaded to do what he should do to be saved.
- The preacher has no responsibility to tell the lost what he needs or to attempt to persuade him to act upon his need.

Brethren, that's too many assumptions! Gospel preaching takes nothing for granted and seeks to persuade sinners to obey Jesus without delay (2 Cor. 6:2)!

### Conclusion

"What must I do to be saved?" is asked and answered in the New Testament of Christ. Although controversy has swirled around it for centuries, neither the question nor its answer is beyond our understanding: "The word is near you, in your mouth and in your heart (that is, the word of faith which we preach)" (Rom. 10:8). Men have resisted the answer, opposed the answer and rebelled against the answer. Others have believed the answer and obeyed the God-given conditions of belief, confession of faith, repentance and baptism. The test of faith comes in humbly and fully obeying the Lord's plan of salvation (Luke 17:10). Men's false plans of salvation will never save the lost. Christ alone is "the author of eternal salvation to all who obey Him" (Acts 4:12; Heb. 5:9).

### Bibliography

Bercot, David W. *Will the Real Heretics Please Stand Up.* Scroll Publishing.

Brents, T. W. *The Gospel Plan of Salvation.* Guardian of Truth Foundation.

Hiscox, Edward T. *The Hiscox Guide for Baptist Churches.* Judson Press.

Leith, John H., Editor. *Creeds of the Churches.* Knox Press, Third Edition.

Lucado, Max. *The 3:16 Promise*, Thomas Nelson Publishing.

Pendleton, J. M. *Baptist Church Manual, Revised,* Broadman Press.

Sproul, R. C. "Augustine and Pelagius" (www.leaderu.com/theology/aug-pelagius.html), Ligonier Ministries.

*The Book of Discipline of the United Methodist Church* (1980). The United Methodist Publishing House.

# Whosoever Will May Come:

## The Tension Between Divine Grace and Human Freedom

### Ethan Longhenry

> Blessed be the God and Father of our Lord Jesus Christ, who hath blessed us with every spiritual blessing in the heavenly places in Christ: even as he chose us in him before the foundation of the world, that we should be holy and without blemish before him in love: having foreordained us unto adoption as sons through Jesus Christ unto himself, according to the good pleasure of his will, to the praise of the glory of his grace, which he freely bestowed on us in the Beloved (Eph. 1:3-6).

> This is good and acceptable in the sight of God our Saviour; who would have all men to be saved, and come to the knowledge of the truth (1 Tim. 2:3-4).

One of the most contentious and long-lived disputations in the history of "Christendom," particularly in the West, involves the tension between divine grace and human freedom. The Scriptures speak both of a sovereign God who is able to accomplish His will and human beings who are called upon to serve and obey Him. The disputations involve how these two realities relate.

---

**Ethan R. Longhenry** was born on May 30, 1981, in Rockford, Illinois. In 1999 he was led to Christ by his now wife, Sarah (Sutherland) Longhenry. Ethan has preached part time for churches in Illinois, Indiana, and Texas, and has served as the full-time evangelist for the church of Christ in Norwalk, Ohio, since 2006. Ethan has a bachelor's degree in Hebrew & Semitic Studies and Classics from the University of Wisconsin-Madison. Ethan and Sarah have three children: Julianna (6), Maia (4), and Nathaniel (1). Ethan is the author of *Churches of the New Testament*, the editor of *Renewed in Spirit*, a frequent contributor in many publications, and the author of the online devotional *Spiritual Manna*. He can be reached at deusvitae@hotmail.com.

Everyone in all the disputations has affirmed that God is sovereign and has provided grace to mankind, and that mankind has some type of free will. But can man's free will invalidate or alter God's will? If God is sovereign, does that mean that His will is absolute? If God's sovereign will is absolute, is it necessary for God to have predetermined who would be saved and who would be condemned? How far does God's grace extend? Can man really come to God in the first place, or is God entirely responsible for man's regeneration? What is the relationship between God's will and God's foreknowledge? Can God predestine the elect to salvation without predestinating the rest to condemnation? How can God desire all men to be saved and yet have some be condemned?

Western "Christendom" has been disputing the answers to these questions for over 1,500 years. The discussions have been complicated immensely by the perspectives and presuppositions of those who have participated in them; any attempt to come to an understanding of these disputes must also take into account the philosophical presuppositions of their participants along with their perspectives of those who came before them. Many times the arguments have more to do with the worldviews of the disputant and his traditional loyalties than they do with what the Scriptures have revealed on the subject.

Let us attempt, as best as we are able, to navigate through the dispute as it transpired over a 1,500 year period. In so doing we will confront oversized personalities in "Christian" theological history and the doctrinal consequences of misplaced confidence in shaky theological premises. The story of the dispute involving divine grace and human freedom always has as much to do with the theological climate of the day as it does with the message of the Scriptures. The dispute has value in expressing not just what is right and true about how the Scriptures present divine grace and human freedom, but also in avoiding excesses and imbalances that come about from overemphasizing one attribute to the detriment of the other.

## Fatalism, Responsibility, and Foundations: 100-400

Significant disputations about the relationship between divine grace and free will are not recorded until the disputes of Augustine with Pelagius in the early fifth century. Other, more pressing issues consumed the energies of "Christendom" in the first three centuries after the Apostles.

One of the most significant and most pressing needs in those first three centuries involved a strong defense of the claims of Christianity against the paganism of the Roman Empire. Greeks and Romans of the day had lost much of their confidence in their gods, and were more resigned to fate. In Greek and Roman mythology, the only all-powerful forces were the three Fates: even Zeus and the other gods were subject to them. Human responsibility and freedom were entirely undercut by these impersonal forces of fate and fortune in popular thinking. This not only deeply influenced the paganism of the day but even the heretical opponents of Christianity; many Gnostic groups held strong beliefs regarding original sin and man's subjection to destiny. In the pagan worldview man was not responsible for his fate—it had already been decreed, and he was merely acting out the role assigned for him.

Since most of their pagan neighbors maintained a very fatalistic worldview, the first Christian apologists strongly emphasized man's responsibility and free will. Many worked diligently to show that even though God had foretold the life, death, and resurrection of Jesus, His accomplishments were not based on fate. Judgment was the fate that awaited all mankind, and judgment was based on the decisions that men and women made. While God certainly foreknew what would take place, such did not cause men to act as they did. These were the positions of Justin Martyr, Irenaeus, Clement of Alexandria, Tertullian, and Origen in the second and third centuries. Even Augustine, who in general strongly overemphasized God's sovereign will and divine grace to the detriment of man's free will, established against the pagans that man did have free will, even if, in his mind, it was subject to God's grace. Fatalism, therefore, was universally denounced, and in the early centuries, man's free will and responsibility were emphasized in order to oppose it.

Another significant disputation that began at this time involved the nature of Jesus as the Christ. In the disputes regarding the nature of humanity, the very nature of humanity and sin were brought into question. The fact that God the Son, the *Logos*, took on flesh, indicated that flesh could not be intrinsically evil, according to Athanasius and others. The universality of death on account of Adam's fall was fundamental, not the idea that sin was inevitable. While most would resolve the contradiction between original sin and Jesus' incarnation with the idea of the immaculate conception, focusing on the Son taking on flesh indicated that "original sin" involved the inheritance of a nature, not actual sin. Since the *Logos* took on flesh and "progressed" or "developed" in obedience, man also could progress and develop godlike attributes, and thus was not intrinsically evil. These emphases led eastern "Christendom" to come to vastly different conclusions about grace and freedom than the West.

Meanwhile, other doctrinal developments were being established that would have significant bearing on future discussions of grace and freedom. Beginning in the middle to late second century, some of the churches began baptizing infants. Not long after, it gained notice from Tertullian: he considered it an unnecessary novelty. Infant baptism was never well-grounded in the Scriptures, but beginning with Origen in the middle of the third century, it was considered to be an "apostolic" practice. He attempted to base the practice on John 3:5 and the necessity of baptism in order to enter the Kingdom, even though he could find no justification for saying that infants had sinned.

Tertullian, who considered infant baptism an unnecessary novelty, nevertheless laid the groundwork for the other doctrinal development of the day: the concept of original sin. Tertullian spoke regarding the condemnation of man that followed from partaking of the fruit of the tree in Genesis 3. He considered Adam as the "pioneer of sin" (*Exhortation to Chastity* 2.5). Since he saw no value in infant baptism, it is hard to say that Tertullian truly believed in what would be called "original sin."

The groundwork, however, had been laid: Tertullian spoke of the condemnation that came about because of Adam, yet found no value in infant baptism; Origen believed infant baptism to be an apostolic practice, but could not justify it in terms of atonement from sin. Cyprian, a few decades later, began the synthesis by arguing that infant baptism ought not be delayed since "being born physically according to Adam, he has contracted the contagion of the ancient death by his first birth" (*Letter* 64.5).

Ambrose of Milan, Augustine's mentor, added another piece in the middle of the fourth century. Based upon the developing idea of original sin, and David's expression of iniquity from birth in Psalm 51:5, Ambrose provided a different perspective on the virgin birth of Jesus. Jesus' sinlessness was based, at least in part, on His birth from a virgin: He did not contract original sin since He was not conceived in the normal way. Thus the doctrine of the immaculate conception was born in order to justify Jesus' sinlessness in the face of the promotion of the doctrine of original sin that justified the practice of infant baptism. These three beliefs—infant baptism, original sin, and the immaculate conception—would strongly influence Augustine's view of man and therefore his perspective on the matter of grace and freedom.

### Augustine and Pelagius (400-430)

The dispute over grace and freedom *per se* was invented in the conflict between Augustine and Pelagius in the early fifth century. The rest of the history of the dispute flows from this original conflict.

For better or for worse, Augustine of Hippo is the most influential person in "Western Christendom" outside of the Bible. His intelligence and literary output were rarely matched; from his death until now he has been venerated by many denominations. Augustine's writings defined the discussion of grace and freedom in the West until 1600, and have significant bearing on the discussion even until this day. Calvinism and its TULIP acrostic simply represent a sixteenth century resurgence of Augustinian doctrines.

His positions were highly influenced by his path and his worldview. His mother was a believer, but he did not initially accept Christianity. In his younger days he was a Manichee; later, through the influence of his mother and Ambrose of Milan, he converted to Christianity. For a long time he accepted the tenets of Neoplatonism, the popular modified version of Platonism developed in the third century A.D., as his philosophical bridge from Manichaeism to Christianity.

Before we can understand Augustine's view on grace and freedom, we must understand the two streams of thought that converged to create it: Augustine's view of man and Augustine's view of God.

Augustine's view of man derives from his conclusions based upon the virgin birth and original sin. As established above, Ambrose his mentor established the concept of the immaculate conception from the virgin birth. It was a short step for Augustine to come forth with the inverse of Ambrose's claim: if Jesus was born without the taint of original sin by the virgin birth, mankind in general is subject to original sin on account of the means of their procreation. In Augustine's synthesis, all of mankind inherited sin from Adam through being born of the sexual union, and thus started off condemned unless saved through God's election and infant baptism. From his Manichee and Neoplatonic background, he believed that the source of evil was the absence of good, and the absence of good comes from human sin, which was passed down to each person through Adam.

Since humanity is sinful and condemned from the beginning, according to Augustine, man is incapable of coming to God. The doctrine of total depravity, therefore, derives from Augustine's justification of infant baptism by the doctrine of original sin and the immaculate conception.

Augustine's view of God derives from his singular emphasis on God's sovereignty. God is omnipotent, and therefore His will must be done. God is not under compulsion to do anything; therefore, anything He does represents a gift—or grace— to those upon whom He bestows it. The creation is an act of grace. The atonement is an act of grace. Everything that God provides is grace.

In Augustine's view, therefore, God's omnipotence and sovereignty mean that His will must be executed, and therefore reality exists by His will. There can be nothing that He did not will; Augustine never let go of the Neoplatonist belief that God is the absolute cause of everything.

When Augustine's view of man and his view of God meet, the result is the Augustinian view of divine sovereignty and grace: total depravity, unconditional election, limited atonement, irresistible grace, and perseverance of the saints, even if Augustine did not describe them in as many words. God is completely sovereign and, therefore, what He wills must take place. The Bible describes that man has sinned and fallen short of God's glory; God must have willed it. The Bible indicates that some will be saved and others will be condemned; God must have willed it. Thus we have not just the doctrine of "predestination," but in fact "double predestination": if God is sovereign and His grace is sovereign, according to the Augustinian synthesis, then God has already willed who will be saved and who will be condemned. It was considered anathema to believe that Christ's sacrifice could be in vain for anyone; therefore, Jesus' blood was shed only for those whom God predestined as the elect. God would draw the elect to Him in His church, and by His sovereign power they were definitively saved.

These views were all conditioned by Augustine's belief in God's unchangeability and impassibility, and were extreme, to say the least. Augustine would not entirely deny that man had free will, considering it part of the "order of causes" in divine prescience: man may freely choose to make the decisions he does, but God knew of them in advance and, in effect, willed them also. To Augustine, it was impossible for man to alter or change God's will, and it was contrary to God's omnipotence for Him to in any way adapt His will on account of the decisions of man. After all, in that situation, God is bending to man, which simply could not be.

Augustine's logic is stark and consistent. Augustine established that God predestined some to condemnation to manifest His wrath and to demonstrate His power (*Exposition of Genesis According to the Letter* 11.8). Infants who were not baptized were consigned to hell. When pressed on the matter on a theological basis, he demurred, saying that it was a great mystery why God would redeem some and consign others to condemnation. In all things, divine grace was the basis, not human merit or action.

Augustine's views were troubling to many, and one of the first to take exception was Pelagius. Not much is known about Pelagius: he and the doctrines that would later be considered under his name were often abused and maligned in later literature, and it is difficult to ascertain exactly what he believed.

Pelagius was a British monk who was universally respected for his piety. He traveled to Rome and even met with Augustine once in Africa and seems to end up in the east by the end of his life. Pelagius was concerned that Augustine's emphasis on divine grace weakened Christian obedience and relegated man to being a puppet in the divine play.

Pelagius perhaps, but certainly Pelagianism, taught that man needed to become perfect. Jesus made the command in Matthew 5:48, and it was believed that, if God made the command, He expected His followers to be able to carry it out. Sin was a personal issue: each man would be responsible for his own sins. Man was not only able but expected to respond to God's commandments and to follow them. Pelagians would not deny election, but believed that it was based upon God's foreknowledge of those who would believe.

The flash point of the controversy involved the difference in the definition of grace between Pelagius and Augustine. To Pelagius, it would seem that grace involved God's gifts through nature and, therefore, man's ability to turn to God had been granted to him by God as part of his intrinsic nature. To Pelagius, a disparagement of nature was a disparagement of grace, and Augustine's view of the corrupted nature of humanity and creation certainly represented a disparagement of nature. Augustine understood grace as the knowledge of, joy in, and capacity to will that which is good; to Pelagius, grace involved the ability God gave man to will and to act, but to will and to act involved man's will alone.

Thus, to Pelagius, Augustine's view of original sin might as well have been a restatement of pagan fatalism. If man was not free to decide, then he bore no responsibility. In the Pelagian perspective, original sin did not mean the actual transfer of sinfulness, for sin required a decision to do the evil.

As Augustine overemphasized divine grace, so Pelagius' followers, at least, overemphasized man's freedom. According to Celestius, a disciple of Pelagius, Adam would have died had he sinned or not, and mankind was not at all tarnished by Adam's sin. Not all of mankind dies on account of Adam's transgression. Furthermore, the law and the Gospel both lead to the Kingdom, and there were persons without sin before Christ.

Eastern Christendom did not really understand what all the fuss was about. Much of what Pelagius and the Pelagians taught could be reconciled with eastern church fathers. Furthermore, since Pelagius *et al* maintained Trinitarian orthodoxy, those in the East had little difficulty with them: in the Synod of Lydda-Disopolis in 415, Pelagius was officially considered orthodox in his beliefs.

The West was not exactly prepared for the disputation that was taking place. Orthodoxy versus heresy had previously involved questions of Christology, the nature of the Godhead, or the nature of the church; the dispute between Augustine and Pelagius involved none of these. In the end, however, Pelagius' and the Pelagians' opposition to the concept of original sin ended up being their undoing. Infant baptism had become entirely enmeshed in "catholic" orthodoxy. Even though Pelagius affirmed the validity of infant baptism, testifying with Origen that it allowed infants to enter the Kingdom, the authorities of the day agreed with Augustine that original sin was the only sufficient justification for the practice of infant baptism. The Synod of Carthage of 418 condemned Pelagianism, and one of its canons involved the need to confess original sin as the reason for infant baptism. Celestius was condemned as a heretic by the Council of Ephesus in 431, and thus Pelagianism, as a whole, was condemned. Augustine seemed vindicated.

## Initial Reaction to Augustine (420-530)

The condemnation of Pelagianism did not mean a wholesale acceptance of Augustinianism. Augustine had gone well beyond the contours of Christian tradition, not only eastern but also western, in his views on predestination and the irresistibility of grace. Opposition to Augustine's views came not just from the Pelagians but also from fellow "Christians" who shared many of Augustine's views on grace. This opposition would later be called "Semi-Pelagian," but such labels are not very helpful, since they do not accurately represent the beliefs of the critics.

Augustine accepted that there were many "brethren" who disagreed with him yet were not themselves Pelagians. They agreed with him on almost everything but his view on predestination. They would not deny that man had fallen in Adam's sin and required God's grace to be redeemed.

The most prominent of these critics were John Cassian, Vincent of Lérins, and Faustus of Riez. Augustine found proponents in Prosper of Aquitaine, Caesarius of Arles, and later in "Pope" Gregory the Great. While his proponents could not understand how his critics could not accept the necessary conclusions of God's sovereignty and grace, his critics returned to the Scriptures to point out problems in Augustine's positions.

Augustine's critics clearly perceived how Augustine overemphasized divine sovereignty and grace to the detriment of human will and responsibility. As Faustus said, "through the pages of the Scriptures sometimes it is the power of grace and at other times it is the assent of the human will that is asserted" (*On Grace* 1.13). The critics perceived the tension in the Scriptures between divine grace and human freedom, yet did not believe that this tension should be resolved in the favor of either over the other.

Augustine's doctrines seemed just as fatalistic to his "orthodox" critics as it did to Pelagius. In Augustine's view of divine sovereignty, God wills evil and God wills sin. Yet, above all, Augustine's concept of "double predestination" could not be immediately reconciled with Paul's statement to Timothy that God willed for all men to be saved (1 Tim. 2:4). Augustine's doctrines meant that God did not really will for "all men" to be saved, merely "all the elect." In time, proponents of Augustine would argue just that: when Paul speaks of "all men," they would say, "he really means 'all the elect,' since the elect involves persons from every gender, nation, and class."

Augustine's doctrines also questioned the value of preaching. Augustine did teach that God predestined Judas for condemnation while predestinating the rest of the Apostles for the Kingdom. If all of this happens according to God's will alone, why bother preaching to anyone? God will save or condemn them regardless. Why, in fact, should anyone pray, anyway? God's will is going to be accomplished regardless of your prayer, and in Augustine's view, there is no reason to believe that God would change His will, either before or presently, because of your petition.

In short, Augustine's critics clearly perceived a fundamental flaw in Augustine's reasoning: he was so carried away by the "logical consequences" of his view that he departed from God's actual revealed will. Augustine's presuppositions about the way God "must be" did not square with how God actually revealed Himself to be according to the Scriptures.

Augustine's extremely dim view of humanity was also criticized. Paul indicated that some Gentiles, by nature, did what God required (Rom. 2:14); this required man to have some ability to come to God's truth.

According to John Cassian and others, the Bible provided plenty of examples of people who, by their own will, turned to God, including Zacchaeus and the thief on the cross. Yes, the Bible also described accounts of God calling persons, like Matthew and Saul/Paul. One could not so easily confine the working of God to a specific system like Pelagianism or Augustinianism.

Augustine's proponents would point to God's secret counsel to support their positions, but did not really find good arguments to combat the critics of their teacher. They could not be tied to the Pelagians. On account of this, many of the early Augustinians felt compelled to moderate some of their teacher's more extreme views, and bring Augustinianism back into the fold of "catholic orthodoxy."

To do so, Augustinians affirmed the universal will of God for salvation by positing that every soul does hear the Gospel in some form and those who will be condemned, in some way or another, refuse it. Their refusal would free God from having decreed their condemnation arbitrarily. While Augustine would disallow God's prescient will from being bent by His foreknowledge of man's actions, Prosper of Aquitaine would say that predestination to condemnation was based in God's foreknowledge of their impenitence. The "essential rule of faith" would not be God's eternal predestinating will, but God's universal will for man's salvation. Predestination was relegated to a "more profound and more difficult point" of theology that was not necessary to describe God's grace (Prosper of Aquitaine, *Call of All Nations*, 1.25).

The end of the first round of disputes on the tension of grace and freedom came with the Synod of Orange in 529, whose decrees relied heavily on Prosper's *Book of Sentences from the Works of St. Augustine* and Caesarius of Arles' *On Grace*. In this synod, essential Augustinianism was vindicated, but not every tenet that Augustine taught. There was a lack of clarity on the relation between predestination and the universal saving will of God, and while Caesarius' writings would lead to the conclusion of double predestination, he did not do so in establishing doctrine for the church; instead, the Synod anathematized anyone who would teach predestination to condemnation. The Synod also affirmed that baptized believers can be obedient to salvation. Nevertheless, in all instances, God's grace was affirmed over human will: no one comes to God by his own will, but all come by gifts of divine grace.

The Synod of Orange did not fully justify Augustine, but it certainly did not affirm his opponents, either. Augustinianism, by in large, became official Catholic teaching. His specter would always loom over the discussion to follow. For the next millennium in "Western Christendom," all disputants speaking on grace and freedom would invoke Augustine. Both sides in every dispute would claim Augustine. Augustinianism became the framework for the entire discussion. When everyone seeks to be more like Augustine than his opponent, the outcome is really without doubt.

**From the Synod of Orange to the Reformation (530-1500)**

While Augustinianism, by in large, ended up representing the doctrines of "Western" Christendom, it would not be so in the east. By the time of Augustine it was evident that Christianity was dividing into two spheres: the "western" sphere, which looked preeminently to Rome and involved the Latin-dominated lands of Britain, France, Spain, Italy, and North Africa, and the "eastern" sphere, which still looked to historic patriarchates and involved the Greek-dominated lands of Greece, Asia Minor, the Levant, and Egypt.

Much of Augustine's works were not translated into Greek until much later. Furthermore, there were strong tendencies in eastern patristic authors toward "Pelagian" or "Semi-Pelagian" views, strongly affirming man's free will. Since there is no Augustine-like figure in eastern "Christendom" that strongly asserted God's sovereignty and divine grace, there was no real dispute in the east like there was in the west. Yes, Pelagianism was officially condemned at the Council of Ephesus in 431, but such was probably more of an accommodation to Rome and the West; Photius preserved the meeting articles of the Synod of Lydda-Diospolis of 415, justifying Pelagius, and these enjoyed more popularity in later days in the east. Furthermore, disputations on the question tended more toward the opposite end of the spectrum, with John of Damascus opposing the dualistic theology of the Bogomils and Manichees.

Therefore, there was no difficulty for Maximus the Confessor in the seventh century to affirm that "the Spirit does not generate a will that is not willing," but "a will that has the desire" (*Questions to Thalassius on the Scripture*, 6). Photius, two centuries later, could say that "God never does violence to the power of free will" (*Amphilochia*, 1.24). Salvation depended on man's own will. Yet this was not sheer Pelagianism; Photius established that salvation presupposed union and collaboration between grace and freedom. This is made evident in the confession of Jesus having two wills, the human and the divine: if the human will did not align with the divine will, Jesus would not have been the willing sacrifice required by Isaiah 53. In the east, Christians freely held to both divine grace and human freedom, did not see a contradiction between the two, and refused to emphasize one over the other.

They were able to do this despite believing in infant baptism and original sin. The reason for this—one which would be tested by interactions later with Reformation churches—was the belief that original sin was really "ancestral sin," sin that needed atonement but which did not hinder free will or God's inherent goodness. While it would seem discordant to hold to both original sin and free will, the Eastern Orthodox continued to maintain both beliefs. Free will was too necessary and profound, and the idea that a good God could be responsible for an evil nature was anathema.

The dispute regarding divine grace and human freedom, therefore, would be a heritage of "Western Christendom" only. And forces were at work in the early medieval period that would set the tone for the discussion for many years.

The decision of the Synod of Orange vindicated most of Augustine's doctrines regarding divine grace and human freedom, and while it anathematized the idea of "double predestination," it never went so far as condemning or censuring Augustine himself for holding the position. This lack of condemnation would have serious implications for the future.

Augustine's reputation as perhaps the greatest theologian since biblical times was solidified by the writings of Prosper of Aquitaine, Caesarius of Arles, and "Pope" Gregory the Great, who, as with the Synod of Orange, confirmed what they approved of Augustine's teachings and mollified or minimized his more difficult teachings.

The two hundred years from the death of Gregory until the Carolingian Renaissance (roughly 600-800) were extremely difficult times in the Western world. Hordes of invaders came through, little hope of political unity existed, and people were simply trying to survive. During this period, the writings of Augustine himself were not as well known as were the *Sentences* of Prosper and the discussions of Augustine's ideas in Gregory's works and others. During this period, Augustine's greatness was being exalted without any consideration of the difficulties of some of his doctrines.

On account of this, when theologians returned again to Augustine's actual writings during the Carolingian Renaissance in the ninth century, they happened upon his view of "double predestination," yet without having much indication that Augustine had gone beyond orthodoxy in presenting the doctrine. Therefore, in the bitter disputes between Hincmar of Rheims and Gottschalk of Orbais, the issue involved what Augustine "really taught."

Gottschalk, along with his supporters, Ratramnus, Servatus Lupus, and Florus of Lyons, affirmed, on the whole, Augustine's view of divine grace and human freedom. Gottschalk went so far as to deny mankind the ability to do anything good beyond God's grace, a position his supporters even did not defend. People must have some type of free will so that they are without excuse.

Gottschalk accepted Augustine's view of God entirely: God is the ultimate cause, God is impassible, and God does not change. God's will could not be altered in any way; therefore, all which took place was already determined by God.

Hincmar, Rabanus Maurus, and others attempted to make room for free will and to condemn the concept of double predestination. In their view, God's predestination did not compel anyone. Free will was sluggish, but it still existed. Hincmar accepted the same definition of God and predestination as Gottschalk, yet defined predestination as distinct from God's foreknowledge. Hincmar followed Prosper of Aquitaine, asserting that God's predestination was based in His foreknowledge of who would believe and who would not believe, and therefore Hincmar attempts to extricate Augustine from the negative implications of double predestination: punishment of sin is predestined, not the sinner. Gottschalk and others denied this, because if God's decision were on human merit, it could not be by grace. Gottschalk also argued that since God is timeless, to speak of *fore*knowledge would be inaccurate: there would be no interval between God knowing and God deciding. Hincmar's attempt to extricate Augustine was also seen as just an evasion: predestination "of" punishment was not to be distinguished from predestination "to" punishment.

The entire discussion was hindered with texts being cited that were really pseudepigraphic; the views of Augustine and others was that much more difficult to ascertain in the midst of competing documents teaching different things.

During the discussion, Florus of Lyons set down "seven rules of faith," that God's foreknowledge and predestination is eternal and unchangeable, no act of God was not foreknown and foreordained, God did not foreknow some but foreordain others, good works belong to the creature in a way that are altogether the works of the Creator while evil works are foreknown but not predestined, and "God did not impose necessity on anyone by His foreknowledge and predestination" (*On Three Epistles* 1-3). Such "laws" were designed to maintain Augustine's views of divine grace while attempting to free God from being responsible for evil deeds and imposing on free will.

Another participant in the discussion, aligned with Hincmar, was John Scotus Erigena, who argued against double predestination as being against reason as it was against Scripture and tradition. His approach was quite philosophical for the time. He was willing to compare various authorities with each other, including Augustine in that mix, and was quite taken with the eastern fathers. He would be condemned for his philosophical leanings, willingness to question certain authorities, and his Greek-leaning views, especially on the possibility of universal salvation. Nevertheless, he demonstrates that when and if one could get beyond Augustine and consider other sources, one would recognize the great difficulties that Augustine's doctrines created.

It is not surprising that Gottschalk and his supporters would, on the whole, fare better than Hincmar, considering that no one was willing to question whether Augustine truly spoke for "the faith" with his doctrine of double predestination. But the one matter of difficulty for Gottschalk and his supporters involved "limited atonement." The Bible made very clear statements about Christ's blood being able to atone for all sin, and while it was generally displeasing to believe that Christ's blood would be "wasted" on anyone, it was hard to square the idea that Christ's blood was shed only for a few with the Bible. Nevertheless, Gottschalk and Florus devised different sets of categories of "redemption," and in so doing attempted to demonstrate that all New Testament passages could be understood as saying that Christ's blood was shed only for the elect. The real problem was the value of sacraments: Augustine himself championed the efficacy of sacraments, and to believe that baptism, the Lord's Supper, and the other "sacraments" developed by Roman Catholicism were useless for those who were really unregenerate would undermine the authority of the Church. Gottschalk conceded that the grace of baptism would forgive anyone's past sins, but since it does not redeem from future sins, the judgment of the condemned would not change.

Hincmar convened a synod of his supporters at Quiercy in 853, codifying his understanding of divine grace and human freedom. In 855, a synod at Valence condemned Quiercy and affirmed double predestination instead, and this was confirmed in 859 at a synod in Langres. It was alleged that the pope, Nicholas, affirmed the synod at Langres and the belief in double predestination and limited atonement, but this has never been able to be confirmed.

The dispute of the ninth century was the first of many flashpoints over the doctrine of divine grace and human freedom that focused more on what Augustine taught than what the Bible really said. It is not surprising that when the issue became focused more on Augustine, the pendulum swung more toward Augustine's perspective, and it would stay there for the next 800 years. Had the Synod of Orange or Gregory or some other respected individual censured Augustine for his "double predestination" as, say, Origen was condemned for his belief in eventual universal salvation at the second Council of Constantinople, the dispute might have turned out quite differently.

Nevertheless, the disputes of Hincmar and Gottschalk opened up the issues of the nature of Christ's atonement and the nature of the authority of the fathers. The former issue would be taken up with Anselm and others in the eleventh century, and it is beyond the purview of our discussion to consider it in detail; the latter would be better analyzed and systemized by the Scholastics of the thirteenth century, who would set forth the neo-Augustinian doctrines that Luther and Calvin would pick up.

The period between the ninth century and the thirteenth century did not see much in the way of disputations on divine grace and human freedom, but there were many who continued to try to "work out" some of the issues. Some in the eleventh century found no room for human will in man's salvation. Anselm of Canterbury, on the other hand, saw grace working alone on behalf of infants, but saw "natural free will" assisting with those who were more "mature." Anselm also facilitated a type of reconciliation of predestination with God not being the author of evil by asserting that God caused deeds but not the evil in them. Predestination was not incompatible with freedom, because God can foreknow sin without forcing man to sin, and God is timeless anyway. Nevertheless, the eleventh century's focus was more on the free gift of atonement in Christ than on the particular question of the relationship between that grace and human freedom.

The thirteenth century was the great age of the Scholastics, men who worked diligently to systematize religious matters. Thomas Aquinas, Bonaventure, and others took the fruit of Augustine, Anselm, and others, and presented the first coherent form of systematic medieval theology. Part of their task involved systemizing the various presentations of the discussion of divine grace and human freedom.

The Scholastics, following Hincmar, understood predestination in terms of foreknowledge: God did not predestine people to sin, but foreknew that they would reject His grace. Nevertheless, these same Scholastics went along with Augustine's more "mature" judgment that God's predestination did not have its determination in human merit, despite the tension between these two views. Divine predestination was not seen as placing constraints on free will. God did not harden people's hearts. Being unchangeable, God has already determined who will be the elect. Thomas Aquinas attributed predestination to the divine intellect; Bonaventure attributed it to the divine will.

The Scholastics also had to wrestle with Augustine's "double predestination" viewpoint. Pseudepigraphic works of Augustine were brought into the discussion as in previous disputes. God's predestining persons to condemnation was not seen as a positive act of election as much as a negative act permitting condemnation. The Scholastics followed after Hincmar, asserting that the punishment for sin was predestined, not men for that punishment.

Why God chose some men for redemption and let others be condemned was one of the mysteries that men would not be able to understand, but it was nevertheless accepted as true. Even though God loved all men and wished all some good, He did not wish the same good to all men, and the decision was of "His own accord" (Thomas Aquinas, *Summa Theologica* 1.23.3).

Another innovation of the Scholastics involved answering the challenge of 1 Timothy 2:4 and God's desire for "all men" to come to the truth. While using the same answers as before, the Scholastics also appealed to different forms of God's will: it was God's "antecedent" will for all men to be saved, which is relative to man's decisions, and not his "consequent," or fixed and absolute, will.

The Scholastics, in attempting to systematize the faith, found recourse to the same types of arguments that Hincmar put forward four hundred years earlier. No one sought to deny the mantle of Augustine, but it was clear that his doctrine of double predestination did not sit well with most theologians.

The discussions did not end with the Scholastics. The period leading up to the Reformation (1300-1500) involved another phase in the discussion, this time swinging back more toward Augustine's original intentions. While Thomas Aquinas and others were more amenable to Hincmar's attempts to reconcile Augustinianism with "Catholic orthodoxy," later theologians felt more compelled, for various reasons, to more strongly emphasize Augustine's perspectives.

Other issues were clarified. Duns Scotus focused on the concern that predestination in some way confined God's freedom. To do so, he argued that, being the first cause, God caused things to take place by contingency, not by necessity, since God always had the freedom to not predestine anything. Mankind is confused about God's freedom because we do not understand how God is timeless: strictly, no divine act is in the "past," and God can freely will as He desires now as if He never had predestined anything.

Yet what of divine foreknowledge of future contingents? Both divine knowledge and future contingents stood without abolishing the other, as Giles of Rome attempted to explain, *contra* the Scholastics, who felt that contingency and necessity only involved "lower" and not "higher" causes.

Scotus, by placing divine will as the centerpiece of his definition of predestination, could establish God's foreknowledge as immutably necessary without being deterministic. The foreknowledge of God's intellect did not compel God's will to be determined; therefore, Scotus would deny that God predestines election or condemnation based on foreknowledge of man's actions.

It should be noted that throughout this discussion we have focused on the dispute as it was carried on in the writings of various monks, scholars, and theologians of the day. We have less information about what the "common believer" thought about divine grace and human freedom. Nevertheless, based upon the information in the writings of many theologians in the fourteenth and fifteenth century, it is apparent that many believed and/or were teaching views that were considered "neo-Pelagian." The exact contours of this "neo-Pelagianism" are not known, but it meant that there were many who were willing to emphasize human freedom—or, at the least, were not willing to relegate it to obscurity.

Thomas Bradwardine and Gregory of Rimini represent those who returned to strict Augustinianism, advocating double predestination, and with Scotus, that predestination was entirely by divine will without consideration of human merit. The "absolute sovereignty of God" was again being emphasized.

Even the forerunners of the Reformation, John Wycliffe and Jan Hus, thought highly of Augustine. Wycliffe added a new dimension to the discussion, one that would feature prominently in the Reformation: the concept of the church as the congregation of the predestined, *contra* the definition of the church as the institution governed by the pope that the Roman Catholic church promoted. Wycliffe promoted Augustinian double predestination to the point of fatalism, going so far as to say that Adam's sin was "necessary" because it led to the exaltation of man in Christ. He did believe, however, that one could only be part of the church if he or she did so by his own free will. Wycliffe also emphasized that even though no one could really know if he were elect or reprobate, each believer had the obligation to hope that he was part of the elect, even if he were, in truth, deceived. The reprobate would be condemned regardless of whatever "virtue" they had; the elect would be saved regardless of their sinfulness. These emphases would return in the Reformation.

As in discussions past, the nature of man's free will vexed theologians in the fourteenth and fifteenth century. They used the Scholastic delineations of "wills" to address 1 Timothy 2:4. Bradwardine went so far as to say that God commanded intercession for all men because of all the "simple people" who believed that God's will could be changed by their prayers and that they would be forgiven of their ignorance and their good intentions. After all, as Augustine had said, the church prays for all men but God only hears them for the elect.

Yet perhaps the oddest development in the discussion during these times was put forward by William of Ockham, who combined free will and determinism into what could be considered "deterministic semi-pelagianism." In this synthesis, the main problem of divine grace and free will—that man could somehow negate God's will—was resolved by saying that while God did predestine all things by His will, He did so in a way that did not negate human freedom. "Predestination" and "reprobation" were not realities unto themselves, but to God, who "caused" each person's ultimate destiny.

The dispute involving divine grace and free will, while seeing developments in definition and argument, was in not much different of a state at the time of Gregory's death as it was when Luther nailed his theses to the church door in Wittenberg. Augustine's doctrines were ascendant, even if there was widespread discomfort with double predestination. Ideas of theologians and the faith of the "common man" may have been quite different. Yet the direction of the dispute was changing, as Wycliffe and Hus made evident. This change would be made quite evident in the Reformation.

### The Reformation and Its Consequences (1500-1715)

Momentous changes came upon western "Christendom" in the sixteenth century, yet the reasons for these changes have been reinterpreted as time has gone on. It has become popular to venerate Luther and Calvin and others for standing up against the Roman Catholic church, and many wonder why it is that Luther and Calvin did not go "further" in their changes.

Yet, at the time, there was no desire to be novel or innovative. Luther especially had no intentions of establishing his own church, but sought to call the Roman Catholic church back to doctrines and beliefs for which it once stood, at least in his opinion. The Reformation was not designed to be a departure from "catholic orthodoxy"; instead, it was designed to be an affirmation of it. Therefore, far from disputing the validity of Augustinian theology, both Luther and Calvin wholeheartedly embraced it. As with before: when the intention is to vindicate traditions and beliefs, it is not surprising to see those traditions and beliefs strongly promoted by its adherents.

While John Calvin and his doctrines are truly representative of Augustine's views on divine grace and human freedom, Martin Luther was just as strongly influenced by Augustine. He perceived Pelagianism as the perennial heresy among Christians and spoke despairingly of his "Pelagian" theological instructors.

Luther's disputes with Desiderius Erasmus focused heavily on the question of man's freedom. Erasmus, by asserting that man has free will, appealed to the authority of tradition; to Luther, he was no better than a Pelagian. Erasmus attempted to frame his view of free will in Augustinian terms, and considered Luther's doctrinal heritage to be the Manichees and Wycliffe.

While the medieval theologians were uncomfortable with Augustine's perspective on human freedom, Luther sought to swing the pendulum fully toward it. Human will, while not evil by nature, was "innately and inevitably evil and corrupt," and not able to "strive to whatever is declared good"

(Luther, *Disputation against Scholastic Theology*, 8-11). While Augustine, when pressed, would concede to the idea that the sinner commits sin by his own free will, Luther would not concede as much to Erasmus: humans act almost entirely by necessity, since free will was "nothing," not able to accomplish anything good, and was confined to "natural matters" like eating and drinking. He would later feel compelled to moderate himself, sensing the legitimacy in the claim that he was reviving Manichaeanism in order to condemn Pelagianism.

Luther remained wedded to original sin and total depravity even after moderating his views. Adam's sin had so corrupted the divine image in man that it was almost entirely lost—Luther's introduction of the idea of man in the "image of the devil" led later Lutherans to posit that original sin involved the loss of the image of God for the image of the devil! Adam's sin now was no longer just the loss of righteousness but was, in fact, the acquisition of evil! Against the charge of Manicheanism, they claimed that the difference was that they posited this depravity after the fall, not in the creation.

Luther's views were extreme because he was arguing against the perceived Pelagianism in others; Philip Melanchthon would later feel compelled to mediate between Luther's and Erasmus' views of free will, and to take the edge off Luther's view of the sin of Adam. Debates within Lutheranism regarding these matters would continue, with later Lutherans striving to disengage from either Manichaean or Pelagian extremes.

It would be left to Calvin to put forth strong positions on both divine grace and human freedom, but Luther set the stage by "out-Augustining" Augustine in matters of human freedom. Nevertheless, while Luther's doctrines would inevitably lead to a position of double predestination, he found little value in contemplating the doctrine: God's hidden will should remain hidden. To consider predestination would lead either to despair or presumption.

Where Luther would not go, Calvin would. Through his *Institutes of the Christian Religion*, Calvin set forth the complete Augustinian position in regards to divine grace and human freedom. He affirmed all that Luther taught regarding human freedom, and paired it with confessing Augustine's double predestination theology.

According to Calvin, as with Augustine, God has an eternal will, to which the eternal destiny of all is referred. God as sovereign Lord decides by His will who will be saved and who will be condemned, and does so without consideration of what humans will do. Romans 9 featured heavily in Calvin's theology—Paul strongly affirms God's sovereign will. The life and death of Christ were all by God's will and counsel: the divine will decreed condemnation just as it decreed life. Foreknowledge involved God's omniscience, but predestination was God's eternal decree "by which he has decided within himself what he wills to happen to each individual human being" (*Institutes*, 8).

Yet Calvin was acutely aware of the determinism that could be seen in Augustine's positions, and set to disentangle foreknowledge, providence, and predestination from it. Predestination involved God's ultimate goals; providence included intermediate goals. God has but one will—therefore, God condemns the reprobate as much as He justifies the elect, a feature of Augustinian doctrine not emphasized since Augustine. Why does God do so? As with Augustine, so with Calvin: that is His business, and who are we to question God?

Furthermore, Calvin found any distinction between "divine action" and "divine permission" frivolous. His devotion to the concept of God as sovereign to the point of the cause of everything meant that one could not distinguish what God allowed from what God did, for they were one and the same. Calvin was willing even to attribute God's active predestination to Adam's sin and the consequent need to condemn "so many peoples, together with their infant offspring" (*ibid.*, 3.23.7).

It is in Calvin that Augustine found his most faithful and dominant proponent, and one whose influence was widespread. The Reformed churches directly proceed from him and his teachings in Geneva; John Knox took Calvinism and converted Scotland to Presbyterianism. English Protestants fleeing from Mary Tudor ended up in Reformed lands; when they returned to Britain, they agitated for Calvinist belief systems, wrote the *Westminster Confession*, and were known as Puritans. *The Heidelberg Catechism* and the *Belgic Confession* were Calvinistic documents; the later Synod of Dort would encapsulate Calvin's (and Augustine's) doctrine into the familiar TULIP acrostic: total depravity, unconditional election, limited atonement, irresistible grace, and perseverance of the saints. Reformed churches, Presbyterianism, and the descendants of Puritanism all held to the Calvinistic viewpoint. Calvin guaranteed that the dispute regarding divine grace and free will would continue in Protestantism.

Calvin's exaltation of Augustine's doctrines, however, also led to the first significant questioning of that tradition in a millennium. While the Roman Catholic church never felt compelled to explicitly censure Augustine for his views on double predestination, and many theologians in that tradition taught little differently on the issue from Calvin, the fact that the Protestants had entirely taken the doctrine over led to significant backpedaling from Catholics. When viewed through polemical lenses, double predestination now seemed to most Roman Catholics as fatalism. Calvin would attempt to argue that the necessity of sinning did not come from compulsion from God but from the fault of man's will. Roman Catholics also argued that Calvin's doctrines would lead to moral laxity, since one's salvation was not dependent on what one did; prayer would also be useless since God has fixed everything anyway. Furthermore, a major problem existed within the Calvinist (and Augustinian) system: confidence in salvation. Calvin exhorted people to trust in their election, yet, based on his doctrines, there would be no basis in that trust without having knowledge of God's hidden will. Against Calvin's exhortation for certainty, Roman Catholics asserted the fact that no one can know with complete certainty that he has received God's grace.

The Roman Catholic church felt compelled to attempt to "rescue" Augustine from both Lutherans and Calvinists. They attempted to establish that Augustine was against both Pelagius and the Manichees, and was not so anti-Pelagian as to again fall into Manicheanism, as the Protestants had done. Yes, man's will was impaired by sin, but it still existed. God's grace did not compel or coerce—free consent was necessary for justification. There was no antithesis between grace and free will, or grace and merit, as the Protestants posited. Roman Catholics again returned to the idea that God's predestination does not impose necessity. On the whole, it is quite interesting that the very arguments offered against Augustine by his fifth century critics, later chastised in medieval literature, were now being offered by the Catholics against Calvin and his fellow Protestants.

Yet some of the strongest opposition would develop within the Reformed community itself toward the end of the sixteenth century and in the beginning of the seventeenth. Jacob Arminius, a Reformed theologian, began to doubt some of the legitimacy of the Calvinist synthesis. His beliefs would be put forth in confessional form by adherents after his death in the *Remonstrance* of 1610. To Arminius, human will had to be free, in some real sense, from "fatalistic necessity." Calvinist predestination undercut both God's and man's freedom, and was equated with Stoic fatalism and Manichaeism. Arminius agreed with Calvin that God foreknew future contingents, and

He was also free to do as He willed for His creation. Likewise, God's grace was undeserved and unmerited, but it was not irresistible. If grace were irresistible, God's offer for reward for obedience and punishment for immorality were vanity. Arminius recognized that the distinction between what God willed and what God allowed was essential—God did not will evil, but permitted evil to allow man to be free. Hardened hearts were due to the impenitence of sinners, not divine initiative.

Furthermore, God's counsel should not be understood deterministically, as Calvin did. According to the Remonstrants, Jesus was the Savior of the world, and His death was for all men—a rejection of limited atonement. It was left for Wesleyans, however, to realize the full import of this, that God's will was a universal will of salvation.

Calvinists responded to the Remonstrant attack with the Synod of Dort, attempting to refocus the issue on God's sovereignty, and having all Scripture understood in those terms, especially 1 Timothy 2:4. Christ only reconciled the elect, not the whole world. God's mercy did not infringe on God's justice. The Calvinist mind set could not imagine the divine will ever being frustrated in its designs.

Yet unlike before, opposition to Augustinian Calvinism continued and was sustained. The dispute was no longer Augustine vs. Pelagius; it was now Calvin vs. Arminius, Calvinists against Arminians. John Wesley would be greatly influenced by Arminius, and Methodism represented one of the strongest Arminian churches. The disputation would not be as one-sided as it had been in medieval times.

The seventeenth century involved the same disputations as the sixteenth. Calvinists responded to Roman Catholic and Arminian arguments with the same responses that had been in use for generations.

Yet even within Calvinistic groups solidarity was not to be found. While double predestination was a satisfactory conclusion to many, others felt that predestination did not contain reprobation, and only referred to election to life, since Scripture never speaks of the condemned as "predestined" to that conclusion. To answer this, theologians of the day used the theology of God's decrees as posited by Calvin and concentrated on how God executed His decrees. The Bible, in this view, demonstrates God's execution of decrees, and not the decree as such.

Against Catholic, Arminian, and Lutheran arguments that God's predestination was determined based on His foreknowledge, Reformed theologians attempted to establish that faith was the effect of God's sovereign choice, not its basis or efficient cause, and used Christ Himself as an example.

The relation of the Fall to predestination was also an issue; many were not comfortable with Calvin's assertion that God actively willed mankind to sin. To counter this, some posited that while God is timeless, and His will is eternal and unchangeable, God's decree of election did take into consideration of Adam's sin, since redemption was the response to Adam's transgression.

This period of time also saw developments in covenant theology among Calvinists. Focus on covenant as demonstrating God's predestined choice went back to Calvin. God is faithful at keeping His covenant, redeeming the elect and condemning the reprobate. The covenant of grace leads to the sanctification of the elect. As God chose Israel and not other nations, so now He chooses the elect, and not other persons. Martin Heidegger made "election" and "covenant" synonymous. The *Westminster Confession* made the covenant concept authoritatively binding on Puritan churches. Jonathan Edwards made Calvinism and covenant the basis of his theology, and federal/covenant theology would have great impact on American religious development. Election, therefore, was considered part of ecclesiology as much as soteriology.

The Roman Catholic church was also sorting out its position on the issue. Cornelius Jansen protested the perceived Pelagianism and Semi-Pelagianism in the Roman Catholic church, demonstrating Augustine's doctrines clearly in his posthumously published *Augustinus*. In 1653, Pope Innocent X issued *Cum Occasione*, officially proscribing extreme Augustinianism. Michael Baius came forth with a strongly Augustinian position on divine grace and free will, and set off another round of discussion on the issue. Pope Pius V, in 1657, condemned his propositions. Baius and Jansen were attacking previous works by Louis Molina and others who were trying to promote, at some level, free will. While it may seem that the Roman Catholic church was strongly moving away from extreme Augustinianism, the magisterium still exhorted that no one condemn any other on the basis of the question of divine grace and human freedom.

Yet the problem of the inconsistent traditions on the question caused great difficulty. Previous testimony was garbled: Augustine had his detractors, the Synod of Orange condemned part of Augustine's teachings without condemning Augustine, and both sides of the dispute claimed all these traditions for themselves. The Council of Trent had enshrined Thomas Aquinas' definition of grace, which preserved essential Augustinianism while making room for free will. Nevertheless, the conflict continued: Molina and Suárez against Baius and Jansen, rehashing the same arguments that had gone on since the fifth century. Nevertheless, all of them condemned Calvin for his extremism.

The dispute had gone on long enough. The process that began with *Cum Occasione* continued, and by 1715, the teaching office of the Roman Catholic church was actively speaking against Jansen and his neo-Augustinianism. This opposition led to the creation of a dogmatic sect within the organization: Jansenism had become not just a doctrinal position, but a movement within the Roman Catholic church.

### The Dispute in Europe (1715-Present)

The eighteenth century involved many watershed moments in the history of Europe and of its religion. The philosophical movement known as the Enlightenment reaffirmed man's capacity to reason, and the questions it would raise would define the conflicts within Christianity for the nineteenth century and beyond.

The dispute over divine grace and human freedom, however, continued on as before. Jansenist Catholics and Calvinists shared no love for one another, and yet both held to Augustine's perspective. The dispute was also present within the Church of England: Puritans tended to be more Calvinist, while the rest of the Anglicans tended more toward Arminianism.

The emergence of so many different positions on the matter of divine grace and human freedom led to confusion in terminology. Terms like "Pelagianism" and "Manicheanism" had been thrown around throughout the life of the dispute; "Semi-Pelagian" was now being used in various senses by various people. It was one thing when there were factions within the Roman Catholic church; now there were Molinist, Jansenist, and Quietist factions in the Roman Catholic church, along with Puritanism, Methodism, Calvinism, Lutheranism, and Pietism among Protestant groups.

Two developments in the dispute both involve the Pietist movement. This movement actually began in the seventeenth century, but much of its fruit came in the eighteenth. Pietism stressed the conversion of the individual believer and a focus on developing personal faith. Its stress on the individual prepared the way for the Enlightenment in many ways; focus on personal belief also served, among many, to undermine a strong emphasis on divine grace. The Pietist movement was trans-denominational; as such, many who could agree on Pietist principles could still disagree on matters of divine grace and human freedom.

Pietist theology strongly influenced John Wesley in the latter part of the eighteenth century, and he was one of the founders of Methodism. Methodism would become one of the strongest defenders of the Arminian position, although its influence was felt more strongly in America than in Europe.

Yet it would be the Enlightenment and its consequences that changed the face of the discussion. In general, the Enlightenment saw the reassertion of reason as the primary authority among men, and involved a much more optimistic view of humans and their capacity than had been seen beforehand.

Enlightenment philosophy, therefore, stood to undermine the doctrine of total depravity that was almost universally accepted in "Christendom." For this and many other reasons many of the religious groups of the day were quite skeptical about the philosophy.

Scotland was abuzz at the time with great developments in thought and science, called the Scottish Enlightenment today. This included Francis Hutcheson and Thomas Reid, who advocated for "commonsense moral reasoning," the belief that God's intentions for man and his morality could be discerned without appeal to traditional authority, and could, in fact, be perceived through investigation of human nature. Such a view militates strongly against the idea that man is incapable of truly knowing the good without divine assistance, and sections of Presbyterianism of Scotland in the middle of the eighteenth century drifted away from its Calvinist heritage. This belief system would become extremely popular in America in the late eighteenth and nineteenth centuries.

The Enlightenment represented a strong challenge to "historic" Christianity. Long cherished beliefs that previous generations could take for granted were now being questioned. The idea of one continuous and overall harmonious history of Christianity was torn to pieces. The Old Testament was being subjected to historical criticism and found wanting. Jesus Himself was not beyond question—it is at this time that the idea of the "historical Jesus" began to be separated from the "Jesus of faith."

The political consequences were also immense—Europe saw the French

Revolution come and go, Napoleon defeated, and constant tumult, exemplified in riots and insurrections in 1848.

In this climate many denominations returned to more conservative positions. In Scotland, Presbyterianism as a whole returned to its Calvinist heritage: Presbyterians there in 1840 believed the same things as did those in 1690. The same was true in Northern Ireland. "Commonsense moral philosophy," beyond the University of Glasgow, found few European adherents.

Meanwhile, in the face of historical criticism, the subjective and personal aspects of faith were emphasized. During much of the past two hundred years, disputes on faith involved matters more weighty than divine grace and human freedom, instead focusing on whether the New Testament truly reflected Jesus and the early Christian movement, and whether miracles did, in fact, happen. It is not as if the dispute regarding divine grace and human freedom had been solved; the same arguments were being made by opposing sides, but the field of conflict had moved to entirely new and different areas.

The twentieth century also saw the rise of the ecumenical movement and attempts to emphasize that which denominations agreed in common. In order to do so, disputations were minimized. It should come as little surprise, therefore, that the dispute over divine grace and human freedom did not progress in many meaningful ways in Europe over the past two centuries: bigger issues were at stake, and the denominations were not as keen to emphasize points of disagreement as much as points of agreement. The relativist influence in postmodernism has also led to the minimization of doctrine among many denominations.

Faith in Europe was sinking. It would be in America that the dispute would maintain its liveliness.

### The Dispute in America (1715-Present)

In the period before the American Revolution, the various denominations in colonial America were very much like their European counterparts. While the Calvinist heritage was being minimized by Presbyterians in Scotland, American Presbyterians emphasized it. Almost everyone agreed that man had little role in his own salvation and that he was entirely dependent on God.

The Puritans of New England represented the most coherent theological force in colonial America, and they were staunch Calvinists. Jonathan Edwards, perhaps the most famous of them, worked to "modernize" Calvinism in the face of the developing Enlightenment philosophy, working out an "experiential" Calvinism. Yet, in his emphasis on conversion and willingness to move away from the strong covenantal stream of Puritan theology, he unwittingly paved the way for the undermining of Calvinism in America.

Edwards was one of the forces behind America's first "Great Awakening" in the middle of the eighteenth century, a realization of Pietist influences in America. Its immediate consequences led to greater Calvinist influence on the country, and stronger ties to the English Reformed heritage. Yet even during these times, many were uncomfortable with Calvinist doctrine, especially among Anglicans.

Nevertheless, colonial American theology represented, by and large, conservative European theologies. Eighteenth century America did not see many great changes in theology; it is notable, however, that the changes that did take place involved groups of Puritans rejecting Calvinism (with many becoming Universalists, Freewill Baptists, or Shakers in the process).

The tumult caused by the American Revolution and its immediate consequences led to the profound shift in American theology in the nineteenth century, and these changes led to a quite different environment for the dispute over divine grace and human freedom. The Augustinian conception of divine grace and human freedom could not provide sufficient answers for the problems of the day: the "commonsense moral reasoning" of Hucheson and Reid, combined with fervent evangelical pietism and attachment to republican principles, did. "Commonsense moral reasoning," with the presupposition that the individual could understand intuitively what was right and wrong based upon the self-evident standard of "common sense," provided a means of justifying Christianity without recourse to the traditional authorities that had previously supported it. Since nineteenth century America was deeply mistrustful of any form of inherited authority, Christianity justified by an appeal to "common sense" would gain greater legitimacy than any appeal to European authorities.

Since the entire Augustinian/Calvinist concept of divine grace and human freedom was based in man's inability to come to God and that mankind was sinful from birth, any idea of man being able to intuitively understand what was right would inevitably lead to friction. It was on this very basis that the

Puritan Calvinists of the middle eighteenth century rejected "commonsense moral reasoning," but by the nineteenth century the latter represented the presupposition of almost all Americans. Without a dim view of humanity, and without the shelter of inherited tradition, Augustinian Calvinism lost the traction that it held in Europe and had previously held in colonial America.

This led to a momentous shift in theology and doctrine in America, and the Restoration movement exemplified the trend.

Barton Stone grew up during the Revolutionary War, and was exposed to most of the historic Protestant churches in America. He eventually ended up as a Presbyterian minister, but the tenets of Calvinism never entirely appealed to him. During the revivalistic campaigns that took place on the frontier from 1796-1803, especially with the Cane Ridge, Kentucky revival in 1801, Stone became convinced of the need for faith as a prerequisite for conversion and that salvation was open to all who would accept it. For his "Arminianism," his association with the Kentucky Synod of the Presbyterian church was severed in 1803. He and some who agreed with him then formed the Springfield Presbytery, yet later concerns would compel them to disband it the next year, issuing the *Last Will and Testament of the Springfield Presbytery*, a call to return to the primitive New Testament church. His movement was known as the Christian church.

Yet it is the story of Alexander Campbell that serves as a microcosm for the momentous changes taking place in American Christianity. Alexander was the son of Thomas Campbell, an Ulster Scot living in Northern Ireland, himself a son of an Anglican French and Indian War hero. Thomas found little value in the "establishment" within Anglicanism, and became a minister of the Seceder Presbyterians. He affirmed Calvinist viewpoints but despaired of the divisions among Christians. His work toward reconciliation eventually forced him to leave Ireland for America, where he remained among Seceder Presbyterians for awhile. Thomas' beliefs were moving him toward antiestablishmentarian views, and he was removed from the Seceder Presbyterians in 1808. The next year he put forth the *Declaration and Address*, a call to no longer accept manmade creeds, but to believe the Bible alone. Nevertheless, he maintained his Calvinist beliefs for the time being.

His son Alexander, meanwhile, grew up in the Calvinist Presbyterian tradition, and, on the whole, accepted it. At fourteen he had grave doubts regarding whether infants were damned. In 1808, Campbell spent the winter at the University of Glasgow where he was exposed to the same teachings regarding commonsense moral reasoning that his father had learned and which was playing such a major role in American developments. He also was greatly influenced by reforming work of the Haldane brothers in Scotland, who pushed for autonomous congregations, weekly observance of the Lord's Supper, and a return to the Bible only. These influences led Alexander to repudiate his tie with the Seceder Presbyterians while in Glasgow.

Alexander joined his father in America the next year, just as the *Declaration and Address* went to press, and both were pleased at how they were reaching similar conclusions independently. Nevertheless, they both continued advancing Calvinist teachings until the winter of 1811.

Alexander had been distressed about the idea of infant baptism for years, and when he learned that his wife Margaret was pregnant, he set himself to a thorough study of the issue. He retrieved all the justifications for infant baptism that he could find, and based on his own research and analysis, found them biblically wanting. Alexander was following his father's guidance, testing the opinions of men on the basis of reason, just as commonsense moral reasoning required.

Alexander's study of infant baptism compelled him to study out the entire basis of his Calvinist beliefs. He went back all the way to Augustine and Pelagius, much like what we are doing, and he also saw Calvin's complete indebtedness to Augustine. Using the popular Baconian method of inductive reasoning, Campbell saw the excesses of Augustine's doctrines; the fact that hyper-Calvinism was prevalent on the frontier only exacerbated the difficulty. He saw that the definition of faith being put forward by both Augustinian Calvinists and Arminian Methodists—the idea that God through the Holy Spirit provided belief in some conversion experience—was not biblical. In the Bible, faith was the belief and confidence of the believer him or herself in God. By the next spring, Alexander had repudiated his Calvinist beliefs. He rejected infant baptism, and his daughter was not baptized. Furthermore, Alexander, his wife, and even his father submitted themselves to immersion in water for the remission of sin.

Nevertheless, Alexander found value in Augustine's view of God providing grace through baptism and the Lord's Supper to demonstrate why baptism was efficacious. He would later confess that he found more difficulties with Arminius and Wesley than Augustine and Calvin; he attempted to navigate the middle road between humanism and fatalism.

The stories of Barton Stone and Alexander Campbell indicate how so many Americans would come to reject the traditional views of divine grace and human freedom so powerfully put forward by Puritans just a generation before.

The new situation in America led to different responses within Calvinist churches. Some entirely rejected Calvinist tenets and formal institutions, like the Restorationists. Others rejected Calvinism, maintained formal institutions, and came to belief in universalism; most such persons were in New England and became Unitarians. Others clung tenaciously to historic Calvinism. Groups developed within both Congregational and Presbyterian churches ("New Haven" Congregationalists and "New School" Presbyterians) whose reasoning led them to deny the core concept involved in original sin: the idea that sin could be transferred. Nathaniel Taylor and Lyman Beecher were the most famous such theologians, and they posited that sin was something that could only be committed, and that by a free moral agent. This led to weakening views on limited atonement also. Such "moderate Calvinism" seemed to be a mediating option between hard-line traditionalism and digression into Unitarianism.

"Moderate Calvinism" is the means by which we can understand the strange Evangelical phenomenon of "faith only" salvation, "once saved, always saved," and the need for individual conversion. This has become a hallmark of much of Baptist theology, although Baptists have been historically divided in different groups over the Calvinist question from their beginning. This perspective can only be understood in terms of nineteenth century revivalist, evangelical, republican common sense moral reasoning based Protestantism. Belief in man's inherent sinfulness and inability to accomplish anything in his own salvation is maintained, along with the comforting idea that no matter what a man may do, he will be saved regardless by God's power. Yet the ideas of unconditional election, limited atonement, and irresistible grace are excised because of the belief that man has enough free will to come to God and believe, and because of the revival's call for anyone to come to this belief. Its theological conundrums are not well considered, and this theology can be considered "half-baked." Nevertheless, it has been a major force in American "Christianity" ever since.

As can be seen, the American climate led to greater traction for the "Arminian" viewpoint. The largest proponents of such views were the Methodists, whose numbers increased mightily between 1790 and 1860. Even though they believed in original sin, positing that God's grace through the atonement is what allows men today to choose God, they opposed Calvinistic doctrines strongly in polemics throughout this period.

The difference is most clearly seen in the second "Great Awakening." While the first such awakening was promoted by Puritan Calvinists and led to stronger Calvinistic positions, the second awakening was pushed strongly by Charles Finney and his brand of revivalism, which was rather Arminian and quite anti-Calvinistic. The pendulum had definitively swung away from Calvinism.

Yet Augustinian Calvinism was not going away. There were many who held to the tradition as firmly in the middle of the nineteenth century as in the middle of the eighteenth. Evangelicalism from that point forward would always feature the tension between Augustinian Calvinist views, "Arminian" free will views, and mediating positions.

All of these developments took place between the Revolutionary and Civil Wars. While the Americans created a new synthesis based upon their unique circumstances, they always derived much of their inspiration from European thinkers and theologians. As the nineteenth century continued, the theological crisis of the Civil War, the development of science in ways casting aspersions on biblical accounts, and the historical criticism of the biblical text eroded popular support for the "self-evident" and "reasonable" claims put forward regarding the Bible in the antebellum period. On account of this, as in Europe, much of the disputation shifted away from "traditional" points of contention, and instead focused on the inspiration and truthfulness of the Bible.

As the nineteenth century turned into the twentieth, modernist and fundamentalist factions of Protestants strongly argued regarding these issues. While most of Protestantism maintained a middle course between the factions, historic denominations eventually moved in the modernist direction, while evangelicals maintained more conservative positions. The ecumenical movement also made inroads in America; as in Europe, among the modernist groups, it led to a minimizing of doctrinal differences among denominations, including matters of divine grace and human freedom, to emphasize what was accepted by all. While evangelical groups did not play as large of a role in the ecumenical movement as a whole, they have always maintained a form of ecumenism of their own: while disputes do continue within Evangelicalism on the competing views of divine grace and human freedom, few believe that their opponents stand condemned for holding to different positions. Such distinctions, to many, now fall under the realm of "differing opinions that do not impact salvation." It was not always so.

While the disputation regarding matters of divine grace and human freedom continue to be discussed, debated, and argued, modern trends have not moved in favor of Augustinian Calvinism, either in America or in Europe. By in large, the state of the dispute itself remains the same today as it did when T. W. Brents argued strongly against Calvinism in his *Gospel Plan of Salvation* in 1874, although there are many fewer denominationalists who would bind Calvinist views as necessary for salvation. As in Europe, so in America: the dispute over divine grace and human freedom was neglected as more weighty arguments came to the fore and as belief in the need for particularity in doctrine was minimized in ecumenism.

**Divine Grace and Human Freedom**

Our survey into the history of the dispute over the tension of divine grace and human freedom has brought many other issues to the fore.

The power of tradition has been a prevailing force in the discussion. The issue was never contentious in eastern "Christendom," because Augustine was not a great force in the east. The east held to a different understanding of original sin, and considered human freedom a doctrine that could not be denied. It was Augustine's exalted position in western "Christendom" that led to the entire discussion. The lack of censure of Augustine regarding double predestination, which clearly deviated from the traditional norms of the "catholicism" of the day, combined with the excessive veneration bestowed upon him, meant that the discussion would never really be balanced until someone was willing to challenge Augustine's hegemony. That person seems to be Arminius in the late sixteenth century. Therefore, it should come to no surprise that Augustine's perspective consistently held weight throughout the medieval period, and Calvin was content being Augustine's sixteenth century Protestant mouthpiece.

Nevertheless, ever since Augustine put his double predestination views forth, there has always been discomfort with them. From John Cassian to Hincmar to Thomas Aquinas, disputes always saw one side attempting to mediate away from the excesses of Augustine's views. Even within Calvinism there have been constant disputations regarding the legitimacy of various points of Augustine's synthesis.

Yet, thanks in large part to the events of the past two hundred and fifty years or so, we can look at the tension between divine grace and human freedom without having to defer to any inherited tradition, and can do so based in our own understanding of the Scriptures.

The disputation has gone on for many generations before us, and the various Scriptures used in the discussion are all but fixed. Adherents of total depravity cite Psalm 51:5 and Romans 3:10-11; Matthew 18:1-4, Mark 10:14, and Ezekiel 18:20 are offered against it. Those favoring unconditional election cite John 15:16, Ephesians 1:4-8, and 2 Thessalonians 2:13; Deuteronomy 30:19, Joshua 24:15, and Romans 2:11 are offered in opposition. For limited atonement, proponents say that John 10 and Matthew 26:28, among other passages, validate the belief, while John 1:29, 1 Timothy 2:4, and Titus 2:11 deny it. Irresistible grace is justified by John 6:37, 39, 44-45; John 12:32 and Galatians 5:1-4 justify the opposite. Perseverance of the saints is "proven" by John 10:28-29 and Romans 8:31-39, and disproven by Hebrews 3:12-14; 6:4-6; 10:26-31 and 2 Peter 2:20-22. Those who align themselves on the Augustinian-Calvinist end of the spectrum try to interpret the Scriptures in terms of the TULIP system, and those who align themselves on the other end of the spectrum do the opposite.

With both groups claiming scriptural justification, how can we sort through what is right and what is in error? As we have seen, the disputation involving divine grace and human freedom involves people's presuppositions as much as it involves what the Scriptures actually say. Therefore, if we will understand what God has truly said, we must first analyze whether the Scriptures justify the presuppositions of those who come to it.

Since Augustine and his perspective have been so dominant in the discussion over the past 1,500 years we would do well to consider the presuppositions of his positions on divine grace and human freedom. As we have seen, Augustine held firmly to Neoplatonic views of divinity—God as the absolute cause of everything. It was inconceivable, in Augustine's perspective, for God's will to bend to humanity or be contradicted by humanity. For God to be omnipotent, according to Augustine, He must have willed all things as they take place.

There are no Scriptures that can be offered in defense of this presupposition because it is entirely foreign to them. We agree that God is omnipotent, and that God does indeed have the ability to do as He wishes (cf. Rom. 9). But this does not require that God *must* do anything in a certain way! Ironically, in an attempt to glorify God's sovereignty, Augustinianism actually places God in a box—everything must already be established by His decree, and even God is not able to change whatever has been previously established.

We cannot justify any position with presuppositions that counter what the Scriptures of God reveal. And the Scriptures reveal, perhaps to Augustine's chagrin, that God's will is not so fixed as to be entirely unchangeable. Consider 1 Samuel 23:10-13, where God tells David that Saul will come to Keilah. Yet David departs, and Saul does not go to Keilah. Did God lie? By no means—if David had not departed, Saul would certainly have come. Events changed based upon man's actions.

Matthew 19:8 represents a powerful challenge to the Augustinian presupposition. Here Jesus says that it was not God's will for the Israelites to be able to divorce their wives, but He permitted it. This verse clearly shows that there is a distinction between what God wills and what God permits, despite Calvin's protestations. If Augustine's view is correct, then God indeed willed the Israelites to divorce their wives, or Jesus is in serious error about the nature of God. Neither perspective accords with the Scriptures!

Examples of God adapting His will on account of the actions of men are legion—1 Kings 21:20-22, 29; Jeremiah 18:7-10; Jonah 3; Acts 27:10, 21-24; among many others. Therefore, while God certainly *could* have predestined all things before the creation of the world, according to His revelation, He has done no such thing. According to God's revelation, it is not an affront to God's sovereignty for God to modify His will based upon the humility or sinfulness of men.

This also stands true in terms of man's standing before God. The Scriptures nowhere assert that God, based upon His grace alone, predetermined who would be saved, regardless of how they would act. Romans 8:28-30 indicates that, even if God predetermined those who would be saved, it was done on the basis of His foreknowledge—the foreknowledge of those who would be obedient servants of the Son (Matt. 10:22; Rom. 6:16-23, etc.). This foreknowledge and "predestination" were not accomplished in opposition to man's will, but on the basis of the decisions of men. God's sovereignty is in no way maligned by this!

The Augustinian picture of God does seem to present a tyrannical sadist. Their defense of such in the idea of the wonderful nature of God's mystery is quite telling (Rom. 11:33-34): since such a picture of God is never really found in the Scriptures, they must act as if He never revealed it! According to such a view, God knowingly created millions, if not billions, condemning them without any hope of renewal or redemption. The story of Jesus and the cross, far from being glorified, becomes tantalizing: a wonderful hope for the "elect" while the "reprobate" have no prayer of redemption in Him. In such a view, there is little point in evangelizing; most of the New Testament would be irrelevant, because there is nothing we can do to better ourselves. Truly, if this were the picture that God wished to present, we would expect the Bible to look quite different than it does!

All of this shows that the Augustinian picture of God is distorted by their presuppositions. While God is just and sovereign, He is also loving and merciful. While He certainly could have created mankind to be robotic, serving Him or rejecting Him purely on the basis of His decree, He did no such thing. Had He done such a thing, it is hard to see how we could deny that God was the author of evil and sin in the reprobate!

But such is not the case. God is not the author of evil—He does not tempt anyone (Jas. 1:13). God provides a way out from every temptation to sin—no one is forced to sin (1 Cor. 10:13). By His sovereign will, God created man with free moral agency: God created man and gave him the choice to obey His guidelines or to disobey them, as is seen in the Garden of Eden (Gen. 2-3). God gave Israel the choice to serve Him or to serve other gods (Deut. 30:19; Josh. 24:15). God desired—and desires—for all men to come to Him, serve Him, and live (1 Tim. 2:4; 2 Pet. 3:9), but because man has the capacity to choose against God, many will not be saved by their own disobedience. On the day of Judgment, God will not arbitrarily condemn anyone; those who will be condemned suffer that fate because of their own sinful disobedience, not God's personal eternal decree for them (Rom. 2:5-11).

Not only are the presuppositions of Augustinian Calvinists regarding God not in accordance with Scripture, but also their presuppositions regarding the condition of man. Augustine consolidated the doctrines of infant baptism and original sin that had been recently established, yet from the beginning it had not been so. Patristic evidence demonstrates that early Christians did not believe in original sin and did not baptize infants. There are no Scriptures that show infants being baptized: everyone who was baptized in the New Testament did so as a result of his personal belief (cf. Acts 2:36-38; 16:31-33; etc.), and infants manifestly cannot have personal belief. Infant baptism represented an innovation in the church, even if it later was clothed with the mantle of "apostolic tradition."

Since original sin as a doctrine grew as a justification of infant baptism, if the practice is illegitimate, then its doctrinal justification is at least suspect. It is hard to reconcile the idea of the utter depravity and sinfulness of small children with Jesus' appeals for them to come to Him, "for to such belongs the Kingdom of God," and the only way anyone will enter the Kingdom is if he is childlike (Mark 10:14-15). This means that the Kingdom belongs to sinfully depraved brats or that children are innocent; the latter is in better alignment with the Scriptures. Psalm 51:5 involves poetry, and David speaks in hyperbole as a reaction to his own feelings of sinfulness; to base our entire view of humanity on such a passage is not wise.

The idea of "original sin" abuses the nature of sin as revealed in the Scriptures. In the Bible, sin involves acts of lawlessness, attributable to a moral agent who chooses to accomplish such deeds (Ezek. 18:20; 1 John 3:4). Sin is never described as something inherited or transmitted. The manifest embarrassment of Ambrose and Augustine that led to the doctrine of the immaculate conception is testimony to the innovative nature of the doctrine of original sin: in order to extricate Jesus from it, they needed to reinterpret the virgin birth as demonstrating Jesus' sinlessness from birth, and for good measure, Mary also was often seen as conceived immaculately. The New Testament is entirely silent on these matters, and for good reason; God did not imagine Jesus as being able to obtain sin through being born! The dim view of sexuality that developed as a consequence of the belief that original sin was transmitted through conception also stands against what God revealed on that particular subject (Heb. 13:4).

While advocates of original sin believe Romans 5:12-18 justifies them, a close reading of the passage demonstrates the opposite. Yes, on account of Adam's sin, sin and death were introduced to the world, and all are under its sentence. But this does not mean that humans are born sinful—they are born into a world marred by sin, and they may suffer the consequences of sin, but sin is nowhere portrayed as something inherited. Children die not because they have sinned but because sin is in the world, and the creation is subjected to futility (cf. Rom. 8:20-22).

The Scriptures nowhere demonstrate that man is thoroughly and entirely depraved. Yes, all people who develop free moral agency will sin and fall short of God's glory (Rom. 3:23), but this does not mean that everything humans do is sinful. Gentiles can be a law unto themselves when they do God's will (Rom. 2:14-15). Paul could find commendable elements of Greek thought (Acts 17:22-31). As assuredly as Christians are able to sin, non-Christians are able to do good works. Yet, without the blood of Christ, there is no redemption from the evil that everyone inevitably does; therefore, it is only through the blood of Christ that anyone can be saved (Rom. 5:8-11).

The presuppositions that undergird Augustinian-Calvinist theology, therefore, are faulty. Faulty presuppositions lead to faulty dogmas. Yet Augustinian Calvinists are not entirely wrong, either. What do the Scriptures reveal about the tension between God's grace and human freedom?

The Scriptures make it abundantly clear that humans are entirely indebted to God's grace. God provides the creation and all of its bounty, without which we would have no life (Gen. 1-2). God created us in His own image, giving us the capability of thinking and understanding His will (Gen. 1:26-27). Despite our sins, God, by His grace, sent His Son to die on the cross that we could have the forgiveness of our sins and be reconciled to Him (Rom. 5:8-11; Tit. 3:3-8). There is nothing that humans have ever done or could ever do in order to deserve these blessings. They are provided freely by God.

Yet the Scriptures also make it clear that God created man to be free to decide to serve God or to turn away from Him (Gen. 2; Deut. 30:19). All men are to hear the Gospel of Christ (John 12:32, Matt. 28:18-20), and they are to decide whether to accept the message, believe in Jesus, and become His obedient servant, or to reject the message, and be liable to condemnation for their sins (Rom. 10:17; Acts 2:36-38; Rom. 6; 2 Thess. 1:6-9). While God has done all that is necessary to allow for man's salvation through the death of His Son, it is incumbent upon mankind to accept this salvation in obedient faith for God to purify them (Jas. 2:14-26; 1 Pet. 1:22). It is God's will for all men to do this, yet He knows that not all will do so.

Christians also have the obligation to constantly serve God, and Christians should not expect to obtain their final salvation if they have been disobedient to their Lord (Matt. 7:21-23; Heb. 10:26-31). This does not somehow make God's promise void: God's promise has always been conditioned on man's obedience to His will, as the example of Israel abundantly proves.

In the end, God is not a tyrant; He never compels anyone. Even when He provides more grace to some, obedience is expected. It is true that Saul of Tarsus received an opportunity that not everyone obtains; he still needed to be obedient, and he certainly could have entered Damascus and rejected the message he received (cf. Acts 9). Jesus Himself was expected to fulfill the will of the Father, and had ample opportunity to refuse to do so. He proved His obedience by doing the will of the Father willingly, and not under compulsion (cf. Matt. 26:39; Heb. 5:7-9). God freely provides His grace, but does so to free moral agents according to His sovereign will: they must choose whether to accept it or reject it, and to endure the consequences of their actions.

Human beings sin (Rom. 3:23), but still maintain the image of God (Gen. 1:26-27). Since Adam's sin, the natural will of man easily gravitates toward sin (Rom. 8:1-11; Gal. 5:17-24), but this does not deny that all human beings have some good in them, as even Jesus confesses (Matt. 5:46-47; Luke 11:11-13). God has placed it within the soul of everyone to seek after Him (Acts 17:26-28); anyone, therefore, is able to come to God, if he so desires, to fulfill His will for them (1 Timothy 2:4).

What of foreknowledge and predestination? The New Testament does speak of foreknowledge and predestination, but only in terms of encouraging the saints (Rom. 8:28-30; Eph. 1:3-12). There is no hint of "predestination to reprobation," for condemnation is on the basis of sin. God's predestination of the elect must be understood in terms of His eternal plan in Christ Jesus (Eph. 3:11). For God to have an eternal purpose in Jesus Christ means that He must have known that man would sin and need a Savior. An eternal plan is eternal both in terms of what came before and in terms of what will be, and since it is God's eternal plan for His wisdom to be known through the church (Eph. 3:10), the church was, by necessity, foreknown and predestined. And yet it is hard to deny the idea that believers are predestined in these passages, but this does not mean that God has done so apart from man's will or by some unalterable divine decree of the ages. Instead, as Romans 8 makes clear, any predestination of Christians would be based in God's foreknowledge of who would serve Him; likewise, the calling, justification, and glorification of these believers will be accomplished as God has otherwise established in the Word, through their obedience to God's will (1 Peter 1:22; *et al*). This message is designed to encourage suffering Christians—God has foreknown their faith and has appointed them in Jesus Christ for adoption as sons and conformity to the image of the Son. This does not require that God has chosen others for condemnation or any other such permutation of the Augustinian distortion of what Paul taught. Paul does speak of predestination, and this predestination involves believers being adopted as sons of God and to be conformed to the image of Jesus His Son (Rom. 8:28-30; Eph. 1:3-12). This is in harmony with, not in opposition against, man's need to come to God, to obey the Gospel, and to continue to be faithful until death (Rom. 6; 10:17; Rev. 2:10). As we have seen throughout the disputation regarding divine grace and free will, imbalance on one side hardly justifies imbalance on the other.

This need not require that God knows everything, only that He can know all things and chooses to know regarding His eternal plan in Jesus Christ (Eph. 3:11). Other passages seem to indicate that God might not know all things (cf. Gen. 18:20-21; 22:12). Divine grace and human freedom are biblical doctrines held in tension with each other: to focus too strongly on one doctrine leads to a neglect of the other, and the truth of God is missed.

The disputation regarding divine grace and human freedom has been a fixture in "Christian" history for most of its existence, and it is unlikely to entirely go away before the Lord returns. The historical imbalances from Pelagius to Augustine to dualism and universalism help us better understand the consequences of drifting too far into one extreme. Let us be judicious in how we handle the Scriptures, recognizing how so many have misunderstood the Scriptures on account of their presuppositions which they did not examine. Let us trust in God, even if we do not have perfect understanding. Let us not be swayed by traditional authorities of any persuasion, but instead rest entirely in Jesus Christ. As it is written,

> As therefore ye received Christ Jesus the Lord, so walk in him, rooted and builded up in him, and established in your faith, even as ye were taught, abounding in thanksgiving. Take heed lest there shall be any one that maketh spoil of you through his philosophy and vain deceit, after the tradition of men, after the rudiments of the world, and not after Christ: for in him dwelleth all the fulness of the Godhead bodily (Col. 2:6-9).

## Bibliography

Brents, T. W. *The Gospel Plan of Salvation*. Bowling Green (KY): Guardian of Truth Foundation, 1987 (1874).

Harrell, David Edwin Jr. *Quest for a Christian Nation, 1800-1865: A Social History of the Disciples of Christ,* Volume I. Tuscaloosa: University of Alabama Press, 2003 (1966) (5, 28, 46).

Noll, Mark. *America's God.* New York: Oxford University Press, 2002.

_____. *The Old Religion in the New World.* Grand Rapids: Eerdmans, 2002.

Pelikan, Jaroslav. *The Christian Tradition: A History of the Development of Doctrine, 1: The Emergence of the Catholic Tradition (100-600).* Chicago: The University of Chicago Press, 1971 (278-331).

_____. *The Christian Tradition: A History of the Development of Doctrine, 2: The Spirit of Eastern Christendom (600-1700).* Chicago: The University of Chicago Press, 1974 (11-12, 182-183, 221-224, 294-295).

_____. *The Christian Tradition: A History of the Development of Doctrine, 3: The Growth of Medieval Theology (600-1300).* Chicago: The University of Chicago Press, 1978 (50-51, 83-104, 272-277).

_____. *The Christian Tradition: A History of the Development of Doctrine, 4: Reformation of Church and Dogma (1300-1700).* Chicago: The University of Chicago Press, 1984 (25-35, 139-145, 217-240, 258-259, 283-289, 363-379).

_____. *The Christian Tradition: A History of the Development of Doctrine, 5: Christian Doctrine and Modern Culture (since 1700).* Chicago: The University of Chicago Press, 1991 (35-59).

Wrather, Eva Jean. Ed. by D. Duane Cummins. *Alexander Campbell: Adventurer in Freedom.* Fort Worth: TCU Press, 2005 (1-85).

# My Kingdom Is Not of This World

**Keith Greer**

## Introduction

"We can believe because a Supreme Power, Almighty God, prepared the earth with everything needed to satisfy what we want. He made the earth just perfect for us! And He created man and woman in the best way for them to enjoy life to the full in this earthly home—forever" (Psalm 116:16)" (*You Can Live Forever in Paradise on Earth*, 7). Wow—we can live on the earth forever! Is that right? Wait a minute.

In the minds of many religious people, the concept of the Lord's kingdom

---

**Keith Greer,** one of four sons born to Glen and Carole Greer, was born May 2, 1954 in Gary, Indiana. In 1983, Keith married Rita Boothby, a native of Huntington, West Virginia, whom he met at church in Peru, Indiana. They are the parents of four children: Tara Riffe of Kings Island, Georgia; Jessica Shapley, who resides in Lowell, Indiana with her husband Steve and their two children—Austin and Brooke; Keith Greer of Lowell, Indiana; and Lesley Salyers, who resides in San Antonio, Texas with her husband John and their two children—Natalie and Elijah.

A member of the United States Air Force for over twenty years, Keith was stationed in Lakenheath, England; Tucson, Arizona; Peru, Indiana; and Las Vegas, Nevada. He retired from active duty in 1992. He began preaching while living in Las Vegas, and preached at the Vegas Drive church for nine years before moving to Beavercreek, Ohio where he has worked with the Knollwood congregation since August 1997.

Keith has gone on six overseas preaching trips since 2000. The last five were to the Philippines, where he is scheduled to go again in 2010. He also holds five meetings per year in various states. He has written in several of the periodicals and has edited the monthly *Knollwood Messenger* since January 1998.

Keith has an Associate Degree from the Community College of the Air Force. While preaching in Las Vegas, he attended, and was the first graduate of, the Las Vegas School of Religion, a three-year upper-level Bible school. Before moving to Ohio, He taught several classes in the school.

on earth involves an as-yet-future golden age when He will return to temporarily reign and rule for a thousand years. It will, they say, be a time of universal righteousness. Some go so far as to describe this period as a return to Eden when men will once again walk and talk on earth with their Creator.

This misconceived doctrine is known as Premillennialism, thus called because believers perceive themselves to be living now in an age before (*pre*) the millennium (*thousand years*).

Many in the Lord's church fail to realize how profoundly this doctrine has influenced their neighbors and friends. Nearly every major denomination accepts some elements of Premillennial thinking. Nor has the Lord's church escaped the influence of this false interpretation of Scripture.

### What is Premillennialism?

It is humanly impossible to define all the different terms that all millennialists would accept. Different approaches and theories exist within this broad group of false teachings. Following are a few of the prominent views:

**Historical Premillennialism** holds that Christians who constitute the church will go through a Great Tribulation, at the end of which Christ will come with great power and glory to raise the righteous dead and rapture the saints. These will be caught up to meet Him in the air, but almost immediately return with Him to earth. His coming destroys the forces of the Antichrist in the battle of Armageddon and then He establishes His kingdom.

**Dispensational Premillennialism** teaches that Christ's coming will occur in two stages:

- First, Jesus will come to rapture the saints, raise the righteous dead, and gather them with the living saints to meet the Lord in the air for a seven-year period.
- Second, at the end of the seven years, Jesus will come with His saints to destroy His enemies in the battle of Armageddon and subsequently establish His earthly millennial kingdom in Jerusalem. This is the most prominent view held today.

**Post-millennialism** holds that Christ will come after the millennium. Consequently, it teaches that we are now living in the millennium and that Christ will return at its end. The post-millennialist does not believe the thousand years is a literal period. Rather, he contends that the millennium is a generic time when righteousness will prevail due to the preaching of the gospel. He expects the world to get better and better. Since the world is generally seen to be deteriorating, post-millennialism has lost its influence.

**Amillennialism** holds that there will be no earthly millennium and that the 1000-year reign mentioned in Revelation 20 does not refer to establishment of a kingdom upon this earth or to a literal 1000-year reign to commence at Christ's second coming. The amillennialist regards the millennial period as a reference to the exaltation of the martyrs and faithful saints after death.

Now, let's look at some of the scriptural problems with Premillennial doctrines. If, as Premillennialism teaches, Jesus is coming in the future to reign for 1000 years in Jerusalem on David's throne, that would make Him an earthly king, ruling over an earthly kingdom. Jesus told Pilate, "My kingdom is not of this world" (John 18:36). If He has not yet established His kingdom, where does that put Him today? And what does this say about the church or Jesus' mission when He was on earth? Someone must provide the answers to these questions in such a way that they reconcile with the Divine record!

Premillennialism teaches there will be a seven-year tribulation, the battle of Armageddon (final battle between good and evil), purging of evil from the earth, and resurrection of the Old Law. It teaches Jerusalem will again be the center of worship, that there will be a return to fleshly laws and rites, and that the Old Testament pattern—a physical kingdom with a physical king—will be restored after centuries of absence.

**Let's Take A Closer Look!**

In light of the Scriptures, can the above teachings be correct? Can they be made to harmonize with the rest of Divine revelation? Since the Bible is a complete book of unity and harmony, everything must agree. The honest examiner will find this to be very difficult. Doesn't this tell us something about the theory?

These doctrines create havoc with *Christ and His kingdom*. If all this is yet to come, what is Christ doing now? What role, if any, does His church play? What does this do to His statement in John 17: "I have finished the work You sent me to do"? Are we to believe that Jesus uttered a false statement? Was He unaware that He had unfinished work left to do? Who can believe it?

The Premillennial doctrine needs to be exposed for what it is—blasphemy! Why? Such teaching undermines God's eternal plan, contradicts past prophecies, and makes the Bible a book of flaws and confusion. Would God be the author of such a book (1 Cor. 15:33)?

### Voices From The Past

Some have misrepresented Restoration-era preachers, such as J.W. McGarvey, as having taught that the throne was a literal throne in Jerusalem. In fact McGarvey, said:

> He made him Lord by causing him to sit on God's own throne, to rule over angels and men; and he made him Christ by causing him to sit on the throne of David according to promise. It was God's throne because it was the throne of universal dominion; and it was David's throne, because it was the lineal descent from David which made Jesus rightful king. From this conclusion the Jewish hearers of Peter learned that, contrary to their previous conception, the promised Christ was to sit, not on an earthly throne, however glorious, but on the throne of the universe (*Commentary on Acts*, 36).

It sounds to me like McGarvey had a good understanding of what the prophets taught concerning the kingdom, and Christ fulfilled those prophecies!

On the other hand, we can look at the teaching of William Miller, a Baptist preacher at the forefront of the nineteenth-century Adventist Movement, and founder of the Seventh Day Adventist denomination. He taught a version of the earthly-kingdom theory and manufactured a prophetic chart that declared—in 1843—that Christ would return in 1844. When 1844 came and went without the Lord's advent, Miller revised his calculations, admitted he made a mistake, and said the Lord would come in 1845. Following great humiliation because of two failed predictions, he stopped setting dates and disappeared.

Another famous millennial believer was Ellen G. White, one of Miller's disciples. She tried to resurrect and repair his mistakes. She added a Sabbath-Day focus to the Advent theology. She claimed to have seen a vision of the Ten Commandments, with a halo around the fourth commandment. Declaring herself an inspired prophetess, she explained that God knew all along that Miller was wrong, but placed a lie in Miller's chart, using him as His mouthpiece to lie for Him! (Think about that: God placed a lie?) She claimed, however, that her prophecies, from the same source, were right. Such statements are pure blasphemy and clearly show why she cannot be believed.

Premillennialism made its way into the Lord's church in the 1920s. In a series of articles written in the *Gospel Advocate* during 1914 and 1915, brother R.H. Bolls of Louisville, KY, began to strongly advocate his own, slightly different, version of Premillennialism. Men, such as Foy Wallace, Jr. and others, discussed, debated, and refuted the subject. Sadly, this resulted in a division of the church, with some churches adopting Premillennial thinking. This split came in the late 1940s and early 1950s. There are still some premillennial churches in southern Indiana and around the Louisville area. A college in Winchester, KY still trains young men to teach this error.

This movement within the churches of Christ led to the introduction of serious errors. Like denominational versions of the doctrine, brethren taught that Jesus will reign as a literal king on a literal throne in Jerusalem for 1000 years. Likewise, they taught that Jesus will sit on David's literal throne, that He will rule over a material kingdom, and that the Jews will return to Palestine. They have taught that the 1000-year period will occur between Christ's second coming and the final judgment of all men.

Brother Bolls said: "The latter term is borrowed from the language of Revelation 20:1-7. This passage speaks six times of a period of 1,000 years, which follows the personal descent of Christ from heaven, and during which Satan is imprisoned, and Christ reigns with his saints . . . . I think the majority of brethren have always believed in a millennium, a period of bliss and triumph, in the future. . . ."

In the Neal-Wallace Debate in 1933 at Winchester, KY and Chattanooga, TN, Charles Neal said, "The Bible clearly teaches that after the second coming of Christ and before the final resurrection and judgment, there will be an age or dispensation of one thousand years during which Christ will reign on the earth."

Division and confusion always result from false teaching. A careful study of Scripture clearly demonstrates what the Bible teaches concerning God's kingdom.

### God's Promises to Abraham

Man's sin in the Garden of Eden separated him from God. Many years later, the world had become so wicked that God determined to destroy it with a flood. In Genesis 6-9, we have the account of the flood that occurred during Noah's lifetime. Following that, we are introduced to a man named Abram. God appeared to him at his home in Ur of the Chaldees and called him to leave for a place He would show him.

God made three promises to Abram: "Now the Lord had said to Abram: Get out of your country, from your family and from your father's house, to a land that I will show you. I will make you a great nation; I will bless you and make your name great; and you shall be a blessing. I will bless those who bless you, and I will curse him who curses you; and in you all the families of the earth shall be blessed" (Gen. 12:1-3).

Abraham did not live to see any of the promises fulfilled. Yet, he believed God would keep them. The scheme of redemption, the Bible story, develops around the three promises which God repeated in Genesis 17:8; 18:18; 22:17, 18. They were contingent on Abraham's faith. In Genesis 22, God tested Abraham's faith by commanding him to offer his son Isaac as a sacrifice. Abraham passed the test, and God spared Isaac's life. The Premillennial teacher affirms that God's promises to Abraham have not yet been completely fulfilled and that something still lies ahead for Abraham's physical descendants—namely Israel. However, Scripture clearly shows that all three promises—creation of a nation (Israel), a land wherein that nation's citizens would reside (Canaan), and the blessing that would come to all mankind through Israel's seed (Christ)—have been fulfilled. The Premillennial teacher fails to rightly divide the Scriptures.

**Promise 1: The Nation Promise.** God promised to make Abraham a great nation, whose citizens would be as innumerable as the dust of the earth, stars in the heavens, and sands along the seashore (Gen. 13:16; 15:6). All three promises were also given to Isaac (Gen. 26:15) and Jacob (Gen. 28:3, 4). God kept this first promise as the Jewish nation multiplied and encountered severe bondage in Egypt. At the proper time, God called Moses to lead them out of Egypt.

Following the ten plagues that God brought upon Egypt, He allowed the Jews to plunder their Egyptian captors and to leave Egypt as free people. After crossing the Red Sea (Exod. 14), God's people were free, and the Egyptians were dead. Thus, the nation promise was, and remains, fulfilled.

**Promise 2: The Land Promise.** Because of their unbelief, the first generation that left Egypt wandered forty years and died in the wilderness. Then, during the days of Joshua, God fulfilled the land promise. This particular promise is important to Premillennial believers. They claim that God gave Israel only part of the land (the west bank) and that He will keep the remainder of the second promise at the millennium. Is this true?

Consider Joshua's words. "*So the Lord gave to Israel all the land of which*

*He had sworn to give to their fathers*, and they took possession of it and dwelt in it. The Lord gave them rest all around, according to all that He had sworn to their fathers. And not a man of all their enemies stood against them; the Lord delivered all their enemies into their hand. Not a word failed of any good thing which the Lord had spoken to the house of Israel. All came to pass" (Josh. 21:43-45). Notice the text says *all* the land, not part of it!

Joshua later reaffirmed this fact, "Behold, this day I am going the way of all the earth. And you know in all your hearts and in all your souls that *not one thing has failed of all the good things which the Lord your God spoke concerning you*. All have come to pass for you; not one word of them has failed. Therefore it shall come to pass, that as all the good things have come upon you which the Lord your God promised you, so the Lord will bring upon you all harmful things, until He has destroyed you from this good land which the Lord your God has given you. When you have transgressed the covenant of the Lord your God, which He commanded you, and have gone and served other gods, and bowed down to them, then the anger of the Lord will burn against you, and you shall perish quickly from the good land which He has given you" (Josh. 23:14-16)

Note the conditional nature of the promise. Yes, God gave them the land, but in order to keep it, they had to obey His commandments. Listen carefully to His words: "Then it shall be, if you by any means forget the Lord your God, and follow other gods, and serve them and worship them, I testify against you this day that you shall surely perish. As the nations which the Lord destroys before you, so you shall perish, because you would not be obedient to the voice of the Lord your God" (Deut. 8:19, 20).

When they disobeyed and failed to fulfill their part of the covenant, God removed them from the land and gave it to their enemies. People need to be very careful not to confuse God's promises. Some confuse His promise to restore the remnant after the seventy-year captivity with His original land promise to Abraham. The two are *not* the same. The following passages document the return of the remnant: Isaiah 10:20-24; Jeremiah 30:3, 4; 50:3, 4; Deuteronomy 30:1-10; Haggai 1:12, 14; 2:2, 3; Ezra 1; 9:13-15; Nehemiah 1:3-11. God did not promise that, after captivity, the remnant would inhabit the same amount of land the entire nation did before the captivity. Premillennialists need to find another promise—one that says God would give back all the land that He took away. No such promise or prophecy exists in the pages of God's word! This is a paramount Premillennial-theory flaw that is easy to expose.

**Promise 3: The Seed Promise.** The first glimpse of this promise was given in the garden (Gen. 3:15). Its fulfillment was accomplished in Christ. "Now to Abraham and his Seed were the promises made. He does not say, 'And to seeds,' as of many, but as of one, 'And to your Seed,' who is Christ. And this I say, that the law, which was four hundred and thirty years later, cannot annul the covenant that was confirmed before by God in Christ, that it should make the promise of no effect. For if the inheritance is of the law, it is no longer of promise; but God gave it to Abraham by promise. What purpose then does the law serve? It was added because of transgressions, till the Seed should come to whom the promise was made; and it was appointed through angels by the hand of a mediator" (Gal. 3:16-19).

All this is vitally important to those who hold Premillennial views. For Jesus to rule in Jerusalem on David's throne, the Jews must possess the land on which the original throne was located. The Old Law and Judaism would have to be resurrected. The Bible says the Old Law was nailed to Jesus' cross (Col. 2:14). If one carefully studies Galatians 3:16-29, he learns that Moses' Law endured until the cross. The Jewish nation's only hope today is in Christ—not sitting on an earthly throne, but a spiritual one in heaven!

### The Kingdom Prophecies

One of the gravest problems attached to Premillennial theory is what to do about the kingdom prophecies in the Old Testament. If the theory is true and can be proven, then the prophecies concerning the establishment of God's kingdom were false. This is a serious flaw that Premillennialists cannot answer.

The first question to consider is whether the Old-Testament prophets were inspired? The Apostle Peter said they were: "Knowing this first, that no prophecy of Scripture is of any private interpretation, for prophecy never came by the will of man, but holy men of God spoke as they were moved by the Holy Spirit" (2 Pet. 1:20, 21). Moses warned that every prophet should be given a test. "When a prophet speaks in the name of the Lord, if the thing does not happen or come to pass, that is the thing which the Lord has not spoken; the prophet has spoken it presumptuously; you shall not be afraid of him" (Deut. 18:22). Did the kingdom prophecies pass the test?

In the *Schofield Reference Bible,* whose notes promote Premillennial doctrine, some illuminating statements precede the book of Isaiah: "It is necessary to keep the Israelite character of the prophet in mind . . . and their glorious future . . . the Church corporately, is not in the vision of the

Old Testament prophet (Ephesians 3:1-6) . . . A Great Mystery . . . but to them (prophets) it was not revealed . . . that consequent upon the Messiah's rejection, the New testament Church would be called out" (883). Schofield believed the prophecies had nothing to do with the future kingdom of God; he affirmed that the kingdom and the church are two different things. He is incorrect, and the Bible proves it.

Not only did Daniel prophesy, about the establishment of God's kingdom, he also told us *when* it would come into existence. "And in the days of these kings the God of heaven will set up a kingdom which shall never be destroyed; and the kingdom shall not be left to other people; it shall break in pieces and consume all these kingdoms, and it shall stand forever" (Dan. 2:44.) Notice the phrase "*in the days of these kings*." Daniel was referring to the kings of the Roman Empire. Rome was the fourth part of the image Nebuchadnezzar saw in his vision, which Daniel subsequently interpreted. He gave us the exact time period when God would establish His kingdom.

Did Daniel's prophecy come to pass? "Now after John was put in prison, Jesus came to Galilee, preaching the gospel of the kingdom of God, and saying, The time is fulfilled, and the kingdom of God is at hand. Repent, and believe in the gospel" (Mark 1:14, 15). Jesus said, "The kingdom of God is at hand" (Mark 9:1). That meant it was near. Jesus also said the kingdom would come during the generation of those who heard Him speak. By the way, during what time period did Jesus live? "And it came to pass in those days that a decree went out from Caesar Augustus that all the world should be registered" (Luke 2:1). Rome and the Caesars ruled during the first century when Jesus was born, lived, died, and ascended back to glory.

The Jews' rejection of Jesus came as a result of their expecting restoration of an earthly kingdom and freedom from Roman oppression. Their expectations were eerily and erroneously similar to Premillennial hopes. The Jews were wrong when the Lord was on earth, and those who believe the Premillenial theory are wrong today for the same reason—they misunderstand the difference between a physical and spiritual kingdom.

Daniel gave another prophecy concerning Christ's kingdom. "I was watching in the night visions, and behold, One like the Son of Man, coming with the clouds of heaven! He came to the Ancient of Days, and they brought Him near before Him. Then to Him was given dominion and glory and a kingdom, that all peoples, nations, and languages should serve Him.

His dominion is an everlasting dominion, which shall not pass away, and His kingdom the one which shall not be destroyed" (Dan. 7:13, 14). Daniel was previewing the Lord's ascension back into heaven. The fulfillment is recorded in Acts 1:9-11. According to this, the Father gave Jesus the kingdom—when He ascended and appeared before Him. By the way, before Jesus ascended, He told the apostles to wait in Jerusalem until power came upon them (Acts 1:8).

Why is this important? Isaiah gave additional information about the kingdom. "Now it shall come to pass in the latter days that the mountain of the Lord's house shall be established on the top of the mountains, and shall be exalted above the hills; and all nations shall flow to it. Many people shall come and say, 'Come, and let us go up to the mountain of the Lord, to the house of the God of Jacob; He will teach us His ways, and we shall walk in His paths.' For out of Zion shall go forth the law, and the word of the Lord from Jerusalem" (Isa. 2:2, 3). On the day of Pentecost, the Holy Spirit fell on the apostles, and they preached the first gospel sermon in the city of Jerusalem (Acts 2). We have the right time, the right place, and the right message!

Premillennial theory says that the church was *Plan B*, the result of the Jews' rejection of Christ. Yet, the prophets clearly foretold that not only would Jesus be rejected, He would also be put to death (Isa. 53). For the momentary sake of argument, let's assume Premillennial theory is correct. What assurance do we have that mankind could not again thwart God's plans?

The truth is that the kingdom is the church—the one Jesus promised to build (Matt. 16:18, 19).

- By pouring out the Holy Spirit (Acts 2:1-4), Jesus gave His apostles the "keys of the kingdom" (to unlock God's word). This fulfilled another Old Testament prophecy given in Joel 2:28-32.
- The apostles preached the gospel, people obeyed, and the Lord added them to the church (Acts 2:47).
- Those who are in the church have been translated into God's kingdom (Col. 1:13).
- Jesus is head of the church and king of His kingdom (Eph. 1:22, 23; 1 Tim. 6:15).

In every one of these points, the New Testament record of the establishment of the church-kingdom agrees with the words the prophets spoke in the Old Testament. Every detail came to pass. Premillennial theories can't get around this fatal flaw in their teaching that the kingdom is yet to come. The kingdom has come; Christ is ruling and reigning in that kingdom, and we are part of it (Acts 2:29-36). Anything less would make the Bible contradict itself, prove the prophets to be false, and render God unwilling and unable to keep His promises. Such reasoning would negate inspiration and weaken confidence in the Holy Scriptures. Who can believe such nonsense?

### A Study of Matthew 24

Premillennialists misunderstand and abuse Jesus' teaching in Matthew 24. Numerous television evangelists read from Matthew 24, discussing the signs of the times and Christ's imminent return. Many base their millennial conclusions on their interpretations of this chapter. Sadly, some commentators have added to the confusion with their prophetic speculations concerning the chapter's true meaning.

First, let's look at the chapter's context. To arrive at a proper understanding of what Jesus was saying, we need to consider both the immediate and remote contexts. Jesus did use strong language, but biblical prophecy has a long history of using this type of *judgment language*. (For similar language, see Isaiah 13 and 19.) In Matthew 21, the Bible speaks of the Jews having been cast out. Jesus said that harlots and publicans would go into God's kingdom before the Jews (21:28-32). He further stated that because of their unbelief (21:33-45), the kingdom would be given to another nation. In Matthew 22, we read of Jesus' debate with the Herodians about whether it was lawful for the Jews to pay tribute to Caesar (22:15-22). The Sadducees debated with Him concerning marriage after the resurrection (22:23-33). And, He debated with a Pharisee about which commandment was the greatest (22:34-39). He always used questions to silence His opposition (22:42-46).

In Matthew 23, Jesus pronounced a judicial sentence. The hostility between Him and the Jews had reached a climax. He pronounced a series of woes—describing them as hypocrites, blind guides, fools, whited sepulchers, and a generation of vipers (22:13-33). He accused them of "shutting up the kingdom of heaven against men." Their personal judgment lacked mercy and compassion. With their rejection of Jesus, they exhausted God's patience. The Lord knew His death was at hand. One might refer to this as a death sentence on national Israel. Listen closely to the ending verses of Matthew 23: "Assuredly, I say to you, all these things will come upon this generation.

O Jerusalem, Jerusalem, the one who kills the prophets and stones those who are sent to her! How often I wanted to gather your children together, as a hen gathers her chicks under her wings, but you were not willing! See! Your house is left to you desolate" (vv. 36-38). He described God's house as one of desolation and declared its destruction inevitable!

In the next chapter, Jesus foretold the destruction of the temple and the holy city of Jerusalem. The millennial reign does not fit into this context. Matthew 24 records Jesus' answers to two or three questions. The chapter opens with the disciples showing and admiring the temple buildings. To most Jews, the temple was an important part of Judaism. What did Jesus tell them? " And Jesus said to them, do you not see all these things? Assuredly, I say to you, not one stone shall be left here upon another, that shall not be thrown down" (Matt. 24:2). He was prophesying about the temple's destruction, which occurred in A.D. 70 at the hands of the Roman general, Titus.

Notice the disciples' reaction to this astonishing revelation. "Now as He sat on the Mount of Olives, the disciples came to Him privately, saying, tell us, when will these things be? And what will be the sign of Your coming, and of the end of the age?" (Matt. 24:3). The disciples asked two questions (some think three). From the wording of the questions, it might appear that they thought all these things would transpire at once. But a closer examination shows that Jesus answered their questions in the order He received them.

He gave certain signs that would signal that fulfillment of His prophecies was at hand. Note carefully the phrase "*all these things*." His answer to their first question concerned the destruction of the temple buildings, which they were admiring. Jesus began to enumerate a number of signs that would alert the disciples when this event was about to occur.

- Deceivers would come (vv. 4, 5).
- There would be wars and rumors of wars, and nation would rise up against nation (v. 6).
- He also spoke of earthquakes, pestilence, and famines in various places (v. 7).
- Persecution would arise against the disciples, causing many to become unfaithful (vv. 9, 10).
- False prophets would come, causing the love of some disciples to wax cold (vv. 11, 12).

- The gospel would be preached to the world (v.14).
- The "abomination of desolation" would be observable in Jerusalem (cf. Dan. 11:31; Luke 21:20).

He told them that when these signs appeared, the righteous should flee to the mountains (v. 16); those on the housetop or in the fields should not return to the city (vv. 17, 18). He warned that travel would be difficult for those with child, or if it occurred in the winter or on the Sabbath (vv. 19, 20). Destruction would be great, but the time would be shortened (vv. 21, 22), while false Christs would arise with false signs and wonders to deceive mens' hearts (vv. 23-26). His coming would not be a secret event (see Rev. 1:7, as well as v. 27). Jerusalem would become like a carcass over which the eagles would fly (v. 28).

Then the text reverts to Old Testament style judgment language concerning the sun, moon, and stars (v. 29), and the sign of the Son of Man in heaven (v. 30). Understand that the signs are from heaven, meaning they are from God. These signs would accompany and signify the coming destruction under discussion in Matthew 24 (vv. 31-33). *Please note, these are clear visible signs that all will see and hear. Scripture does not affirm any such signs at Christ's second coming for final judgment* (1 Thess. 5:2; 2 Pet. 3:10).

Premillennialists ignore, misapply, or otherwise misconstrue what Jesus said in Matthew 24. They ignore the clear time designation given and that He was addressing more than one question.

The false teachers of our day teach that these are signs that will precede Christ's second coming and His establishment of an earthly kingdom. But, let's reread verse 34: "Assuredly, I say to you, this generation will by no means pass away till all these things take place." Notice the phrase "*all these things*." When Jesus uttered these words, He was looking at the temple buildings. He was telling that present generation it would not pass away until it witnessed Jerusalem's destruction. Thirty-seven years later, in A.D. 70, the temple and Jerusalem were destroyed. Jesus predicted that it would happen during their lifetime. How could this be referring to His second coming and the establishment of an earthly kingdom? The generation to which Jesus spoke is dead and gone. The predictions were fulfilled at Jerusalem's destruction; they were not meant to refer to the end of the world.

Jesus forcefully declared His answer to the first question and then proceeded to deal with the second. Why were signs to be given at the times of the destruction of the temple and Jerusalem? They were given to provide sufficient time for the Christians to flee the city and be saved before the Roman army destroyed it.

Then the subject matter of chapter 24 changes as the terminology follows a different approach. "But of that day and hour no one knows, not even the angels of heaven, but My Father only" (Matt. 24:36). At the time of Jerusalem's judgment, there would be visible signs of impending destruction; but at the second and final judgment, there would be no such signs! Only by twisting, perverting, and ignoring the context can one reach the conclusion that Matthew 24 is discussing *signs* that will occur at the end of the world. Sadly, many of today's television preachers are confused about the two different judgment types. They reach numerous conclusions, which they attribute to Christ's second coming; in reality, the teaching was addressing the destruction of Jerusalem.

### Christ's Second Coming

Christ's resurrection declared His deity with power (Rom. 1:4). He now sits at God's right hand, on David's throne, ruling and reigning over His kingdom (Acts 2:29-36). He has all power in heaven and on earth (Matt. 28:18).

Will He come again? Jesus promised, and the inspired writers assured us, He will (John 14:1-3; Acts 1:9-11; 1 Thess. 4:16, 17; Heb. 9:27, 28; Rev. 1:7; 22:20).

The Premillennialist allows his imagination to work overtime and run wild when it comes to what he believes and teaches concerning Christ's second coming. Below is a sampling of Premillennial teaching:

1. When the Lord returns the second time, the righteous dead will be raised to meet Him in the air. They refer to this as the *rapture*.
2. Then, there will be *tribulation* on the earth for a period of seven years.
3. During this period, there will be a great conflict—the battle of Armageddon—with Satan.
4. When the conflict ends, the earth will have been purged of evil, the nations conquered, and the Jews returned to Palestine. Supposedly, Jesus will then bring the righteous back to the earth, set up national

headquarters in Jerusalem, and literally reign on David's throne for 1000 years.

5. Then the end of time will come (this time, it's really the end). Christ will raise the rest of the dead, execute the general judgment, and direct the wicked and the righteous to Heaven or Hell.

The one great problem with this teaching is that it is unscriptural. It has no biblical foundation on which to stand. Let's examine the true Bible teaching concerning Christ's second coming.

**The Certainty of His coming.**

In Peter's day, the scoffers argued, "All things continue as they were before . . . where is the promise of His coming?" (2 Pet. 3:4). Peter told them they had willfully forgotten some things—for example, the fact that in an earlier age, God destroyed the world with water (Gen. 6-9). Peter went on to explain that time is not an issue with God (2 Pet. 3:8). He works on His timetable, not man's. Many passages, including 2 Peter 3:9, 10, plainly tell us He keeps His promises and will return as a "thief in the night." (Also see 1 Thess. 5:2.)

Other passages assure us that Jesus is coming back. Following are a few to consider:

- He said He would come back (John 14:1-4).
- At His ascension, the apostles were told that He will return in the same manner He left (Acts 1:9-11).
- We are told that God has appointed Him to return to judge the world (Acts 17:31).
- Every eye will behold Him (Rev. 1:7).
- He will come with His angels, in flaming fire (2 Thess. 1:7-9).
- He is coming back to be glorified with His saints (2 Thess. 1:10).

The time of His return is unknown to man, angels, or even the Lord Jesus Himself (Matt. 24:34-36; Mark 13:32). Men have rejected these plain statements of truth and set dates for His return. The Jehovah's Witnesses did so seven times and were wrong every time! Many claim that *signs* will be given before His return. The plain truth is that life will be proceeding routinely, just as it did in the days of Noah before the flood came. This is why the Bible emphasizes the need to be prepared.

What will be the manner of His coming? He will return the same way He left (Acts 1:9-11). He will come in person (1 Thess. 4:16, 17), and He will come in visible form (Rev. 1:7). He is coming in power and glory to redeem the saved (1 Cor. 15:50-53).

Christ is *not* coming back to . . .

- Establish His kingdom; that establishment has already occurred (Dan. 2:44, 45; Mark 1:15; 9:1; Acts 1:8; 2:1-4).
- Sit on David's throne; He already occupies that throne in heaven and is now ruling and reigning over His kingdom (2 Sam. 7:12-14; Acts 2:29-36; Eph. 1:19-23; 1 Cor. 15:25, 26).
- Restore Palestine to the Jews. God already fulfilled every land promise He made to Israel (Josh. 21:43-45; 23:14-16). And besides, for this to occur, other things would also need to be restored.

    —There would be a need to restore the Law of Moses; but that can't be, because it was nailed to the cross (Col. 2:14).

    —And restoring Israel to Palestine would necessitate restoration of the Levitical priesthood; it also was taken away at the cross.

How could Israel reoccupy its various tribal territories, since the genealogies and records were destroyed in A.D. 70? And can a Christian really believe in a return to temple worship and blood sacrifices? That's wrong because Christ's blood has now taken the place of those animal sacrifices. Remember, the Law of Moses was given to bring us to Christ and His once-forever sacrifice (Gal. 3:24, 25).

### Events That Will Occur at His Coming

Some important events that will take place at the Lord's coming are worth our attention. These include:

1. Preparation will end. When Jesus descends from heaven, the time for preparing and waiting will be over forever (Matt. 25:1-13; John 9:4).
2. The dead—righteous and unrighteous—will be raised (John 5:28, 29). When we carefully read John 6 and notice the phrase "*the last day*," we observe another conflict with Premillennial thought. If the Premillennial theory is correct, many days will still be left; but the term "*last day*" precludes such.

3. The final judgment of all men will take place before Christ (Matt. 25:31-46; 2 Cor. 5:10; Rom. 14:10-12; Rev. 20:11-15).

4. The world and its material elements will melt with fervent heat. With the earth destroyed, where would they set up an earthly kingdom (2 Pet. 3:10-12)?

5. The kingdom and all rule will be given back to the Father. Notice this point carefully. It does not say Jesus will set up a kingdom; rather, He will give one back to His Father! How do you give something to someone unless you first have it in your possession (1 Cor. 15:24-26)?

### Why Bring Christ Back to Earth?

Does the Premillennalist really understand God's eternal purpose in His Son? "To the intent that now the manifold wisdom of God might be made known by the church to the principalities and powers in the heavenly places, according to the eternal purpose which He accomplished in Christ Jesus our Lord, in whom we have boldness and access with confidence through faith in Him" (Eph. 3:10-12).

Allow me to suggest some things that the Father has already accomplished through Christ:

1. His mission of redemption is complete (Eph. 1:7-10).
2. His revelation is complete (2 Pet. 1:3; Jude 3).
3. He now has all authority in heaven and on earth (Matt. 28:18; Col. 1:16-20).
4. He is head of His church (Eph. 1:19-23).
5. The kingdom is complete and Christ is its king (Col. 1:13; Rev. 1:9).

What more could be accomplished by bringing Christ back to earth? By the way, no passage in the entire divine record says He will again step foot on the earth!

### Consequences of Premillennial Theories

Finally, let us look at some of the consequences if Premillennial doctrine is true. Please give careful and sober attention to these points; they are by far the strongest evidence that the Premillennial teaching came from men and not God.

**1. This teaching invalidates the prophecies of the Old Testament prophets.** What about Daniel's prophecies? Isaiah's? The promises made to David in 2 Samuel? It would mean that these men were false prophets and that the Bible contains errors. Couldn't we argue that the entire inspired record should be held in question?

**2. It limits God's power.** It implies that the creature is greater than the Creator. Premillennialists tell us that because the Jews rejected Christ, God had to come up with *Plan B*—the church age. Does God ever need a Plan B? Please read Isaiah 55:8-11; Jeremiah 10:23; Proverbs 14:12.

**3. It dethrones Christ.** The Bible clearly says that He is now ruling and reigning on David's throne in His kingdom (Dan. 7:13, 14; Acts 2:29-36). Why would God remove His Son from David's spiritual throne in heaven and place Him on an earthly throne in Jerusalem? He would be moving down (backward) a step.

**4. It demonstrates that some men are seeking an earthly kingdom.** This is the same mistake the Jews made when Christ came the first time. They were expecting the Messiah to establish an earthly kingdom and free them from Roman oppression. Jesus knew nothing of such a plan (John 18:36). The Jews were wrong then, and Premillennialists are wrong today.

**5. It means that Christ's glorious church is little more than a substitute.** Think about this seriously. Do you belong to an organization that came about because God's original plan failed? The church was in God's mind before the world began; it's part of His eternal plan (Matt. 16:18, 19; Acts 20:28; Eph. 3:10, 11). Did Christ die for a substitute?

**6. It leaves the New Testament writers appearing to be confused.** If the Lord's kingdom is yet to come, the inspired New Testament writers were confused concerning this truth. Paul said the Colossian Christians were translated into the kingdom of God's dear Son (Col. 1:13). During the first century, John thought he was part of that kingdom (Rev. 1:9). John also thought that Christ's sacrifice had redeemed men (Rev. 5:9, 10). How could these people be part of an institution that is yet to come?

**7. It annuls the dispensation the Bible refers to as the "last days."** Paul said that Christ is now (in the last days) God's spokesman (Heb. 1:1-3). When Peter preached the first sermon on the Day of Pentecost, he said men were living in the "last days" (Acts 2:16-21). We are now living in the last days. How can that be if there is going to be a future 1000-year reign of Christ on earth?

**8. It makes God a liar.** Jesus promised to build His church, the kingdom, and give its keys to the apostles (Matt. 16:18, 19). Jesus and John the Baptist both taught that the kingdom was near (Matt. 3:2; 4:17). Daniel said that in his inspired vision he saw the Lord stand before the "Ancient of Days" and receive a kingdom (Dan. 7:13, 14). Jesus said all things written about Him in the Law, the Prophets, and the Psalms must be fulfilled (Luke 24:44). God cannot lie (Hebrews 6:18). He always keeps his word!

**9. It interchanges Judaism and Christianity.** The Premillennial view interchanges the types and anti-types given in the Scriptures. The book of Hebrews contrasts the Old Testament with the New, and tells why the New is superior to the Old. Why would God resurrect an inferior system, which He has already replaced with a superior one? Such reasoning is pure foolishness.

**10. It revokes the Great Commission.** Before Jesus left the earth, He sent out the disciples with a message that would give men hope (Matt. 28:18-20; Mark 16:15, 16; Luke 24:44-47). Human reasoning and Premillennial doctrine have made Him a prospective king who has no authority, power, or kingdom. Why teach men to become part of the church, if it is nothing more than an afterthought?

**11. It presents Jesus' incarnation, crucifixion, and resurrection as a failed work and mission.** When Jesus was praying in the garden, He said He had finished the work His father sent Him to do (John 17:4-8). His main reason for coming to earth was to die to provide a remedy for man's sin problem. What did our Lord say just before His death on the cross? "So when Jesus had received the sour wine, He said, 'It is finished!' And bowing His head, He gave up His spirit" (John 19:30). If the Lord left unfinished work, He knew nothing about it.

### Concluding Thoughts

The doctrine of Premillennialism totally ignores and contradicts God's eternal purposes for Christ Jesus and His church. It would appear that God is more dependent on man than the other way around. What does this say about Christ's cross and crucifixion? It implies they were totally unnecessary and that all His pain, anguish, and suffering were unnecessary. How can anyone believe that the Lord died for a church that was nothing more than an afterthought in God's mind?

The serious Bible student could never accept this flawed thinking concerning God's kingdom. Only by taking passages out of context, and twisting and perverting them, can we arrive at such an unbelievable theory. God's kingdom was never intended to be a physical kingdom on earth—not in the days when Christ was here, or when He returns. Such reasoning makes the Bible a book of confusion and places God's power in question. I think I'll stick with Paul's words written long ago, under the Holy Spirit's inspiration— " . . . Certainly not! Indeed, let God be true but every man a liar" (Rom. 3:4).

Christians owe a debt of appreciation to those valiant preachers and elders who believed and taught the truth when the premillennial conflict blossomed in the early twentieth century. Many of those who led the battle were castigated by their peers as being mean-spirited and vicious. However, their stand for the truth focused attention on the correct interpretation of Bible prophecy and led brethren away from the dangers associated with unrestrained prophetic speculation common to such denominations as the Jehovah's Witnesses and Seventh Day Adventists. The truth that was learned in the crucible of controversy is a precious truth that brethren still appreciate to this day.

### Bibliography

Adams, Connie. *Premillennialism: True or False?* Bowling Green: Guardian of Truth Foundation Publications, 1985.

Numerous writers. *Apocalypticism Explained, The Book of Revelation.* Website WGBH 1995-2008.

Highers, Alan. "A Study of Premillennialism," *The Spiritual Sword*, Vol. 30 (January 1999), No.2.

McGarvey, J.W. *Commentary on Acts.*

Mosby, Ron. *A Biblical Response to the Doctrine of Premillennialism.* Louisville: Religious Supply Company, 2006.

Smith, J.T. *Premillennialism and the Rapture.* Louisville: Religious Supply Company, 2nd printing tract.

Wallace, William E. *No Millenium Ahead.* A Truth Tract. Bowling Green: Guardian of Truth Foundation.

Wallace, Foy, Jr. *God's Prophetic Word*, Foy E. Wallace Publications, 1946.

Wells, Wayne. *Study of Matthew*, godofmercy.com, 2005.

White, Michael. *Christian Millennial Expectation through the Centuries*, website, WGBH, 1995-2008.

# There Is One Body

**Justin Monts**

> There is one body and one Spirit, just as you were called in one hope of your calling; one Lord, one faith, one baptism; one God and Father of all, who is above all, and through all, and in you all (Eph. 4:4-6).

In Ephesians 4:4 we find four words that boil down to a single concept: *There is one body*. Few words have generated more controversy than these four words. Critics have long asserted that it is rather narrow-minded or egotistical to believe that there is just one body to the exclusion of other bodies. We are told that a man may be a bigot or acting like a Pharisee if he maintains there is just one body. Yet parallels to this truth are found throughout Scripture. God said to Noah, "Build me an ark of gopher wood"

---

**Justin Monts** was born in Sacramento, California on January 14, 1979 but was raised in Derby, Kansas, outside of Wichita. The Monts family moved to Issaquah, Washington in 1991. When Justin was sixteen years old he studied his way out of the institutional church of Christ and began worshipping with the Manitou Park church of Christ in Tacoma, Washington. It was here that he had his first experiences in preaching, speaking once or twice a month as part of a rotation of men. In 2004 he received his B.S. degree in Cellular and Molecular Biology at the University of Washington and shortly thereafter moved to Glasgow, Kentucky. Justin has also studied the biblical languages of Hebrew and Greek at Western Kentucky University. In November 2004 he began his first full-time work with the Peters Creek church of Christ where he has labored ever since. Justin has preached in the Philippines and India and most recently in Moldova (April 2009). He is very grateful to his mother, Elma, for her zeal and dedication to the Lord, her tireless efforts in teaching her children, and for her fine example of courage under the most difficult of circumstances. In addition, Justin has a wonderful brother Steven who currently preaches at the 31-W North church of Christ in Franklin, Kentucky and a precious sister Shannon who worships faithfully at the Manitou Park church of Christ in Tacoma with Elma. In light of these remarkable influences Justin is honored to say he is a most fortunate young man.

and that ark proved to be "for the saving of Noah and his household" (Gen. 6:14; Heb. 11:6). Undoubtedly, there would have been many boats in the days of Noah yet Noah had the only boat that would survive the world-wide flood. In Joshua 1 we read of the spies who entered Jericho. Rahab hid them and protected them and they promised that her house would be spared if she hung a red ribbon from the window. There were many houses in Jericho, potentially even many within the wall. But Rahab's house was the only house that would be spared when the wall crumbled and tumbled and the city was destroyed. Even so, there are many religious bodies today; many man-made denominations numbering in the thousands, but it is only the church of our Lord and Savior Jesus Christ that shall stand when this world is destroyed.

Members of the church of Christ are mocked and teased by others who say, "Do you really believe that only those in the church of Christ are going to heaven? That's ridiculous!" Let us be quick to point out that it is God's holy word that teaches plainly that only men and women who are part of the New Testament church shall be saved (Acts 2:47). And if our friends and loved ones are in churches that cannot be found in Scripture, we call upon them to have the honesty of heart to become members of the New Testament church. One might reply, "Where exactly do we read about the church of Christ?" The Bible tells us in Romans 16:16 that "the churches of Christ greet you" or "the churches of Christ salute you" (KJV). So yes there is book, chapter, and verse for the name church of Christ. But understand this much too, not every time you see the name church of Christ hung on the door or every time you see the title church of Christ on the front lawn would that indicate that that is a true church of Christ. We must look at what is taught. We must look at what is practiced at that particular group to find out if it is in fact the New Testament church.

### The Way

In John 14:6 we have this familiar and fundamental statement made by our Lord: "I am the way, the truth, and the life; no man comes to the Father except through me." Jesus did not say he was "a" way; he did not say he was "one of several ways." If Buddha had encountered the apostles he might have declared that he was merely "a" way. But Jesus said, "I am *the* way, *the* truth, and *the* life; *no one* comes to the Father but by me." Is that all-inclusive? Is it all-encompassing? Even a passing consideration reveals that it is rather narrow. Yet Jesus is *the* way, the *only* way.

Let's now consider a number of passages in the Book of Acts that demonstrate the oneness of the body and therefore its exclusive nature:

Saul of Tarsus, before he became a Christian, was seeking to destroy the disciples. The record tells us:

> Then Saul, still breathing threats and murder against the disciples of the Lord, went to the high priest and asked letters from him to the synagogues of Damascus, so that if he found any who were of *the Way* (emphasis mine, jnm), whether men or women, he might bring them bound to Jerusalem (Acts 9:1-2).

Christians belonged to *the* way – not a way.

In chapter 16 of the same book we find that Paul, Silas, and Luke are preaching in Philippi and the Bible tells us in verses 16-17,

> It happened, as we went to prayer, that a certain slave girl possessed with a spirit of divination met us, who brought her masters much profit by fortune-telling. This girl followed Paul and us, and cried out, saying, "These men are the servants of the Most High God, who proclaim to us *the way* of salvation."

There were many religious beliefs in Philippi; many that were given to mysticism and mythology and idolatry, but Paul, Silas, and Luke proclaimed *the way* of salvation. Even a demon, working through a little slave girl, confessed that.

In Acts 19 Paul is found at Ephesus. A great harvest of souls will eventually be reaped but observe verses 8-9:

> And he went into the synagogue and spoke boldly for three months, reasoning and persuading concerning the things of the kingdom of God. But when some were hardened and did not believe, but spoke evil of *the Way* before the multitude, he departed from them and withdrew the disciples, reasoning daily in the school of Tyrannus.

Christians were a distinct group that men either accepted or rejected but there was no middle ground. Christians belonged to *the* way.

In verses 23-28 of the same chapter we meet a man who became very difficult in the life of Paul.

> And about that time there arose a great commotion about *the Way*. For a certain man named Demetrius, a silversmith, who made silver shrines of Diana, brought no small profit to the craftsmen. He called them together with the workers of similar occupation, and said: "Men, you know that

> we have our prosperity by this trade. Moreover you see and hear that not only at Ephesus, but throughout almost all Asia, this Paul has persuaded and turned away many people, saying that they are not gods which are made with hands. So not only is this trade of ours in danger of falling into disrepute, but also the temple of the great goddess Diana may be despised and her magnificence destroyed, whom all Asia and the world worship." Now when they heard this, they were full of wrath and cried out, saying, "Great is Diana of the Ephesians!"

What message did the apostle Paul have? He said that idols and images do not represent real gods! There is one true and living God but there are no gods which are made with hands. That was rather exclusive, was it not? It's not as though he said that Jesus was just one of several great lights, and that the pagans may have some great lights too, and that all could just start an inter-faith movement. No. There was to be no compromise. Truth has always been controversial but the truth is the truth!

Truth is truth even if no one were to accept it! Paul said, "Let God be true and every man a liar" (Rom. 3:4). If a thousand preachers taught something different than what God's word reveals, those preachers are all wrong, every last one. If all in the world professed to believe the Bible and yet contradicted the Bible, they'd be wrong and the Bible would be right. Truth is truth even if hypothetically *no one* in this world would accept it.

**Church History**

What is interesting to me as I think about this topic is that, whereas today our society has an ecumenical mind set of compromise, a mind set that would say we don't want to hurt anybody's feelings and that everybody is okay, historically that has not always been the case. When you go back to the first century you find that men were dedicated to what they believed and defended what they believed. The apostle Paul was preaching *the* way, not *a* way but *the* way. And I think most would agree if we go back just a hundred years we would find, percentage wise, more who were concerned about being religiously right than in the present.

Even in the first great departures from the New Testament church in the formation of what is called the Roman Catholic Church and the subsequent Eastern Orthodox Church, we find men at least claiming to be religiously right. Let me explain. The word Catholic means "universal." So in the centuries following the first century we could conceivably hear a Roman Catholic declare, "I am a Catholic. I am a part of the *universal* church." But then an Orthodox man could also declare, "I am an Orthodox man" – *ortho* meaning right, and *dox* or *doxadzo* meaning praise or worship. So what he'd be saying is, "I'm a part of the right praise or *right worship* church." Individuals maintained by their adopted names that they were right and others wrong. Yet little discussion today ensues as to who accurately represents the New Testament church and few, unfortunately, seem to care.

Near the end of the Dark Ages (420-1000) the corruption in the Catholic Church reached an all-time high. In the 1450s the printing press was invented and papers were put out that exposed the error within Catholicism. During this period there was a great clamor among men to learn more about the Bible and to get back to the Bible. A number of reformers came onto the world scene – reformers with names that loom large like Martin Luther (1483-1546) or John Calvin (1509-1564). And yet while the reformers sought to purge Catholicism of her many moral and doctrinal impurities, the reformers fell short of getting back to the Bible entirely. Incidentally, as a consequence, more religious bodies were created.

King Henry VIII of England made a break from Roman Catholicism in 1534 and began what is known today as the Anglican or Episcopalian Church. In 1538 he commissioned a translation of the Bible into English. An element within the Church of England became vocal and dissatisfied with the Church of England, arguing that there were yet many practices within the church that smacked of Catholicism and were therefore unauthorized. They did not care for the relics, images, and idols found in cathedrals scattered throughout England, nor were they fond of the veneration of saints. They argued essentially that the church needed to rid itself completely of all vestiges of Catholicism for that would be necessary to get back to the one body of the New Testament! What happened? Their voices were not heard satisfactorily so some left for the New World – they became known as the Pilgrims. What I am illustrating by this is that men were making strides in the right direction during this period. Many sought to reform the Catholic Church with their creeds, but it eventually became widely recognized on a large scale that what was necessary was to restore the New Testament church. In order to restore the New Testament church human creeds would have to be abandoned. This phenomenon became known as the Restoration Movement.

### Abandoning Human Creeds

Human creeds are uninspired documents drawn up to define religious beliefs and practices. They have a long history going as far back as the fourth century in the Apostles' Creed (which is a misnomer for the apostles of Christ never produced such a creed). One of the most famous creeds is the Nicene Creed which affirmed the deity of Christ (A.D. 325). Human creeds can affirm some statements of truth but they are dangerous for they are unauthorized by the Bible and they establish a most perilous precedent and trend. They represent a division of loyalty. A group that endorses an uninspired confession of faith finds themselves bound to the tenets of that document. If even one tenet proves to be a contradiction of biblical truth, the group generally chooses to uphold their creed and all the while still insist that they believe the Bible.

Further, endorsing human creeds has led to the fragmentation of religiously-minded people. For when an element within a group takes issue with portions of the creed they may separate and draft another creed to characterize their beliefs. And, if years later, an element within that newly formed group objects to the new creed, they may also break away and compose a different creed altogether. The Bible is not the source of religious division but human creeds are!

What does the Bible say about this divided loyalty? In Matthew 15, Jesus chided the Pharisees for setting aside the word of God for their human tradition.

> Thus you have made the commandment of God of no effect by your tradition. Hypocrites! Well did Isaiah prophesy about you, saying: "These people draw near to me with their mouth, and honor me with their lips, but their heart is far from me. And in vain they worship me, teaching as doctrines the commandments of men" (Matt. 15:7-9).

By following their tradition over and above the word of God the Pharisees nullified the word of God and so stood condemned.

In 2 Timothy 3, the apostle Paul gave a succinct and concise statement about God's word; something that we need to take stock of: "All Scripture is given by inspiration of God, and is profitable for doctrine, for reproof, for correction, for instruction in righteousness, that the man of God may be complete, thoroughly equipped for every good work" (2 Tim. 3:16-17). Human creeds will not help us to become complete! The Bible is what makes us complete in God's sight. It will help us to be the man God wants us to be. And that's exactly what Paul was teaching Timothy. Scripture is inspired, not the writings of men, not the doctrines of men.

In 1 Corinthians 4:6, Paul wrote, "These things I have figuratively transferred to me and Apollos for your sakes that you may learn in us not to think of men above that which is written." In promoting and quoting human creeds individuals are thinking of men beyond what is written for human creeds often contradict the doctrines of our Lord.

### Creeds Contradict God's Word

As an example of creeds contradicting the Bible let us just consider the *Book of Common Prayer*. Perhaps you have heard of the *Book of Common Prayer*. I am not convinced that's the best title for this work for while it contains many liturgical prayers there are also many mandates that have to do with church doctrine. It is the official creed book for the Episcopalian Church. What does the *Book of Common Prayer* say about baptism? The *Book of Common Prayer* teaches that, when you are sprinkled as an infant or when you have water poured on you as an infant, that baptizes you into Christ even though you haven't yet believed in Jesus. What does the Bible say about baptism? When you examine the cases of those who were baptized (immersed) in the Bible, every last soul who was baptized was also an adult who believed. Take for instance the Ethiopian Eunuch in Acts chapter 8. He said, "See, here is water. What hinders me from being baptized?" What was Philip's reply? "If you *believe* (emphasis mine, jnm) with all your heart, you may" (Acts 8:36-37). The Eunuch had to believe before he was baptized. The Bible is consistent on that topic. Belief comes before baptism and baptism is not nor has it ever been sprinkling or pouring. It means immersion (Vine's *Expository Dictionary of New Testament Words*, 98). Yet what do human creeds do? Human creeds contradict the word of God.

In Proverbs 30:6, Agur the son of Jakeh tells us, "Do not add to his words, lest he rebuke you, and you be found a liar." This truth is so foundational that it is repeated at the very last chapter in the very last verses of the last book of the Bible. Revelation 22:18-19:

> For I testify to everyone who hears the words of the prophecy of this book: If anyone adds to these things, God will add to him the plagues that are written in this book; and if anyone takes away from the words of the book of this prophecy, God shall take away his part from the Book of Life, from the holy city, and from the things which are written in this book."

We dare not add to God's word. We have to be content with it for it is this word that shall judge us in the last day (John 12:48).

### John Mulkey and the Old Mulkey Meeting House

I had an opportunity to go to the Old Mulkey meeting house in Tompkinsville, Kentucky. The meeting house has actually become a state shrine

**Old Mulkey Meeting House in Tompkinsville, KY.**

and it can be located on any *Rand McNally Road Atlas*. If you have not had a chance to visit I would encourage you to do so. John Mulkey was the preacher for that congregation in the early 1800s. You may read about his story and the story of the congregation on the plaques at the site there. Mulkey began as a Baptist preacher laboring with a Baptist church but in the year 1809 he called upon the church to abandon human names, creeds, and doctrines. This was a group of about 200, very sizeable for the early 1800s. On November 17, 1809, fifty who were not happy with the prospect of breaking from the Baptist Association departed to start their own local Baptist church. The 150 who remained with Mulkey gave up denominationalism altogether and pursued the pure pattern of the New Testament. In the aftermath Mulkey made an announcement that has resonated with me ever since I first read it:

> Finally brethren our light will shine and the truth will prevail. Indeed, brethren, we have reason to rejoice that notwithstanding the floods of opposition and torrents of abuse that have poured forth from various quarters, yet truth is prevailing. Gospel light is shining. Error and sectarian bigotry are in many instances giving way; and the kingdom of the Redeemer is spreading.

What did he mean by saying we have "reason to rejoice" – especially when fifty in the congregation had just left? You see if we uphold the Bible in one hand and human creeds in the other hand we have divided loyalty and divided interests. We are defeated from the outset. Jesus said, "A house divided against itself cannot stand" (Matt. 12:25). And if, as mere men, we create a creed and then appeal to it as a source of authority for our souls, we cannot also claim that the Bible is the sole authority in matters of faith. In the Bible and in the Bible alone we have all things that pertain to life and godliness (2 Pet. 1:3)! Jude tells us in verse 3 of his book that the faith has "once for all been delivered to the saints." That faith was given in the first century and it has been sufficient for every century after the first century and it is sufficient for the 21st century. And when we follow this all-sufficient word of God the truth shall always prevail in our lives as well.

**Restoring New Testament Christianity and Locating God's People**

Let me here confess that I do believe personally that God has always had His people on this earth. They may have been very few, but I am convinced they have been here. Biblically speaking we know that God in times past has set aside a remnant. He did so with Noah. He did so with Jeremiah and Daniel. When Elijah thought he was the last faithful man on earth God revealed, "I have reserved seven thousand in Israel, all whose knees have not bowed to Baal, and every mouth that has not kissed him" (1 Kings 19:18). Paul alluded to this in Romans 11 saying,

> God has not cast away his people whom he foreknew. Or do you not know what the Scripture says of Elijah, how he pleads with God against Israel, saying, "Lord, they have killed your prophets and torn down your altars, and I alone am left, and they seek my life"? But what does the divine response say to him? "I have reserved for myself seven thousand men who have not bowed the knee to Baal." Even so then, at this present time there is a remnant according to the election of grace (Rom. 11:2-5).

And as I contemplate this topic I am reminded of something that happened not long ago. On November 10 and 11 of this past year I preached at the Ebenezer church of Christ in Tompkinsville. A fine man, Danny Shirley, typically preaches there but he also rotates out with his son, Jason. Meeting them has been one of the most encouraging experiences of my life. Danny had first come out to the Peters Creek church of Christ a few months prior to this when we had a gospel meeting with brother Jarrod Jacobs. He was impressed with the solid Bible-based teaching and so he came in future weeks. After hearing me preach a few times he approached me and asked if I'd be willing to do a meeting for them at Ebenezer. I had earlier asked folks at Peters Creek if they knew where the Ebenezer church of Christ was located and no one seemed to know for sure. So, naturally, there was a tendency to be unsure as to what the brethren there as a body believed or practiced. Thus, when I was approached about a meeting I said, "Well, let me first explain some of my beliefs to you and then you can decide if you'd still like to have me." I explained how I came out of a background of the social gospel – and I properly defined what that was. He listened carefully and at the end I told him, "I inform you of this so that you know there is a marked difference between a church like Peters Creek and a church like the Columbia Avenue church of Christ in town, which fully endorses the social gospel." In answer he said, "Well, on account of the things you talked about, that's why I don't go to Columbia Avenue either. And, I reckon that's why you meet here and the Dry Fork church of Christ is further down the road." I answered, "That is correct." He later revealed that one of the things that first impressed him about Peters Creek was how we did not have a so-called "fellowship hall," party room, or banquet room in our parking lot.

I knew I had met an outstanding man in Danny Shirley and the meeting was scheduled. Currently there are eleven members and six children at Ebenezer. I was honored to have been asked to preach for them and I have grown closer to Danny Shirley and his family since that time. I believe what I may have found at Ebenezer is something comparable to the "7000 who have not bowed the knee to Baal." How many other little groups like Ebenezer are out there, out in remote places? Elijah evidently did not know about the 7000, but God knew them. Little churches like Ebenezer or Peters Creek don't make the history books but that does not mean we have not been a part of history!

Yet what occurred in the 1800s in the Restoration Movement is something that happened on a large scale where men and women began to give up human creeds and go by just the Bible. There is no question that in America today such interest has fizzled and faded and all but been forgotten. My prayer is that one day we may see a revitalization of the restoration plea among men and that they will seek to speak where the Bible speaks and be silent where it is silent and to do Bible things in Bible ways and to call Bible things after Bible names (cf. 1 Pet. 4:11).

The Restoration Movement is an excellent model for us and all men. We must make sure that we're building all things according to the pattern no matter who we are or where we live in the world (Heb. 8:5). The Psalmist reveals: "Unless the Lord builds the house they labor in vain who build it" (Ps. 127:1). There is one body with one head – Jesus Christ (Eph. 1:22). Anything with no head is dead and anything with more than one head is a monstrosity. Equally so, anything with one head and many bodies does not live long or well. All in the biological realm illustrate that truth. All that we see in Scripture support that truth. Let us acknowledge the singular nature of the church: There is one body.

### Entrance into the One Body

So how do we get into this one body? Again, we shall not consult a human creed. There are some who would want to tell us, "Well, if you look over here at our creed book, this will tell you how to get into the body." No, let's go just to the Bible because the Bible is sufficient to answer that question. Let us define properly that the church is this body. In Ephesians 1:22-23 the apostle Paul said, "And he put all things under his feet, and gave him to be head over all things to the church, which is his body (singular, jnm), the fullness of him who fills all in all." In Colossians 1:18 Paul says of Jesus, "And he is the head of the body, the church, who is the beginning, the firstborn from the dead that in all things he may have the preeminence." And in Acts 2:47 we read the Lord added to the church daily those who were being saved. There is a mantra heard that "salvation is not found in the church, but only in Christ." Yet we read consistently that the church *is* the body of the *saved!* How can one get into Christ without getting into His body? The two go hand in hand.

Those in the first century heard the word (Acts 2:37), believed in Jesus (John 3:16), repented of sin (Acts 3:19), confessed Christ (Acts 8:36-39), and were immersed in water for the remission of sins (Acts 2:38). Baptism was effectively the doorway into the church. Why not seek to become a member of the Lord's church today and find the harmony and peace and assurance that comes with knowing that you are in the one body?

### Bibliography

The Holy Bible. All quotations from the NKJV unless otherwise noted.

*The Book of Common Prayer and Administration of the Sacraments and Other Rites and Ceremonies of the Church According to the Use of The Episcopal Church.*

Barker, W. P. *Who's Who in Church History*. Grand Rapids: Baker Book House, 1977.

Boles, H. L. *Biographical Sketches of Gospel Preachers*. Indianapolis: Faith and Facts Press.

Eerdmans, W. B. *Eerdmans' Handbook to the History of Christianity*. Grand Rapids: Lion Publishing, 1982.

Halley, H. H. *Halley's Bible Handbook*. Grand Rapids: Zondervan Publishing House, 2002.

Rogers, W. C. *Recollections of Men of Faith*. Indianapolis: Faith and Facts Press, 1994.

Vine, W. E. *Vine's Expository Dictionary of New Testament Words*. Peabody (MA): Hendrickson Publishers.

West, Earl. *The Search for the Ancient Order Vol. 1*. Delight (AR): Gospel Light Publishing Company, 2002.

# *Sola Scriptura* . . . The All-Sufficiency of Scripture

**John Gibson**

The expression, *sola Scriptura,* may appear strange to the person that has had little contact with the history of the Sixteenth Century Reformation Movement, but its importance is discovered in the fact that it became a foundational doctrine of that period and fueled a change from the Catholic position on scriptural authority. *Sola Scriptura* is a Latin expression (*sola* meaning "alone" and *scriptura* meaning "Scripture," thus "the Bible alone") that asserts that the Bible is self-authenticating, clear to the reader, its own interpreter, and sufficient of itself to be the only authority for the Christian. The basic meaning would, of course, eliminate creeds, councils, statements of faith, oral tradition, church tradition, church interpreter, and the need for a personal illumination of the Holy Spirit to discover God's will. The interesting aspect of this study is that as this truth surfaced in

---

**John A. Gibson** was born on September 21, 1950 in Cambridge, Ohio to Earl and Billie Gibson. John attended Kent State from 1969 to 1970 and in the spring of 1970 married his high school sweetheart, Linda Emslie. They honeymooned to Florida where John completed two and one-half years of study at Florida College. John began preaching while attending his last year at Florida College in Dunedin, Florida. From there he moved and preached for the church of Christ in Alliance, Ohio (1973-1974), the Platt Woods church of Christ in Kansas City, Missouri (1974-1976), the Geyer Road church of Christ in Kirkwood, Missouri (1976-1978), and the Cemetery Road church of Christ in Hilliard, Ohio (1978-1989). He is currently working with the Parkview church of Christ in West Lafayette, Ohio (1989 to present). He has done preaching work outside the country in Tula, Russia. John and Linda have three sons: Scott, Jonathan, and Jeremy. All three boys are married with families and work faithfully with the church in West Lafayette. They have provided John and Linda with five lovely grandchildren.

debate many rejected it outright while others accepted it in principle but denied it in application.

## The Reformation Period

Most historians agree that the Protestant Reformation period began in 1517 when Martin Luther (1483-1546) nailed his Ninety-Five Theses to the door of the Castle church in the university town of Wittenburg, Germany. Such a posting was common practice of the day and served as an invitation to debate. Luther, a Catholic priest, courageously questioned the corrupt practices of the Catholic Church, but wasn't the first to do so. John Wycliffe (1324-84) and John Huss (1369-1415) had blazed the trail before him in denouncing the specific areas of the sale of indulgences, pilgrimages, the excessive veneration of saints, and the moral and intellectual standards of ordained priests as corrupt. Corruption in the Catholic Church in the fourteenth and fifteenth centuries prompted these men to protest it practices. The corruption reached all the way to the papacy and surpassed anything that had gone before.

Luther's objections were simple and not all that controversial. He wanted religious teaching at the university where he taught to focus more on the Bible and less on the speculations of the canon lawyers and the scholastics. Even though it was the selling of indulgences by the church that brought his protests to a head, the underlying principle that fueled his protest was the belief that the Bible was the only true authority in religion (*sola scriptura*) in contrast to the pope or church council. His study led him to believe the teachings of the Catholic Church were not based on Scripture. His efforts turned to discovering once again the true essence of Christianity in its teaching that salvation is by grace through faith in Christ (*sola fide*), and not through a system of works as manifested in the Catholic system of sacraments. His protest also questioned the Catholic concept of the priesthood, believing the New Testament taught the priesthood of all believers.

Philip Schaff agrees and states in his history of the Christian Church that there were three fundamental principles of the Reformation period: "the supremacy of the Scriptures over tradition, the supremacy of the faith over works, and the supremacy of the Christian people over an exclusive priesthood" (Schaff, 16).

Prominent figures who followed Luther in his quest for reform were Ulrich Zwingli (1484-1531), a Swiss theologian and leader of early reforms in Switzerland; John Calvin (1509-1564), a French theologian and reformer who fled religious persecution in France and settled in Geneva in 1536; and John Knox (1513-72), an ardent follower of Calvin in the region of Scotland.

Obviously, many factors came together to produce the Protestant Reformation. The truth that surfaced from this period of controversy was: (1) the Bible is our sole source of authority and (2) each person has the right to study the Bible for himself and not be bound by someone else's interpretation of it. Yet the men who fought for this truth and those who followed them were flagrantly guilty of repudiating it in their practice of formulating human creeds. The very existence of human creeds restricts the right of private study to determine God's will. If the right of private study is not a right belonging to all, then Luther, Calvin, Zwingli and others likeminded were wrong in breaking away from the Catholic Church. If we do not have the right of private study, then these "protesters" simply changed masters. As the Catholics were bound by a Pope, Luther, Calvin, and others who followed them bound themselves with paper "Popes" called "Creeds."

### The Scriptures Are All-Sufficient

"All-sufficiency" is best defined when recognized as a compound word composed of two basic words: "all" and "sufficiency." "All" means "total, whole, complete, or without limitation." "Sufficiency" means "enough; equal to the end proposed; adequate to wants; as much as is needed" (*Webster's Online Dictionary*). To refer to the Scriptures as "all-sufficient" is to say that they are complete enough to accomplish the end for which they were designed by the God who gave them. That design is expressed by Paul's statement to Timothy concerning the inspiration of the Scriptures, "All Scripture is inspired by God and profitable for teaching, for reproof, for correction, for training in righteousness; that the man of God may be adequate, equipped for every good work" (2 Tim. 3:16, 17). "All-sufficiency" is actually a "double affirmative," which is an attempt to stress the adequacy, efficiency, and competency of the Bible.

As we will see shortly, many have denied the all-sufficiency of the Scriptures and in doing so have denied God's power and will. If we believe that God has the power to create the world and the universe out of nothing, can we not believe that God has the power to prepare His revelation so the common man can understand? To deny that is to deny that God is God! He has supplied us completely "for every good work" (2 Tim. 3:17), by His "all-sufficient Scriptures." James W. Adams wrote,

> It should be obvious to them that to deny, either theoretically or practically,

> the all-sufficiency of the Scriptures is tantamount to affirming that God was not wise enough to produce a revelation of Himself and His will that would complement man's nature, capacity, spiritual and fleshly needs in his present, earthly environment, and his eternal destiny in the world to come. On the other hand, if it be acknowledged that God was wise enough to produce such a revelation, we may conclude that He did not possess the power to do so. If it be admitted that He had the power to do so, but did not, we are forced to conclude that He did not will to do so. This would impeach His benevolence – His goodness. It is almost universally agreed among believers that man is a responsible and accountable being who will one day answer to God in judgment for "the deeds done in the body" (2 Cor. 5:10; Rom. 14:12). Hence, to repudiate the all-sufficiency of the Scriptures would be to impugn the justice of God. Under a system of justice, responsibility and accountability emanate from and their extent is determined by a universally available, intellectually intelligible, and totally inclusive standard of human conduct. Therefore, it is with supreme confidence that we affirm the all-sufficiency of the Scriptures with reference to the conviction and conversion of the alien sinner and the sanctification, and eternal salvation of the child of God (Adams, 323).

### Positions on the All-Sufficiency of Scripture

The Roman Catholic Church has historically claimed that it is the one true church and, therefore, the ultimate authority in all religious matters, even in the area of Scripture. It claims infallibility and the ultimate judge of the meaning of Scripture and tradition. This places it above correction and judgment and above Scripture. Therefore the Catholic position is that God's will to man comes from not only Scripture but Tradition, with the Church being the ultimate authority as the infallible interpreter of both. Therefore, the Roman Catholic position rejects the truth of *sola Scriptura.*

The Roman Catholic view of Scripture is a two source position: Tradition and Scripture being interpreted by the infallible Catholic Church (see chart on next page).

The chart illustrates that Christ gave the "Faith" to the Apostles, having promised that the Holy Spirit would come and "guide them into all truth" (John 16:13). The Roman Catholic position is that the Faith is then transmitted by two sources, by written tradition (Scripture) and unwritten tradition. The Roman church believes that it alone can infallibly interpret Scripture and tradition. It equates both with the same authority. This is based upon their belief that the Holy Spirit protects them from error, thus making them the ultimate and final authority for the Christian. This view is often referred to

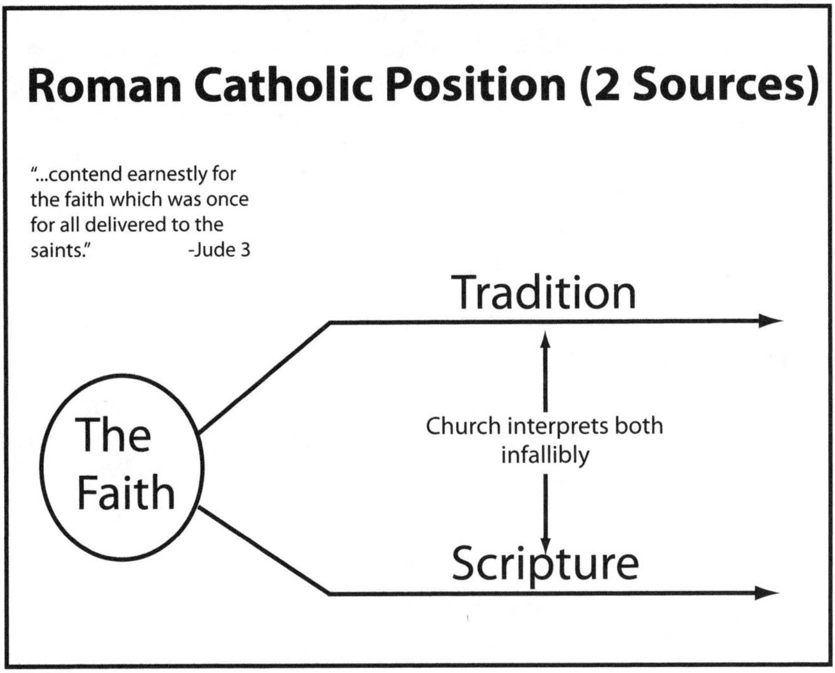


as *sola ecclesia* (the church alone). The Roman Catholic Church declaring herself to be infallible, in effect, becomes a law unto herself, able to say and do anything under the guise of being directed by God. An example of this is Catholic theologian Silvester Prieras' 1519 response to Martin Luther,

> . . . the Church means the Church of Rome, headed by the pope, who is infallible and thus more authoritative than councils and even the Holy Scriptures themselves. There is no authority higher than the pope; and he cannot be deposed, even if he were to give so much offense as to cause people in multitudes . . . to go to the Devil in Hell (Mathison, 94).

Tradition interpreted by the Church has become the guiding force for Catholics. Scripture must be made to fit the long established Tradition. This is seen in a statement made by Father John Whiteford,

> The Holy Scriptures are the summit of the Tradition of the Church. But the greatness of the heights to which the Scriptures ascend is due to the great mountain upon which it rests. Taken from its context within Holy Tradition, the solid rock of Scripture becomes a mere ball of clay, to be molded into whatever shape its handlers wish (Whiteford, 45).

From the Council of Trent (1564) to the latter part of the eighteenth century, it was the unanimous view of the Roman Catholic Church that Scripture did not contain the totality of revelation but needed to be supplemented by Tradition. But if Tradition is a reliable source of revelation from God and is properly interpreted by the Church would it not agree with the Scriptures? It is not difficult to see that Tradition actually contradicts the Bible.

- The Bible teaches that the office of bishop and presbyter are the same office (Tit. 1:5-7), but Tradition says they are different offices.
- The Bible teaches that all have sinned except Jesus (Rom. 3:10-12; Heb. 4:15), but Tradition says that Mary was sinless.
- The Bible teaches that Christ offered His sacrifice once for all (Heb. 7:27; 9:28; 10:10), but Tradition says that the priest sacrifices Christ on the altar at mass.
- The Bible says that we are not to bow down to statues (Exod. 20:4, 5), but Tradition says that we should bow down to statues.
- The Bible says that all Christians are saints and priests (Eph. 1:1; 1 Pet. 2:9), but Tradition says that saints and priests are special caste within the Christian community.
- The Bible says that Jesus is the only Mediator between God and man (1 Tim. 2:5), but Tradition says Mary is co-mediator with Christ.
- The Bible says that all Christians should know that they have eternal life (1 John 5:13), but Tradition says that all Christians cannot know that they have eternal life.

This next view represents the typical Protestant position on Scripture (see chart on next page).

It is obvious that the Catholic Church views the Scriptures as subordinate to Tradition and the word of the Church. Plain and simple, it denies the doctrine of *sola Scriptura*. But the Protestant position is equally a denial of *sola Scriptura*, although they refuse admit to this. Remember, *sola Scriptura* simply means "the Bible alone." They protest and say they hold to the true meaning of the Reformation doctrine: that the Bible is their only rule of faith and practice, to the exclusion of all canons, decretals, traditions, and philosophies.

The following are examples of creedal statements supporting *sola Scriptura:*

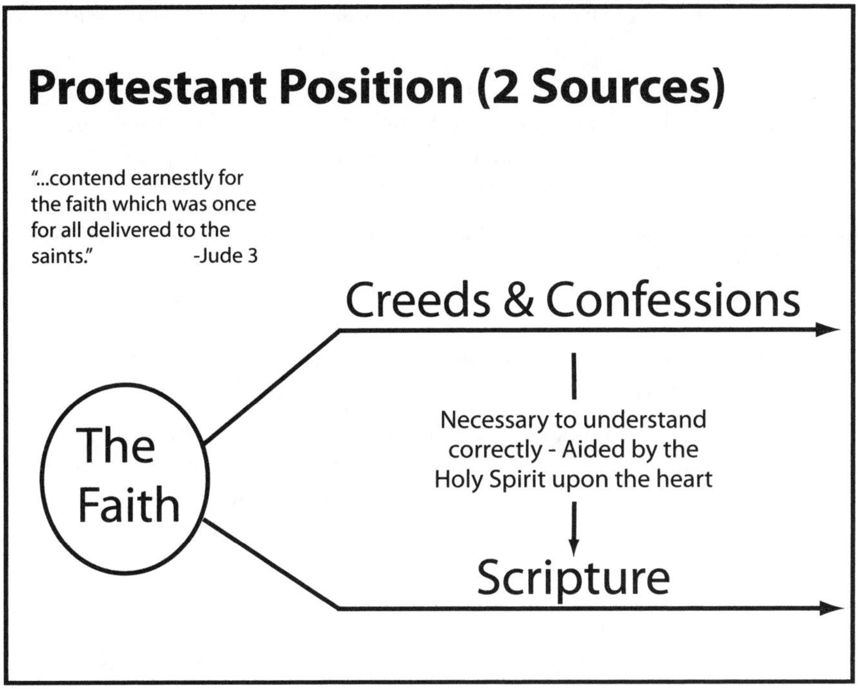


> The Holy Scriptures contain all things necessary to salvation; so that whatsoever is not read therein, nor may be proved thereby, is not to be required of any man that it should be believed as an article of faith, or be taught requisite or necessary to salvation (*Methodist Discipline*, 56).

> The whole counsel of God, concerning all things necessary for his own glory, man's salvation, faith, and life, is either expressly set down in Scripture, or by good and necessary consequence may be deduced from Scripture: unto which nothing at any time is to be added, whether by new revelation of the Spirit, or traditions of men (*Presbyterian Confession of Faith*, 28).

> We believe that the Holy Bible was written by men divinely inspired, and is a perfect treasure of heavenly instructions; that it has God for its author, salvation for its end, and truth without any mixture of error for its matter; that it reveals the principles by which God will judge us; and therefore is, and shall remain to the end of the world (*Baptist Manual*, 173).

No doubt, most all could agree with the above statements from these three church manuals. Yet with a little searching, it becomes obvious that what is said in these statements is denied by the rest of their creeds. The following are just a few examples of what these creeds continue to say that is obviously opposed to their claim that nothing should be added to Scripture.

> Original sin is the corruption of the nature of every man, that naturally is engendered of the offspring of Adam, whereby man is very far gone from original righteousness, and of his own nature inclined to evil, and that continually (*Methodist Discipline*, 57).

> They (our first parents) being the root of all mankind, the guilt of this sin was imputed, and the same death in sin and corrupted nature conveyed to all their posterity, descending from them by ordinary generation. From this original corruption, whereby we are utterly indisposed, disabled, and made opposite to all good, and wholly inclined to all evil, do proceed all actual transgressions (*Presbyterian Confession of Faith*, 49).

> All those whom God hath predestinated unto life, and those only, he is pleased, in his appointed and accepted time, effectually to call, by his word and Spirit, out of that state of sin and death in which they are by nature, to grace and salvation by Jesus Christ: enlightening their minds, spiritually and savingly, to understand the things of God, taking away their heart of stone, and giving unto them an heart of flesh; renewing their wills, and by his almighty power determining them to that which is good; an effectually drawing them to Jesus Christ; yet so as they come most freely, being made willing by his grace (*Presbyterian Confession of Faith*, 71-72).

> There are two Sacraments ordained of Christ our Lord in the Gospel; that is to say, Baptism and the Supper of the Lord. Sacraments ordained of Christ are not only badges or tokens of Christian men's professions, but rather they are certain signs of grace, and God's good will toward us, by which he doth work invisibly in us, and doth not only quicken, but also strengthen and confirm, our faith in him (*Methodist Discipline*, 59).

> Dipping of the person into the water is not necessary; but baptism is rightly administered by pouring or sprinkling water upon the person. Not only those that do actually profess faith in and obedience unto Christ, but also the infants of one or both believing parents are to be baptized (*Presbyterian Confession of Faith*, 129-130).

If it is found that these creeds contain more than the Bible (which we have just shown), they contain too much; if it is found that they contain less than the Bible, they do not contain enough; if it is found that they contain the same thing as the Bible, then they are unnecessary. The conclusion one must reach based on what we have just seen is that either the Protestant principles of the Reformation must be eliminated or the creeds eliminated. But I don't suppose we can expect creeds to be eliminated any sooner than the Catholics eliminating their pope.

Oblivious to this reasoning, most Protestants continue to believe that there is a genuine need for creeds and confessions of faith while holding theoretically to the doctrine of *sola Scriptura.*

The following is a quote form Dr. C. Matthew McMahon which fairly presents the traditional Protestant view of *sola Scriptura.*

> It is unfortunate that a false view of *Sola Scriptura* today is aiding the modern church in further schism, rather than unifying the church. *Sola Scriptura* should not be used as a "me and my bible" hermeneutic which allows "each individual Christian" to maintain their own theological view on a given doctrine. That is not what the Reformers intended, and it is not what the doctrine of *Sola Scriptura* teaches. If you believe that *Sola Scriptura* means "each individual Christian should, on an individual level, use the Bible alone in understanding and determining the corpus of biblical truth" you have completely missed the idea and point of the doctrine itself (McMahon, 1).

The "false view of *sola Scriptura*" that McMahon refers to is that the Bible is understandable to any and all individual(s) unaided by creeds or church statements. He believes that one cannot understand (interpret) Scripture in a "historical vacuum," apart from traditions past and present. To do so would bring error that would further add to the division in the religious world.

"Tradition" becomes a tricky word for McMahon and others like him. Understandably, tradition is a New Testament word. The apostle Paul told the Corinthian church to "hold firmly to the traditions, just as I delivered them to you" (1 Cor. 11:2; also 2 Thess. 2:15; 3:6). The word "tradition" here comes from the Greek word *paradosis*, which refers to that which is handed down or passed on. What is handed down or passed on is what was revealed by Jesus and written down by the apostles and prophets through the work of the Holy Spirit. But for McMahon "tradition" is not what is passed down or revealed by Jesus but a "statement," "creed," or "confession" that is framed by the church as to what is to be believed. Note another of McMahon's statements.

> The Christian Church, as a divine institution, takes the Word of God alone, and the whole Word of God, as her *only* rule of faith. However, she must also frame a statement of what she understands the Word of God to *teach*. This she does, not as arrogating any authority to suppress, change, or amend anything that God's Word teaches, but in discharge of the various duties which she owes to God, to the world, and those of her own com-

> munion. So a Confession of Faith is *not* the very voice of divine truth, but the *echo* of that voice from souls that have heard its utterance, felt its power, and are answering to its call. And, since she has been instituted for the purpose of teaching God's truth to an erring world, her duty to the world requires that she should leave it in no doubt respecting the manner in which she understands the message that she has to deliver. Without doing so, the Church would be no teacher, and the world might remain untaught, so far as she was concerned (McMahon, 3).

McMahon continues.

> The Church must discharge and produce a form of sounds words, in order both to promote and confirm their knowledge, and also to guard them against the hazard of being led into errors. . . . This is the *regula fidei* of the church. It is the basic summary of the orthodox position of the Bible. The formation of a Creed, or Confession of Faith, is imperatively necessary, and thus it appears that a Church *cannot* adequately discharge its duty to God, to the world, and to its own members, without a *Confession of Faith* (McMahon, 4).

The conclusion one gets from this position is that no one will come to understand God's Word without the church expressing it in the form of a creed or confession of faith. To use McMahon's words, "this is the *regula fidei* of the church." *Regula fidei* or "rule of faith" was first used by Irenaeus (130-300) as he confronted the Gnostic heresies of his day. It consisted of a summary of the faith taught by the Apostles to counter the secret unwritten tradition of the Gnostics. This may have seemed innocent to begin with and appropriate in light of the Gnostic influence, but it gave way for Councils and creeds to be developed. Keith Mathison tries his best to give creeds an acceptable basis by erroneously linking them with the faith taught by the Apostles.

> The patristic (early Christian theologians, jag) attitude toward the authority of the Councils, the creeds, and their predecessors also plays into this debate. The discussion of Irenaeus and Tertullian illustrated the importance of the *regula fidei* in the early decades of the Church's history. It is interesting to note the gradual way in which the earliest creeds built upon the rule of faith (Mathison, 45).

Though the Scriptures were to be accepted alone, Protestants have instead looked to the Church and its interpretation of Scripture through various Council decisions and creeds. Mathison believes that no one can be trusted to find truth by taking the Bible alone.

> The Scripture was to be interpreted by the Church and in the Church within

> the context of the *regula fidei*. If it was taken out of its apostolic context, it would inevitably be mishandled. Yet neither the church nor the *regula fidei* were considered second sources of revelation or equal authorities on par with Scripture. The Church was the interpreter and guardian of the Word of God, and the *regula fidei* was a summary of the apostolic preaching and the hermeneutical context of the Word of God. But only the Scripture *was* the Word of God (Mathison, 48).

Berkeley Mickelsen in his book, *Interpreting The Bible*, "pulls back the curtain" and reveals how and why creeds among the Protestants came into existence.

> From the death of Calvin (1564) to the end of the sixteenth century, we see the beginning of creed and system making. The Council of Trent, which was in session off and on between 1545 and 1563, drew up a list of degrees and canons anathematizing the Protestants. With such an extensive production, the Protestants began to reply in kind. New writings were geared to attract all who were dissatisfied with the church of Rome. The Council of Trent clarified the extent and nature of the reforms the Roman Catholic Church would accept. As a result Protestants in the last part of the sixteenth century prepared a great quantity of literature consolidating their biblical data. This literature continued into the seventeenth and eighteenth centuries. We must remember, however, that these theological statements forged in the heat of controversy often lacked the balance that comes from comprehensive exegetical study based on a dispassionate study of the Scriptures (Mickelsen, 41).

Keith Mathison and Protestants like him loudly proclaim that they hold to the doctrine of *sola Scritpura* but at the same time argue endlessly that creeds and confessions are necessary for the Church. Their double talk reveals their allegiance to their creeds and confessions rather than the Holy Scriptures. They refuse to admit as Mickelsen has in the above quote that their creeds were "forged in the heat of controversy" and are nothing more than a human response to Catholic writings, unnecessary and dangerous. Yet so many try and fail. For example, Dr. Samuel Miller goes to great lengths to prove that creeds and confessions are of vital importance. The following are the seven arguments he makes in defense of them. His attempt is futile.

> 1. Without a creed explicitly adopted, it is not easy to see how ministers and members of any particular church, and more especially a large denomination of Christians, can maintain unity among themselves.
>
> 2. The necessity and importance of creeds and confessions appear from the consideration that one great design of establishing a church in our

> world was that she might be, in all ages, a depository, a guardian, and a witness of the truth.
>
> 3. The adoption and publication of a creed is a tribute to truth and candor, which every Christian church owes to the other churches, and to the world around her.
>
> 4. Another argument in favor of creeds, publicly adopted and maintained, is that they are friendly to the study of Christian doctrine, and, of course, to the prevalence of Christian knowledge.
>
> 5. It is an argument of no small weight, in favor of creeds, that the experience of all ages has found them indispensably necessary.
>
> 6. A further argument in favor of creeds and Confessions may be drawn from the remarkable fact that their most zealous opposers have generally been latitudinarians and heretics.
>
> 7. The only further argument in support of creeds on which I shall dwell is that their most zealous opposers do themselves virtually employ them in all ecclesiastical proceedings (Miller, 2-10).

It's obvious that these seven arguments say simply, "The Bible is not enough; it cannot be understood alone!" The claim is made that the Bible alone can't bring about unity; can't be set alone before the world by the Church as truth; that the Church doesn't owe the world just the Bible; and that the faithful can't be content with just the Bible. Who, among God's faithful, can believe this?

So we have seen that Protestants have brought a challenge to the teaching of the Catholic Church by insisting that Scripture is the ultimate authority for the Church. But at the same time they inconsistently uphold the authority of creeds and councils and then turn right around and say they must be subordinated and held accountable to Scripture. How can any sane person argue this way and be taken serious? In reality, they place their creeds and councils right along side of Scripture as being authoritative. Thus, as the above chart shows, Protestant denominations adhere to two sources of authority. Their position requires Scripture to be interpreted according to the accepted creeds and councils of the early church.

But one obvious objection remained. Fallible men were writing these creeds. How could they be trusted to guide the church? The Scriptures were inspired by the Holy Spirit, a truth that all accepted. To trust the creeds then required that they too be inspired by the Holy Spirit. This became a necessary conclusion whether it could be supported biblically or not.

Therefore, most Protestant churches believe the Bible cannot be understood without the direct illumination of the Holy Spirit to guide the individual to the correct interpretation. Yet, like the Catholic Church, they also believe the Holy Spirit guides the corporate church to a correct understanding of truth. All these churches heavily endorse the use of creeds, both historic and modern which they believe to be "functionally equivalent" to Scripture. Some say their creeds are revelations of the Holy Spirit, while others would deny this; yet all believe creeds are an acid test of orthodoxy. These churches claim to use the Bible only, yet in practice do not since creeds are faithfully upheld.

Mathison explains the place the Holy Spirit plays in bringing forth reliable creeds. He says the Holy Spirit is the ultimate criterion of truth, but bears witness through this reciprocal relationship between Christian Scripture, the Christian Church, and the Christian Creed. Each of these three relates to the other two in a unique way. The Scripture is the Spirit-inspired Word of God that bears witness to the truth of the *regula fidei* and bears witness to the identity of the church, Notice these two quotes,

> It is only within the Church that we find Scripture interpreted rightly, and it is only within the Church that we find the gospel (Mathison, 268).

> The ecumenical creeds represent the hermeneutical consensus already reached by the Church. They declare the basic essential truths which have been confessed by all Christians from the first days of the Church until today. They represent that which the entire Church has seen in Scripture. . . . if the Holy Spirit has been promised to guide the Church into the knowledge of the truth of Scripture; if the entire Church for thousands of years confesses to being taught by the Spirit the same essential truths in Scripture, then it follows that those truths are what Scripture says (Mathison, 267).

This last chart (next page) expresses the true meaning of the Scriptures being all–sufficient (*sola Scriptura*).

This position says that Scripture is the sole basis and authority in the life of the Christian. Man-made tradition is useless and misleading and creeds and confessions are the result of man's attempts to clarify and ultimately supplant God's word.

The Bible claims to be an all-sufficient book. Not only does the Bible claim inspiration for itself, it also declares that it is all-sufficient. The recognition and acceptance of the Scriptures as authoritative in the realm of

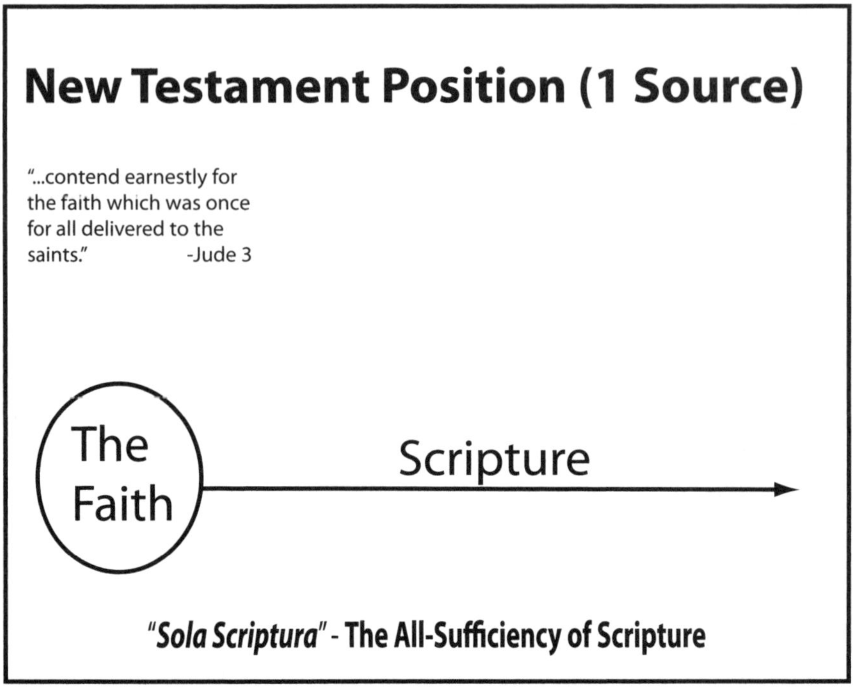


religious faith and practice demand an acceptance of their "all-sufficiency." Being divinely revealed and verbally inspired by the Holy Spirit, the Scriptures represent themselves as being infallible, imperishable, and authoritative. The New Testament Scriptures themselves are an inerrant and complete record of the words of Christ, either spoken in His own person while on earth or through His Holy Spirit inspired apostles and prophets after He ascended to His throne in heaven. They likewise represent themselves as being the standard of eternal judgment.

### Jesus Affirmed the All-Sufficiency of Scripture

Jesus affirmed that the Scriptures are all-sufficient and understandable by all when he spoke to the young lawyer in Luke 10:25-37. After being tested with the question, "What shall I do to inherit eternal life?" Jesus responded with His own question for this lawyer, "What is written in the Law? How does it read to you?" This lawyer didn't need to inquire of the latest consensus or the best interpretation of the chief priests or scribes; there were no "creeds" to turn to for the proper understanding. He knew how to respond because the law which he had studied was understandable. Jesus' response is indicative of three important truths about Scripture. (1) One can find in Scripture the answer to life's questions, such as, "What must I do to inherit eternal life?" (2) Every man is responsible for reading for himself. (3) The Scriptures give the same answer to all who faithfully read them. Jesus' response destroys the argument for creeds and councils.

### The Apostles Affirmed the All-Sufficiency of Scripture

These passages from Paul and Peter speak clearly to the all-sufficiency of Scripture. "All Scripture is inspired by God and profitable for teaching, for reproof, for correction, for training in righteousness; that the man of God may be adequate, equipped for every good work" (2 Tim. 3:16, 17). "That by revelation there was made known to me the mystery, as I wrote before in brief. And by referring to this, when you read you can understand my insight into the mystery of Christ, which in other generations was not made known to the sons of men, as it has now been revealed to His holy apostles and prophets in the Spirit" (Eph. 3:3-5). "For we write nothing else to you than what you read and understand, and I hope you will understand until the end" (2 Cor. 1:13). ". . . and that from childhood you have known the sacred writings which are able to give you the wisdom that leads to salvation through faith which is in Christ Jesus" (2 Tim. 3:15). "Grace and peace be multiplied to you in the knowledge of God and of Jesus our Lord; seeing that His divine power has granted to us everything pertaining to life and godliness, through the true knowledge of Him who called us by His own glory and excellence" (2 Pet. 1:2, 3). The Scriptures, inspired by the Holy Spirit, are understandable by every man on the planet in the same way a common newspaper is. No human creed or interpretation from a council of fallible men is necessary to understand God's will from the Scriptures. The gospel as God gave it is perfectly adapted to man as God made him and totally adequate for the accomplishment of the purposes for which God gave it, therefore "all-sufficient."

### Example of the Bereans

Consider the story of Paul in Berea (Acts 17:10-12). Paul preached there in the synagogue and many Jews responded to his preaching with eagerness. We are told that, after they listened to Paul each day, they examined the Scriptures to see if what Paul said was true. How did Paul react? Did he say that the Scriptures were not clear and that only he as an apostle or the rabbis or the Sanhedrin could tell them what the Scriptures really meant? Or did he say that they should not expect to find the truth in the Scriptures because they were incomplete and needed to be supplemented by tradition? Or did he say that they were insulting his apostolic authority and that they should simply submit to him as the infallible interpreter of the Bible? Or did Paul say that they should defer to Peter as the only one who could interpret the Bible? No! He did not say any of these things. The practice of the Bereans is praised in the Bible. They are called "noble" because they evaluated everything on the basis of the written Word of God. If we are to be faithful children of God, we must proceed as the Bereans did.

**The Restoration Period**

The influence and corruption of Catholicism and denominationalism seemingly had free reign until shortly after the turn of the nineteenth century. Various men were at work in religious circles in America to bring about not another reform but a restoration of the New Testament principle of the Bible and the Bible alone. Among the Methodists there was James O'Kelley; among the Baptists, Abner Jones and Elias Smith; among the Presbyterians, Barton W. Stone; and among the Baptists there was Alexander Campbell. These men became increasingly discontent with the religious denomination that they were a part of and sought for New Testament authority with new groups that called for a "thus saith the Lord." There was a similar call for Bible authority and a realization that the Bible was all-sufficient.

How did the "Protestant Reformation" differ from the "Restoration Movement"? James R. Cope explains it best as follows:

> The difference between policy and principle may properly be considered the basic difference between the "Protestant Reformation" begun in the Sixteenth Century and the "Restoration Movement" of the Nineteenth Century. The word policy often conveys the idea of human wisdom, sagacity or shrewdness in the management of affairs. Whereas the word principle, derives from the Latin *princeps, principis* whence come the English word, "prince," meaning "first" or "chief"; hence, "a fundamental truth; a primary or basic law, doctrine, or the like." Policy may change when in fact principle is "a settled rule of action; a governing law of conduct" (Webster). Compromise is a way of life with persons who consider truth and right as policies. With men of principle, truth and right are never negotiable! (Cope, 1).

James O'Kelley, as early as 1775, began hearing sermons that spoke of the all-sufficiency of the Bible. Earl West in his first volume of *The Search for the Ancient Order* gives this quote,

> They (certain ministers) came to us under the direction of John Wesley, whose name to me is of precious memory. His writings magnified the Bible, and gave it preference and honor; he declared he regarded the

> authority of no writings but the inspired. He urged the sufficiency of the Scriptures for faith and practice, saying, "We will be downright Christians" (West, 7, 8).

Another example is that of Barton W. Stone. As a Presbyterian preacher, Stone along with four others like him voiced their objections to manmade creeds, particularly the *Westminster Confession of Faith*, and made their break with the Presbyterian Church in 1803. When they withdrew, they set up a Presbytery of their own called the Springfield Presbytery. They made known to all churches their total abandonment of all authoritative creeds except the Bible. They soon dissolved this Presbytery seeing it as a "party spirit" and issued in 1804 "The Last Will and Testament of The Springfield Presbytery."

> The Last Will and Testament contains less than eight hundred words, but it is one of the classical documents coming out of the restoration movement. It showed the sincerity and honesty which characterized Stone in wanting to give up everything of human origin in religion and take only the Bible. Once having planted their faith upon the Word of God they found themselves led farther and farther from human elements in religion (West, 25).

One of the most famous meetings of the restoration period according to West was held at the house of Abraham Altars between Mt. Pleasant and Washington, Pennsylvania. At this famous meeting, the speech that Thomas Campbell gave ended with the famous motto: "Where the Bible speaks; we speak; where the Bible is silent, we are silent." Even though this motto was not new, Campbell and others applied it to Protestant creeds and confessions of faith denouncing their existence (West, 47).

### The Meaning of *Sola Scriptura* is Lost to Many Yet Today

The Christian Church and the Disciples of Christ who claim the Restoration Movement as their "roots" have repudiated the all-sufficiency of the Scriptures by committing themselves to the principle that the "silence of the Scriptures" authorizes such things as instrumental music in worship, church supported missionary societies, recreational activities, celebration of unauthorized holy days, and a host of other things.

Our "liberal-minded" brethren among the churches of Christ insist on the all-sufficiency of the Scriptures, but their actions speak louder than words. They denounce the all-sufficiency of the Scriptures when they pervert the work of the church by involving the church in the social gospel that manifests itself in church supported colleges, hospitals, and homes for unwed mothers, the aged, and orphans. They continue their denial by involving the church in recreational activities that require gymnasiums and "fellowship halls." The organization of the church is distorted when they funnel funds of multiple churches to one centralized body in the sponsoring church arrangement. When the authority of the Scriptures is no longer appealed to for the authority to act, the floodgates are thrown open to all forms of apostasy. The transformation, though subtle, is taking place where soon many will look like mainstream Protestant churches.

If *sola Scriptura* really means "Bible alone" and men preach and teach this, why is there so much division among Bible believers? The Catholics believe it's because the doctrine of *sola Scripture* is flawed and cannot be supported. Protestants claim that division exists because not all adhere to the "rule of faith" of the early Christian writers. But division comes when God's Word is abandoned for man's wisdom. Among our own brethren, we see this has occurred for the following reasons: (1) In years gone by, many young preachers have been trained by teachers who have received their training in modernistic seminaries where the Bible no longer is considered all-sufficient. (2) The churches where they preach are largely composed of second and third generation Christians who have had little to no study of New Testament authority. They know nothing of or openly repudiate direct commands, approved apostolic examples, necessary inferences, general and specific authority, and the silence of the Scriptures as "patternism" that no longer applies to them. (3) Biblical authority is replaced with an appeal to denominational practices that "shout" success.

Our only hope is to return to the true meaning of *sola Scriptura*. Let us take our Bibles, study them diligently, and "contend for the faith which has once for all been delivered."

## Bibliography

Adams, James W. "The All-Sufficiency of the Scriptures." *Guardian of Truth* XXX: 11 (June 5, 1986), 323-325.

*Baptist Manual, The Hiscox Standard.* Valley Forge: Judson Press, 1965.

Brumback, Robert H. *History of the Church Through the Ages.* Lufkin: Select Books, 1957.

Cope, James R. "The Restoration Principle." *Guardian of Truth* XXX: 11 (June 5, 1986): 321, 358.

D'Aubigne, J. H. Merle. *History of the Reformation in the Sixteenth Century.*

New York: Putnam & Sons, 1872 (Facsimile edition, Powder Springs Press).

King, David T., and William Webster. *Holy Scripture: The Ground and Pillar of Our Faith, Vol. I, II, III.* Battle Ground: Christian Resources, 2001.

Litmer, Greg. *History of the Church Though the Ages.* Bowling Green: Guardian of Truth Foundation, 2005.

Mathison, Keith A. *The Shape of Sola Scriptura.* Moscow: Canon Press, 2001.

McMahon, Dr. C. Matthews. *The Doctrine of Sola Scriptura in a Nutshell* from A Puritan's Mind Website (http://www.apuritansmind.com/Creeds/McMahonSolaScriptura.htm) (November 1, 2008).

Mickelsen, A. Berkeley. *Interpreting the Bible.* Grand Rapids: Erdmans Publishing Company, 1989.

Miller, Dr. Samuel. *The Utility and Importance of Creeds and Confessions* from A Purtan's Mind Website (http://www.apuritansmind.com/Creeds/MillerSamuelImportanceCreedsConfessions.htm) (November 11, 2008).

Nagler, Arthur Wilford. *The Church in History.* Nashville: Abingdon Press, 1929.

*Presbyterian Church, The Confession of Faith of the.* Richmond: Board of Christian Education, 1965.

Riggs, David, and Michael Lopez. *Sola Scriptura Debate* from Steve Rudd's web site (http://bible.ca) (July 10, 2008).

Schaff, Philip. *History of the Christian Church, Vol. VII.* Grand Rapids: Eerdmans Publishing Company, 1970.

Salmon, George. *Infallibility of the Church, A Refutation.* Grand Rapids: Baker Book House, 1959.

Stevens, Eldred, and Eric Beevers. *Stevens-Beevers Debate on The New Testament and Roman Catholicism.* Nashville: Published by Eldred Stevens, 1952.

*United Methodist Church, The Book of Discipline of the.* Nashville: The United Methodist Publishing House, 1984.

Waiss, Fr. John R., and James G. McCarthy. *Letters Between a Catholic and an Evangelical.* Eugene: Harvest House Publishers, 2003.

Warfield, Benjamin B. *The Inspiration and Authority of the Bible.* Phillipsburg: The Presbyterian and Reformed Publishing Company, 1948.

*Webster's Online Dictionary* (http://websters-online-dictionary.org) (October 17, 2008).

West, Earl I. *The Search For The Ancient Order: A History of The Restoration Movement 1849-1906.* Nashville: Gospel Advocate Company, 1964.

White, James R. *Scripture Alone.* Minneapolis: Bethany House, 2004.

Whiteford, Fr. John. *Sola Scriptura: An Orthodox Analysis of the Cornerstone of Reformation Theology.* Ben Lomond: Conciliar Press, 1996.

# “In Vain Ye Do Worship Me”

**Charles Willis**

One of the greatest of all religious controversies is the question of whether instrumental music in worship is approved of God. My purpose in this lesson is to examine the extent of this controversy over the last two thousand years and bring to light its importance to believers still giving answer by the truth of God in the twenty-first century. Many today, even most today, are participating in vain worship by including instruments.

I am thankful to be asked to speak on this specific topic. I hold a Bachelor’s Degree in Music Education from Sam Houston State University, and labored as a band director in the public schools for ten years. During the course of my collegiate studies, I was required to examine the history of music for four semesters. During this time I could not help but be impressed with many truths regarding our topic of instrumental music in worship. Therefore I choose to begin my thoughts on this controversy many hundreds of years ago.

---

**Charles Willis** had a gift for music from an early age. His mother enrolled him in piano lessons at age four. He continued his interest in music by joining the band in his school years. He went on to study tuba and piano at Sam Houston State University earning a Bachelor’s degree in Music Education in 1988. Charles taught Junior High School Band for ten years in the Clear Creek I.S.D. (just south of Houston, Texas) with many award winning bands and hundreds of accomplished students. In 1998 he left the public schools to begin preaching full time. He has been with the New Caney Church of Christ since 2003. He is actively involved in teaching Bible Classes in public and in private. Charles has recently published a book entitled *Effectively Teaching Adult Bible Class.* Charles is married to his wife of twenty years, Deanna. The Lord has blessed them with two children: Joshua and Rachel.

## Catholic History

My college text book was the *History of Western Music*. Donald Grout writes on page thirteen: "Hymn singing is the earliest recorded musical activity of the Christian church." He goes on to say the early church "excluded music from the public worship" (26), meaning instrumental music. The "Christian church" is the historian's way of referring to the Catholic church. It must be said at this point that our modern system of musical notation was invented by Catholic priests around A.D. 1000. Man has no idea what musical performance was like or how it was conveyed to musicians prior to the invention of musical notation. This standard music history text affirms that singing was the only activity originally in the Catholic church.

This fact is verified in the *Catholic Encyclopedia* which reveals, "For almost a thousand years Gregorian chant, without any instrumental or harmonic addition, was the only music used in connection with the liturgy (657). *Westermyer* agrees, "For a thousand years the church in the East and the West followed this example of being purely vocal" (805). Thomas Aquinas, a Catholic monk and celebrated theologian who lived from 1225-1274 wrote, "Our church does not use musical instruments, as harps and psalteries, to praise God withal, that she may not seem to Judiaze" (Kurfees, 176).

Catholic history teaches us that the earliest religious groups understood that music in worship was acappella. The earliest form of written Catholic worship music is in the form of Gregorian Chants. This form of music saw a revival in our pop culture during the middle of the 1990s. Sporadic use of the organ is seen beginning around A.D. 650 but not till A.D. 1300 do we find the organ in wide use. As an instrument, the beginning of the organ can be traced to the times of the Roman Empire. It is therefore wrong to conclude the church adopted the organ when it was invented. Logic demands that the religious men of that time understood instruments were not to be included in worship to God. A study of the early church fathers will readily demonstrate that the use of instruments was associated with concerts offered to the idols as worship. Tertullian said Christians were to hate and abhor these things.

When the great renaissance of art and literature began in Europe, the main forms of music being composed were religious in nature. This tradition continued throughout the classical music periods with works such as Handel's *Messiah*, and Mozart's *Requiem Mass*. The Catholics have long accepted instruments in the worship assembly, even though their documents say it is only an aid and should not detract from the voice. They retain a claim on the supposed importance of vocal music in worship. As late as the sixteenth century they did not use instrumental music in worship when the Pope was present (Price, 81). I find it hard to believe anyone can listen to some of the great composers and the orchestral use in their pieces and maintain an emphasis on the vocal parts. Truly they are taken as a whole – a combination of the vocal and instrumental. This is the case any time an instrument is added.

It is interesting to note that in the 1300s the Catholic church divided into what are now referred to as the Roman Catholic Church and the Eastern Orthodox Church. Many things led to the division, but it is interesting that, at just the point in time when the organ is being accepted into Catholic practice, we see a major division. The *Schaff-Herzog Encyclopedia* records, "In the Greek Church the organ never came into use. But after the eighth century it became more and more common in the Latin Church; not, however, without opposition from the side of the monks" (Kurfees, 152) The *Concise Cyclopedia of Religious Knowledge* agrees, saying, "The organ has never been used among the Greeks. From the time of Charlemagne organs seem to have come more and more into use in the West, though protests were made against them, and the monks were very averse to their use" (Kurfees, 154). In *Christian Antiquities*, J. E. Riddle states, "In the east, organs were never approved as instruments of sacred music, nor did the use of them continue without opposition in the west" (Kurfees, 161). Though unstated in Catholic sources I was able to examine, it appears that one of the controversies which led to the division of the Roman Catholic and Eastern Orthodox Church was the acceptance of instrumental music in the worship.

### Other Religious Controversies Over Music

The Catholics were by no means the only religious group to struggle with the acceptance of instruments into the worship. J. S. Curwen writes in his *Studies In Worship Music,* "Men still living can remember the time when organs were very seldom found outside the Church of England. The Methodists, Independents, and Baptists rarely had them, and by the Presbyterians they were stoutly opposed. . . . Yet, even in the Church of England itself, organs did not obtain admission without much controversy" (Kurfees, 146)

In 1521, Andreas Bodenstein of Carlstadt, a friend and supporter of Martin Luther, "rejected the use of musical instruments in Christian worship. His overarching thesis was an historical argument in which he connected the fall of the church in the Middle Ages with the increased use of music. Carlstadt maintained that the increase of ecclesiastical music from the time of Pope Gregory, including the use of instruments, was one of the marks of the apostasy of the church" (Price, 88). During this same period of history, John Calvin "vehemently objected to the use of musical instruments in Christian worship, believing that they were part of the Temple ceremonies that had been abolished by Christ" (Price, 93). These were some of the arguments that led the way in the Reformation period when people were pulling out of Catholicism and looking back to the Bible rather than the Pope.

In his *History Westminster Assembly of Divines,* William Hetherington describes a Church of England convocation in the year 1562. He writes, "six alterations were proposed . . . (one of which was) that the use of organs be laid aside. . . .The final state of the vote being fifty-eight for, and fifty-nine against. Thus it was determined . . . that the Prayer book should remain unimproved, that there should be no more reformation, that there should be no relief granted to those whose consciences felt aggrieved by the admixture of human inventions in the worship of God" (Kurfees, 173). It must be seen that as many people objected to the introduction of instruments into the worship as were in favor. This is virtually a forgotten fact in the modern Episcopalian Denomination (Church of England).

We again see controversy over instruments in early America. "The first Puritan church to have an organ was the First Congregational Church in Providence, Rhode Island, in 1770. The organ was installed only after much debate" (Price, 129).

"The first organ in a Baptist church was about 1820 in Pawtucket, Rhode Island" (Price, 130). W. K. Pendelton, in an article in the *New York Herald* in 1868 informs us, "The Baptists, only, as a great body, have held aloof and kept to the letter of their original simplicity, and these will no doubt gradually soften and mingle with the general pulp!" (Lewis, 134). "The exclusion of musical instruments from Christian worship by Benjamin Keach and Hanser Knolly is of great significance to Reformed Baptists today. These men were two of the most prominent leaders of the Particular Baptists of the late seventeenth century" (Price, 120). The Baptist denomination, which so strongly supports and promotes instrumental music today, did not do so 125 years ago. The popular nineteenth century Baptist preacher Charles Spurgeon did not allow instrumental music in the worship assemblies where he taught, and spoke openly against their introduction (Kurfees, 196-197; Price, 132).

"Prominent leaders among the Southern Presbyterians . . . refused to admit musical instruments into the worship of their churches into the late 18th century" (Price, 135). "The Irish Presbyterian Church maintained the simple singing of praise without musical instruments from the time of the Reformation to at least the end of the 19th century" (Price, 105).

My point is that the inclusion of instruments into the worship assembly has *always* been a point of controversy anytime they are introduced. This is not a unique issue to our time, nor to the Lord's church. Nevertheless, it is a very important issue which has been greatly discussed among saints for more than the last one hundred years. Sadly, this issue has always caused strife and division.

**Issues of the 1850s-1900s**

In considering lessons learned from controversies, the question over instrumental music in the worship assemblies must bear in mind the problems surrounding this issue during the Restoration era. I speak of the mid to late 1800s in America. Many in the Lord's church today do not know of the issues that have gone before. I am thankful for the opportunity of these lectures to address these things in a public fashion.

"The mechanical instrumental music controversy was the most vehement one of the period and became the major contributor to division. The first instrument known to have been introduced into any now identifiable congregations was at Midway, Kentucky in the late 1850's" (Willis, 74). This eventually led to a division between members of the Church of Christ and members of the Christian Church.

Some will argue that the role of instrumental music in the division of 1900 was small and insignificant. I would kindly disagree. It was not the only issue, for that of Missionary Societies was also of great concern, but the addition of the organ in the worship assemblies caused many problems. A quotation from a sermon by Benjamin Franklin appeared in the *Gospel Preacher* around 1860. It reads eerily similar to things being written today:

> If any one had told us, forty years ago, that we would live to see the day when those professing to be Christians; who claim the Holy Scriptures as their only rule of faith and practice; those under the command, and who profess to appreciate the meaning of the command, to 'observe all things whatsoever I commanded you', would bring any instruments of music into a worshiping assembly, and use it there in worship, we should

> have repelled the idea as an idle dream. But this only shows how little we know of what men would do; or how little we saw of the power of the adversary to subvert the purest principles, to deceive the hearts of the simple, to undermine the very foundation of all piety, and turn the very worship of God itself into an attraction for the people of the world, an entertainment or amusement (Lewis, 152).

Clearly in the 1860s there was controversy among believers. This controversy grew stronger in the coming years as the proponents of instrumental inclusion refused to back down.

"There is little question but that 1870 was the 'year of the organ'. Organs were in churches all over the land and the number was growing. Issac Errett and James S. Lamar were the foremost leaders of the organ advocates. They wielded their pens with 'amazing graciousness'" (Choate/Woodson, 31-32). No one can read of the Restoration period without recognizing one significant fact: men starting paying attention to something other than the Word of God. Prominent preachers promoted the error of instrumental music both in their preaching and their writings. The influence of these men carried weight and many placed their trust in men rather than clinging to what was revealed in Scirpture. Religious journals influenced brethren on both sides of the issue, as the introduction of missionary societies and mechanical instruments of music in worship drove a wedge in a formerly united fellowship. Isaac Errett, editor of the *Christian Standard*, promoted and defended the use of the organ. Papers such as the *Gospel Advocate* (edited by David Lipscomb) and the *American Christian Review* (edited by Benjamin Franklin) opposed it. ". . . The whole organ matter began in Lexington, Kentucky, and the larger adjacent region where Christian Churches flourished and which were informed by the religious papers of outstanding editors and writers" (Choate/Woodson, 39). The influence of men swayed the thinking of some believers to accept error in the late nineteenth century.

One of the lessons to be learned from the instrumental music controversy is that we must beware of paying more attention to men than to the Word of God. We are inundated with daily religious materials through e-mail and web sites. It is possible to spend a great portion of a day examining religious blogs which good men are writing. Some congregations send bulletins to people in other places. Many continue to receive religious journals because of the value of the teaching. Men who teach in many gospel meetings still tend to draw a larger crowd. We listen to religious radio, watch religious television shows, and read books on religious subjects. Some even pay money to take a religious course in college. Influence is being brought to bear upon us through all of these media. That influence can be good or bad depending upon the content of what is preached (or not preached). The more influence held by the speaker, the greater is the potential for good or evil. We must remember how the influence of prominent men led people astray in the 1850s-1900s. The same dangers face us today. We must be certain that we do not repeat their mistakes. "See to it that no one misleads you" (Mark 13:5, NASB).

There is great potential for abuse through any of these media. Just consider this: how much time during our typical week is spent looking at these sources when compared with how much time we spend reading our Bible? Which has the greater influence on us? "Let him who thinks he stands take heed that he does not fall" (1 Cor. 10:12, NASB).

"By the early 1870's the instrument question had become a flaming issue that eventually would burn away the cords of brotherliness" (Willis, 81). "In April of 1870, Errett rolled out his heavy artillery. He laid down a barrage of articles favoring the organ in the churches whose reverberations continue to this day. . . . There was no end to Errett's 'plausible' reminders that harps in the hands of angels surely were not wrong in heaven, and how could it be wrong on earth" (Choate/Woodson, 33-34). Fellowship was maintained by some who did not see the addition of the instrument as indicative of breaking unity. Much effort was afoot to get the instrument accepted and not cause a break in the brotherhood. McGarvey wrote, "The question of instrumental music is becoming a serious one. There are many who favor it, and who will listen to no argument against it. By the cry of progress and conformity, it is making its way over the heads and hearts of many of our best brethren and sisters . . . " (West, II: 84). We must be impressed with similar attitudes and concepts being promoted today. Those in favor of including instruments in the worship are using the same arguments as Errett's in regard to angels using harps in heaven, therefore it cannot be wrong to use them today. We similarly face a modern push by many to accept instruments. Many favor it and will listen to no argument against it. We cannot read of the problems in the nineteenth century without hearing a strong echo in the twenty-first century.

"Ominous warnings of church division rumbled on through the 1880s. Libscomb, Harding, and other *Advocate* writers were cast mainly in the roles of observers and commentators. The organ advocates in the Christian Church largely ignored the opposition with hardly a response" (Choate/

Woodson, 80). "After 1880, a veritable flood of articles was appearing in the *Gospel Advocate* in opposition" (Choate/Woodson, 37). This opposition rightly examined scriptures and demanded that men speak where the Bible speaks and be silent where the Bible is silent. This motto had been held by all for almost a hundred years, but was then only heard by those opposed to the organ.

George P. Slade was the first to put forth a false argument that the word "sing" "used by Paul, included musical instrument in the song service. Slade had written articles in the *American Christian Review* to prove that the apostle, by using the word *psallo* or *psalmos* (Eph. 5:19 and Col. 3:16) implied the use of a stringed instrument in the worship. Slade asserted that the use of the Greek word always conveyed the idea of instrumental accompaniment to singing even if the instrument is not mentioned" (Choate/Woodson, 45). "Slade made it amply clear there was no middle ground on the issue" (Choate/Woodson, 47). *Psallo* became a rallying cry for those in favor of the organ. The argument was worn out by writers over the next ten years.

"By March, 1897 . . . many congregations had now been split over the organ and missionary society questions, which usually resulted in conservatives having to find another meeting place" (Willis, 134). This division was officially recognized in the National census published in 1910 when two separate groups filled out forms for the report. The Christian Church accepted the organ, the Church of Christ did not. What a terrible state the believers were in. How awful to consider the lack of love being shown to God and fellow brethren. Yet today men are seldom aware of these controversies from the past.

Reflective of the struggle over instrumental music is a series of debates between those who opposed and those who supported using instruments of music in worship. Here is a partial list of them:

Otey-Briney Debate (1908)
Hardeman-Boswell Debate (1923)
Clubb-Boles Debate (1927)
Hunt-Smith Debate (1953)
Hunt-Inman Debate (undated)
Book-Miller Debate (1955)
Bunting-Marian Debate (1957)

Many others could be added to this list. The point is that the introduction of instruments of music into the worship of the church created dissension and divsion within the body of Christ resulting in the full severance of the fellowship between those who chose to use mechanical instruments of music in worship (variously known as Disciples of Christ, Independent Christian Churches, and Churches of Christ [instrumental]) and those who opposed their use (Church of Christ [non-instrumental]).

"McDougle made a surprise announcement in 1905, which he thought would win favor for the organ. He had written Dr. J. H. Thayer of Harvard University for his scholarly opinion on the meaning of *psallo*. The letter was passed on to Dr. J. H. Ropes as Dr. Thayer had died. . . . The harp was not inherent in *psallo* even as far back as the Septuagint (250 B.C.)" (Choate/Woodson, 116). What was thought to sway people to the organ actually disproved Slade's entire argument. As difficult as it is to believe, few if any were swayed away from the organ by this scholarly information, and men today still proudly tout Slade's argument as if it is a fresh idea.

"We still say that not one new dimension of meaning and information has been added to the 'rivers of words' on the subject since Isaac Errett gave his thoughts in 1870 and George P. Slade startled his brethren with the *psallo* position in the late 1870's" (Choate/Woodson, 123-124). I agree with Choate and Woodson. Men today in the twenty-first century are using the same arguments first begun over one hundred years ago. Their arguments have not changed. Their validity is no stronger now that it was then. Men believe they are hearing a new teaching which is in fact old. It is an argument without scriptural authority.

In my preparation I was startled by these statements about the late 1800s: "Probably not over ten percent of the congregations opposed the liberal trends that had invaded the churches" (Willis, 187). "Otey, while at Shelbyville, called attention to the fact that New Testament authority had not been found for instrumental music that caused brethren there to begin to practice it. Instead brethren decided and began to use it without finding authority for it. After it was called in question, then they began to seek scriptural justification for it. Otey suggested this process was exactly backward to what it should be" (Willis, 237). This apparent pervasive attitude seems to have prevailed once again in the minds of the Lord's people in the 1950s and even to this day. Certainly the Missionary Society issues of the late 1800s were revisited in the middle of the twentieth century when brethren began questioning supporting institutions from the Lord's treasury, but some did not question the practice till after it had begun.

### Modern Issues

So it is that many today are not questioning the use of instrumental music until it has entered the worship assembly or is announced it will be brought in. I am thankful that you are concerned about these things, for this is not just an interesting historical phenomenon, but is all around us today. The lessons learned from the controversies should be strong and revisited often – but sadly they are not. As I said earlier, many Christians today know nothing of these issues from the past. Few even know of the division which occurred in the 1950s or what the issues were about. By studying these issues in the past we gain great insight into the word of God. We benefit from the study of God's word by people in the past.

"In this you greatly rejoice, even though now for a little while, if necessary, you have been distressed by various trials, so that the proof of your faith, being more precious than gold which is perishable, even though tested by fire, may be found to result in praise and glory and honor at the revelation of Jesus Christ" (1 Pet. 1:6-7). The testing of our faith produces endurance (Jas. 1:3). The faith of many Christians today must be classed as weak and lukewarm. Their knowledge of Scripture is vague at best. Their personal application is haphazard. Their resistance to temptation is poor. Faith comes by hearing the word of God (Rom. 10:17), but it is when our faith is under trial that we are *forced* to grow. Men in the past were forced to study God's word and reach a conclusion about whether a practice was authorized. Examining these modern issues through the writings of men who have been through them will only increase our faith! I would that more Christians would be concerned enough to read of the past issues and see how good men stood fast. We also must stand like men of God in the midst of our trials. The need is great. John Price, a Reformed Baptist preacher wrote in 2005, "As we look back over the entire history of the church, there are only two periods in which musical instruments have had great prominence in worship. The first was the dark ages of Roman Catholicism in the $14^{th}$ and $15^{th}$ centuries, and the second is our own generation" (Price, 143). At a time when some groups with Church of Christ on the sign are bringing instruments into the worship, some named Baptists are removing them from worship.

More change can be observed in religious music in America in the last thirty years than in the last one hundred years. Adherents of the use of instruments in worship tell us this is a dead issue or a "non-issue." They want to remove the argument from the realm of authority and side-line it into a realm of opinion or interpretation. Please understand the introduction of instruments into the worship assembly has always been a matter of authority, and those in favor of their use have always tried to seek approval through the false argument of opinion. We must see in history that this argument has been successful, at least as far as creating strife and dividing believers.

A truth learned through the study of this historical issue is that the silence of scripture must be honored. *A lack of approval in Scripture does not authorize.* Yet that is exactly the issue being taught today for acceptance of instruments. When Rick Atchley brought three lessons to the North Richland Hills congregation about the elder's decision to include instruments in worship, he said, "You can't open your Bible and show me where God forbid it" (Miller, 53). He goes on saying, "I can't believe God will send me to hell because I didn't discern His inference or silence" (Miller, 105). The congregation did accept the use of the instrument and this lesson was received with shouts of "Amen," whoops, and three minutes of applause.

"Some of the arguments in support of the organ included its rising popularity among the churches, its appeal to the younger members of the church, and its supposed usefulness in evangelism" (Price, 128). This sounds like a modern argument, but in reality it was written about the history of the late 1700s! Today we hear people saying we need to appeal to young people through a medium they want to listen to. If we do not use guitars and drums why would they listen? They will instead turn to the music of the world which has more appeal. The fallacy of this proposal is that it sets aside the authority of God and makes the thinking of men more rational. Anybody can fill a room with a group of good musicians, but that denies the purpose of the church as a pillar and support of the truth (1 Tim. 3:15). If we run past the limit of God's authority, the church is no longer supporting the truth. "Church bands" might create a good sound, but it is not a sound pleasing to God. He is the one for whom all this noise is supposedly being made. Truly in vain some worship Him.

The controversy continues in our time. The "Quail Springs congregations (calling itself 'Quail Springs Family Of God') adopted a 9AM worship service with instruments starting in January of 2008. The membership dropped from 900 to 600. They made the move 'to be able to reach out to a larger group of people'" (May). This argument is made not only at Quail Springs, but almost verbatim at Richland Hills (Ross). It is touted as a plausible and effective argument, but it makes no sense. It would be like the apostles trying to get Jesus to feed the thousands every time they assemble, yet Jesus said, "You seek Me, not because you saw signs, but because you ate of the loaves and were filled. Do not work for the food which perishes, but for the food which endures to eternal life. . ." (John 6:26-27, NASB). Jesus did not feed the crowd on this occasion. As a result of this and His further teaching about being the "bread of life," "many of the disciples withdrew and were not walking with Him anymore" (John 6:66, NASB). Adherents to instrumental music in worship are not willing to teach as Jesus did because they fear the result Jesus got. Their concern is not about being a pillar and support of truth but being the largest in the community. Instrumental music is merely one tactic they use, but in this we see their attitude toward God's authority. "Outreach" is a good work, but when done through unauthorized, unlawful means, God cannot approve. Men will continue to call it the work of God, but it stops being God's work when it is not authorized. "Not everyone who says to Me 'Lord, Lord' will enter the kingdom of heaven, but he who does the will of My Father who is in heaven" (Matt. 7:21, NASB).

The reality is that modern religious music is an entertainment as admitted by many. Erasmus (1466-1536) wrote, "Men run to church as to a theatre, to have their ears tickled" (Price, 86). They are hearing what they want to hear, just as Paul warned: "for the time will come when they will not endure sound doctrine; but wanting to have their ears tickled, they will accumulate for themselves teachers in accordance to their own desires, and will turn away their ears from the truth and will turn aside to myths" (2 Tim. 3:3-4, NASB). How true of the instrumental music proposal. People want them and make any argument imaginable to justify their use. When shown the truth of Scripture, when faced with the reality of a lack of authority, these close their ears and blind themselves to the truth in order to continue to do what they desire. Their conscience is not pricked by the truth.

Consider also the very modern trend of "Christian Music" as part of the pop culture. "Christian Music" is a genre and style now in its own venues like rock bands of the 1980s. There is a question among brethren as to whether we should listen or abstain from such entertainment. It cannot be missed that this genre has appeal to many Christians, and many choose to listen, some avidly. They have told me, "it is not harming me," "it is better than the worldly stuff on the radio," "I'm not worshipping." While this question remains in the realm of personal judgment, we must not blind ourselves to the potential dangers. Consider this statement from the Elders of the Norway Church of Christ to their congregation:

> It is difficult to be consistent with the a cappella only position. We let our children sing spiritual songs in choruses with music at school but they have been not been allowed to do this at church. We go to concerts and praise God and are uplifted by Christian musicians but we will not do this in the assembly. We know a number of people who are avid supporters of the a cappella-only position but they listen to the Gaithers or have a hymnal on their piano at home or listen to Christian music on the radio. Furthermore, when people ask us to explain this inconsistency we have no Biblical explanation – we point to our own human tradition and we feel that we have been inconsistent and now we want to align our practice with our current beliefs (Norway).

In aligning their practices they expanded the use of instrumental music from their Monday and Wednesday night services to include the Sunday morning worship assembly. The Norway Church of Christ justified its decision to add instruments of music to its worship, not on the basis of what Scripture authorizes, but from the practices of its members who allowed their children to participate in programs at school that featured singing spiritual songs with instruments of music and their participation in "Christian music" concerts.

What are we teaching our young people? Do we at least warn them of the dangers of listening to "Christian Radio"? We cannot bury our heads in the sand about this issue. "Christian Music" as a genre is here to stay. It is a modern development of an old issue and every generation must be taught the truth of God. Music is an influential medium which reaches us at an emotional level. It has the ability to influence us away from the truth if we do not know the truth and stand firm in the faith.

### In Vain Ye Do Worship Me

Vain (useless) worship is accomplished when it is not "in spirit and in truth" (John 4:24, NASB). Jesus' condemnation is over the teaching of men's doctrines as if they are the command of God (Matt. 15:8-9). In verse seven Jesus calls this hypocritical conduct. We cannot honor God with our lips while practicing the precepts of men. We dishonor God in this type of worship which makes it vain.

Nadab and Abihu stand as horrific examples to us about vain worship. "Now Nadab and Abihu, the sons of Aaron, took their respective firepans, and after putting fire in them, placed incense on it and offered strange fire before the Lord, which He had not commanded them. And fire came out from the presence of the Lord and consumed them, and they died before the

Lord" (Lev. 10:1-2, NASB). Their strange fire was only strange because it was not commanded of God. It was a foreign addition to the worship practice of the Old Covenant. God's condemnation is obvious when He stated, "By those who come near Me I will be treated as holy, and before all the people I will be honored" (Lev. 10:3, NASB). Nadab and Abihu disdained the holiness of God and dishonored Him by offering strange fire. In a similar way Moses was not allowed to enter the promised land "because you did not treat Me as holy in the midst of the sons of Israel" (Deut. 32:51, NASB). When Ananias and Sapphira tested the holiness of God by lying to the apostles, God struck them both dead (Acts 5). Vain worship dishonors God by its disobedience.

It is no different when men want to include strange things in the worship of God which He has not commanded. The Corinthians twisted the observance of the Lord's Supper into a common meal, which Paul condemns in chapter eleven. They went too far and did not abide in the doctrine of Christ (2 John 9). The North Richland Hills congregation has added instrumental worship to a Saturday evening assembly during which they observe the Lord's Supper. Why would we expect any different response from God for including these strange things in worship which is vain? God has not commanded them.

Believers are told to "teach and admonish" one another in "psalms, hymns and spiritual songs, singing with thankfulness in your hearts to God" (Col. 3:16, NASB). If I must teach with the use of an instrument (the false argument regarding the word *psallo*), then everyone in the congregation must play an instrument. We must teach "one another." The problem is with teaching and admonishing. These cannot be done without the voice. Instruments have nothing to do with the command. They in fact get in the way of the command and are an addition to the command to "sing." God placed the emphasis on the words.

Sing is a specific word, even in the Greek. It falls under the general category of "music." It sits beside the sub-category, "instrumental." Visit any University Music Department and see how it is divided. The world recognizes the truth of specific authority. No one would walk into the "instrumental office" at the university when taking something to the head of the vocal department. They would only be confused if they were directed to take it to the "music" office. That is a generic. Those who would promote instrumental worship simply ignore the truth of this basic argument.

As a specific, "sing" automatically excludes everything else. Anything more than singing is an addition. God did not have to tell us we cannot use guitars, we cannot use drums, because God said sing. The same truth is evident when God told Noah to use gopher wood (Gen. 6:14). He did not have to name every other species of wood, it was automatically excluded. All parents and children understand this simple concept. If I send my son to the store for a loaf of bread and he comes back with a loaf of bread, a candy bar, and a soda, he will be in trouble. I did not authorize anything but the loaf of bread. Yet those who promote the false understanding of *psallo* tell us we can include instruments and it is only an aid to singing. This is not good scholarship, nor is it good logic. This is merely an effort to tickle ears to promote the desires of some who want to worship with instruments.

God says "sing" (Col. 3:16; Eph. 5:19). He says teach "one another." There is no room in this language for anyone to be a spectator. We all teach and admonish concurrently as we sing. It is concluded then that performers in the worship assembly are "strange" (unauthorized) and therefore vain worship. We cannot adopt choirs and soloists, concerts and special music groups into the worship. It denies the whole concept of edification through singing. It destroys one of God's purposes in demanding corporate worship.

What is missing and what is needed by those who would worship God vainly with instruments, is embodied in the simple statement of Paul: "Let the word of Christ richly dwell within you. . . . Whatever you do in word or deed, do all in the name of the Lord Jesus" (Col. 3:16-17, NASB). The word is not richly dwelling in us when we worship without the authority of Jesus. We are in fact outside the doctrine of Christ which results in our not having God (2 John 9). If His word is "richly" dwelling in us, we would be outraged that some would want to bring instruments into the assembly. Just as outraged, and for the same reasons, as why we would never consider using milk at the Lord's Table. It is not authorized because the Lord's specific (fruit of the vine) automatically excludes everything else. "In the name of" speaks of His authority which is required if we desire to please Him. Whatever we do must have His approval in Scripture. Instrumental music in worship does not.

These are some of the arguments which have been constantly put forth by those opposed to instrumental worship. It is a question of authority, not opinion or interpretation. This is an issue which must be opposed. Good men must stand for the truth or the way of truth will be maligned.

## Conclusion

I must concur with Dabney (a Presbyterian of the late 1800s) who spoke of the inclusion of the organ, "I know, by an intuition which I believe every sensible observer shares, that the innovation is merely the result of an advancing wave of worldliness and ritualism in the evangelical bodies. These Christians are not wise but simply more flesh-appealing and fashionable . . . " (Price, 147).

This "innovation" is being brought about by some who desire to see changes in the Lord's church. Their motivations are suspect, or should be. One of the great leaders of the Missionary Society push in the 1800s was Andres I. Myhr. He believed this new innovation was necessary. In 1910, *The Tennessee Christian* wrote a commemorative piece about Myhr, but stated,

> there is yet another side to the Myhr story. Dr. Herman Norton, distinguished Restoration historian of the Disciples of Christ, tells us something else that Myhr had done: "But what he did not tell the delegates was that during this same period of time the work for which he had administrative responsibility engendered a bitter partisan spirit in almost every congregation in the state. He, himself, had helped sow seeds of discord. Strife, bitterness, and alienation had followed in the wake of his program activities. Where there had been one communion, admittedly with discord, when he arrived in the state, there were now two separate and distinct bodies with no meaningful communication between them. Myhr's role in bringing this about had been a major one" (Choate/Woodson, 123).

Myhr was successful in bringing about innovation, but at great expense to the church and through the sin of creating strife (1 Cor. 3:3; Gal. 5:20). Men today are also trying to innovate the work and worship of the church. History teaches us to be suspect.

Lynn Anderson wrote in *Wineskins*, "So we must dance lightly on the balls of our feet and constantly change strategies and formats to connect with an ever changing culture" (Woodson, 106). This sounds appropriate enough. It makes sense to change with the culture, but Anderson is proclaiming much more than merely keeping up with the times. He continues saying, "Profound and speedy changes have catapulted us into new realities which make the old rules obsolete" (Woodson, 107). Which old rules? There can be no understanding except God's rules. "New realities" (like "Christian Music Radio") make the old rules obsolete. Says who? This is simply situation ethics on a national scale! Rather than conforming to the societal changes, God demands we be "transformed by the renewing of your mind, so that you may prove what the will of God is, that which is good and acceptable and perfect" (Rom. 12:2, NASB). It is our responsibility to prove what God says is good, acceptable and perfect (complete). When this is discovered through study (study to show yourself approved), we must renew our mind. We must change our thinking to conform to God's will. We transform ourselves away from the world to become what God desires. Mr. Anderson would have us ignore the word of God, keep our mind set on the things we desire and conform ourselves to society. The "new realities" we are really dealing with are false teachers promoting sinful things, drawing away disciples after themselves. "Many will follow their sensuality, and because of them the way of truth will be maligned" (2 Pet. 2:2, NASB).

Calvin Warpula in the journal *One Body* writes, "Some of our people affirm that Christians who use instrumental music in worship will go to hell. . . . Most of us have seen the folly of making such a strong asseveration because the Bible does not say that as we want to 'be silent where the Bible is silent . . . '" (Woodson, 282). What awesome skills as a writer. This almost sounds right because of the "be silent where the Bible is silent" phrase. It will convince some. It already has. Yet he says "most of us have seen the folly," as if everyone agrees there is nothing wrong with instrumental music in worship. Rick Atchley stated, "We all know thousands and thousands of sincere members of churches of Christ who have studied their Bible, and they no longer believe instrumental praise offends God" (Miller, 103). I find these statements abusive of Scripture and brethren. It is assumptive, coercive, purposeful, and sinful. Men like Warpula and Atchley know exactly what they are doing.

Rubel Shelly must be counted among this group since he argues, ". . . whatever else one can say about pianos and organs in worship, he cannot find their explicit condemnation in the Bible. Acceptance of their use certainly does not repudiate any one of the seven essential items of Christian faith identified in Ephesians 4:4-6" (Woodson, 171). Mr. Shelly has for many years been leading the way in attempts to reunite the Church of Christ with the Christian Church. "The problem was (and still is) that the Christian Churches will not stop using instrumental music in worship, and Shelly refuses to accept it in worship. How can a way around this impasse be found? The answer is: redefine the content of scripture which is authoritative for unity so that instrumental music is relocated outside the parameters essential to unity; the problem is solved! This was and is the heart of the Shelly's effort, an effort driven not by Scripture teaching but by a goal embraced outside Scripture and imposed as a grid on the New Testament to enable unity with the Christian Churches" (Woodson, 169-170).

The Lord's church does not need innovation. The word of God does not need updating. "All scripture is inspired of God and profitable for teaching, for reproof, for correction, for training in righteousness; so that the man of God may be adequate, equipped for every good work" (2 Tim. 3:16-17, NASB). In a study of instrumental music in worship it cannot be missed that men relied on Scripture as God's inspired word. Every time the Bible is examined and is the sole source of authority, men stand opposed to the introduction of instruments in the worship. Further, God's Word is used to teach the truth on this subject, to reprove those who would bring it in, to correct those who have brought it in, and to train those in righteousness who have not yet brought it in. It is only in this way that a man of God may be "adequate" (complete).

In the coming years may we all strive to know God's will and apply it fully in our own lives. We must stand apart from our society as God's distinctive people. We must use the written Word to teach on every issue, which includes the use of instrumental music in worship. We live in a trying time when virtually all the voices around us proclaim God's approval of instrumental worship, but that simply means we need to stand firm (Eph. 6:11-13). "Be on the alert, stand firm in the faith, act like men, be strong. Let all that you do be done in love" (1 Cor. 16:13-14, NASB). May God bless our efforts in His Kingdom.

### Bibliography

*Catholic Encyclopedia*, Volume 10, Encyclopedia Press, Inc. (1915).

Choate, J. E. and William Woodson. *Sounding Brass And Clanging Cymbals* (Freed Hardeman University, 1991).

Dabbs, Matt. mattdabbs.wordpress.com/2008/01/26/reflections-on-gulf-coast-getaway-instrumental-music/

Grout, Donald. *History of Western Music* (W. W. Norton & Co Inc., 1980).

Lewis, John T. *The Voice of the Pioneers on Instrument Music and Societies* (Gospel Advocate, 1932).

Kurfees, M.C. *Instrumental Music in the Worship* (Gospel Advocate, 1950).

May, Joe. gospelnews.wordpress.com/2008/01/28/quail-springs-uses-instrument.

Miller, Dave. *Richland Hills & Instrumental Music: A Plea To Reconsider* (Sain Publications, 2007).

Norway Avenue Elders statement, www.norwayavenue.org/instrumental_music10-16-05.pdf

Price, John. *Old Light On New Worship* (Simpson Publishing, 2005).

Ross, Bobby, Jr. christianchronicle.org/article555~Nation%27s_largest_Church_of_Christ_adding_instrumental_service

West, Earl Irvin. *The Search For The Ancient Order* (Religious Book Service, 1950).

Westermyer, Paul. "Music," *Encyclopedia of Christianity*, Ed. Bowden (Oxford Press, 2005).

Willis, Cecil. *W.W. Otey, Contender For The Faith* (Truth Publications, 1964).

Woodson, William. *Change Agents and Churches of Christ* (Sain Publications, 1994).

# The Church is the Pillar and Ground of Truth (1 Timothy 3:15)

**Tom M. Roberts**

> These things write I unto thee, hoping to come unto thee shortly: But if I tarry long, that thou may know how thou ought to behave thyself in the house of God, which is the church of the living God, the pillar and ground of the truth (1 Tim. 3:14-15).

Writing to Timothy from somewhere in Macedonia, Paul encouraged him (and also Titus) to be bold and faithful in their work as evangelists. Evidence points to two imprisonments of Paul in Rome. The letter of 1 Timothy would have been written after his first term in prison and subsequent release. Uncertainty marked this period of his life as he hoped to travel to Spain but he also hoped to be united with Titus (Tit. 2:12) and, from our text, with Timothy as well. None can be sure as to his success in reaching Spain. But

---

**Tom Roberts** was born in Gladewater (northeast), Texas on February 8, 1935. He married Pauline Kelley the year he graduated and attended Florida College during the 1954-55 school year. Together, they had three children: Curtis (1956), Tommy, Jr. (1957), and Paula (1964). Tommy was accidently killed in a motorcycle accident in 1981 at twenty-three years of age. Tom and Pauline have been married over fifty-five years (1953- ). They currently reside in Arlington, TX where he works with the Northside church in Mansfield, in the Dallas-Fort Worth metroplex area.

Tom began preaching full time in 1956 in south Texas and has preached continually since then, having lived in North Carolina (twice), Texas, and Florida. He has been a staff writer for *Truth Magazine*, co-editor for *Watchman Magazine,* and co-author and editor of *Neo-Calvinism in the Church of Christ.* He has preached in gospel meetings across the nation, preached on radio and television, and helped start congregations in Sherman, TX, Morehead City, NC, and Fort Worth, TX.

"if I tarry long" indicated his resolve to instruct in a pressing matter: how men should "behave themselves in the house of God." The great principles of truth contained in his letters to Timothy certainly fulfilled that desire. There continues to be a great need today in the same sphere. In the past, as in our own lifetime, controversies and strife and wranglings have characterized churches of Christ. Even as Paul wrote Timothy that he must "charge some that they teach no other doctrine" (1:3), the need continues today. Paul warned that some, "desiring to be teachers of the law, understand[ing] neither what they say nor the things which they affirm" (1:7).

How we ought to "behave" in the house of God is not contemplating parliamentary procedure (though that would certainly be an improvement over many business meetings we have witnessed), a particular order of worship (two songs and a prayer, etc.), or whether mothers should take their children out for some "birch tea" when too boisterous. Paul has in mind how brethren respect God and other brethren in spiritual matters before the church. There is a "walk worthy of our calling" (Eph. 4:1) and this should characterize our relations with God and one another. Shameful and disgraceful actions have often occurred when brethren disagree with others, both in doctrinal and judgmental matters.

A church in Texas was known for the trouble which erupted when a night watchman was suspected of bringing a hidden gun with him into the assembly. One of the brethren tackled him to find out, a sister took off her shoe and beat the man nearly unconscious with it, and, in the melee, the gun went off. The police were called. No one was injured but the townspeople were heard to ask, "What happened at the church of Christ?" every time a car backfired during the next week! While I daresay that this church did not "behave" itself, Paul had more in mind than such ungodliness.

The text of 1 Timothy is rich in meaning and cannot be ignored if we claim to behave ourselves before God. Certainly "how thou ought to behave" would include a submission to sound doctrine (1:10), praising God (1:17), waging a good warfare with a good conscience (1:18-19), prayer for all men (2:1ff), women in subjection and modesty (2:9-15), appointing elders and deacons (3:1-13), watching against apostasy (4:1-11), personal dedication of evangelists (4:12-16), care of widows (5:1-16), support of those who teach (5:17-18), respect of elders (5:19-20), relations between masters and servants (6:1-2), teaching and exhorting (6:2b-5), proper use of wealth and material possessions (6:6-10, 17-19), personal dedication of those who teach (6:11-16), and guarding that which is entrusted to our care

(6:20-21). All this, as well as the teachings of 2 Timothy and Titus, would instruct all of us in godly behavior.

But our assignment has to do with "great truths learned from historic controversies." While we cannot ignore the immediate controversy stirred up by Hymenaeus and Alexander (1:20), Hymenaeus and Philetus (2 Tim. 2:17), Jannes and Jambres (in Moses' day, 2 Tim. 3:8), and Alexander the coppersmith (4:14), our concerns are with the more modern problems which some mistakenly wrest from our text, 1 Timothy 3:15.

### What 1 Timothy 3:15 Teaches

Paul affirms the Lord's church to be the "pillar and ground of the truth." A "pillar" is a column supporting the weight of a building (Thayer, 184). In this analogy the church supports the truth which has been sent by God through revelation of the Holy Spirit. "Ground" is from *hedraios* which means "steadfast, firm, thus a support, bulwark, stay" (Thayer, 181). It is a truism that the truth of God's word stands alone, without the need of any support. I mean by this that the Bible, and the Bible alone, contains the *truth* and men may learn the truth of God without the help of any man. Give someone a Bible and you give him the truth of God, illustrated by the success of the "Restoration Age" in America. However, through the wisdom of God, He has assigned the church as the pillar and ground of the truth. The church, *by its existence*, by its unity, by its divinity, evidences and exemplifies the truth contained in the Bible. It enhances the truth and supports the truth by its very existence. When men fully understand the plan of redemption, they will come to see Jesus and the body of Christ as the "end" (purpose) of God's plan (Gal. 3:23-27).

But which church fulfills this role? Is it any given *local* church, or the church *universal?* May I suggest that we need to think again if we think it is any local congregation? In what sense could the church at Laodicea be the pillar and ground of truth in the light of its condition? God was ready to "spew them out of his mouth." Likewise, Pergamos had those who taught the "doctrine of Balaam" and the "doctrine of the Nicolaitians," while Thyatira allowed Jezebel to beguile members to commit sexual immorality and call herself a prophetess (see Rev. 2-3). Could Corinth be the "pillar and ground of truth" when a brother scandalized the city with his immorality (1 Cor. 5)?

On the other hand, Jesus had no local church in mind when He promised to "build my church" (Matt. 16:18). This is the divine body of Christ of which Jesus is its head (Eph. 1:22-23) and will forever be the ideal which correctly represents the revealed truth of the gospel. When Paul asserted that the "manifold wisdom of God might be made known by the church to the principalities and powers in the heavenly places according to the eternal purpose which He accomplished in Christ Jesus our Lord" (Eph. 3:10-11), He had in mind the church in the sense of Matthew 16:18. "Principalities and powers in heavenly places" had no need to have the gospel preached to them. However, when the church came into being, its divine existence explained the "mystery" of the gospel to those who "desired to look into" those things (2 Pet 1:12). (Note: Whether or not one agrees with my assessment of the pillar and ground of truth as being the church universal and not any given local church, the effect is the same. 1 Timothy 3:15 is not a proof-text in either sense for denying Christians the right to teach, sing, pray, edify, or practice benevolence outside the local church.)

With this truth before us, it is easy to agree with those who teach the "all-sufficiency of the church." Yes, the church is sufficient to do all that God has planned for the church to do. Thus, a church-supported missionary society is wrong because it usurps the role of the Lord's church and reduces the work of the church by draining resources from the church to empower the missionary society. I know of no brother among us who denies that the church is all-sufficient to do the work God has assigned to it. The church-supported missionary society idea presented a sharp contention in the past generation but it was soundly defeated among faithful churches and is not a present danger among brethren.

### Great Truths Learned from the Restoration Era

What is usually referred to as the "Restoration Era" reflects a period of time in which a great spiritual awakening took place in America during the late 1700s and well into the1800s. Along much of the eastern seaboard and into the Western Reserve (Ohio), human creeds were abandoned and the cry was heard: "Speak where the Bible speaks, and be silent where the Bible is silent." Thomas Campbell and his son Alexander, along with Barton W. Stone, Elias Smith, Abner Jones, Walter Scott, "Racoon" John Smith, Tolbert Fanning, David Lipscomb, and many others, independently returned to New Testament Christianity and abandoned denominationalism. Thousands of early Americans responded to the pure gospel and were baptized into Christ.

Sadly, the unity and fervor of the Restoration Period did not last. If we must learn any lessons from this for our profit, we must learn that, just as people can turn to the Lord, people can turn away from the Lord. Apostasy in any age is an ever present danger. Just as in the days of the apostles, even so throughout history, men depart from the "old paths."

The rocks upon which the Restoration Period floundered were the creation of the American Christian Missionary Society and the introduction of instrumental worship into local churches. Leaving the issue of instrumental music in worship to other studies, we will spend our time considering what we may learn from the controversy over church-supported missionary societies.

Central to this issue is the misconception that the universal church of Christ is composed of a collectivity of all local churches. The pioneers of the Restoration came from denominations which had structures of their churches that were larger than a local church, but smaller than the church universal, *i.e.* Baptist denomination, Presbyterian denomination, etc. Their ecclesiastical organizations confused early disciples and it took much work to learn differently. Early examples of this confusion among restoration leaders were the Mahoning Baptist Association (Thomas and Alexander Campbell) and the Springfield Presbytery (Barton W. Stone). For example, Alexander Campbell argued, "A church can do what an individual disciple cannot, so can a district of churches do what a single congregation cannot" (*Millennial Harbinger* [1831], 237). From the discussions between brethren of this era, we have learned to appreciate that the church universal is composed of individuals, not churches (Heb. 12:22-23). Each local church is independent and autonomous under Christ (Acts 14:23; 1 Pet. 5:1-2; Acts 20:28). The church universal has no earthly headquarters, treasury, collective work, or structure.

Working under the erroneous concept of the universal collective of churches, brethren met on October 23, 1849, in Cincinnati, Ohio, in a convention of churches to create a "general church organization for the furtherance of the work by the church collectively." The result was the "American Christian Missionary Society" (ACMS). None other than Alexander Campbell (though absent from the convention) was elected its first president. D. S. Burnet expressed satisfaction with his influence in the formation of the Missionary Society when he wrote, "I consider the inauguration of our society system which I vowed to urge upon the brethren . . . as one of the most important acts of my career" (F. M. Greene, *Christian Missions and Historical Sketches of Missionary Societies Among the Disciples of Christ*, 172). While acceptance of the missionary society was not universal, it would be safe to state from that convention forward, churches of Christ have had a studied fascination of such societies. Furman Kearly, editor of the *Gospel Advocate* stated at the Dallas meeting (1990) that the "*Gospel Advocate* is a missionary society" and urged brethren to send funds to them to disperse (see http://lowerrichlandchurch.org, *Dallas Meeting — Institutional Issues*, Day 3, Summations [July 12-14, 1990]).

W. K. Pendleton, son-in-law of Alexander Campbell, explained his expectancy of the work of the ACMS: "We met . . . to consult the best ways for giving efficiency to our power . . . . There are some duties of the church which a single congregation cannot, by her unaided strength, discharge. . . . A primary object being to devise some scheme for a more effectual proclamation of the gospel in destitute places, both at home and abroad, the Convention took under consideration the organization of a Missionary Society" (W. K. Pendleton, "The Convention of Christian Churches," *Millennial Harbinger*, Third Series, VI:12, pp. 689, 690).

Objections to the society quickly arose. Ben Franklin stated:

> The circumstance that they had no missionary societies in the first age of the church, of itself, does not prove that we may not have them. But the fact that the Lord ordained the congregations, with their officers, and made it their work to convert the world with the additional fact that we have their example in sending out preachers, with the circumstance, that they had no missionary societies, but the churches, proves that it is wrong for individuals to create missionary societies, separate from local churches, as substitutes to do the work which the Lord appointed for the churches . . . . The simple question is, whether we shall honor the churches in working in them and making them effective as the Lord's appointed societies, in converting the world, or declare them insufficient to do the work which the Lord committed to them, and substitute a creation of our own hands, to do the work of the churches ordained by the Lord . . . ("Explanation for brother G. W. Elley," *American Christian Review*, X:19 [May 7, 1867], p. 148).

David Lipscomb was another outspoken critic, especially of those who contended that the society could do a better job of preaching than the local church. He said, "To operate through an institution of man's devising in preference to the church of God is, in our esteem, to exalt man as of superior wisdom and power to God . . . " (David Lipscomb, "Destroying Church Cooperation," *Gospel Advocate*, IX:6 [Feb. 7, 1867], 115). (A comment needs to be made about this point. I know of no brother who agrees with the right of Florida College or Truth Foundation to provide facilities for lectures who will state that these efforts "can do a better job of preaching than the local church." In fact, I would emphatically deny such a proposition. There is no competition between efforts of a local church to teach the Bible and efforts by individuals to teach the Bible. The local church is authorized to teach the Bible. The individual is authorized to teach the Bible. It is ludicrous to compare such efforts as one better than the other for in many cases, the same preacher will preach in a local church and, later, preach in a lectureship provided by individual brethren. Though advocates of the missionary society made such a claim in their zeal to promote the ACMS, we have certainly learned that such is not true and is, within itself, inherently contradictory.)

As the twentieth century opened, a climactic debate between J. B. Briney and W. W. Otey took place in Louisville, Kentucky during September 14-18, 1908 (*The Otey-Briney Debate).*

Arguments for the all-sufficiency of the church included:

• *The missionary society is an indictment against the all-sufficiency of the church.* The church, as planned by God and built by Christ, is a perfect church. As a perfect church, the church has

- A divine architect (Eph. 3:10-11).
- A perfect blueprint (Heb. 8:5).
- A perfect builder (Matt. 16:18).
- Perfect preparations (Mark 1:14-15; Gal. 4:4).
- A perfect head (Eph. 1:20-23).
- A perfect law (Jas. 1:25).
- A perfect mission (Eph. 4:12).

The chart on the next page was widely used during the discussions on institutionalism in the 1950s and 1960s. The copy quoted is from *Passing The Torch*, by Mike Willis (10).

Please note that the support of the society was to be taken from churches, not from individuals. Daniel Sommer, we will see, was more narrow in his view in that he did not approve of any group effort which was supported by either churches or individuals. This important distinction must be realized in today's world as we grapple with the same issue. While most sound churches will refuse to support efforts to preach the gospel through a church-supported missionary society (a collectivity of churches), others, like Sommer, label any effort to preach, teach, do benevolence, or worship outside the context

| The Church | The Missionary Society |
|---|---|
| 1. Originated in the mind of God (Eph. 3:21) | 1. Originated in the mind of man |
| 2. Is blood-bought (Acts 20:28) | 2. An organization that is not blood-bought |
| 3. Money raised through contributions (1 Cor. 16:1-2) | 3. Money raised through contributions |
| 4. Organization: elders and deacons (1 Tim. 3) | 4. Organization: Board of Directors, President |
| 5. Does its own work (Eph. 4:12) | 5. Does work in place of church |
| 6. Local church is only functioning unit (Phil. 1:1) | 6. A collectivity of churches; an organization larger than local church, smaller than universal church |
| 7. Local church represents only itself | 7. Considered official functioning organ of a brotherhood of churches |
| 8. Competent to accomplish its God's-given mission (Eph. 1:23; 3:10-11) | 8. Designed to give the church greater efficiency in accomplishing its mission |
| 9. Can accomplish its mission (1 Tim. 3:15) | 9. Proposes to do what local church cannot do |
| 10. Creed and by-laws: The New Testament (James 1:25) | 10. Makes its own creed and by-laws |
| 11. Each local church oversees its own work | 11. Oversees the work of a brotherhood of churches |
| 12. Unity in the body (Eph. 2:16) | 12. Divided brethren |
| 13. No universal structure, organization, or mission | 13. Seeks to activate the universal church through this functioning unit |

of a local church (even by individuals) as apostate.

We can summarize what we have learned from the Restoration era as follows:

1. Denominational terminology, methodology, and structure are not the same as the New Testament order.
2. A misunderstanding of the church universal permits egregious practices to arise which will never be addressed until a distinction is made between that and the church local.
3. It is impossible to activate the universal church. All such efforts are futile and self-serving.

4. Church-supported societies are sinful in that they drain funds and personnel from local churches and compete with it to exist. Local churches exist merely to fund the collective and the collective controls the churches.
5. Church conventions are unscriptural in themselves and dangerous.
6. Noble Christians can be misled into alliances and practices which contradict their own teaching (Alexander Campbell, e.g.).
7. The local church is capable of doing all that God assigned to it. It is absolutely all-sufficient and needs no collectives of churches to function.
8. The individual is capable, also, of doing all that God assigned him to do. There is no conflict between areas of service within the local church and service outside the local church as individual disciples.

**Great Truths Learned From Battles With Daniel Sommer**

Daniel Sommer was born in Queen Ann, Maryland on January 11, 1850 to parents who were Lutherans and German immigrants. They had Daniel sprinkled as an infant. Raised in abject poverty, he nevertheless had an indomitable spirit which led him to seek an education. Born only three years after the death of Alexander Campbell, he became acquainted with Bethany College and Benjamin Franklin and was influenced greatly by the "Restoration Movement" concept. Widely known for his preaching ability, he became a sort of "fire brand" who permanently affected and hastened the division between churches of Christ and the Christian Church. Seeing the missionary society and instrumental music as innovations, he led many to walk out of churches that utilized either. The Sand Creek "Declaration and Address" (Sand Creek, Ohio, August 17, 1889) marked opponents as digressives and made their actions tests of fellowship. The division among churches was officially recognized in the 1906 U.S. census.

Prominent in the thinking of Daniel Sommer was the idea that the church, and the church alone, had the authority and obligation to preach the gospel. This led to a repudiation of Bethany College – or any organization – which, in his view competed with the church to do that work. We read:

> In Daniel Sommer's debate with J.N. Armstrong entitled, *A Report of Skirmishes Between a Religious Journal and a Religio-Secular College,* Sommer argued:
>
> 'Fourth. Then, in the next place we oppose this institution and

> pronounce it unscriptural because of what the apostle Paul says in his first letter to Timothy, third chapter, 15th verse, where he says to Timothy: 'But if I tarry long, that thou mayest know how thou oughtest to behave thyself in the house of God, which is the church of the living God, the pillar and ground of the truth.' So then, my hearers, he says the Church of God is the house of the living God, and adds, which is 'the pillar and ground of the truth.' So, if the Church of God, without any such appendage as this, is the pillar and ground of the truth, we object to this institution, established for the purpose of teaching mankind in religion'" (*"J.T. Smith and the Re-Birth of Sommerism"* by Mike Willis, Truthmagazine.com/collectivities).

Please note the use of 1 Timothy 3:15 in his argumentation.

To further illustrate the issue: D. Austen Sommer (Daniel's son) made the following argument in his debate with J.C. McQuiddy entitled *The College Question Discussed:*

> Now these things are true: 1. The "Bible colleges" are organizations. 2. They are teaching the Bible. . . . 3. Teaching the Bible is "the Lord's work." 4. Therefore, the human organization of the "Bible college" to do "the Lord's work" is to say the least superfluous; and inasmuch as it is a tradition of man, we may add in the words of Christ, "In vain do ye worship me, teaching for doctrines the commandments of men" *(Ibid.).*

These brethren were not discussing whether or not church support of these organizations was scriptural; they were discussing whether or not these organizations could exist separate and apart from church support. This same approach is being used in our time. Thus a revival of "Sommerism" is an accurate assessment of our present situation. Apart from the institutional churches, there are no efforts at all among us to activate the church universal or to create church collectivities to utilize a church-supported missionary society.

A common thread that has characterized the Sommer issue all through the years and that is usually assumed with no proof is this: that teaching the Bible is ***exclusively*** the work of the church. It is also assumed that edification and benevolence to needy saints are ***exclusively*** the work of the church. But logically, we must ask, to be consistent, "Are singing and praying ***exclusively*** the work of the church?" "Is benevolence ***exclusively*** the work of the church?" If we have learned anything from the discussion among brethren in the early twentieth century, we have learned to question the assumption that these actions are exclusively the work of the church. If this is true, what Scripture teaches it? Certainly, it is not found in 1 Timothy 3:15!

Daniel Sommers' objections to individually supported efforts to teach the Bible confused brethren and divided churches needlessly. The logic and truthfulness of his objections to church supported missionary societies were diminished because of this inconsistency. Another inconsistency that likewise diminished his influence was the fact that, even while he opposed any organization other than the local church to teach the Bible, Sommer published *The American Christian Review*, in which periodical he taught the Bible! During the Armstrong-Sommer Debate, this glaring contradiction was forcibly argued by his opponent. We will notice this inconsistency by others as we examine our present-day controversies about 1 Timothy 3:15 later. Claiming that only the local church can teach the Bible does not seem to hinder some from using their own institutions to do the very thing to which they object.

We may summarize what we have learned from the discussions about Daniel Sommer as:

1. Some brethren assign exclusive works to the church and deny the right of any except the local church to do these works.
2. In their view, teaching the Bible and helping the needy (benevolence) are the exclusive works of the church.
3. No collective effort of these works is allowed except through the local church.
4. This approach is different from the ACMS of previous years in that the missionary society was supported by a collectivity of churches, thus activating the universal church.
5. Sommer allowed neither groups of individuals nor church collectives to teach the Bible.

Sommer's "spiritual heirs," W. Carl Ketcherside and Leroy Garrett, were the last loud voices to keep pushing these hobbies past the mid-century point, principally by debating and writing. Ketcherside debated such men as Rue Porter, G.C. Brewer, and G.K. Wallace, and Garrett's opponents were Bill J. Humble and George W. Dehoff. The greatest influence of this strain of "anti-ism" was in the states of Pennsylvania, Indiana, Illinois, and Missouri, and it is largely dead even in those areas. Ironically, Ketcherside (in 1957) and Garrett (in 1959) reversed themselves completely, leaving the extreme narrow view of fellowship demanded by their hobbies, and began championing the most liberal kind of open fellowship and ecumenism.

**Great Truths Learned from the 1950s and Institutionalism**

While Sommer and his companions questioned the right of such organizations to exist whether church supported or not, the issue of the 1950s saw church-supported institutions arise again as the focal point of the battle. The conflict was focused on church support of colleges and orphan homes, but it was a revival of the issues associated with church supported missionary societies. Actually, the seeds of this battle began in the 1930s with the issue of church-supported colleges, but the battle soon incorporated many parallel issues: church-supported orphan homes, old folks' homes, centralized evangelism (Herald of Truth), etc. Brother G. C. Brewer spoke at the lectures at Abilene Christian College, calling for support for the college from congregations. Many brethren objected and it was ten years before N. B. Hardeman, President of Freed Hardeman College again defended the practice. Batsell Barrett Baxter stated it very plainly: "It is my conviction that the schools need to be dependent upon the churches for their financial life blood in order for the schools to remain permanently loyal to the goals and principles the Bible teaches" (*Questions and Issues of the Day*, 30). Ironically, those church-supported schools have not remained loyal to biblical teaching, although brother Baxter thought their dependence upon church support would be what secured their loyalty to God's word.

> Abilene Christian College remained at the center of the institutional debate because it was the most visible and recognizable human institution supported by members of the churches of Christ. As early as the 1930s, the college's leadership began making impassioned pleas to local churches for financial support. A minority of brethren, mostly in the North, were suspicious of the college, and a few people made it clear that they believed it was wrong for the college to ask for funds. C.R. Nichol said in the *Firm Foundation* magazine, *"No, it is not right to take the money contributed by the church of Christ . . . and use it for schools"* ("Religious Digest," Nichol, *Firm Foundation*, [August 11, 1931], 1). The debate became even more serious when G.C. Brewer, an influential preacher from Lubbock, Texas, became the figurehead for A.C.C. monetary support. He made several appeals in the early 1930s to churches and their elders to put Abilene in their regular church budgets (http://wwwsweethome.com/Institutionalism%20History.htm "Institutionalism – A Historical Perspective," Ryan Goodwin).

When it became clear to many preachers that the subject would not remain in the category of "expediency," those who supported the institutions suddenly became impatient and wanted the matter settled. N.B. Hardeman pressed his opponents on the matter by pointing out supposed inconsistencies in their logic. Having supported orphan homes for years, many men like Foy E. Wallace, Jr. were taken to task for arguing so vehemently against colleges. Ed Harrell wrote,

> In his 1947 defense of church contributions to colleges, N.B. Hardeman seized the orphan home argument, noting that support for colleges and the homes "must stand or fall together" (*The Churches of Christ in the Twentieth Century*, 90).
>
> In the late 1940s, preachers scrambled to find a consistent position, and the only right way to argue against the colleges was to throw in orphan and convalescent homes as well (*Ibid.*).
>
> The major figures in the debate over institutionalism were men like Fanning Yater Tant (son of J.D. Tant, the respected Texas frontier preacher), Roy E. Cogdill, and Foy E. Wallace, Jr. representing the non-institutional perspective, and G.C. Brewer, N.B. Hardeman, and B.C. Goodpasture, representing the institutional persuasion (*Ibid.)*.
>
> "Numerous debates were conducted on these issues, some of the most crucial of which were those between W. L. Totty and Charles Holt (1954), E. R. Harper and Yater Tant (1955, 1956), Guy N. Woods and W. Curtis Porter (1956), Guy N. Woods and Roy E. Cogdill (1957), and G. K. Wallace and Charles Holt (1959). (A History Of "Anti-ism" From The Nineteenth Century To the Present by Dub McClish, http://www.scripturecache.com/resources/HISTORY+OF+ANTI-ISM.pdf )

Quotations abound from those who raised warning cries about institutionalism in general and church-supported colleges in particular.

> Institutionalism has destroyed the life and energy of the church today! . . . The next religious war will be fought around the issue of institutionalism (W. E. Brightwell, *Gospel Advocate* [November 29, 1934]).
>
> The ship of Zion has floundered more than once on the sandbar of institutionalism. The tendency to organize is a characteristic of the age. On the theory that the end justifies the means, brethren have not scrupled to form organizations in the church to do the work the church itself was designed to do. All such organizations usurp the work of the church, and are unnecessary and sinful (Guy N. Woods, *Abilene Christian College Lectures*, 1939).

> A great apostasy, maybe, is being planned unaware in the various things that local churches are doing under the eldership. Institutionalism is dangerous because it is a departure from the apostolic way. Human societies to do missionary work is wrong, but no more so than some human organization to take care of the orphans or old people or even the young folks (*Life and Works of C. M. Pullias*, 577).

The first orphanage established by churches of Christ was the Tennessee Orphan Home in Columbia, Tennessee. The Tennessee Orphan Home was chartered in 1909 and officially opened in September 5, 1910. Notice that prior to 1910, church supported orphanages were not a practice.

There seemed to be a concerted effort to gain support from the churches for the college by tying the college to the orphan homes. While discussions about church support for colleges was heated, they were nothing compared to the heat generated by the discussion of institutional "orphan" homes. Those who opposed such support of Boles Homes, Tiptons' Home, Tennessee Orphan Homes, et al, were designated as "anti's," "orphan haters," and "church splitters," or worse. Cartoons appeared in various bulletins and papers showing "anti's" refusing abandoned babies admission to church buildings, kicking babies out of "church" boats that were used to rescue victims of a flood, allowing churches to pay for fertilizer for the lawn but denying money to orphans, etc. It was much easier to generate sympathy for a "poor, helpless orphan" than for an institutional college. "Another miss in the logic of those seeking sanction for unlawful practices *is the assumption that orphan homes furnish a premise* without *fault or criticism* from which to draw the conclusion that any and all other institutions may be included in the budgets of the churches" (Foy E Wallace, *Torch,* [August 1950], 11).

Batsell Barrett Baxter argued, "The orphan home and the Christian school must stand or fall together" (*Questions and Issues of the Day*, 29).

Foy E. Wallace, Jr., known for his reasoned attacks on premillenialism, soon waded into the fight against church-supported colleges (cf. *Bible Banner*, *Gospel Guardian*, etc.).

> Today any man or group of men can start any institution they may please, put it in a benevolent basket, label it "your baby," and place it on the doorstep of the church with the appeal: "Please take care of it!" That is taxation without representation. Again, I say the delegate system of the digressives is better than that, for in that case there would be a voice in what is started. The church is about to become the unwitting and unwilling victim of Institutionalism. And Institutionalism is about to become

> a racket. Where is there *scriptural* precedent or precept for scouring the country for orphans, transporting them from sections far and wide to an institution that was not created by orphans in a particular community, but which a promoter created by searching for orphans. Is this editor against taking care of orphans? *He is not!* But he is against the institutionalism racket. It is the duty of the church to care for their dependents and they should provide means for doing so under their own supervision. If individuals wish to operate hospitals, inns, homes or schools, it is their right to do so. But the church cannot operate institutions. If the church can do its benevolent work through a board of directors, why not its mission work through a board of directors? If one is a society, why not the other? There is no such thing as "our" institutions, if by "our" you mean the church. (*Bible Banner,* [July 1939], 3).

> Nearly fourteen years ago the original *Gospel Guardian* appeared, titled and formatted by my brother Cled and me after we had read together Paul's appeal to Timothy. "O Timothy, guard that which is committed to the trust" (I Timothy 6:20) with the added and final charge, "that good thing which was committed unto thee guard by the Holy Spirit which is in us." (II Timothy 1:14) . . . But to the menace of millennialism there was then added, as an incipient issue, the inroads of secular institutionalism into the sacred precincts of the church. The *Bible Banner* met this issue then and there, has met it ever since, is meeting it here and now, and we shall "continue to meet it hereafter and forever, for the life and duration of the *Banner* and the *Guardian* or the tenure of their successors . . . ." So in the might of the God of Israel and in the name of the Christ of the church, in the spirit of the indomitable Paul, with an all-out effort to stem the tide of digression again, to stay the subversive influences of compromise, and to uphold the truth in the midst of the multiplied defections and departures that confront and surround us, that the pure church of Christ may be preserved unto our children, let us all who honor this heritage and espouse this cause, and who are thus likeminded, say together in resounding unison—THEY SHALL NOT PASS! (Foy E. Wallace, Jr., quoted by Cecil Willis *Truth Magazine* VIII: 11 [August 1964], p. 3).

Of course, the challenge by brother Wallace that "they shall not pass" was a declaration of warfare. He intended that it be, and it was received by his critics as such. These opening salvos against institutionalism introduced decades of debate and increasing hostilities.

> As a matter of record and a reminder of the facts in the case request is here made for all to refer to the May and July issues of the *Bible Banner*, in which will be found editorials of my own dealing with the church-supported college question. These editorials discussed the issue, injecting

nothing unrelated to the issue. But the ire of certain brethren was aroused, precipitating the onslaught of personalities, and a veritable barrage of character assault was laid down against us. We have replied. We stand by the replies. We have stated the facts and told the truth about all matters related. From these positions we shall not recede, and not one point at issue shall we surrender.

In the current controversy among the brethren over the sphere of the school, the college and the church, certain colleges are themselves the aggressors. The controversy will be just as easily stopped as it was started—just let the schools abandon their departures, discontinue their objectionable practices, reform their worldliness, cease to infringe on the divine principle of the independence of the church from all human institutions, and quit imposing on congregations, and all will be well. In short, let the college stay in its place, and let the church alone.

For an example of the aggression mentioned, one of the leaders of the campaign to put the college in the budget of the churches closed an article with the statement that if it is not right to put the college in the budget, then he would join Daniel Sommer and be done with it. In other words, he will have it this way or no way! It is that "this way or no way" spirit that has always driven the wedges, forcing issues upon the brethren, then blaming those in honest opposition to their schemes for resultant dissensions. It was so in the digressive movement that split the church. It has been so in the "Boll movement" which says: "we will have our theories." It is now so in the present controversy with the colleges whose leader and mouthpiece says "we will have the budget or nothing." In that case the brethren should see to it that it will be nothing—from the churches. With this announced attitude the colleges can blame no one but themselves for the growing opposition to them or for any division or alienation that may arise over the discussions (*Bible Banner*, X: 1 [January 1948], pp. 2-4a).

But the name "Bible college" has caused so much confusion in the minds of so many that it becomes necessary to discuss the relation of the school and the church. Let us compare the work of the church with the work of the school in seeking to obtain the correct answer to the question involved. The Bible teaches that the work of the church is twofold. First, missionary, pertaining to the spread of the gospel—the salvation of souls. Hence, the church is called "the pillar and ground of the truth." Second, benevolent, pertaining to the care of the poor, orphan, or aged. This is referred to as "pure religion." The Bible further teaches that the church is all-sufficient to carry out this divine mission without the aid of human machinery. Any organization larger or smaller than the local congregation is an unscriptural organization through which to do the work of the church, and takes

> away from it the praise and glory. Therefore, we condemn the missionary society as an auxiliary to the church, a human machine seeking to do the work that God has commanded his church to do. We pronounce it, without further argument here, unscriptural.
>
> What, then, "is the 'Bible college?" It is an auxiliary indeed, but not to the church (*Ibid.).*

It was abundantly clear that opposition to Bible colleges, as well as "orphans homes," etc., was only because of the drive to put these institutions in church budgets. They were not viewed by Wallace and his brethren as inherently sinful. However, when they made a grab for financial support from church treasuries, they overstepped their bounds. Church-supported institutions were the focus of the battle.

> These principles are fundamental. Let us draw the lines clearly. We have pointed out the central thought of the subject—namely, the school as an auxiliary of the home. This being true, it is not the business of the church to run it. The church is not in the school business. The only way the church can scripturally do its work is through the elders of the local congregation. Appeals made to churches, therefore, in behalf of schools are wrong—fundamentally wrong—wrong in principle. Let the school stand where it belongs, apart from the church, as an aid to, and adjunct of, the home. Let parents and individuals realize their duty and feel their responsibility in the support and maintenance of them, thus making it possible for our children and our neighbors' children to have the training and influence they so much need and deserve. —(In the *Gospel Advocate*, 1931) (*Bible Banner*, "The Issues — Then And Now," Part 1, X: 1 [January 1948], pp. 2-4a).
>
> Periodically defeated in the deliberate plans to get in the budgets of the churches, as in 1935-38 and again in 1945-48, already we are hearing *post mortem* gasps with threats to try again . . . and in less than a decade it will be necessary to fight the battle all over again, for some are saying already that they will win it in the next campaign *(Torch,* Aug. 1950, p. 7).
>
> It appears certain that the fight against organizations and digression made in Texas and Tennessee fifty years ago must be fought all over again. If this sounds like an over-statement of the situation, just take a look at the picture: A central eldership in the United States overseeing institutional boards in foreign countries through which to do the work of the church, with all other churches working through this central eldership of one church, which in turn works through the man-made boards of human organizations somewhere else! (*Ibid.*, 20).

Brother Floyd A. Decker, a preacher well-known for leaving the Christian Church eighteen years previously due to their multiplied errors, saw the same errors becoming a reality within the church and raised his voice against them.

> Before leaving the "Christian Church", I learned many lessons concerning the evils of the United Christian Missionary Society (UCMS). I learned that the thing itself was evil and amounted to nothing more or less than a political machine with all the ruthless tactics of the same, rendered more evil because of the guise of religion. The UMCS was a giant octopus with tentacles running out in every direction—into every congregation grasping and choking until what little respect for New Testament authority remained was released. The manhood of the preachers and elders was sapped and their faith in God drained off until what started out to be a movement to advance the Cause for which Jesus died ended up in decay and death. The only advancement made is material unless it is in the realm of worldliness. They advanced now to where the inspiration of the Bible and the divinity of Christ is denied by many of the very ones who launched the program to advance the will of God on earth.
>
> Much has been said recently concerning the right of a local congregation to support institutions. Institutionalism has such an evil reputation and has resulted in such great corruptions, especially when connected with churches or religious movements, that it seems to me we should know enough without further discussion to turn away from them. Speeches supporting the idea of the "College in the budget" come with very poor grace from those who are to be benefited. Why not leave the discussion to those whose motives can not be charged? Oh, I see now! You say if we did that there would be none to make the speeches!
>
> There is no scriptural argument for a local congregation, as such, supporting any kind of an institution, as such. When churches of the Lord become tributary to an outside institution, by whatsoever name called, it will eventually become subsidiary to the same (*Bible Banner*, X: 1 [January 1948], pp. 12-13).

Brother Decker had a clear view of error, having renounced it when he left the Christian Church. He recognized the gathering speed with which the apostasy was moving and appealed, fruitlessly, for brethren to learn from his own experience.

> May God help us take the warning from the Christian church. They have gone far astray from the word of God. Since I left them they have gone farther faster than I thought they would. There is yet hope for many individuals within that body but as a body there is no hope of recovery.

> Brethren let us think now and stop the downward plunge. We are not drifting—we are plunging! Back to the Bible, back to the church of the Bible, back to the organization of the Bible, back, back, BACK to where we started and where we must be found and where we will wish we were when the world is on fire (*Ibid.).*

Cled, the brother of Foy E. Wallace, added his voice and pen to the fray, making it clear that institutions must leave the church alone. He stated succinctly that he did not oppose private institutions so long as they operated without church funds.

> What do I mean by institutionalism? I mean anything in the way of an organization that comes between the church and its appointed work. A church has no right to turn its obligations and responsibilities over to any kind of an institution. Now that's New Testament teaching (Cled Wallace, *Bible Banner*, X:9 [Sept. 1948], pp. 1-7, 10).

> All right, if a man's going to conduct a school, and if it's going to grow into an institution, and it's a private affair, an adjunct of the home, to be supported by individuals, just like a publishing house, a hardware store or something else, well and good; but it must not assume power and reach out to control churches. It must leave the church's business strictly alone. The church is the independent body of Christ, a divine organization, and we oppose the efforts to farm out its work to the colleges and turn it over to the institutions among us (Cled Wallace, *Bible Banner*, X: 9 [Sept. 1948], pp. 1-7, 10).

It was clear to some who had historic ties to colleges that they did not begin with the purpose of operating with church funds. A. B. Barret selected the site for the college in 1906 and called for brethren to help build a school.

> Indeed, the founder of Abilene Christian College recognized the colleges were not proper recipients of church funds. "There were no 'brotherhood colleges,' 'church papers,' 'church orphanages,' 'old folk's homes,' and the like, among apostolic congregations. . . . Individual Christians, any number, may scripturally engage in any worthwhile work, such as running colleges, papers, and orphanages, and other individual Christians may properly assist them in every proper way; but no local congregation should be called upon as such, to contribute a thing to any such enterprise. Such a call would be out of harmony with the word of the living God. And if any congregation so contributes, it transcends its scriptural prerogatives" (*Gospel Advocate*, March 13, 1930).

In spite of the frequent, insistent, and repetitive challenges of brethren to the church-supported colleges to produce Scripture or give up their dependency on church treasuries, most colleges operated by brethren today look to churches for funds to operate. So far as can be determined, only Florida College in Temple Terrace, Florida, refuses church contributions as a matter of conscience. Additionally, children's homes and other institutions continue to operate among "institutional" churches at church expense. As in 1906, a definite division among institutional (I) and non-institutional (NI) churches exists. History has repeated itself.

We may summarize what we have learned from the controversy fifty years ago as follows:

1. Many do not learn from the past and, thus, are doomed to repeat the mistakes of years gone by.
2. Promoters of institutions see church treasuries as fertile opportunities to fund their activities. Most are not willing to limit their fund-raising to individuals.
3. Creators of institutions are ruthless and cunning in their allegiance to their creations. If objections are raised, the standard response is to attack the personality of the one objecting (*ad hominem* argument), "orphan haters," "you don't believe in evangelism," etc.
4. All church-funded institutions stand or fall together; there is no difference between church supported missionary societies and church supported benevolent societies.
5. The church universal is composed of individual saints, not local churches.
6. The local church (Phil. 1:1) is able to fulfill the work that God intended for the church to accomplish.
7. Individuals, whether alone or in groups, have functions to do outside the parameters of the local church and in no sense compete with the local church.

## A Present Controversy
## Can We Apply The Lessons Learned?

This brings us to our present age and the continuing battle against institutions, missionary and benevolent societies, and the relationship between the local church and individuals. It seems somewhat easier to sit in judgment over previous generations and their activities than to apply what we have learned to our own activities. But we have been warned to "examine yourselves, as to whether or not you are in the faith. Prove yourselves" (2 Cor. 13:5). If we are to be honest with those brethren who have gone before us, and honest with ourselves, we must apply the Scriptures equally to them and to us. Are we free from institutionalism? Are we forming missionary and benevolent societies? Are we trying to activate the universal church? Are we forming unscriptural collectivities?

It has been charged that we are making the same mistakes of the past.

> What is wrong with brethren pooling their resources and forming privately funded missionary societies, edification orders, and relief for needy saints organizations? In the first place, God has told us what organization to use, the local church. I remind all of the simple hermeneutic rule that when a specific is supplied, all that constitutes a different matter is excluded and is to be viewed as an aberrant. "Let the Church be the Church – A Review."
>
> **Addendum**: This review is not denying individual action (cp. I Tim. 5:16). Also, the review is not addressing two Christians concurrently teaching another, etc. The material is focusing on Christians forming an organization with full entity structure and a treasury through which to preach the gospel. Other than the local church, there is no observed teaching either in precept, example, or necessary inference for privately supported missionary societies. The neo-institutional mind-set of many today thinks one can be a member of such an entity as the **Guardian of Truth Foundation** or even **Truth Magazine** as a staff writer and still only individually function. Alas, such thinking is patently flawed (Don Martin, http://www.bibletruths.net/Archives/BTAR296.htm).
>
> The question is, are we free to form religious, or spiritual, collectivities as we may please, or has God *specified* the religious collectivity through which we are to worship and serve Him? The answer is, God has called us together in *the church! (Gospel Anchor,* Nov. 1977).
>
> If individuals may form collectivities to preach the gospel, may they not form societies for collective worship and edification? But why would Christians want to do this, seeing we have a perfectly good arrangement—a divine arrangement—in the church? (*Ibid.*).

Currently, men such as J. T. Smith (*Gospel Truths*) and Gene Frost (*Gospel Anchor*), and a few others, continue to make the same argument as Sommer, questioning the right of Florida College and Truth Foundation to teach the Bible. Don Martin argued,

> Many changes are occurring among my brethren, as well. One matter that has of late occupied more of my focus has been the privately funded societies to offer the climate and milieu for brethren to pool their resources in and through which to collectively preach the gospel, institutions while not local churches, are doing the work God has assigned to the local church (I Tim. 3: 15) (http://www.bibletruths.net/archives/BTAR330.htm).

In such plain language as this, the errors of Sommerism are being repeated today. None likes to be labeled a "Sommerite," but the similarity of the arguments is unmistakable.

Under the guise of 1 Timothy 3:15, and with the argument of the all-sufficiency of the church, some brethren are reviving arguments from the past and denying to others the right to act as individuals in efforts such as this lectureship. They continue to assert that teaching the Bible is the exclusive work of the church. They deny the right of group activity to anything save the local church. Even benevolence as a group activity is attacked as unscriptural. Meetings have been cancelled and support has been denied to evangelists whose name appears on this lectureship program. The subject has been debated and various books have been written in defense of both sides. Among those who have supported both the Truth Lectures and the lectures of Florida College, *We Have A Right* (a book by Mike Willis and Dan King, with an addendum by Thomas G. O'Neal) has been published and is available today. On the other hand, Gene Frost (*Gospel Anchor*) has written extensively against such lectures in general and the *Truth Foundation* in particular and an index to much of his material can be located at http://www.brotherhoodsocieties.com/ArticleIndex.htm.

We are told that it is *sinful* for brethren to do what we are doing today. Likewise, it is *sinful* for brethren to arrange a situation in which prayer, singing, and Bible teaching take place outside of the local church. We are told that such spiritual action is solely and only the work of the local church. Is preaching the work of the local church only? Is singing the work of the local church only? Is praying the work of the local church only?

> A failure to properly distinguish between individual action and joint action has been a constant source of confusion in the churches of Christ and detrimental to its peace and harmony. For the sake of clarity, we define *individual action* as conduct involving solely the volition of the individual or individuals involved. When several individuals are involved, the action is *concurrent* as distinguished from *independent* action when the individual acts alone. *By joint action* we mean action in which individuals cooperate,

> each acquiescing his own volition in favor of the collective will. It also may be called *collective action,* a term we prefer and will use henceforth in this study (Gene Frost, *Gospel Anchor*, October 1977).

In the above quote, brother Frost uses a dictionary to give a very limited definition to "individual action" and then judges everything according to this limited definition. The confusion comes from the fact that the dictionary does not stop where brother Frost stops. While he limits "individual" to "one person," the dictionary goes on to say, "6. of which each is different or of a different design from the others: *a set of individual coffee cups* . . . 10. a group considered as a unit" (*The American College Dictionary*, 618). Please note this distinction carefully. Brother Frost wants to limit an individual as one person while the dictionary recognizes that individual may include a "*set*," or a "*group*." Nothing is truer than the old saying, "If you let your opponent define the terms he will always defeat you." Brother Frost wants us to accept his terms, but I want the full dictionary terminology. It is possible to have **group** action or action of a **set**, while still operating in the realm of the **individual**. Sommer, Frost, Smith, et. al., refuse to allow such action and seek to force every "group" to compete with the local church.

| Frost's Definition | American College Dictionary |
|---|---|
| Individual | Individual |
| One Person Only | Set |
| | Group |

Though Daniel Sommer softened in his stance in later years prior to his death, identifying the college issue as a matter of opinion, the issue became prominent in the thinking of some brethren and it has disquieted brethren until this day. It is more than a little ironic that Sommer fought doggedly against the Bible being taught by any group other than the church in his early life but became more tolerant as he aged. But the same objections to Bible teaching by any other than the local church has now been revived by men such as Gene Frost and J. T. Smith. Both J. T. and Gene would agree with us in our opposition to the church-supported missionary society, but by affirming that the church has the exclusive right to teach the Bible, they make the same arguments as Sommer!

Of course, the phrase "individually supported missionary society" is a prejudicial term and it is uniformly rejected by all of us. We could call the local church a "missionary society," but we don't because it carries a connotation of confusion and division. Is the church a society of brethren who are "missionary"? Of course, but we have a scriptural term which we use: the local church. Why confuse some with nomenclature that has historic "baggage"? Prejudicially, some continue to charge us with believing in an "individually supported missionary society." This is a charge straight out of Sommerism. In fact, what do we believe? We believe and teach that in addition to the work performed by a local church, individuals also have a responsibility to teach, pray, sing, edify, and practice benevolence. Though we may act as a "group," it is still in the individual realm and does not compete with or contradict the work of any local church.

### Thou That Judgest Others, Condemnest Not Thyself? Romans 2:1

The Jews took great glee at Paul's condemnation of the Gentiles in Romans One, but did not recognize their equal (if not greater) guilt in God's sight. They judged others, but could not see their own condemnation.

There is a parallel in this discussion before us. Critics of Florida College and the Truth Foundation are vehement in their condemnation of human societies that teach the Bible, not acknowledging that they are, likewise, human societies that teach the Bible!

> What we oppose are collectivities—companies or societies, incorporated or unincorporated— which solicit the pooling of resources of individuals or churches for the teaching of the gospel (in supporting preachers, broadcasting over radio or TV, distributing literature, etc.) under the oversight of a human board. This supplants the church, wherein individuals pool resources for the teaching of the gospel, which treasury is under the oversight of elders! (Gene Frost, private publication 2/22/79).

While it is fully understood and agreed that no collectivity should solicit the pooling of resources from churches for the teaching of the Bible (which collectivity would be a church-supported missionary society), there remains the stubborn opposition by brothers Frost, Smith, and others to collectivities which operate in the realm of the individual. Sommer opposed them. Gene Frost opposes them. J. T. Smith opposes them. Yet, in no uncertain terms, as diagrammed below, the opposition by which they judge us to be unscriptural points the finger of accusation at themselves!

Again, "Thou that judgest others, condemnest not thyself?" How is it possible to look at these human institutions side-by-side and not recognize their identical structures? While Florida College (for some reason) has not

| Truth Foundation Collectivity | Florida College Collectivity | Gene Frost Collectivity: Gospel Anchor | J.T. Smith Collectivity: Gospel Truths |
|---|---|---|---|
| Not the church | Not the church | Not the church | Not the church |
| Takes no money from churches | Takes no money from churches | Takes no money from churches | Takes no money from churches |
| A human institution | A human institution | A human institution | A human institution |
| Writes own creed and by-laws | Writes own creed and by-laws | Writes own creed and by-laws | Writes own creed and by-laws |
| Organized to teach the Bible | Organized to teach the Bible | Organized to teach the Bible | Organized to teach the Bible |
| Incorporated | Incorporated | Incorporated | Incorporated |
| Has officers and board | Has officers and board | Has officers and board | Has officers and board |
| Accepts donations, money and manuscripts from individuals (pooled resources) | Accepts donations, money and manuscripts from individuals (pooled resources) | Accepts manuscripts from individuals (pooled resources) | Accepts manuscripts from individuals (pooled resources) |
| Teaches the Bible Sells its Services | Teaches the Bible Sells its Services | Teaches the Bible Sells its Services | Teaches the Bible Sells its Services |

been the focal point of criticisms for teaching the Bible (as in past years), vehement attacks against Truth Foundation fill the internet, sermons and papers. Some churches have decided that any individual appearing on the Truth Lectures cannot hold meetings, receive support and participate in fellowship with those churches. Rather than leave this issue where it belongs, in the area of expediency and personal conscience, some continue to attack Truth Foundation as unscriptural. But if the Truth Foundation is unlawful to exist, why is Gospel Truths and Gospel Anchor lawful? Those who are so vocal against Truth Foundation, why have you given respite to Florida College for doing what it is doing? I hope Florida College is enjoying its moment of quietude; Truth Foundation hasn't found the same rare quality of acceptance.

The truth of the matter is that all the human institutions above have a right to teach the Bible! I would defend the right of Florida College, Gospel Truths, and Gospel Anchor to continue their right to publish and teach the word of God. But even so does the Truth Foundation have a right to teach the Bible, both in the printed medium and orally.

We have a right as individuals acting together to do what all these human institutions are doing (teach the Bible), without interfering or competing with any local church. Teaching the Bible is not the exclusive work of any given local church. Allow the church to operate in its realm, but also allow the individual to operate in his realm.

### What 1 Timothy 3:15 Does Not Teach

There is a vast difference between agreeing that the church is all-sufficient to do the work God has assigned to it which opposes the church-supported missionary society and denying brethren the right to participate in lectures in which singing, praying, and teaching are an integral part. Such efforts do not comprise a missionary society, usurp the work of any local church, or drain the resources of any church. *If any brother contends otherwise, let him name the church that has had its autonomy usurped or its treasury drained of a single penny.*

### The Church Is All-Sufficient To Do Its Work!
### Is The Individual Not Also All-Sufficient To Do His Work?

While agreeing with the all-sufficiency of the church, we must insist on the *right of the individual* to be all-sufficient as well. While there are items of worship peculiar to the local church (the Lord's supper and church contributions), there is much work and worship that God has assigned to the individual. It is my understanding that much of this controversy would cease if brethren would grant the right to individuals that God has assigned to them.

• **Is it right** for brethren to practice free enterprise and establish businesses as individuals? May such a business be incorporated without ceasing to be individual enterprise? May such a business provide opportunity for friends, employees, or others to teach the Bible, sing, pray, or practice benevolence?

• **Is it right** for brethren as individuals in their free enterprise to use part of their funds to teach the Bible, sing, pray, or practice benevolence?

• **Is it right** for a plurality of brethren to act together as individuals without usurping the work of a local church? We need only refer Bible students to Matthew 18:15-17 to show the difference between one individual, a group of two or more, and the church. Clearly, a group of two or more is not the same as a single individual, nor is it the same as a church. Yet, Jesus authorized a group (two or more) to work together in a spiritual activity.

• **Is it right** for brethren to pray individually and collectively outside the local assembly? Is prayer exclusively the work of the local church?

• **Is it right** for brethren to sing individually and collectively outside the local assembly? Is singing exclusively the work of the local church? Did Paul and Silas sin while singing and praying outside the assembly (Acts 16:25)?

• **Is it right** for brethren to preach and teach individually and collectively outside the local assembly? Is preaching and teaching exclusively the work of a local church? Did Acquila and Priscilla sin when they taught Apollos "more accurately the way of the Lord" (Acts 18:26)?

• **Is it right** for a family of Christians (mother, father, children, kinfolk) to pray, sing, or teach outside the assembly? Is it right for them to pool their money to support evangelism, edification, or benevolence? Does a married couple sin when they take money from a joint bank account to support an evangelist?

• **Is it right** for brethren to practice benevolence individually and collectively outside the local assembly? Is benevolence exclusively the work of the local church? Did Dorcas sin when she performed works of charity (Acts 9:36)?

• **Is it right** for brethren to help one another financially in order to support a good work outside the local assembly? Can brethren ever pool money as individuals without usurping the local treasury? Did Mary Magdalene and other women sin when they pooled money to help finance the work of Jesus (Luke 8:1-3)?

These and other questions are pertinent to our controversy today.

### The Local Church Is Limited

We agree that the local church must have either generic or specific authority from God before it may engage in any particular work or spend any of its funds. Such authority must exist before the church has a right to act. This has been successfully debated over many years and we are generally agreed on the principles that authorize the local church to act. Whether in worship, evangelism, benevolence, or edification, authority must precede action.

### The Individual Has More Liberty

In the first century, Ananias and Sapphira lied to the Holy Spirit about their financial contributions and were slain by God for their sins. In rebuking Ananias for his lies, Peter asked, "While it remained, was it not your own? And after it was sold, *was it not in your own control?"* (Acts 5:4, italics for emp.). Clearly, this passage teaches that any individual has personal control of his/her finances and can act freely under the generic authority granted to individuals. But what does this mean? Simply, that God has granted individuals more liberty in the use of their money and abilities than He has the local church. *This is sadly overlooked by those who wish to bind the all-sufficiency of the church to the exclusion of individuals.* I believe this to be the crux of our differences on this subject. Are individuals authorized to teach, sing, pray, or practice benevolence outside the local church? As ludicrous as it sounds, some are denying individuals these rights. Is it right for this lectureship to exist outside the auspices of a local church? Is it right for us to pray together outside the local assembly? Is it right for us to sing together outside the local assembly? Is it right for the Bible to be taught without a local church being in charge? Must we yield to the strident voices of those who object? Have we not learned from past controversies in which some objected to Bible classes and individual communion cups? Misdirected zeal and misapplication of scriptural principles has haunted us in the past and will continue to haunt us until we learn to make proper application of God's word.

### Authority for Individuals

Much of the New Testament is written to individuals to encourage them to serve in the kingdom of Christ.

- Sermon on the Mount – Matthew 5-7
- Evangelism – Acts 8:4; 8:35; 2 Timothy 2:2, 4
- Benevolence – 1 Timothy 5:16; James 2:15-16
- Edification – Acts 18:26; 2 Timothy 2:2
- Prayer – Acts 16:25; 1 Timothy 2:1
- Singing – Acts 16:25; Ephesians 5:19
- Use of money – Acts 5:4

In fact, the individual is not the church and cannot be limited as the church is limited (1 Cor. 12:14; 1 Tim. 5:16).

We may summarize:

| Congregational Action | Individual Action Alone or With Others |
|---|---|
| Singing (Heb. 2:12) | Singing (Eph. 5:19) |
| Praying (1 Cor. 14:16) | Praying (Acts 12:12) |
| Teaching, Preaching (Acts 15:22-33) | Teaching, Preaching (Acts 8:35) |
| Contribution (1 Cor. 16:1-2) | |
| Lord's Supper (Acts 20:7) | |
| Evangelism (Phil. 4:15) | Evangelism (2 Tim. 2:2) |
| Edification (1 Cor. 14:26) | Edification (Acts 18:26) |
| Benevolence (2 Cor. 8, 9) | Benevolence (Acts 9:36) |
| Use of money (2 Cor. 8:23) | Use of money (Acts 5:4; Luke 8:1-3) |

Some brethren have arbitrarily made a rule that individuals cannot pool their money in any spiritual enterprise without violating Scripture. *I ask, "What Scripture?" Where is this rule found in God's word?* Yes, we agree that churches cannot pool their money, but the individual is not bound by such restrictions in the light of Acts 5:4. At Gladewater, Texas, during the 1950s controversy, I heard some express the rule against individuals acting apart from the local church thusly: "Any money spent by individuals to support evangelism, benevolence, or edification must be deposited in the local treasury so that God can get the glory through the church." The scriptural "proof"? You guessed it: 1 Timothy 3:15, along with Ephesians 3:21. Are we not able to see the fallacy of such reasoning? Yes, the church is the "pillar and ground of the truth." But a misconception of this passage forces it to refer to a local church only and makes null and void the work of individuals in the service of Christ, whether alone or with others. If 1 Timothy 3:15 is interpreted in such a manner that it violates other passages of Scripture, that interpretation must be wrong! The work of the church does not negate the work of individuals. Just as it is wrong to teach that the local church can act as individuals, even so is it wrong to state that individuals are bound by the rules governing local churches. Individuals have liberties that are not allowed to congregations.

Mike Willis related a conversation he had with his brother Cecil about the subject of opposition to the Bible department at Florida College. Cecil stated that institutional brethren had argued that the church can do anything the individual can do to defend church support of human institutions (orphan homes and colleges). On the other hand, some brethren were arguing that whatever the church cannot do (support orphan homes and colleges), the individual cannot do (operate a college which teaches the Bible). Both views are mistaken.

Much of our history reflects the misunderstanding of these principles. If one argues for a "pattern" which prohibits pooling of funds among individuals to do various spiritual works, that one is obligated to produce the scriptures that establish the pattern. A single example otherwise will show that the pattern is not, indeed, a pattern. We will note later the action of Jesus' disciples in Luke 8:1-3 of a "pooled" treasury. This alone would destroy the so-called "pattern." The practical results of such a theory would condemn a married couple who would pool their money in a joint bank account to make a joint contribution to the church treasury, to practice benevolence, or support an evangelist, or do other spiritual works. *Remember, the contention is that no individuals can pool their money outside the local treasury to do a spiritual work.* We have shown this to be invalid and erroneous.

This difference between the individual and the local church is a basic scriptural principle. It is not feigned or a stretch of the imagination. No Scripture must be forced beyond or outside of its context to substantiate this principle. Thus, those who are objecting to such individual activity as we are practicing are honor bound to deal forthrightly with this principle. It will not do to just wave one's hand and dismiss the argument. It is not right to ignore reasoned, biblical, and sound discussions of Scripture simply because they differ with another's judgment. We call upon those who disagree to recognize a biblical realm of service (individualism) which does not violate any part of the work of the local church. Acknowledge this principle and the controversy ceases!

Let us pose some questions that might help us to get to the heart of the controversy.

- May an individual pray, sing, teach, and practice benevolence?
- May two individuals together, pray, sing, teach, and practice benevolence?
- May individuals pool their funds to provide opportunities to pray, sing, teach, and practice benevolence?
- May these individuals form an organization to maintain order and provide opportunities for their actions?
- May these individuals incorporate under civil law to protect themselves from law suits?

*At what point did the action of these individuals become corporate (collective) action which competes with the local church? Is it not possible to act as a "group" of individuals without being a church or competing with the church?*

If an objection is made at the point of "pooling their funds," I would remind you that individuals in a marriage relationship pool their money into a joint bank account and may utilize this arrangement for teaching the Bible and benevolence.

If an objection is made at the point of "forming an organization," brethren form all kinds of organizations constantly under the free enterprise system. Even a secular business enterprise may spend part of its funds to promote Bible study.

If an objection is made at the point on "incorporating," I would remind you that individuals, families, and churches often incorporate as a matter of civil procedure to protect themselves in case of a law suit against them.

All of this points to the separation of the local church from the individual. The simple act of brethren working together does not compete with the local church. While they may be acting together, it is yet in the realm of individual action and not congregational.

Ron Halbrook distinguished individual action, joint action, and church action in some material he distributed at the 2008 Truth Magazine lectures. From that material, the following chart was prepared:

**Principle of Two Are Better Than One**

| Work | Individual Action | Joint Action | Church Action |
|---|---|---|---|
| To provide one's needs | Eph. 4:28 | Acts 18:3 | 1 Cor. 16:1-2 |
| To correct the erring | Matt. 18:15 | Matt. 18:16 | Matt. 18:17 |
| To pray | James 5:13 | Acts 16:25 | Acts 2:42 |
| To sing | James 5:13 | Acts 16:25 | Col. 3:16 |
| To teach | Acts 8:5 | Acts 18:26 | 1 Tim. 3:15 |
| To support teaching | Gal. 6:6 | Acts 16:15 | Phil. 4:15 |
| To help the needy | James 1:27 | 1 Cor. 16:15 | 1 Cor. 16:1-2 |
| To care for widows | 1 Tim. 5:16 | 1 Tim. 5:16 | 1 Tim. 5:16 |

Halbrook concluded by making these observations:

- The local church is authorized to function only through its divine organization, it may not centralize its work by donating its money to human organizations (missionary society).
- Christians may teach alone or jointly without violating the unique nature of the church
- Schools, businesses, and other groups which provide occasions for Bible teaching are not comparable to a missionary society. They are comparable to the synagogue and Jesus' joint work with the disciples in Mosaic Age, and comparable to joint activities recorded in the New Testament.

## Other Important Considerations

While we have carefully examined the issues from a historical and scriptural basis, we have, to this point, advanced little in the way of positive arguments for our actions. Most of the text has been analyzing and answering objections rather than presenting a positive case. Now, let us present some Bible facts to provide a Bible basis for our actions. We would be remiss if we did not use this opportunity to show clearly that the work we are doing is eminently scriptural.

Please note that the accusation against us is that any group that operates outside the local church is a violation of Scripture since God assigned the church as the only (exclusive) collective by which the Bible can be taught.

To prove false the proposition that the church has the exclusive authority to teach the Bible, one need only to provide Bible authority for one other collectivity to teach the Bible. Please consider the following:

**The Synagogue.** What do we know about the synagogue? Here is what historians tell us:

> (Gr. sunagoge, i.e., 'an assembly'), found only once in the Authorized Version of Ps. 74:8, where the margin of Revised Version has 'places of assembly,' which is probably correct; for while the origin of synagogues is unknown, it may well be supposed that buildings or tents for the accommodation of worshippers may have existed in the land from an early time, and thus the system of synagogues would be gradually developed.
>
> Some, however, are of opinion that it was specially during the Babylonian captivity that the system of synagogue worship, if not actually introduced, was at least reorganized on a systematic plan (Ezek. 8:1; 14:1). The exiles gathered together for the reading of the law and the prophets as they

> had opportunity, and after their return synagogues were established all over the land (Ezra 8:15; Neh. 8:2). In after years, when the Jews were dispersed abroad, wherever they went they erected synagogues and kept up the stated services of worship (Acts 9:20; 13:5; 17:1; 17:17; 18:4) (http://www.biblegateway.com/resources/dictionaries/dict_meaning.php?source=1&wid=T0003545).

Later scholarship disputes some of the assumptions about an early beginning for the synagogue and a good source for study on this subject is Mike Willis' response to Gene Frost in *We Have A Right, Revised* (259-273). Many sources not available to most of us are considered and valuable insights to its origin and function are presented.

Of one thing we can sure, the synagogue was not the church! Furthermore, there is no divine commandment, approved example, or necessary inference that the synagogue existed prior to the completion of the Old Testament canon. A synagogue was an authorized liberty, not a divinely required arrangement for worship and work. Most commentators agree that the origin of the synagogue is lost in ancient history, but they existed both in the Old and New Testament eras (Acts 15:21) and were not condemned by God. Yet, the synagogue was an *organized collectivity*, with officers (Mark 5:22, etc.) and members, in which worship, prayer, and teaching took place on a regular and planned basis. Jesus Christ, Himself, worshipped and taught in the synagogues (Matt. 12:9; Mark 3:1; 6:2) without exhibiting disapproval of the institution itself. The apostle Paul often taught in the synagogues at home and abroad, teaching the Bible in the synagogue arrangement. If, then, as some contend, it is unscriptural for any other collective to teach the Bible or provide a place for worship, what were Jesus and the apostles doing in the synagogues? Is teaching the Bible exclusively the work of the local church or not? It is clear that the synagogue arrangement was utilized by Jesus and the apostles. *Would they have done so if the synagogue arrangement was sinful?* My question is not: Would Daniel Sommer approve? Would Gene Frost or J. T. Smith approve? I cannot tell you since I know not their answer, but the definitions they use would condemn the synagogue as a collectivity that competed with the local church. Would their objections be as vocal if we named our gathering today Synagogue Lectures instead of Truth Lectures?

It also needs to be emphasized that the synagogue was not the same as the Temple. The Temple was an exclusive place of worship for the Jewish nation and the sacrifices were to be offered here and at no other place (Exod. 25:8-9; 16, 22; 30:1; Deut. 12:11-14). Worship was acceptable at the

Temple, as a place of prayer (Isa. 56:7). The Samaritan woman understood that Jerusalem was the "place where one ought to worship" (John 4:19). Now, what does this mean? Was it sinful for Jews to worship collectively at any other location? Surely not, for Jesus, the apostles, and thousands of Jews worshipped at synagogues all over Israel. Did the synagogue compete with the church? No. Did the synagogue compete with the Temple? No. The synagogue was a collectivity in every place where it was established, it had officers (was organized), made provision for prayer and worship even in Jerusalem where it co-existed side by side with the Temple. If Daniel Sommer had lived in those days, his beliefs, if logically applied, would have denied the synagogue the right to exist! Those today who ridicule the "synagogue argument" have no real answer to the fact of the synagogue in relation to the Temple and the church.

**School of Tyrannus:** Is it a sin for brethren to teach the Bible in a college? The apostle Paul, who wrote 1 Timothy 3:15, did not see it as a contradiction. It is recorded in Acts 19:9 that Paul withdrew the disciples from the synagogue and began teaching daily in the "school of Tyrannus." We know so little about the school, its organization, or its purpose that I will not make of this more than the Bible does. It is possible that Paul utilized the school by renting space/rooms for his teaching. I doubt seriously that he was part of the paid staff, but who can be sure? But we can know that he was present at the school and was identified by his teaching there because he was at the school for two years and "all who dwelt in Asia heard the word of the Lord Jesus, both Jews and Greeks." Paul taught the Bible in a school. Can the *Truth Foundation* also rent rooms and invite people to come study the Bible? Can one person rent rooms in a school/college today and teach the Bible? Can two or more people on an individual basis (a "group") also rent rooms and teach the Bible? Well, not if we use the definition of Daniel Sommer or Gene Frost. But if we use the legitimate definition found in a dictionary, where is the sin?

**Roberts' Real Estate Company:** At one time, though not now, I had a real estate broker's license to sell real estate. Since, as a Christian, I want to include opportunities to teach wherever I am, would it be scriptural for me to have a tract rack in my real estate office and give away tracts? If not, why not? Would it be scriptural for me to invite my co-workers and friends to meet with me every day at lunch and have a Bible study? If not, why not? If my real estate company succeeded and made a profit, would it be scriptural for me to take part of my money and send it to a gospel preacher (Acts 5:4)?

If not, why not? Mind now, that the real estate is an organized business, it is incorporated, and I might even have partners who are Christians as well. Does this make it a collectivity which competes with the church? Is the church the only collectivity which can teach the Bible? Would teaching the Bible make my real estate company a missionary society? Brethren, I appeal to you to apply the knowledge of the word of God which you have studied and recognize that all that I do as listed here is nothing more than the work of an individual and does not take away one scintilla of glory from the church nor does it compete with the church in any fashion.

While we are on the subject of private companies which might use part of their resources or personnel or funds to teach the Bible without violating Scripture, let me make reference to a practice universally accepted by all of us. Of course, universal acceptance does not make it right, but we do it because we universally believe it to be right! Which preacher among us has not been contacted by a nursing home (or who contacted a nursing home himself) in order to arrange a worship service in the nursing home? In this situation (which I would defend vigorously), a group of brethren (Matt. 18:15-17) convene at a nursing home (a human institution, not the church) to use their facilities, assisted by their personnel, without financial cost to anyone, in order to teach the Bible. In what substantive way does this differ from what Truth Foundation, Gospel Anchor, or Gospel Truths is doing? Gospel Truths, not the church but a human institution (J. T. Smith, with his board), invites a group of individuals to use his facilities, assisted by their personnel, without financial cost to anyone to teach the Bible (write articles). Gospel Anchor, not the church but a human institution (Gene Frost, with his board), invites a group of individuals to use his facilities, assisted by their personnel, without financial cost to anyone to teach the Bible (write articles). Truth Foundation (not the church, but a human institution) invites a group of individuals to use rented facilities to teach the Bible (written and oral). A nursing home (not the church, but a human institution) invites a group of individuals to use their facilities, assisted by their personnel, without financial cost to anyone, to teach the Bible. I would like to know how it is righteous to teach the Bible in a nursing homes while denying that it is righteous for the Bible to be taught in other institutions?

**Noah's Other Boat:** In Genesis 6, God informed Noah that the earth had become so wicked that He intended to destroy all mankind. Only Noah, his wife, his three sons, and their wives were going to survive. In order for them to be saved from the flood, Noah was instructed to build an ark (a boat) "to the saving of his house." The dimensions of the boat, its particular characteristics, and the type of wood (gopher) with which it was to be constructed were plainly given to Noah. Faithful to God, Noah built the ark and he and his family survived the flood. "Thus did Noah; according to all that God commanded him, so did he" (6:22).

As an individual with common needs and necessities, would it have been scriptural for Noah to build another boat? Be sure that you understand that we agree about Noah and his faithfulness in obeying God's command with regard to the ark. But if Noah had decided, for his own pleasure or as a means for livelihood, to build a fishing boat, another boat than the ark, would that have been sinful? If this fishing boat were made with wood other than gopher wood, would that matter? Was Noah not free as an individual to do in his personal life whatever liberties God allowed? Would a fishing boat compete in glory with the ark of God? Would it show disrespect to God for Noah to have a fishing boat in addition to the commanded ark?

I don't know that Noah had another boat. But my point is that *he could have had one without violating any precept concerning the ark of gopher wood.* As an individual, Noah could do anything to support his family that was decent and good without competing with his work of building the ark. Individual enterprise is generically authorized in the Scriptures (Eph. 4:28) and does not violate corporate work (the church).

Brethren today need to understand this analogy. As an individual, Noah had the liberties of free enterprise to earn a living and support his family in any decent manner. As individuals today, we have liberties to decide in a broader sense what we want to do to serve God than we do when specific authority for the church is concerned. Now, if Noah had decided to build another ark "for the saving of his house" and use another wood than gopher wood, Noah would have sinned. But a fishing boat in no way conflicted with the divine purpose of the Ark of God. It is easy to dismiss the analogy if one's mind is set and impenetrable by facts. But the fact remains that Noah could have had a fleet of boats which did not impede his obedience to God regarding the Ark.

| The Ark of God | Noah's Other Boats |
|---|---|
| Divinely Designed | Of Human Origin |
| Exclusive to God's Purpose | Used As Noah Had Need |
| Made of Gopher Wood | Made of Any Kind of Wood |
| To Save Noah and His Family | For Fishing, Ferry, Pleasure, Cargo |

**Luke 8:1-3:** Luke records,

> Now it came to pass, afterward, that He went through every city and village, preaching and bringing glad tidings of the kingdom of God. And the twelve were with Him, and certain women who had been healed of evil spirits and infirmities – Mary called Magdalene, out of whom had come seven demons, and Joanna the wife of Chuza, Herod's steward, and Susanna, and many others who provided for Him from their substance.

We are told that the situation described by Luke is unscriptural for us to imitate. Yes, it was in the life-time of Jesus while He was on earth and, thus, under the Old Testament age. However, this example is exactly the same as some today condemn. You have Jesus teaching about the kingdom and there is pooled money to support Him. So far, the only answer that has been made to this Scripture is to ridicule it. What the text teaches is:

- group activity
- an organized group, with a treasurer
- pooled money, a treasury
- money used to support teachers of the Bible
- money that was also used to support benevolence (John 12:5-6)

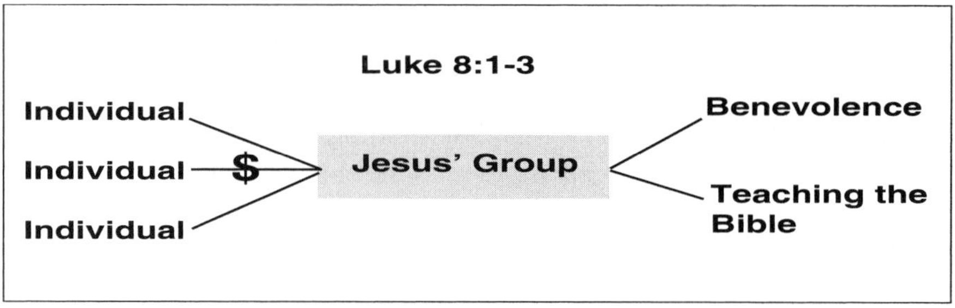


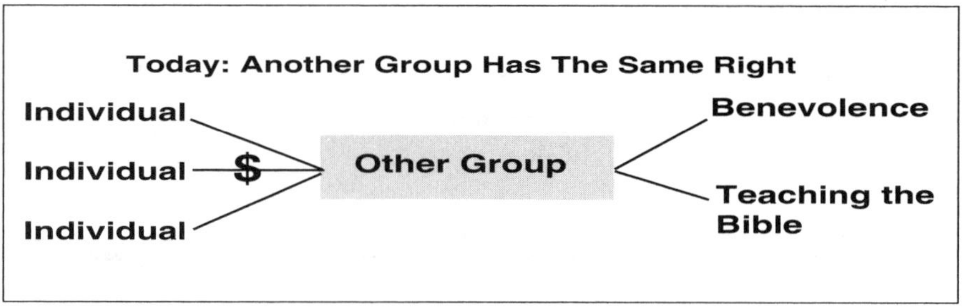


Listen to Gene Frost:

> A human religious collectivity is the collective action of individuals who

> contribute into a treasury overseen by a human board to accomplish a work God gave His divine religious collectivity (the church) to do! The foundation of *Truth Magazine* is a religious collectivity in that it solicits money from individuals which it oversees in teaching. What we oppose are collectivities—companies or societies, incorporated or unincorporated—which solicit the pooling of resources of individuals or churches for the teaching of the gospel (in supporting preachers, broadcasting over radio or TV, distributing literature, etc.) under the oversight of a human board. This supplants the church, wherein individuals pool resources for the teaching of the gospel, which treasury is under the oversight of elders! I understand the argument to be—
>
> 1. Individuals contributed into a treasury, pooled their resources;
> 2. The treasury was *not* the funds of individuals acting concurrently;
> 3. Judas was in charge of the funds; he was the treasurer.
>
> The funds were used to support preachers, including Jesus. He argues that Jesus had an *individually supported missionary society,* which received funds and with these funds supported men to preach the gospel! That is his argument—I did not dream it up, and he knows that I am telling the truth about it! He argues it, but he will not defend it . . . he will not defend what he claims Jesus did! Amazing! (private publication 2/22/79).

Please note that no one I know has ever called this an "individually supported missionary society" except brother Frost. I don't believe anyone has to call it anything. The question is: "Is it right or wrong?" Did Jesus allow these women to pool their money in a common treasury overseen by a treasurer and finance His teaching and benevolent activities? The answer is **yes!** The only reason anyone would call it an individually supported missionary society is to cast prejudice on the practice. But, friends, this is a simple statement of what Jesus did. ***Did He do wrong?*** I deny that He did any wrong (Heb. 4:15) or that we do any wrong when we do what He did. Individuals acting together in such a fashion do not take away from the work of the church, do not deny it the glory that it deserves, and are not creating another organization to compete with the church. Whether five women, or individuals who publish *Truth Magazine*, do what Jesus did, there is no sin involved.

Mike Willis explains:

> When human institutions are organized and maintained without involvement in local church's work, I do not see how they deny the all-sufficiency of the church. *They are organized to do a work separate and apart from a local church's work; they are supported without involvement of church*

> *funds; they are not organized to do the work of any given congregation; they are not overseen by any given congregation; they are not promoted by any given congregation; they are not attached formally or informally to any given church or churches.* Consequently, on what basis can such organizations be considered to be a denial of the all-sufficiency of the church? The only way that I see that they could possibly be considered a denial of the all-sufficiency of the church would be to speak of the church's work on universal terms, something which we have sought to avoid in all of our discussions on institutionalism and the sponsoring churches works. Yet, my brethren, some among us have concluded that men do not believe in the all-sufficiency of the church in the event that several of them pool their resources to conduct a tent meeting in an area which does not have a local church! (Mike Willis, *Truth Magazine,* March 1, 1979).

## Conclusion

It needs to be made very clear, before this treatise is concluded, that whether or not one does or does not attend the lectures here or at Florida College, or participates in any other work supported by a group of individuals does not decide your spiritual fate. No one even hints that you must attend these lectures to be a faithful child of God and to go to Heaven. *It is not now, and never has been, a test of our fellowship with those who decide not to come.* We recognize that some brethren, after due and careful consideration, have decided that their conscience will not allow them to participate in any fashion. That does not make any of us your enemy, nor is fellowship considered less important with you because of your conscientious absence. However, it is believed that the study that has been made on these issues allows us the right to attend and to participate without being in violation of the will of Christ, or in any way denying the efficacy of the local church in any and every place. We ask that prayerful consideration be given to our honest arguments and defenses. If our defense is not crystal clear to you, surely you will grant that enough Bible study has been presented to allow us a liberty to exercise our conscience, even as you do yours.

The problem arises over the issue of Florida College teaching the Bible and conducting a lecture program and the Truth Magazine lectures when some brethren make their conscience on this issue a condition of salvation and fellowship. The issue is parallel to the issues of using one cup in partaking of the communion and using Bible classes in a church's teaching program. No one believes that a church which chooses to use one cup when partaking of the communion or decides not to have Bible classes for different age groups is sinful for making that choice. Nor would fellowship with each other be broken by their choosing to do either. However, the issue becomes a problem when brethren make their personal conscience a condition of salvation and fellowship. This was the problem Paul faced when he wrote in 1 Timothy 4:1-3 as follows:

> Now the Spirit speaketh expressly, that in the latter times some shall depart from the faith, giving heed to seducing spirits, and doctrines of devils; speaking lies in hypocrisy; having their conscience seared with a hot iron; forbidding to marry, and commanding to abstain from meats, which God hath created to be received with thanksgiving of them which believe and know the truth.

Paul obviously did not believe one was out of fellowship with God if he chose to live a life of celibacy, because that was the choice that he had made. Nor did he condemn one who decided to abstain from meats. *What he condemned was those who made these things conditions for salvation and fellowship.* Paul said that those who teach such have departed from the faith and are teaching doctrines of devils.

Daniel Sommer, Leroy Garrett, and W. Carl Ketcherside created problems among brethren by making their opinion about colleges that taught the Bible a condition of salvation and a test of fellowship. In more recent years, those who hold a similar position among us have kept their personal opinions as private judgments and we have worked and worshipped together in peace, with brethren on both sides of the issue respecting each other's personal convictions. But now, a new spirit of Sommerism has arisen in which brethren are drawing lines of fellowship with each other over these opinions, making one's participation in the Florida College and Truth Magazine lecture program a test of fellowship for whether or not that church will send benevolent assistance to a brother or financial support for a preacher, be invited for a gospel meeting, or recognized as a brother in fellowship with the Lord. This is what I view to be intolerable and, therefore, oppose.

There have been, and will be, recurring efforts to create church-supported missionary and benevolent societies. There will continue to be efforts at sponsoring churches and centralized control that seek to activate the church universal and denigrate local churches of Christ. It is our plea that we continue to fight every innovation of man while allowing individuals the right to be active in the service of Christ without further dividing brethren. In the meantime, we keep our arms and hearts open in the fervent desire that continued study will lessen our differences and bring us closer to the oneness for which Jesus prayed (John 17:20-21).

# All Authority Has Been Given Unto Me

**Ray Warfel, Jr.**

The question of authority was hotly debated in the New Testament. The Jews of Jesus' day clearly understood that God had sent Moses with authority as the lawgiver. The authority of Jesus however, was not readily accepted. The fact that Jesus spoke "as one having authority, and not as [the] scribes" was obvious (Matt. 7:29). Did Jesus speak from Himself however, or did His authority come from God (John 7:16-17)? This was the issue during Jesus' ministry. After Jesus' death, and resurrection the

---

**Ray Warfel, Jr.** is the second of six children born to Raymond and Darlene (Brooks) Warfel. Ray was born in 1977 at Camp Lejeune, North Carolina while his father was serving in the Marines. He grew up in parts of Illinois and Indiana. At the age of twelve he became a Christian, and he matured under the preaching of his father.

In 2000, Ray married Erin (Hardy) of Frankfort, Kentucky. Together Ray and Erin have three children, twin daughters Molly and Megan, and a son Charles Raymond.

Ray began preaching after attending one year of college. He accepted opportunities to study and work with more mature preachers in Kentucky and Indiana. Following this study and a stint in pest control, Ray devoted himself fully to preaching. Ray has worked with several churches since in Illinois, Indiana, and Kentucky. Ray has also spent time working in Ethiopia.

For several years Ray has wanted to help boys navigate their way into manhood. The unexpected passing of his grandfather spurred Ray to action. The result is a workbook titled, *Boy It's A Circus*. Ray intends it to be a tool for fathers and sons as they discuss various challenges in becoming men.

Ray was able to return to the classroom in 2007. He is steadily working towards a degree. Though he is undecided on a major his interests lie in the fields of History and Classics.

disciples faced another issue – What was the place of the Law of Moses within the law of Christ?

As a result of these historical controversies Christ's supreme place was reaffirmed. As a note of clarification, these debates did not establish Christ's authority. God, not Jesus' disciples, gave Him authority and headship (Eph. 1:22). The struggles with these issues however, helped the disciples to understand this fact.

Today the echoes of these controversies are being heard. Judaizers once rejected Christ's supremacy by demanding that those who would come to Christ first submit to the Law of Moses, even though it was powerless to save them. Today there are men who are rejecting Christ's authority by demanding that we interpret His will by a hermeneutic just as helpless to bring understanding of the Scriptures or unity to estranged brethren.

The aim of this paper is to reaffirm the supreme place of Christ for a new generation, and to stress the biblical mode of understanding His will.

### Christ Has All Authority

"All authority has been given to Me in heaven and on earth. Go therefore and make disciples of all the nations, baptizing them in the name of the Father and the Son and the Holy Spirit, teaching them to observe all that I commanded you; and lo, I am with you always, even to the end of the age" (Matt. 28:18-20).

God gave Jesus the right, the power, and the authority to command. Coming to this realization was a challenge for many Jews. Some saw and accepted Him early (John 1:39, 45-49; 6:68). Others understood, but were unwilling to boldly acknowledge Him (John 3:1-2; 12:42). After many convincing proofs however, no one could honestly deny Him, His victory, or His authority (Matt. 28:11-15; Acts 1:3).

### The Jews Recognized the Authority of Moses

"The Lord your God will raise up for you a prophet like me from among you, from your countrymen, you shall listen to him" (Deut. 18:15).

When the wilderness wandering is nearly over and Moses preaches the sermons of Deuteronomy, the people listen to him. They repeat a resounding "Amen" to his words (Deut. 27). Clearly God chose Moses to be the leader and lawgiver.

The rebellions of the past had been divinely and decisively addressed.

God plagued Miriam with leprosy when she challenged the preeminence of Moses (Num. 12). God caused the earth to open and swallow Korah and his family when he and two hundred others rose up against Moses (Num. 16:1-35). God also slew many more for blaming Moses for Korah's death. The people should have blamed the rebels. Yet Moses commanded Aaron to make atonement for the people and "the plague was checked" (Num. 16:48).

The authority of Moses from that time forward is solidified in the mind of the Israelites. In New Testament times the Pharisees of course are content to set Moses aside when it suits them (Mark 7:10). Still, they recognize and offer an outward respect for the authority of Moses. This can be seen in their challenges to Jesus. When they ask Jesus about divorce "for any cause at all," Jesus responds, "What therefore God has joined together, let no man separate" (Matt. 19:3, 6). In the Pharisees retort we can hear them quibble, "*But Moses said* . . . give her a certificate of divorce and send her away" (Matt. 19:7).

On another occasion Jesus is in the Temple. The Pharisees bring a woman they had "caught in adultery, in the very act" (John 8:4). The redundancy of the statement "in the very act" indicates that her guilt cannot be avoided. They ask Jesus therefore, what they should do with her. The Pharisees are also sure to remind Jesus that "in the Law Moses commanded us to stone such women" (John 8:5). We could point out that, if they were interested in adhering to the authority of Moses, they would not have stopped to seek Jesus' counsel on the matter. However, the point to be stressed is that Moses is viewed as sent by God with supreme authority in matters pertaining to life, death, and as we will see, the resurrection.

The Sadducees approach Jesus with a question about the reality of the resurrection. They unfold a hypothetical situation by citing a provision in the Law. They say, "Teacher, Moses wrote for us that if a man's brother dies, and leaves behind a wife, and leaves no child, his brother should take the wife, and raise up offspring to his brother" (Mark 12:19). The answer Jesus gives is not as pertinent to our study at this time as is the basis of the Sadducees question – Moses wrote. It is also interesting that Jesus responds by citing Moses (Mark 12:26).

### Jesus Shows Himself To Have Greater Authority Than Moses

The question that Jews were facing then was not so much about authority, but whose authority came from God. Was Jesus the prophet like Moses to whom the people were to listen? Jesus, the apostles, and prophets of the New Testament address this in a series of comparisons between Moses and Jesus.

One of these comparisons is drawn the day after Jesus feeds the five thousand. Jesus challenges them to believe that God sent Him (John 6:29). The multitude responds, "What then do You do for a sign, that we may see, and believe You? What work do You perform? Our fathers ate manna in the wilderness; as it is written, 'He gave them bread out of heaven to eat'" (John 6:30-31). They are arguing that the manna in the wilderness is evidence that God sent Moses. Their line of reasoning would continue that, if God sent Jesus, He would again feed them on this day. Jesus however replies, "It is not Moses who has given you the bread out of heaven, but it is My Father who gives you the true bread out of heaven. For the bread of God is that which comes down out of heaven, and gives life to the world . . . I am the bread of life" (John 6:32-35). The bread Moses gave lasted only one day (it rotted if kept over night, Exod. 16:20), but that which Jesus gives, even Himself, is the sole source of continual nourishment.

Stephen takes up the comparison when he is accused of speaking "blasphemous words against Moses and against God" (Acts 6:11), and preaching Jesus who would supposedly, "alter the customs which Moses handed down" (Acts 6:14). Stephen reviews some well-known history for the high priest and Council, making some obvious but unstated comparisons. He reminds them that, "This Moses . . . is the one whom God sent to be both a ruler and deliverer" yet his people and his generation "disowned" him saying, "Who made you a ruler and a judge?" (Acts 7:35). Subsequently Moses "led them out [of Egypt], performing wonders and signs" (Acts 7:36). Next Stephen reminds them that Moses "received living oracles to pass on to you. And our fathers were unwilling to be obedient to him" (Acts 7:38-39).

The point is that while the high priest and Council revere Moses, Moses had prophesied that God would send another prophet like him. Jesus is that prophet. God sent him, and He preformed greater wonders and signs than Moses (Acts 2:22). Still, His people and His generation rejected Him, and even more they killed Him.

Jesus came fulfilling the law and giving a perfect law (Matt. 5:17; Heb. 10:1-9; Jas. 1:25). Jesus came to deliver His people from an oppressor older than the Egyptians, stronger than the Babylonians, and crueler than the Romans. Jesus came to free men and women from sin (Luke 4:18; John

8:32-36; Rom. 8:2; Gal. 5:1), but Stephen's audience, like their forefathers, was unwilling to be obedient.

This debate continues for the first Christians. They know that God sent Moses with authority. These Christians also recognize that God sent Jesus with authority. The question for the disciples is "What place does the authoritative commands of Moses have within those of Jesus?" Circumcision is the issue that this debate finally centers on.

Luke records that, "some men came down from Judea and began teaching the brethren, 'Unless you are circumcised according to the custom of Moses, you cannot be saved'" (Acts 15:1). What follows conclusively shows that Jesus has all authority. His authority is not contingent on Moses. He does not share authority with Moses, but possesses all authority. We will take a closer look at this situation in a moment.

### Christ's Authority Is Dispensed Through Command, Example, and Necessary Inference

It is one thing to acknowledge Jesus' word and will as authoritative. It is quite another matter to seek to understand and obey this authoritative will. Hermeneutics is the bridge between these peeks.

Our discussion must now move to asking what means of interpretation, or what hermeneutic should we use? Grant Osborne correctly observed that, "Only a carefully defined hermeneutic can keep one wedded to the text" (Osborne, 6). In other words only clearly defined rules about understanding the Bible can keep us consistent in applying the text in modern circumstances. Thomas Warren argues a similar point saying, "To accurately interpret the Bible, it is not enough merely to know what the evidence is—one must properly *interpret* that evidence. This means that one must have some *method,* some approach to the *handling* of the evidence" (Warren, 21).

### Command, Example, and Necessary Inference

Command, example, and necessary inference (or the acronym CENI) is the hermeneutic I believe to be both right and biblical. It is also however, the method many challenge.

Better words might be chosen for this means of understanding and interpreting God's will. For instance Warren suggests the phrase "account of action" be used instead of "example" (Warren, 105-107). I particularly like the use of "example" because it is a biblical word (1 Pet. 2:21), and using biblical language, Bible names for Bible things, is always preferable.

The word "command" might be replaced with the word "statement" because not every call to action is given in the form of a command (Mark 16:16; John 3:16, the call to believe and be baptized is issued in these verses but not in the form of an order). Cogdill chooses the word "precept" when discussing this direct mode of teaching (Cogdill, 14).

I have no quarrel with using different words to express these concepts. When we talk about the work of the church we may classify it, as it often has been, as evangelism, edification, and benevolence (Cogdill, 58, 62, 66). The work of the church may also be described as: saving the lost, standing firm in the truth, and sharing with needy Christians. Though the words here are replaced, the concept and biblical truth remains the same.

As I said, I do not have so much a problem with using other words when discussing biblical ideas, but abandoning these truths is a serious problem. Some are not just criticizing how we phrase this hermeneutic – CENI. Some reject the hermeneutic itself.

**Many Reject This Hermeneutic**

Reuel Lemmons said, "We have glibly tripped off our tongues for the past hundred years the slogan that things are proven to be scriptural in three ways: (1) divine command, (2) necessary inference, and (3) approved example. The more we dig into this matter the more we are convinced that the only way to prove a thing essential is by divine command. We are afraid of necessary inference because we do not always trust the ability of the inferer to make infallible inferences. We do not trust approved examples because there are a lot of approved examples that all people agree are not binding examples" (Lemmons, 786).

Michael Casey wrote, "The second challenge is that the traditional hermeneutic of command, example, and necessary inference is not found in the Old and New Testament, but is grounded in the human history of Reformed theology, Scottish Common Sense philosophy and logic, and nineteenth century American culture. It is not a 'divine' hermeneutic insulated from the 'chaos' of history" (Casey, 268).

Cecil Hook simply asserts, "No examples are binding" (Hook, 14).

As an initial response to these attacks, the words of Dave Miller are appropriate. He states, "It matters little to what extent churches of Christ have demonstrated an affinity with so-called 'Enlightenment' principles—which is beside the point anyway. The issue is simply—to what extent have churches of Christ demonstrated an affinity with New Testament principles? Have members of the church learned and obeyed the gospel? Drawing lines and tangents to some sociological current in human history is irrelevant. The real issue is whether we can understand the Bible unimpeded and unhindered by our own preconceived notions" (Miller, 41-42).

Similarly Ed Harrell says, "The ability to observe the world around us and make reasonable decisions based on our perceptions was described, not discovered, by Enlightenment thinkers" (Harrell, 28).

Concerning necessary inference, numerous others have pointed out that the only way we know any of the precepts found in the Bible apply to any of us today is by inference. No text states, "Ray Warfel, Jr. must believe." Yet we infer that "whosoever" applies to everyone (John 3:16). The same is true for the great commission. Jesus is specifically speaking to the eleven when He says, "Go therefore and make disciples of all the nations" (Matt. 28:19). Someone has well said though, concerning the King James rendition of the text that "*Go ye* means *go me*."

Reuel Lemmons' complaint also fails. While we may not trust all inferences drawn by fallible men, we should not discard necessary inferences all together. It would be the proverbial throwing the baby out with the bathwater. Besides if we are to reject necessary inferences because some would bind inferences that are not necessary, why retain even commands? Some are quite good at ignoring straightforward commands like, "Repent and be baptized" (Acts 2:38).

**Jesus' Use of the Scriptures**

Jesus' use of the Scriptures demonstrates a respect for command, example, and necessary inference. When, "a certain lawyer stood up and put Him to the test, saying, 'Teacher, what shall I do to inherit eternal life?'" (Luke 10:25). Jesus points to the divine precepts of God's word by responding, "What is written in the Law? How does it read to you" (Luke 10:26)? Ed Harrell discusses how this banter between the Lord and the lawyer is a "clear-cut hermeneutical exchange" (Harrell, 33). Without going into such an exposition it serves our purpose to note that Jesus draws His audience's attention to what precepts were written, "You shall love the Lord your God with all your heart, and with all your soul, and with all your strength, and with all your mind; and your neighbor as yourself" (Luke 10:27; cf. Deut. 6:3; 11:13; Lev. 19:18). The reader might also observe that the lawyer has drawn a inference by summarizing the whole of Scripture this way, just as

Jesus does when he states, "On these two commandments depend the whole Law and the Prophets" (Matt. 22:40). The conclusion is that all of God's commandments fall under the umbrella of these two, and the second even under that of the first.

There are also several instances when Jesus draws or leaves His hearers to draw a necessary inference. Some Pharisees approach Jesus with a question about divorce, "Is it lawful for a man to divorce his wife for any cause at all?" (Matt. 19:3). He answers first by pointing to the precept in the Law, "Have you not read, that He who created them from the beginning made them male and female, and said, 'For this cause a man shall leave his father and mother, and shall cleave to his wife; and the two shall become one flesh'" (Matt. 19:4-5). Jesus then draws the necessary conclusion from God's commentary, "What therefore God has joined together, let no man separate" (Matt. 19:6).

Other conclusions should be drawn from the example of Adam and Eve and God's accompanying statement on marriage. The one I believe most pressing today concerns homosexuality. God created a woman for the man. In His wisdom God brought them together, and approved of them being together. I know that God approves of heterosexual relationships, but there is no evidence that demonstrates that God approves of homosexuality. Even without Paul's explicit denunciation of this sin we can still know what God wants in this regard by the necessary conclusion drawn from what He did and said at creation.

Another instance of Jesus' use of necessary inference is when some Sadducees question Him about the resurrection. Jesus addresses the hypothetical question about what brother will have the woman as wife in the resurrection by discounting the premise. In the resurrection, "they neither marry, nor are given in marriage" (Mark 12:25). Then Jesus shows how the Sadducees had failed to reason properly from the Scriptures. Jesus lays out two propositions about God. The first from God Himself, "I am the God of Abraham, and the God of Isaac, and the God of Jacob" (Mark 12:26). Jesus is sure to remind them also that God said this when He spoke to Moses from the burning bush years after the three patriarchs had died. Jesus then states a second truth about God, "He is not the God of the dead, but of the living" (Mark 12:27). The implication is that Abraham, Isaac, and Jacob must be alive though their bodies are dead. Jesus does not state this fact, but He expects all who hear Him to draw this inescapable conclusion, this necessary inference.

Years ago Bob Crawley concluded an article titled *Jesus' View of the Scriptures* with this penetrating thought: "We cannot reasonably claim to have respect for the life and teaching of Jesus Christ without imitating his attitude of respect for the sacred scriptures" (Crawley, 38). To abandon the means of handling and interpreting Scripture that Jesus used is little different than abandoning the authority of the Savior Himself.

**The Hermeneutic Employed by His Disciples**

The Jerusalem debate is a clear picture of first century disciples coming to understand God's will on a particular subject by the means of command, example, and necessary inference. As was already noted some disciples come down from Judea teaching, "Unless you are circumcised according to the custom of Moses, you cannot be saved" (Acts 15:1). Barclay rightly assesses the repercussions of such teaching saying, "If this attitude had prevailed, Christianity would have become nothing more than a sect of Judaism" (Barclay, 113).

They came together therefore, and debated the matter. McGarvey comments that, "The apostles . . . permitted the judaizers in the church to say all that they wished to say before any reply was made to their position and arguments" (McGarvey, *New Commentary on Acts,* 62). While I doubt that no response at all was made, it is clear that the Judaizers presented their position. When however, the apostles speak they each in turn give a key to the means by which God expects us to understand His word.

Peter begins the recorded discussion by reminding the audience about the facts of his preaching among the Gentiles. God chose him to deliver the gospel to the gentiles and God "made no distinction between [Jews] and [Gentiles]" (Acts 15:9). The audience is left to draw the necessary or unavoidable conclusion that God does not require the keeping of the Law of Moses as a condition of salvation. This is the same conclusion brethren came to when Peter first related the conversion of Cornelius (Acts 11:18).

Paul takes up the defense of truth next by "relating what signs and wonders God had done through them among the Gentiles" (Acts 15:12). Stringer comments on this text saying, "Again, we see that God expected men to learn his will through means other than direct statements or commands. . . . The truth could be learned by the *divinely approved example* of Paul and Barnabas. They had converted Gentiles and God had shown his approval through miracles" (Stringer, 305). God does not need to re-approve His acceptance of Gentiles, so we need not work miracles like Paul, but it is right to follow his example and preach the gospel to Gentiles.

James concludes by quoting the "words of the Prophets . . . 'After these things I will return, and I will rebuild the tabernacle of David which has fallen, and I will rebuild its ruins, and I will restore it, in order that the rest of mankind may seek the Lord, and all the Gentiles who are called by My name'" (Acts 15:15-17). The statement of God's prophet explains His will concerning Gentiles. Gentiles are welcome to Him and it is conditioned on the rebuilding of David's house, not circumcision. Again to cite Stringer, "These three methods of learning truth are not a man-made hermeneutic, as some would teach. They are principles observed by inspired men" (Stringer, 305).

The reason for Paul's going to Jerusalem should be clarified before going on. Paul does not go up to Jerusalem because it is "the headquarters of the Church" and he is seeking a "ruling" from the governing body as Barclay suggests (113). Paul knew the truth. He had received it from the Lord in whom all authority rested (Gal. 2:2). Paul went to Jerusalem because that is where these false brethren had come from, likely claiming to have been sent with apostolic authority. Further the letter the apostles and elders draft and send out is not dictation from the "mother church" (Witherington, 451). The letter is sent to assure those who had been disturbed by these Judaizers that those in Jerusalem gave no such instruction (Acts 15:24).

### Christ's Authority Is Being Undermined

"I am amazed that you are so quickly deserting Him who called you by the grace of Christ, for a different gospel; which is really not another; only there are some who are disturbing you, and want to distort the gospel of Christ" (Gal. 1:6-7).

Commenting on these verses Willis says, "The apostasy at Galatia did not deny the death, burial, resurrection, ascension, coronation, or glorification of Christ. It did not deny that baptism was essential to salvation. However, it was a departure from the one who had called them into the grace of Christ. It was a departure from the gospel of Christ. It resulted in giving up one's hope for eternal salvation in Christ. Those who teach that we need to be united only in the gospel (meaning, the facts pertaining to the death, burial, resurrection and ascension of Christ and the one act of baptism) but can have diversity in the realm of doctrine (all other teachings in the Bible) find their doctrine answered here in the first few verses of Galatians.

The apostasy which Paul was refuting was, by the modern terminology, a 'doctrinal' apostasy" (*Galatians,* 14-15).

Many are preaching a "doctrinal apostasy" today. The remainder of this paper will be a brief examination of such preaching, and the ruin it makes of Christ's authority.

### The Principles of Cecil Hook

Writing about commands, Hook says, "It [the command] is not imperative for us unless the teaching or command is directing the accomplishing of a practical purpose" (Hook, 13). Hook then illustrates his hermeneutic with some observations about the Lord's Supper. He says, "If its purpose is to make us think on the atonement, then what difference does it make at what hour or on what day we do it, or if we do it twice on a day or several times weekly? What is the concern about whether the cup be fresh or fermented, or whether the bread be leavened or unleavened? How could sequence be of importance – whether we break the bread before or after the prayer, whether the bread be taken before the cup, or whether they be served at the same time? Such details have nothing to do with the purpose of participation. If a person derives the benefit of this remembrance on Wednesday instead of Sunday, does it suddenly become a curse instead of a blessing?" (15).

The underlying problem of this hermeneutic is that all authority is now invested in Cecil Hook. The Lord's commands are only commands if Hook, or whoever subscribes to this approach, sees a reason for the command. Walton Weaver in answering *Free In Christ* translates Hook this way, "A 'command' promoting no principle (that I can see) is not really a command" (Weaver, 98).

The repercussions of this thinking go far beyond the Lord's Supper. What is the purpose of the water in baptism? Paul says the purpose is that we might be "buried with Him through baptism into death, in order that as Christ was raised from the dead through the glory of the Father, so we too might walk in newness of life" (Rom. 6:4). Why then must water be used? Why not shut the penitent person in a closet and let them open the door as the stone was rolled away from Jesus' tomb?

Since the purpose of preaching is to save the lost what difference does it make if a woman is standing behind the pulpit? If I see the purpose of the collection to be doing good what difference does it make if it is used to support a Bible college or benevolent society? What difference does it make if such money is collected from Christians? Why not put on a carnival or casino night?

The difference is that all authority rests with Jesus the Christ, not Cecil Hook, or you or me. Even if I cannot recognize a purpose or principle behind some command that does not mean there is no purpose or principle.

### The Core Gospel of Rubel Shelly

"Some people within the Restoration Movement simply don't understand the principles upon which either it or the New Testament church it seeks to restore is founded. We are not commissioned by the Lord to promote a particular name or a particular set of interpretations about organization, worship, and work in the local church. Our commission is built around the universal and essential matters of Ephesians 4:4-6" (Shelly, 89).

Many preach a message similar to Shelly's. They may not agree on what the core or essential matters are, but there is consistence that the core gospel does not include some doctrinal issues.

There is a serious problem with kind of thinking – how do we determine the essential from the trivial? What is the commandment hierarchy? What commandments are we bound to keep and what commandments are we at liberty to ignore? God calls for unity (John 17:21; 1 Cor. 1:10; Phil. 2:2). Is unity therefore, more important than Jesus' teaching on divorce and remarriage or the kind of music used in worship?

### Great and Weighty Commandment

The perception that some of the Lord's commands are more important and that others are less important is an old trouble. Shelly has his contemporaries, but the Pharisees predate them all. Boles comments on the Pharisees' attitude when he says, "The teachers among the Pharisees had decided that no man could observe perfectly all the commandments of the law delivered by Moses; they were sticklers for perfect obedience; but they saw in their own lives that no one kept perfectly all the commandments of the law; therefore they had decided that if one man kept perfectly one commandment his obedience to this one would be accepted as obedience to all of the laws. However, the question arose among themselves as to which one was the most important, or which one should be selected to be kept" (Boles, 437).

The trouble is also fueled by the misuse of several Scriptural phrases. That love is the greatest commandment is one such phrase (Matt. 22:37-38;

Rom. 13:8; 1 Cor. 13:13; Gal. 5:14). I do not doubt that love is the greatest or first commandment, but what do Jesus and Paul mean when they say this? Are they saying that love is more important than all other commandments? Are they saying that so long as we love (however love is defined) other issues may be disregarded?

Love is the first and greatest commandment because it incorporates all other commandments. McGarvey say, "It is called the first and great . . . not because, apart from all others it is great, but because in observing it all others are observed" (McGarvey, *Matthew and Mark,* 193). When Paul writes, "But now abide faith, hope, love, these three; but the greatest of these is love" (1 Cor. 13:13), he is saying the same thing. Love is not more important and therefore as long as we love, faith and hope may be ignored. Rather he is saying that "faith and hope spring from love" (Willis, *First Corinthians,* 384).

A second misused text is Jesus' statement about the "weightier provisions of the law" (Matt. 23:23). Again I have no doubt that there are weightier provisions of the law for Jesus so says. I do though, doubt that there are provisions that are more important and others that are less important.

Jesus makes this comment in a series of condemnations He levels against the Pharisees. Jesus says, "Woe to you, scribes and Pharisees, hypocrites! For you tithe mint and dill and cummin, and have neglected the weightier provisions of the law: justice and mercy and faithfulness; but these are the things you should have done without neglecting the others" (Matt. 23:23). Jesus does not condemn the Pharisees for tithing or for their tedious way of doing so. No, He go so far as to say they should not have neglected to do such. How then are justice, mercy, and faithfulness weightier?

Thayer says about *barus* (926 Strong's Number) that it's second meaning is as a metaphor in which it may mean "burdensome, severe, or of great moment." Thayer then attaches Jesus' statement to this third possibility. This however, is Thayer's commentary (96). Vine notes Jesus' statement too, but simply says, "The comparative degree is used in the neuter plural" (671). The context must determine what kind of comparison is being made.

While Jesus' word choice may be used to compare the importance of two matters I think Jesus uses it to compare burdens, an equally legitimate definition. Jesus is telling the Pharisees that while their tithing may be tedious it is easy. They chose to do what was easy while neglecting the more difficult, the heavier, the weightier parts of the law: justice, mercy, and faithfulness.

Jesus does however, deal with matters of importance in this context. Jesus describes the Pharisees as those who say, "Whoever swears by the temple, that is nothing; but whoever swears by the gold of the temple, he is obligated" (Matt. 23:16). Jesus then asks the question, "Which is more important, the gold, or the temple that sanctified the gold?" (Matt. 23:17). Jesus is not trying to show the Pharisees that they had their hierarchy backwards, that the temple was really the more important of the two. Jesus in fact says that if they swore by either the temple or the gold they were equally bound (Matt. 23:20-22).

Jesus is asking the same kind of question I asked earlier. If there are more important commandments and less important commandments, how do we tell the difference? And if like Shelly, Hook, or the Pharisees we conceive of some system on whose authority do we promote it? Jesus calls the Pharisees blind guides for this very reason (Matt. 23:16). They could not see that these things were equal.

### Conclusion

Hook, Shelly, and men preaching a similar message are akin to the Pharisees and Judaizers of generations past. The Jews sought to bind a law that was helpless to save, and a circumcision that could not sanctify the hearts of men. These modern Judaizers seek to bind a helpless hermeneutic that cannot enlighten the eyes of any man to the word of God, or foster unity between any group of men.

### Bibliography

Barclay, William. *The Acts of the Apostles.* Philadelphia: The Westminster Press, 1976.

Boles, H. Leo. *Matthew*. Gospel Advocate: Nashville, 1989.

Casey, Michael W. *The Battle Over Hermeneutics in the Stone-Campbell Movement, 1800-1870*. Lewiston: The Edwin Mellen Press, 1998.

Cogdill, Roy E. *Walking By Faith*. Bowling Green: Guardian of Truth Foundation, 1984.

Crawley, Bob. *Jesus' View of the Scriptures*. Truth Magazine, VIII (1963): 2, pp. 37-38.

Harrell, David Edwin, Jr. *Christian Primitivism in the Twenty-First Century,*

*Thinking "inside the box" about restoring New Testament Christianity.* Lakeland: Harwell/Lewis Publishing Co., 2007.

Hook, Cecil. *Free In Christ.* 1988.

Lemmons, Reuel. *When Are Examples Binding*, Firm Foundation, XCI: 50, p.786.

Osborne, Grant R. *The Hermeneutical Spiral, A Comprehensive Introduction to Biblical Interpretation.* Downers Grove: InterVarsity Press, 1991.

McGarvey, J. W. *Matthew and Mark.* Abilene: Chronicle Publishing Company.

_____. *New Commentary on Acts.* Delight: Gospel Light Publishing.

Miller, Dave. "A Review of *The Worldly Church*," *The Spiritual Sword*, XX (1988): 1, pp. 41-43.

Shelly, Rubel. *I Just Want To Be A Christian.* Nashville: 20th Century Christian, 1986.

Stringer, Johnny. *The Book of Acts*, Bowling Green: Guardian of Truth Foundation, 1999.

Thayer, Joseph H. *Thayer's Greek-English Lexicon of the New Testament.* Peabody: Hindrickson Publishers, 1996.

Vine, W. E. *Vine's Expository Dictionary of Biblical Words.* Nashville: Thomas Nelson Publishers, 1985.

Warren, Thomas B. *When Is An "Example" Binding?* Jonesboro: National Christian Press, 1975.

Weaver, Walton. *That They All May Be One, Studies on unity, freedom, and authority in the body of Christ.* Bowling Green: Guardian of Truth Foundation, 2003.

Willis, Mike. *First Corinthians.* Bowling Green: Guardian of Truth Foundation, 1994.

_____. *Galatians.* Bowling Green: Guardian of Truth Foundation, 1994.

Witherington, Ben, III. *The Acts of the Apostles, A socio-rhetorical commentary.* Grand Rapids: William B. Eerdmans Publishing Company, 1998.

# Part Three
# The Morning Classes

# Jesus Is the Son of God

**Steven J. Wallace**

> Therefore, having obtained help from God, to this day I stand, witnessing both to small and great, saying no other things than those which the prophets and Moses said would come—"that the Christ would suffer, that He would be the first to rise from the dead, and would proclaim light to the Jewish people and to the Gentiles" (Acts 26:22, 23).[1]

Paul accredited God for helping him in his ministry which was a welding together of two things—the former testimony (of Moses and the prophets) with the witness of Paul. This alliance pointed forward from Moses and the

[1] All verses are from the New King James Version unless otherwise noted.

**Steven J. Wallace** was born October 29, 1970 in Hot Springs, SD. He learned and obeyed the pure gospel of Jesus Christ, November 14th, 1986 while attending and studying with members of the Southside church of Christ in Rapid City, SD. In time he moved to Bloomington, Indiana where he met his wife, Kelly Renee Keene. Steven and Kelly were joined in marriage May 20, 1989. Steven attended college at IUPUI, Florida College, California State University in Long Beach, and Indiana University in Bloomington. For his first work, he moved to preach for the Fairfax church of Christ in the Cincinnati, Ohio area in 1994. In January of 1999, Steven relocated 2400 miles away to work with the church of Christ in Sunnyside, Washington. In September 2005, the church at Sunnyside spawned another work about forty minutes away in Terrace Heights (a suburb of Yakima). Until December 21st, 2008, Steven worked for both churches, preaching and teaching in alternating services along with managing their websites. He has been able to engage in two formal public debates. He debated Kurt Steutker of *Answers In Genesis* on the subject of salvation and Dave Giles over the Sabbath question. Currently Steven continues to preach for the Sunnyside church of Christ and maintains two websites: *www.sunnysidechurchofchrist.com* and *www.revandcreation.com.* He and Kelly have been blessed with three beautiful children: Nickolas Steven, Ethan Gabriel, and Danielle Renee.

prophets and culminated in the retrospective witness of Paul in one very important historical fact that would affect all families of the earth: that the Christ would suffer, rise from the dead and proclaim light to all. Please notice the wording, "the Christ would suffer." Who would suffer? The Christ would suffer. Jesus would suffer as the Christ. In suffering, Jesus was yet the Christ, the *anointed* Messiah.

The apostle, Matthew, recorded, "And she will bring forth a Son, and you shall call His name JESUS, for He will save His people from their sins" (Matt. 1:21). "Jesus" (and its equivalency "Joshua") is of Hebrew origin and means "Jehovah is Salvation." All the former biblical men who were known as "Joshua" in the Scriptures were not named such because they would save their people from their sins. Their names pointed to and looked forward to the great salvation of Jehovah. Jesus is that great salvation of Jehovah. Notice again Matthew 1:21, ". . . you shall call His name JESUS *for* He will save His people from their sins" (emp. mine). Only God can save people from sin. No prophet, angel, preacher, or apostle has that power. Others may save men from some calamity of sorts, but only God can forgive sin and save others from such a death bringer. "Why does this Man speak blasphemies like this? Who can forgive sins but God alone?" reasoned the scribes (Mark 2:6). They were correct in understanding that only God can forgive sins (Isa. 43:25). Yet, they erred in not seeing that Jesus was God, the anointed Messiah, the One who would save people from sin.

Paul said the prophets affirmed that "the Christ would suffer . . ." Matthew asserts in the beginning of his gospel that Jesus, the one who would save His people from their sins, is the Christ. He recorded, "Now the birth of Jesus *Christ* was as follows . . ." (Matt. 1:18). This was not just the birth of a Jesus, but of Jesus the *Christ.* Matthew continued writing by saying, "So all this was done that it might be fulfilled which was *spoken by the Lord* through the prophet, saying: 'Behold, the virgin shall be with child, and bear a Son, and they shall call His name Immanuel,' which is translated, '*God with us*'" (Matt. 1:22, 23, emp. mine). Notice the *Lord* proclaimed through the prophet the *Lord's birth/entrance* into the world. In this prophecy Jesus is proclaimed "Immanuel" which is clarified as meaning, "God with us." J. W. McGarvey correctly observed, "Nature shows God above us; the Law shows God against us; but the Gospel shows God with us, and for us."[2] John accords, "And the Word became flesh and dwelt

---

[2] J. W. McGarvey, *The Four Fold Gospel*, 26.

among us, and we beheld His glory, the glory as of the only begotten of the Father, full of grace and truth" (John 1:14). Later Paul wrote, "And without controversy great is the mystery of godliness: God was manifested in the flesh . . ." (1 Tim. 3:16). Jesus as the Christ, the Messiah was manifested in the flesh and suffered. He suffered as "God with us!" His deity was not somehow lost or robbed in the shuffle, but was manifested to us.

When we see the agony and emotions of the Christ, we often misinterpret these as marks of His humanity. But rather, these are characteristics of the Divine Creator given to those who bear His image. We rightly agonize over evil, love what is good, and weep and rejoice with others because God created us with such a capacity (Gen. 1:27; 6:6; Exod. 20:5; Ps. 119:104; Eccl. 7:29; 1 Sam. 15:35; Ps. 36:7; 1 Pet. 5:7; 1 John 4:19; etc.). Sin will often corrupt that capacity and make us snicker at those who weep; weep at those who prosper, or perhaps agonize over what is good while craving what is wrong (see Isa. 5:20).

### Identity Of Jesus: A Point Of Controversy

> When Jesus came into the region of Caesarea Philippi, He asked His disciples, saying, "Who do men say that I, the Son of Man, am?" So they said, "Some say John the Baptist, some Elijah, and others Jeremiah or one of the prophets." He said to them, "But who do you say that I am?" (Matt. 16:13-15).

The identity of Jesus was not something that was easily understood and universally accepted. His identity was controversial even when Jesus was walking on earth. Some struggled, reading Him as either good or deceitful (John 7:12). Some wondered if He was the Christ, while others countered that the Christ could not come from Galilee (John 7:41). Others perceived that Jesus was one of the prophets or perhaps even John the Baptist (Matt. 16:13-15). Of the many answers that man gave, only one was acceptable. It was that answer that hung on what Matthew's gospel began with: *Jesus is God with us*, hence, *the Son of God* (Matt. 16:16, 17). This is the answer that met with Jesus' approval. Jesus is the Anointed Son of God.

Only confidence in the correct identity of Jesus will permit any of us to be saved. Understanding Jesus is not merely an academic debate; it is pertinent to the very salvation of our souls as the Lord stated, "Therefore I said to you that you will die in your sins; for if you do not believe that I am He, you will die in your sins" (John 8:24). What did Jesus mean by "I am He"? "He" is supplied and is not in the original text. We must believe that Jesus is the "I Am" or we cannot be saved (cf. John 8:58; Exod. 3:14).

Jesus is the great "I Am" or self-existing One. He is the co-existent Son of the Father. "Whoever believes that Jesus is the Christ is born of God, and everyone who loves Him who begot also loves him who is begotten of Him" (1 John 5:1; cf. Acts 8:37).

Jesus would rarely state with frankness that He was God. He said and did things for people to see that He was "Immanuel." Jesus would say things to separate Himself from mere mortals as in John 8:23, "You are from beneath; I am from above. You are of this world; I am not of this world." This would leave His audience asking, "Just who are you?" (see John 8:25). Then Jesus would spell out His relationship to the "Father" as the One who sent Him and who is with Him (see John 8:26-29). Yet, in the course of the discussion, Jesus would call the Father "My Father," making Himself the Son of God, which would set His critics on edge (see vv. 28, 29).

### Controversies in Ancient Times

**Gnosticism.** The controversy over understanding the makeup of Jesus continued to rage through the ages and became the central issue of fiery debate in various circles. One of the first great apostasies in the Lord's church involved a Gnostic approach to understanding Jesus. The Gnostic movement believed that the material world was evil and that we could and must be free from it by learning esoteric spiritual truths. Because of this persuasion, Gnostics would assert that Jesus had not come in the flesh at all, but rather He simply *portrayed* Himself in a body of flesh. So, all that Jesus appeared to do "in the flesh" was really in a phantom body. Because their low view of the material world was so prized, Gnostics ultimately had to deny the humanity of Christ. Through inspiration, the apostle John helped curtail this error and the distortion it created by writing, ". . . every spirit that does not confess that Jesus Christ has come in the flesh is not of God. And this is the spirit of the Antichrist, which you have heard was coming, and is now already in the world" (1 John 4:3; see also 2 John 1:7). Notice carefully, that denying Jesus' correct nature results in being an "antichrist." Simply denying that Jesus came in the flesh makes you an ally of Satan.

**Monarchianism.** The struggle of understanding the "oneness" of God and rightful opposition to polytheism sometimes resulted in other wrong ideas. Monarchianism, set out to defend the monarchy of God, yet, unlike Gnosticism which denied the humanity of Christ, Monarchianism actually denied the deity of Christ. Of the two major brands, *Dynamic Monarchianism* (adoptionism) was taught in the second century by Theodotus of Byzantine and asserted that Jesus was born a mortal and later became divine.

This doctrine denied Jesus as coexisting with the Father and affirmed that the power of God descended upon Him. So, the power to do miracles was granted to Jesus at His Baptism. He later became divine at either His resurrection or His ascension.

In a similar denial of Christ's deity and the trinity, *Modalistic Monarchianism*, as taught by Sabellius (c.a. A.D. 220), asserted that God manifested Himself in three *modes*.[3] These modes are the Father *in creation*, the Son *in redemption,* and the Holy Spirit *in sanctification*. Tertullian in writing a letter against Praxeas for promoting this error, said, "By this Praxeas did a twofold service for the devil at Rome: he drove away prophecy, and he brought in heresy; he put to flight the Paraclete, and he crucified the Father."[4] Tertullian was correct when he argued that, if Jesus was the Father, then the Father was crucified and not the Son!

**Arianism.** Arianism, named after Arius, began another fiery storm of debate in Christology during the fourth century. In A.D. 318, Arius of Alexander claimed that Jesus was the first of God's creation and unlike God, but of *similar* substance. Logically then, since Jesus had a beginning, He was not immutable and self-existing. Arius used a phrase in the Scripture, "only begotten Son" and affixed a definition to it that was not intended. Arius wrote, "For He was not unbegotten. We are persecuted, because we say that the Son has a beginning, but that God is without beginning. This is the cause of our persecution. . . ."[5] He concluded then that there was once a time when Jesus *was not*. In 321 Arius was banned from Alexandria but settled in Palestine where he continued to teach his doctrine. Eusebius of Nicomedia declared his agreement with him as well as having a sympathizer in Eusebius of Caesarea. In 325, the Roman Emperor, Constantine, convoked the council of Nicaea where about 300 bishops attended and condemned the Arian doctrine from which the Nicene Creed emerged. Arius refused to sign it and charged the signees as endorsing Sabellianism (Modalistic Monarchianism above), since that creed affirmed that Jesus was of the *same* substance as the Father. But Sabellianism rejected the three persons of the Godhead, something the Nicene Creed clearly affirmed.

---

[3] Hence the second brand of Monarchianism is *Modalistic Monarchianism.*

[4] Tertullian, *Against Praxeas*, ch. 1. Translated by Dr. Holmes (*http://www.ccel.org/ccel/schaff/anf03.v.ix.i.html*).

[5] Theodoret, *The Ecclesiastical History of Theodoret*, 1:4.

In a seeming prophetic way, John denounced any doctrine that denies the relationship that exists between Jesus and the Father, "Who is a liar but he who denies that Jesus is the Christ? He is antichrist who denies the Father and the Son" (1 John 2:22). To suggest that Jesus is not the same "substance" as the Father is to deny the Father and the Son. Both Gnosticism and Arianism are, therefore, antichrist doctrines. We must accept that the Word became flesh, and fully believe in the humanity and deity of Christ. It may be surprising to know that Arianism is not so far removed from our day. It is alive and working in any religion that doesn't reduce Jesus to "just a man," yet fails to exalt Him as 100 percent God. Consider this quote, "Jesus lived in heaven as a spirit person before he came to earth. He was God's first creation, and so he is called the 'firstborn' Son of God (Col. 1:15; Rev. 3:14). Jesus is the only Son that God created by himself."[6] By such a statement, Jesus is not "just a man" or "fully God" in the sense the Father is. Alas, Arianism lives on!

**Nestorianism.** In the fifth century, another error that gained some ground was Nestorianism. Nestorius (whom the doctrine is named after) believed in two separate persons co-existing in Christ—the human spirit as well as the divine spirit. He and his followers believed that Mary had been the mother of the human Jesus but not the divine Jesus. Yet, Jesus didn't take on a human spirit but took on a body (Heb. 10:5). Nestorianism is still believed and defended today.[7]

### John 1:1-4

All of these fell short of the John 1:1-4 understanding of Christ. We can learn from their departures and take caution lest we do the same. We may not understand how all these things work, but we can believe what the Scripture says plainly:

> In the beginning was the Word, and the Word was with God, and the Word was God.

---

[6] Jehovah's Witnesses Official Web Site, *Who Is Jesus Christ?* (*http://www.watchtower.org/e/rq/article_03.htm*).

[7] "Most Nestorians, numbering about 176,700, live in Iraq, Syria, and Iran, where they are generally known as Assyrians. Headed by a patriarch, at present residing in Iraq, they reject the doctrine, defined at Ephesus, that affirms that Jesus Christ is one single divine *hypostasis* (person), and that consequently his mother, Mary, should be called "Mother of God" (Encarta Encyclopedia, *Nestorian Church* (*http://encarta.msn.com/encyclopedia_761576621/Nestorian_Church.html*).

> He was in the beginning with God.
> All things were made through Him, and without Him nothing was made that was made.
> In Him was life, and the life was the light of men (John 1:1-4).

Five clear points should rise out of these four verses. One, Jesus pre-existed. He existed before coming in the flesh (cf. 1:14). He pre-existed the creation as all things were made by Him. Two, Jesus had fellowship with God in the beginning, hence, "and the word was *with* God." Three, Jesus is God. The Word was *fully* God.[8] Four, Jesus is creator as "all things were made through Him.[9] Five, Jesus has life as an intrinsic component to His nature. He was not given life as a *creature* but was the giver of life as the *Creator.* The Last Adam is a "life-giving" spirit (1 Cor. 15:45). John penned, "For as the Father raises the dead and gives life to them, even so the Son gives life to whom He will" (John 5:21).

### Controversies In Recent Times

In recent years the identity of Jesus has been questioned. Some have tried to make a distinction between the Jesus *of history* and the Jesus *of faith.* In 1977, British theologian, John Hicks and others charged that Jesus never thought of himself as God, but that these were exaggerated concepts written into the gospels.[10] On his official website, Hicks wrote,

> So I'm suggesting that we see the idea of divine incarnation in Jesus of Nazareth as a metaphorical idea. . . . And this [certain statements from the gospel of John, sjw], as we all know, is the theology dominating what has come to be called Christianity. It is not the teaching of Jesus, but was gradually created by later members of the Jesus movement and

---

[8] The Word did not become "a god" as some wrongly translate. Neither is John implying that Jesus was *once* a God and no longer is. He is the "I Am" who was, and is, and is to come (see Rev. 1:8; 22:13; John 8:24, 58).

[9] The charge that this is an exaggerated legendary claim written into the gospels is unwarranted. Paul concurs with this entire passage in his letter written to the Colossians only about thirty years after the crucifixion, "For by Him all things were created that are in heaven and that are on earth, visible and invisible, whether thrones or dominions or principalities or powers. All things were created through Him and for Him. And He is before all things, and in Him all things consist" (Col. 1:16, 17). These letters were written too soon after the crucifixion to be reduced to legendary material.

[10] I fully recommend, *The Case For Christ: A Journalist's Personal Investigation of the Evidences for Jesus,* by Lee Strobel for supplemental reading.

> was finally enshrined in the creeds. . . .This [Nicene Creed, sjw] is not the human Jesus of history but the divine Christ of faith . . . creating the insoluble puzzle of how an historical individual could have both the infinite, eternal, perfect, omnipotent, omniscient, omnipresent attributes of God and the finite, mortal, sinful, limited in power and in knowledge attributes of our humanity.[11]

### Five Arguments That Prove The Deity Of Jesus

The following material is designed in brief to contend against the skeptic's assertion that Jesus was not the Son of God. Five arguments, when sincerely looked at, prove the deity of Christ and answer the modernist.

**1. Credible Witnesses.** There is the area of credible witnesses and this is further broken down into two sub categories: (a) manuscript integrity, and (b) the quality of the witnesses themselves. The testimony that connects someone living today with the witnesses of the first-century is primarily found in the biblical manuscripts themselves that compose the New Testament. There is corroborating testimony from non-biblical sources that clearly implies the death of Jesus and subsequently Him being worshiped as God.[12]

By far the quality of manuscript integrity is owned by the New Testament exclusively. It stands without any parallel from any literary source ever written in undergoing the painstaking efforts to survive the challenge placed on it by time. One can have more confidence in the original authenticity and accuracy the New Testament than any other ancient historical document. The only literary source that can begin to compare with the integrity of the New Testament is Homer's *Iliad.* Yet even in this comparison, Homer's *Iliad* would look like an anthill comparing itself with the scale of Mount

---

[11] John Hicks' Official Website, *Believable Christianity, 2006* (*http://www.johnhick.org.uk/article16.html*).

[12] Josephus, *Antiquities of the Jews*, 20.200, ". . . when, therefore, Ananus was of this disposition, he thought he had now a proper opportunity [to exercise his authority]. Festus was now dead, and Albinus was but upon the road; so he assembled the Sanhedrin of judges, and brought before them the brother of Jesus, who was called Christ, whose name was James, and some others, [or some of his companions]; and, when he had formed an accusation against them as breakers of the law, he delivered them to be stoned. " See also Josephus, *Antiquities of the Jews* 18.63, 64; Tacitus, *Annals* 15.44; Pliny the Younger, *Letters* 10:96 for further corroboration that Jesus existed, died a violent death at the hands of the Romans, and was worshipped as God afterwards.

Rainier. Where Homer's *Iliad* has around 650 Greek manuscripts, the New Testament has over 5500. With the case of Homer's *Iliad*, a 1000 year gap exists between the original manuscript and the oldest known copy. However, the New Testament books stand in contrast with copies and fragments dating within a couple of generations of the very originals. The point is clear, if scholars can believe that the copies of Homer's *Iliad* are authentic, then they certainly can believe in the authenticity of the New Testament. Our Bible is true to the original manuscripts.

It is within the New Testament volume that credible testimony transpires from "eye-witnesses" (Luke 1:2; Acts 4:20; 1 Cor. 9:1; 2 Pet. 1:16; 1 John 1:1-3; 4:14; etc.). There is no better witness than one who saw and heard the things in question. If Jesus was seen and heard by honest witnesses, then His veracity can be known. The New Testament has the testimony of witnesses who lived and died by their testimony. Such elevates their witness far above that of "hearsay." A witness might be a false witness. He might lie about what he saw, but one would hardly be willing to die for a lie that he imagined.

What did they testify? They affirmed that Jesus was the Christ, the Son of the Living God! John the Baptist, for example, was given a mission to turn many to the Lord their God (Luke 1:16). Yet in turning them to the "Lord their God," he turned them to Jesus, "The Lamb of God who takes away the sin of the world!" (John 1:29; cf. v. 34). Andrew affirmed in John 1:41, ". . . 'We have found the Messiah' (which is translated, the Christ)." Philip spoke, ". . . We have found Him of whom Moses in the law, and also the prophets, wrote—Jesus of Nazareth, the son of Joseph" (John 1:45). Nathanael confessed, "Rabbi, You are the Son of God! You are the King of Israel" (John 1:49). A centurion was so impressed with the things that happened on the day Jesus was crucified that he confessed the deity of Christ (see Matt. 27:54). John began his gospel affirming that Jesus preexisted the creation, that He was in fellowship with God, that He is God, that He is creator, and that life is an intrinsic component of Him (John 1:1-4). The list could continue from example after example of the deity of Jesus being affirmed throughout the New Testament. To ascribe to these writers as lining up exaggerated claims that were written into the gospels is to make the gospel writers themselves false witnesses, the very thing that they condemned in their own testimony (cf. Matt. 26:60; John 5:31, 32; 1 Cor. 15:15). What are the odds of any of these witnesses dying or being persecuted for a known deception?

**2. Old Testament Prophecy.** To assert that Jesus was not the Son of God does not only cast reproach on the writers of the first century, but also makes empty those anticipatory statements that speak of the coming Messiah. Paul spoke of two characteristics of the power of God in Romans 4:17, ". . . God, who gives life to the dead and calls those things which do not exist as though they did." Besides giving life to the dead, another proof for God is prophecy—*to call things which do not exist as though they did exist.* Prophecy not only proves the inspiration of the Scriptures, but it also weighs on the question as to who Jesus was. With literally hundreds of prophecies in the Old Testament pertaining to the Messiah, space would only permit a sampling of some significant passages.

| Prophecy | Description | Fulfillment |
|---|---|---|
| Isaiah 7:14 | Born of a Virgin<br>Called Immanuel | Matt. 1:18, 24-25<br>John 1:14; Luke 1:16 |
| Isaiah 11:10 | From the House of Jesse | Matt. 1:6; Luke 3:32 |
| Micah 5:2 | Born in Bethlehem | Matt. 2:1; Luke 2:4-7 |
| Isaiah 9:6 | Government on his shoulders<br>Called Mighty God | Eph. 1:21-22; Rom. 9:5<br>Rev. 1:8; Tit. 2:13; 1 John 5:20 |
| Zechariah 9:9 | Riding on a foal of donkey into Jerusalem | Luke 19:30-37; Matt. 21:7 |
| Isaiah 35:5-6 | Perform miracles | Matt. 4:23-25 |
| Psalm 78:2 | Teach in Parables | Matt. 13:34 |
| Psalm 24:7-10 | King of Glory | 1 Cor. 2:8 |
| Zechariah 11:12 | Sold for Thirty Pieces of Silver | Matt. 26:14-15 |
| Psalm 22:16 | Piercing the hands and feet | John 20:25; Luke 24:39 |
| Isaiah 53:9 | Grave with wicked/rich at death | John 19:38-42; Matt. 27:57 |

In these prophecies we find that Messiah would be born of a virgin, from the family line of Jesse and in the city of Bethlehem. The Gospels agree that these particulars were fulfilled in Jesus. Isaiah 9:6 speaks of the government being on Messiah's shoulders and that one of the things He would be called is "Mighty God." The New Testament books bear out that Jesus is the divine founder and head of the church and is our great God and Savior. Zechariah forecasted that the Messiah would ride on the foal of a donkey entering Jerusalem (Zech. 9:9). Matthew and Luke agree that Jesus fulfilled it. Isaiah 35:5, 6 confirmed that the Messiah would perform miracles, and the New Testament overflows with sign after sign that was done by Christ. Even when the apostles performed miracles, they attributed the power to do such to Jesus Christ (see Acts 3:12, 16). Psalm 78:2 reflects that the Messiah would use a parabolic kind of teaching. Such teaching requires a great understanding of things. One cannot speak a parable about sowing seed in different kinds of soils and relate that to the different kinds of people that there are without first having an understanding of how things grow and likewise possessing a deep understanding of how people behave. Indeed, ". . . He knew what was in man" (John 2:25). Yet the Lord's understanding of man was not limited to His human experience with men, but as omniscient God, He knew all men, "But Jesus did not commit Himself to them, because He knew all men" (John 2:24).

Psalm 22:16. Among other things, David predicted the crucifixion of the Messiah in Psalm 22 before the act of crucifying criminals was even done.[13] Skeptics have alleged, without merit, that Psalm 22:16 has been manipulated by Christians to make it look like a crucifixion passage. They assert the rendition of the Jewish Publication Society as evidence.

> For dogs have encompassed me; a company of evil-doers have inclosed me; like a lion, [they are at] my hands and my feet.[14]

Often ignored, yet something that should cast doubt upon this version is this: The Jewish Publication Society has to add "they are at" with their "like a lion" translation to make any sense at all. That this seems like a copyist error is hinted in the absence of any verb.

The unwarranted conclusion that "pierced my hands and feet" is a Christian manipulation can be dismissed because of a *Dead Sea Scrolls* (DSS) find. The scroll, *4QPsf*,[15] has the Hebrew *karu* (to dig) not *ka'ari* (like a lion). This scroll has been dated to the first-century B.C. Additionally, the *Nahal Hever* discovery, a discovery in close proximity to the DSS, has one scroll of Psalms (*5/6HevPs*), where *ka'aru* is found in Psalm 22:16 and supports

---

[13] "The earliest historical record of crucifixion was in 519 BC when Darius I, the Persian King of Kings, crucified 3000 political opponents in Babylon" (*http://encylopedia.stateuniversity.com/pages/5235/crucifixion.html*).

[14] Jewish Publication Society (1917).

[15] "*4QPs$^f$* equals: 4(cave 4) Q (Qumran) Ps (Psalms) f (sixth manuscript); hence, the sixth Psalm manuscript found in Cave 4. This scroll may also be referred to as "4Q88" (the eighty-eighth manuscript from Cave 4 at Qumran).

"digging through" the hands and feet. While this manuscript is dated later than the DSS, it is still an old rendering that does not agree with "like a lion." Finally, the third-century B.C. Septuagint (LXX), a translation of the Hebrew Bible into Greek also agrees with "piercing" of the hands and feet. All point to the *wounding* of the hands and feet by boring through them. These documents *prove* that Psalm 22:16 is not a Christian problem but a Jewish one. It begs the question, "How could Christians mesh Psalm 22:16 to look like a crucifixion when these ancient source-documents existed before Christianity, before the crucifixion of Christ, and before the church?"[16] Incidentally, the DSS also prove significant in asserting the integrity of the Old Testament scriptures with fragments of every Old Testament book except Esther, pushing the dating of the earliest copies of the Hebrew Bible to the second century B.C.!

In considering another prophecy, Isaiah spoke of the grave of Christ being with the wicked. If you note carefully the wording of John 19:38-42, this aspect was equally fulfilled in the placement of the body of Christ. "Now in the place where He was crucified there was a garden, and in the garden a new tomb in which no one had yet been laid" (John 19:41). His tomb was in a garden; the garden was in or near the place where He was crucified; hence, the Lord's body was literally "laid to rest" where the wicked (criminals) were put to death. Further, Isaiah 53:9 forecasts the rich being at the death, and this was accomplished by Joseph of Arimathea who attended to the body of Jesus by permission of Pilate (see Matt. 27:57).

These prophecies predate Christianity and are anticipatory with specific qualities rather than vague generalities. These prophetic statements were beyond the power of being manipulated by the original composer. Since prophetic statements are realized in Jesus of Nazareth, we ought to join in echoing the sentiments Thomas expressed in John 20:28 when he was presented with the evidence for the living crucified Christ, "My Lord and my God!"

**3. Claims of Christ.** The claims of Christ are significant because they tell us who Christ thought He was. Isaiah 9:6 spoke of the male child who was born of a virgin as being called "Wonderful, Counselor, Mighty God, Everlasting Father, Prince of Peace." Incidentally, the Lord's final words after a confrontational discussion with some of the Jews in John 8 were,

---

[16] For a more detailed study of Psalm 22:16 and how it forecasts the crucifixion of Christ, see *http://www.revelationandcreation.com/pptfiles/psalm%2022.pdf.*

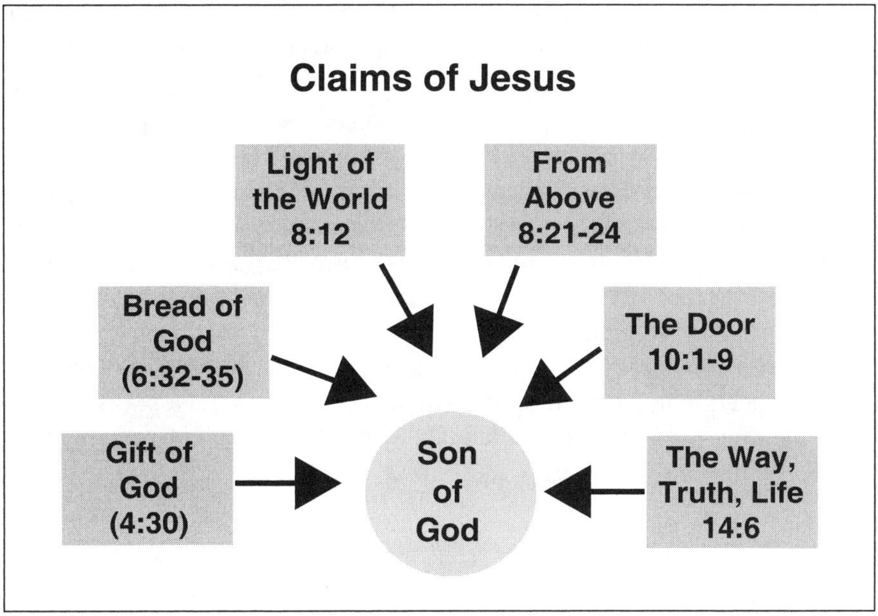


"Most assuredly, I say to you, before Abraham was, I AM" (John 8:58). While the Jews took it as blasphemy and violently tried to squelch Him, Isaiah's prophecy necessitated that Messiah have the quality of the everlasting Father. John 8:58 shows that Jesus clearly recognized this and applied such to Himself. His adversaries responded here in a way consistent with the crucifixion. There has to be a reason why Jesus was crucified. This certainly was one of those reasons.

Some of the other claims that Jesus stated were equally assertive about His nature and self-identity. To show the difference between Jesus and an apostle, consider if any prophet or apostle ever made the claims of being the "bread of God" and the "light of the world" (John 6:32-35; 8:12). An apostle might point to "the way" but he could never claim to be "The Way." He might know how to access the Father, but he could not claim to be the doorway to the Father as Jesus did in John 10:1-9 and 14:6.

Likewise, on one occasion, Jesus spoke of His life, saying, "No one takes it from Me, but I lay it down of Myself. I have power to lay it down, and I have power to take it again. This command I have received from My Father" (John 10:18). While we all have power to lay our life down, none of us has the ability to take it up again. This is impossible for a man to utter who is representing what is true, if he thinks of Himself as only a man. In fact, it is absurd for anyone except God to utter. "No one has power over the spirit to retain the spirit, And no one has power in the day of death . . ." (Eccl. 8:8; see also Ps. 89:48). Yet please note that Jesus claimed to have such inherent power! "For as the Father raises the dead and gives life to them, even so the Son gives life to whom He will" (John 5:21). By stark contrast, Paul could raise the dead and heal the sick, yet he was not able to lay down his life and take it up again. "Therefore we do not lose heart. Even though our outward man is perishing, yet the inward man is being renewed day by day" (2 Cor. 4:16). His outward man (body) was perishing and Paul could not reverse it. Neither was he able, on his own, to save his own life from an evil conspiracy that would have cut it off prematurely. If God had not intervened Paul would have died then (2 Cor. 1:8-11). Nor was he able to give life to whomever he willed, as he evidently was not permitted on his own will to heal Epaphroditus (Phil. 2:27).

This should prove that, if we accept the gospels as honest reproductions of the sayings of Jesus, and there is no valid reason not to, then Jesus was very cognitive of who He was. He clearly understood Himself to be God. "Then they all said, 'Are You then the Son of God?' So He said to them, 'You rightly say that I am'" (Luke 22:70). One more point should resonate with us very clearly as it relates to the claims of Christ: the Lord's accusers were not unclear about who Jesus thought He was, "The Jews answered him, 'We have a law, and according to our law He ought to die, because He made Himself the Son of God'" (John 19:17).

**4. Signs of Christ.** "And truly Jesus did many other signs in the presence of His disciples, which are not written in this book; but these are written that you may believe that Jesus is the Christ, the Son of God, and that believing you may have life in His name" (John 20:30, 31).

Though it was impossible to list them all, the apostle John drew from the wealth of miracles that Jesus had done to record enough for us to reach a conclusion about Jesus of Nazareth. What conclusion should we reach specifically of Jesus? That He is the Christ, the anointed, the Son of God. No one can ever have life without reaching that conclusion. There is a body of evidence encased and presented within the Bible for every person to draw a conclusion about Jesus. Was He a deceiver or not? Was He the Christ or not? If the evidence is real, then there is only one conclusion the honest mind can reach: Jesus Christ is the Son of God!

John presents Jesus turning water to wine, healing a nobleman's son,

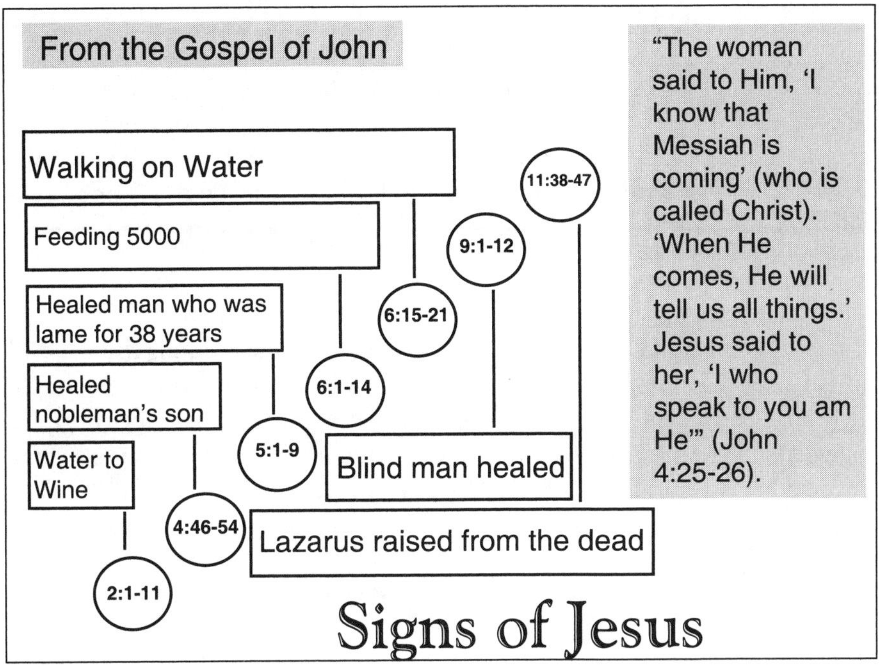


healing a man who was lame for thirty-eight years, feeding 5000, walking on water, making a blind man see, and finally raising Lazarus from the dead. These miracles accord so well with John's point in John 20:31 that one may have life through believing in Jesus as the Christ! If He can raise the physically dead, why not also believe that He can give us life in His name? This life is available if we will immerse ourselves in the evidence for Christ and respond in grateful obedience to the gospel (Mark 16:15, 16).

Perhaps it is summed up well in the example of the Samaritan woman, who while not a Jew, expected the coming of a Great One. She understood that He would have great power to prove Himself in telling us all things. While perhaps slightly skeptical at first, the evidence presented to her won her over to Christ. Jesus not only verbally accepted the place of the Messiah, but displayed the right to that place in telling things about her that only the Messiah could know (John 4:16-18; 25, 26, 28-30, 39-42).

The greatest sign of all was in Jesus raising Himself up from the grave. Prior to His death, Jesus claimed to have the power to lay His life down and raise it up again. He adamantly claimed that no one takes it from Him (John 10:18). The veracity of His claim was vindicated when, on that first day of the week, He burst forth from the chains of death and re-entered into that cold and lifeless body. The expression, "O Death, where is your sting? O Hades, where is your victory?"[17] was pronounced in the chorus of divine deeds when Jesus came forth from the grave. Paul, in the beginning of his epistle to the Romans, spoke of both the humanity and deity of Christ, "concerning His Son Jesus Christ our Lord, who was born of the seed of David according to the flesh, and declared to be the Son of God with power according to the Spirit of holiness, by the resurrection from the dead" (Rom. 1:3, 4).

**5. Relationships of Christ.** It is important to recognize this last body of information as it pertains to any controversy that surrounds the deity of Jesus Christ. The material previously taught should be convincing enough. However, because some have asserted that it is possible that the disciples had used exaggerated claims about the life of Christ and others have argued that Jesus' power was on loan to Him, we feel compelled to offer this last section of information. Would Jesus agree with John's assessment about who Jesus was? Would Jesus, while on earth, agree with John that He was in the beginning and that He was with God as God and created all things?

**The Picture of Christ's Relationships . . .**
**Prove Him To Be The Son of God!**

- **Over Apostles**
- **Greater than John the Baptist**
- **Possessor of Kingdom**
- **Savior of the Lost World**
- **Power to Fulfill and Put Away the Law of Moses**
- **Crucified by the Romans as "a King"**

**The Bottom Line**

[17] 1 Corinthians 15:55.

Was Jesus the Son of God or was He merely an inspired miracle worker like Paul and Moses who tapped into the power of the Holy Spirit? Did Jesus really express the idea that He was the Messiah to the woman at the well or are these kinds of statements merely the product of manmade manipulations of individuals who desperately wanted to believe that Jesus was the Messiah when in fact He never believed Himself to be? A study of the relationships of Jesus seals up the argument that not only did men in the first-century believe He was the Son of God, but Jesus also clearly viewed Himself as God in the flesh. By observing these relationships we see the divine insignia pertaining to the personality of Jesus of Nazareth.

*Christ's Relationship with the Apostles.*

> Now there was also a dispute among them, as to which of them should be considered the greatest. And He said to them, 'The kings of the Gentiles exercise lordship over them, and those who exercise authority over them are called "benefactors." But not so among you; on the contrary, he who is greatest among you, let him be as the younger, and he who governs as he who serves. For who is greater, he who sits at the table, or he who serves? Is it not he who sits at the table? Yet I am among you as the One who serves (Luke 22:24-27).

What is Jesus' relationship to the Twelve? Is He merely a part of this group of men or rather, is He the head, the leader, and organizer of it? Similar to the founding of the twelve tribes of Israel in the Old Testament, Jesus establishes an apostleship by choosing twelve men to serve as ambassadors and representatives of Christ in the kingdom/church. But the Lord's is clearly *over* the apostles, or the expression in verse 27, "Yet I am among you as the One who serves" makes no sense. If He was an equal or less, it has no meaning.

*Christ's Relationship with John the Baptist.* "For I say to you, among those born of women there is not a greater prophet than John the Baptist; but he who is least in the kingdom of God is greater than he" (Luke 7:28).

There is a relationship that Jesus draws from regarding John and all the prophets. Jesus clearly said there is not a greater prophet than John. This should make us see the folly of those who claim Jesus was only a prophet. If He were only a prophet, then John would have been greater than Jesus. Yet, the baptizer clearly understood that he was not greater than Him.

> You yourselves bear me witness, that I said, "I am not the Christ," but, "I have been sent before Him." He who has the bride is the bridegroom; but

> the friend of the bridegroom, who stands and hears him, rejoices greatly because of the bridegroom's voice. Therefore this joy of mine is fulfilled. He must increase, but I must decrease. He who comes from above is above all; he who is of the earth is earthly and speaks of the earth. *He who comes from heaven is above all* (John 3:28-31, emp. mine).

As we think about the significance of Luke 7:28, we find that Jesus also elevates His kingdom above John. The least in the kingdom of God is greater than John. That is because, the least in the kingdom is in the church, the bride of Christ. This would have been a profound statement to enter into the ears of the common Jew. The prevailing view was that physical Israel was the kingdom of God and it would be restored in time (see Acts 1:6). John was certainly a citizen within that kingdom. Yet Jesus clearly shows in Luke 7:28 that physical Israel is not the kingdom of God. While John was a part of the physical kingdom of Israel, he was not member of the kingdom, but a forerunner to it. As great as John was, Jesus is greater than he.

*Christ's Relationship to the Kingdom.* "And I will give you the keys of the kingdom of heaven, and whatever you bind on earth will be bound in heaven, and whatever you loose on earth will be loosed in heaven" (Matt. 16:19).

Jesus is clearly presented as the one who has the keys of the kingdom and can give them to the apostles. He states in Luke 22:29 that He bestows a kingdom upon them. Jesus bestows the kingdom and shares the same nature with the Father who bestowed it upon Him. Note also the possessive quality in Luke 22:30, "that you may eat and drink at *My table* in *My kingdom*, and sit on thrones judging the twelve tribes of Israel" (italics added). The relationship that Jesus has with the kingdom is owner and king.

*Christ's Relationship to the World.* "And He said to them, 'Go into all the world and preach the gospel to every creature. He who believes and is baptized will be saved; but he who does not believe will be condemned'" (Mark 16:15, 16).

This clearly portrays that the world is lost and in need of a savior. It shows that the gospel of Jesus is needed to save and the two critical steps for salvation are herein stated. They must believe that Jesus is the Son of God and respond by being immersed in water into Christ (John 8:24; Matt. 28:18, 19; Acts 2:38; 8:36-38; 22:16; Rom. 6:3-6; Gal. 3:26, 37; etc.). But the very fact that the world needs to believe and be baptized into Jesus to be saved elevates Jesus above the world and all who are in it. Likewise, the fact that Jesus has the power to condemn the world confesses His position above the world.

*Christ's Relationship to the Law.* "Do not think that I came to destroy the Law or the Prophets. I did not come to destroy but to fulfill" (Matt. 5:17).

Who could claim to have the power to fulfill the law as Jesus did? As great as Moses was in *giving* the law, Jesus is greater in *fulfilling* it! No prophet, apostle or even angel could make such a claim. Further, Jesus spoke with authority as to things pertaining to the Law. Yet, He could go deeper than what a surfaced reading of the Law would imply, with "but I say to you" (Matt. 5:22, 28, 32, 34, 44). For example, the law condemned the explicit sexual act of adultery, but Jesus spoke with authority regarding how adultery can exist and be condemned in the halls of the heart (Matt. 5:28).

Jesus had power to modify the Law. The Law of Moses permitted divorce and remarriage for things less than adultery (viz. "some uncleanness," Deut. 24:1-4). The Law of Moses permitted both parties to remarry except that the Law forbade the man to ever take his original wife back if she remarried. Jesus, however, set that law aside for two reasons. One, it was permitted because of the hardness of man's heart. Two, it fundamentally was not agreeable with the creation model. Hence, Jesus exclaimed, ". . . from the beginning it was not so" (Matt. 19:8). Any citizen of the kingdom of Christ will not be ruled by "the hardness of heart" but will persist to please Jesus by abiding in the original creation model of one man to one woman for life.

J. W. McGarvey expounded:

> But Jesus here limits the right of divorce to cases of unchastity, and if there be a divorce on any other ground, neither the man nor the woman can marry again without committing adultery (Mt 19:9). Such is Jesus' **modification** of the Old Testament law, and in no part of the New Testament is there any relaxation as to the law here set forth. It is implied that divorce for unchastity breaks the marriage bond, and it is therefore held almost universally, both by commentators and moralists, that the innocent party to such a divorce can marry again. Of course the guilty part could not, for no one is allowed by law to reap the benefits of his own wrong" (emp. mine).[18]

[18] J. W. McGarvey, *Four-Fold Gospel*, 242.

We also see this relationship to the Law exhibited in Matthew 12 by Jesus referring to Himself as greater than the temple and being Lord of the Sabbath (vv. 5-8). Only one greater than the temple could have authority to modify and expound on the Law the way He did. The fact that Jesus had the power to take away the Law and produce a New Covenant shows that Jesus is altogether greater than Moses and the Law (Col. 2:14; Heb. 9:15-17; 10:9; etc.).

Indeed, there was no identity crisis with the Lord; Jesus fully understood Himself to be the Son of Man of Daniel's ancient prophecy who is seen as ascending to the Father, the Ancient of Days, and receiving a kingdom (Dan. 7:13, 14).

> But Jesus kept silent. And the high priest answered and said to Him, "I put You under oath by the living God: Tell us if You are the Christ, the Son of God!" Jesus said to him, "It is as you said. Nevertheless, I say to you, hereafter you will see the Son of Man sitting at the right hand of the Power, and coming on the clouds of heaven" (Matt. 26:63, 64).

Daniel's prophecy is consistent with the New Testament's portrayal of Jesus.

*Christ's Relationship to the Roman Authorities.* "Pilate therefore said to Him, 'Are You a king then?' Jesus answered, 'You say rightly that I am a king. For this cause I was born, and for this cause I have come into the world, that I should bear witness to the truth. Everyone who is of the truth hears My voice'" (John 18:37).

Those who believe Jesus was only a wise sage of Israel, or who think that Jesus didn't understand Himself to be the king of God's everlasting kingdom collide into an insurmountable problem in dealing with the reason Jesus was crucified under Roman rule. Why would the Romans crucify a Rabbi who merely taught fascinating and soul searching and heart piercing parables? Why the title on the cross, "The King of the Jews"? Either He had made that claim to others or others concluded that He considered Himself a king (see also John 19:19-22). This comprehensive picture is evident proof that Jesus is the Son of God. Focusing on any tangent or doctrine that takes us away from this picture is not of God, nor of the Spirit, nor of the apostles.

### Recent Controversy in the Brotherhood

The controversy over the nature of Christ has also affected the church in recent years. Debates have sprung up touching the subject. In 1995 John

A. Welch debated Gene Frost pertaining to the immutability of the spirit of Jesus. John Welch affirmed that the Lord's spirit did change; Gene Frost denied such.

**Arguments that were advanced for the changed spirit of Christ were:**

- Jesus had to learn things which means He didn't know everything (Isa. 7:15, 16; Luke 2:40; cf. Matt. 24:36; Heb. 5:8, 9). "How does an all wise God increase in wisdom?"

However, care should be given to not assert things which are beyond our finite scope and power to understand. "But of that day and hour no one knows, not even the angels of heaven, but My Father only" (Matt. 24:36). To insist that Jesus *lost* any quality of omniscience because He doesn't know something the Father knows also incriminates the Holy Spirit. The "Father only" excludes the Holy Spirit as much as it excludes the Son (just as "faith only" excludes "obedience"). Rather than questioning the all knowing capacity of Christ and the Spirit, we ought to understand that there are some things in the mind of the Father, the director of all things, which have not been revealed to the other two members of the Godhead. As the Head of the Godhead, the Father has that prerogative.

Regarding the passage in Isaiah 7:15, 16, "Curds and honey He shall eat, that He may know to refuse the evil and choose the good. For before the Child shall know to refuse the evil and choose the good, the land that you dread will be forsaken by both her kings." Jesus was able to go through the process of human growth.[19] As a babe, Jesus could have spoken Greek and performed gymnastics. If He could make a donkey speak in the days of Balaam; He could as a baby speak too! However, Jesus experienced the

---

[19] Matthew Henry correctly stated, "Though he be conceived by the power of the Holy Ghost, yet he shall not therefore be fed with angels' food, but, as it becomes him, *shall be in all things made like unto his brethren*, Heb. ii. 17. Nor shall he though born thus by extraordinary generation, be a man immediately, but as other children, shall advance gradually through the several states of infancy, childhood, and youth, so that of manhood, and growing in wisdom and stature, shall at length wax strong in spirit and come to maturity, so as to know how *to refuse the evil and choose the good*. See Luke ii. 40, 52. Note, Children are fed when they are little that they may be taught and instructed when they have grown up; they have their maintenance in order to their education" (*Matthew Henry's Commentary*, IV: 48).

nature and development of man in strength, wisdom, and stature (Luke 2:40, 52). He would have therefore learned to crawl, walk, read, and talk as a man. Isaiah 7:15, in using the expression, "that He may know to refuse the evil and choose the good" is simply speaking of His childhood development. Verse 16, however, is more than likely speaking of one of Isaiah's children and the impending doom that is connected with the fall of the two kings discussed in chapter 7 and 8.[20]

Yet even as a youth, we see Him knowing things about His mission prior to being baptized. "Why did you seek Me? Did you not know that I must be about My Father's business?" (Luke 2:49). How can an all knowing God increase in wisdom? I confess that I do not have an answer that fully satisfies. But neither do I have a satisfactory answer how an all knowing and all seeing God, who can hear the outcry of Sodom's sin, yet still must go down to "see whether they have done altogether according to the outcry against it" (Gen. 18:21). Despite the limits of my understanding, I still believe and defend that Jehovah is all knowing and all seeing (Jer. 23:24; 2 Chron. 16:9; Ps. 11:4; etc.). How does an all knowing God not know that men could do such vile things as burning their children to Molech (Jer. 32:35)? Evidently, Jehovah, though He is omniscient, has the ability to not see things in our future as well as forget things in our past (e.g. ". . . their sin I will remember no more," Jer. 31:34). Yet, how can the twelve-year old boy in Luke 2:42 know His heavenly Father like Jesus did? How can He know what His business is? How does He derive that He needs to be about doing His Father's business and possess a better understanding of it

[20] Matthew Henry, in the reference above, asserts that "the child" in verse 16 is another child altogether and not the Messiah of 7:14, 15. He contends that it should better be understood as "this child," that is, the child Isaiah had in his very arms named Shear-Jashub, whom Isaiah was commanded to bring with him at his meeting with Azah (see 7:3). Alternatively, it might also be understood as Isaiah's other child who is mentioned in Isaiah 8:3-4, "Then I went to the prophetess [his wife, sjw], and she conceived and bore a son. Then the Lord said to me, 'Call his name Maher-Shalal-Hash-Baz; for before the child shall have knowledge to cry "My father" and "My mother," the riches of Damascus and the spoil of Samaria will be taken away before the king of Assyria.'" That these two identities address the immediate problem facing Ahaz and better parallel the demands of 7:16 seems obvious and can therefore not easily be dismissed. Further, Isaiah viewed his children as "signs" for this immediate calamity, "Here am I and the children whom the Lord has given me! We are for signs and wonders in Israel from the Lord of hosts, Who dwells in Mount Zion" (Isa. 8:18).

than His parents' did? This is equally difficult to explain, save for the fact that He was "God with us."

Hebrews 5:8, 9 conveys the idea of experience. Jesus learned obedience because He experienced it in the things He suffered. Simply, He practiced it. To suggest that Jesus knew nothing about obedience is nonsensical as He knew everything (John 16:30). Reading passages where God needed to know something doesn't mean that He lost his omniscience per se. Just because Jesus asked where Lazarus was laid does not mean that He didn't know (John 11:34). God knows the heart but could choose to test others ". . . to *know* whether you love the Lord your God with all your heart and with all your soul" (Deut. 13:3; emp. mine). Although He knows man and what is in man, He could not let certain things ". . . come into My mind that they should do this abomination" (John 2:24, 25; Jer. 32:35).

| Normal Appetite | Good Satisfaction | Evil Satisfaction |
|---|---|---|
| • Hunger | • Food | • Gluttony |
| • Thirst | • Water, juice | • Alcohol |
| • Well Being | • Rest | • Drugs |
| • Sex | • Marriage | • Fornication |

**Luke 6:45; Mark 7:21-23**

- Jesus was tempted (Heb. 2:17). God cannot be tempted, so Jesus gave up omnipotence/omniscience in order to be tempted.

However, we know that God can be tempted (Exod. 17: 2, 7; Deut. 6:16; Ps. 78:18, 41, 56; 95:9; 106:14; Mal. 3:15; 1 Cor. 10:9; Heb. 3:9). Jesus was tempted and we might also add He overcame the devil and sin in the same measure we can. Some assert that, if Jesus had all of His divine attributes, then He had an unfair advantage. Yet, such an assertion proves nothing and creates as many problems as it tries to solve. For example, one could counter then that Jesus had an unfair advantage against Satan by having the Holy Spirit in the manner in which He did. These assertions wander into the wilderness of mere speculation and away from the path of truth and reason. Jesus being tempted does not require that He lose any share of His Godhood. While God can be tempted, He cannot be tempted *by evil* (Jas. 1:13). God is not tempted by evil because there is no place for evil in Him (1 John 1:5). Likewise, Jesus never developed a lust for evil. "I will no longer talk much with you, for the ruler of this world is coming, and *he has nothing in Me*" (John 14:30, italics added). On the other hand, man is created with an upright heart and later acquires a *desire* for evil (Eccl. 7:29). Jesus lived in the flesh; yet He proved that evil desires are not inherent to the flesh. Bodily appetites can be satisfied in honorable and true ways. But man sins when he desires to satisfy those bodily appetites in ways that are evil.

- Jesus emptied himself (Phil. 2:7). To be like us He must have to walk by faith. If Jesus had all the attributes of deity, He walked by sight and not by faith.

We might ask, "He emptied Himself of what?" Did he empty Himself of love, of righteousness, of any divine attribute? This passage doesn't say Jesus emptied Himself of anything other than "Himself." It is better understood in the translation "but made Himself of no reputation." Philippians 2:7 is speaking of the manner in which Jesus came to earth which is consistent with being a servant. It is not discussing His losing attributes but coming in a humble manner. He came in the form of a man, to serve rather than be served (Matt. 20:28). He abased Himself and is not ashamed to call us brethren (Heb. 2:11).

- Jesus sorrowed as men do. Jesus was *very heavy* in the garden (Matt. 26:37; Mark 14:33). Deity cannot sorrow as a man does. He must have given up some divine attributes to feel sorrow.

But we know sorrow because the capacity for emotion was given to us by bearing the image of God. No other creature on earth sorrows as a man and we experience such emotions as we have, not because we are human, but because we are made in the image of an emotional God (Gen. 6:6; Judg. 10:16; Ps. 78:40; 95:10; Isa. 43:24; Zech. 11:5, 8; Matt. 23:37; Mark 3:5; Heb. 3:10; Eph. 4:30).

### Power Derived by the Holy Spirit?

Another aspect of this controversy has been the assertion that Jesus had no inherent power on earth and all the miracles that He did were exclusively derived by the Power of the Holy Spirit. Jeff Asher penned:

| **Divested or Derived** | |
|---|---|
| IF: | THEN: |
| "I have many things to say and to judge concerning you, but He who sent Me is true; and I speak to the world thongs things which I heard from Him" (John 8:26). | "But when the Helper comes, whom I shall send to you from the Father, the Spirit of truth who proceeds from the Father, He will testify of Me" (John 15:26). |
| MEANS JESUS' POWER WAS DIVESTED AND THEN DERIVED FROM THE SPIRIT | MEANS SPIRIT'S POWER WAS DIVESTED AND THEN DERIVED FROM JESUS |

> The Bible teaches that Jesus exercised divine power delegated to Him by the Father *derived from the Holy Spirit*. Jesus said, and He ought to know, "The Son can do nothing of Himself. . . . I can of My own self do nothing . . . the works which the Father hath given Me to finish. . . . I speak to the world those things which I have heard of Him. . . . I do nothing of Myself; but as the Father hath taught Me . . . the truth which I have heard of God . . . . I proceeded forth and came from God; neither came I of Myself. . . . this commandment have I received of my Father" (see: John 5:19, 22, 26, 30, 36, 43; 8:16, 18, 26, 28, 29, 38, 40, 42, 55; 10:17, 18, 25, 29, 32, 36). *The man does not live that can make sense of these passages and at the same time declare that Jesus exercised power independent of the other members of the Godhead in a fashion that was underived or undelegated* (italics added).[21]

These passages are not discussing the abandonment of ability to work miracles, but rather they speak of the union that exists between the individual members of the Godhead and their seemingly distinct roles: the Father as the director and head, Jesus as the executor and model of the plan, and the Holy Spirit as the revelator and exhibitor of the plan. Jesus came to do the will of the Father and He therefore worked within the command (authority) of the Father. Even if we were to concede that Jesus performed every miracle by the power of the Holy Spirit, that doesn't prove that He had no power to carry out the deed. Further, does the fact that Jesus worked by the Holy Spirit's power imply that the Father was somehow without that miraculous power? I think not.

Because of space, we cannot address every passage specifically cited, but we shall look at some of them. When you consider John 5, several verses

---

[21] Jeff Asher, "Response to Osborne's 'Smooth Things about the Deity of Christ,'" *Bible Talk*, Vol. 1: 17 (1998).

are noted in the above quote as an example of Jesus having the power to work miracles by the Holy Spirit alone. The context clearly shows Jesus is referring to His work being done by the approval and authority of the Father who is His head (1 Cor. 11:3). This is what was contested by the Jews. This doesn't mean any divine attributes are lost from our Lord or that any were derived from another source, any more than human attributes are lost in women when they recognize men as the head and respect that divinely placed authority.

**John 5:26.** "For as the Father has life in Himself, so He has granted the Son to have life in Himself." If anything, this passage affirms the equal ability of Christ to that of the Father. It does not say that He granted the Son to tap into the miraculous ability of the Spirit. Albert Barnes fittingly affirmed:

> This evidently does not refer to the manner in which the second person of the Trinity exists, for the power and authority of which Christ here speaks is that which he exercises as *Mediator*. It is the power of raising the dead and judging the world. In regard to his divine nature, it is not affirmed here that it is in any manner derived; nor does the fact that God is said to have given him this power prove that he was inferior in his nature or that his existence was derived. For, 1st. It has reference merely *to office*. As Mediator, he may be said to have been appointed by the Father. 2[n]d. Appointment to office does not prove that the one who is appointed is inferior in nature to him who appoints him. A son may be appointed to a particular work by a parent, and yet, in regard to talents and every other qualification, may be equal or superior to the father. He sustains the relation of a son, and in this relation there is an official inferiority. General Washington was not inferior in nature and talents to the men who commissioned him. He simply derived *authority* from them to do what he was otherwise fully able to do. So the Son, as Mediator, is subject to the Father; yet this proves nothing about his nature (italics his).[22]

Further, Jesus said, "I have come in My Father's name, and *you do not receive Me . . .*" (John 5:43; italics added). The Jews did not quibble who the power was from. They understood Jesus did the work. Their contention was with what *right* did Jesus have to do this deed on the Sabbath (John 5:10, 11, 16). They clearly thought that Jesus violated the Law. The second point of controversy was that Jesus called God His Father which they *correctly* understood would make him equal with God (John 5:17, 18; cf. 10:33). Amazingly, the passages that brother Asher uses were understood by the

---

[22] Albert Barnes, *Barnes Notes On The New Testament,* II: (Luke, John) 234.

original audience pertaining to the Lord's equality with God. They were in a hard situation as they could not deny the miracle, yet the miracle gave credence to what Jesus taught. These Jews never had the notion that Jesus was before them as one dependent upon another to do anything miraculous at all. They understood Him to be claiming and doing marvelous deeds that they wrongly thought violated Moses' Law. The Lord's actions impeached their whole understanding of the Sabbath Law. Jesus affirmed that He had done His work in the approval of God which indicted their religion as without divine approval. Ironically, they thought that it was easier to try to kill Jesus, the One with Life, than to deal with the discrepancy. In doing so it added another sin upon their showcase of sins: not honoring the Son as they would the Father (John 5:23).

**John 5:19.** "Then Jesus answered and said to them, 'Most assuredly, I say to you, the Son can do nothing of Himself, but what He *sees* the Father do; for whatever He *does*, the Son also *does* in like manner'" (emp. mine). Our Lord tells something that the careful reader does well to pick up on. Jesus "sees" and "does" what the Father in heaven does. This is a careful assertion of the full and comparable divine attributes of the Son to that of the Father. Jesus, while on earth could see (observe, behold) the Father and do in like manner. Again, the passages brother Asher uses, when read carefully, actually affirm the equality of the Son to the Father! The fact that Jesus could, of His own will, see the Father is a mark of deity. No man has seen God that way (John 1:18). Likewise, that Jesus could do things *in like manner* to the Father is again another testimony to the deity of Christ and His inherent power. This testifies to the unity of the Godhead from one member to another. That Jesus had His full array of power at His fingertips, so to speak, cannot be denied by anyone who carefully reads the New Testament, "For as the Father raises the dead and gives life to them, even so the Son gives life to whom He will" (John 5:21).

When we consider the resurrection of Christ, who had the power to raise up Jesus? If we let the Scriptures speak we find:

1. God had the power, "Men of Israel, hear these words: Jesus of Nazareth, a Man attested by God to you by miracles, wonders, and signs which God did through Him in your midst, as you yourselves also know . . . whom God raised up" (Acts 2:22, 24).
2. The Holy Spirit had the power *if* we understand passages like Romans 8:11 to be referring to the Holy Spirit.

3. Jesus had the power, "No one takes it from Me, but I lay it down of Myself. I have power to lay it down, and I have power to take it again. This command I have received from My Father" (John 10:18). Jesus stated in no uncertain terms that He had the power to lay down His life and take it up again. While alive, Jesus had the power to lay down His life. There were many attempts on His life prior to the crucifixion, but He evaded them and escaped (John 8:59; 10:31; Luke 4:29). While dead, Jesus had the power to raise upHimself. Neither the power to lay down His life when alive nor raise it up again after He died was *derived* from the Holy Spirit. It was His power.

**John 8:26.** "I have many things to say and to judge concerning you, but He who sent Me is true; and I speak to the world those things which I heard from Him" was used to promote the idea that Jesus derived His power from the other members of the Godhead. Jesus was sent by the Father to speak to the world those things which He heard from Him. Once again, this affirms the full deity of Christ in human form. Being sent by God, in this sense, is coming from the presence of God.[23] He spoke what He was sent to say. If this necessitates that Jesus somehow became divested of certain powers and needed to resupply that loss from another member of the Godhead, then what shall we make of similar statements that pertain to the Holy Spirit in John 15:26 and16:7, 13, 14? Note, "Nevertheless I tell you the truth. It is to your advantage that I go away; for if I do not go away, the Helper will not come to you; but if I depart, *I will send Him to you. . . .* However, when He, the Spirit of truth, has come, He will guide you into all truth; *for He will not speak on His own authority*, but *whatever He hears He will speak*; and He will tell you things to come" (John 16:7, 13, 14; emp. mine). As Jesus was sent to speak, so the Holy Spirit was sent to speak. Yet who would believe that Jesus sending the Spirit to speak would mean the Spirit was divested of anything? It simply boils down to the respect that the persons of the Godhead place for the authority of each other. The Spirit worked within Christ's authority. Jesus worked within the Father's.

**John 8:28.** Likewise, if we skip down to John 8:28, ". . . that I do nothing of Myself; but as My Father taught Me, I speak these things" and imply that

---

[23] Compare Jesus in John 8:42, "Jesus said to them, 'If God were your Father, you would love Me, for I proceeded forth and came from God; nor have I come of Myself, but He sent Me" with the Holy Spirit with John 15:26, "But when the Helper comes, whom I shall send to you from the Father, the Spirit of truth who proceeds from the Father, He will testify of Me."

Jesus didn't know all things while on earth, then, the Holy Spirit in John 16:13, 14 didn't know all things. If it is true with Jesus, then why would it not be true with the Spirit? What would the Holy Spirit have to lose to be sent by Christ and speak within the authority of Christ? Would He have to "lose" any attribute in order to operate "under" the authority of Christ? Why would Jesus then have to lose anything to work within the authority of the Father? It wasn't so much what He lost, but what He took on—*a body.*

**Acts 10:38.** Sometimes arguments prove too much. For example, Paul stated in Acts 10:38, ". . . how God anointed Jesus of Nazareth with the Holy Spirit and with power, who went about doing good and healing all who were oppressed by the devil, for God was with Him" (Acts 10:38). This passage has been used to show that Jesus was empowered to work miracles by the Holy Spirit. Yet in doing so, one creates the very problem that he is trying to avoid. That problem is this: How could Jesus live as a man, be tempted as a man, and yet have all of His divine attributes? However, why not also assume the Holy Spirit was Christ's agency to *do good?* Jesus was anointed with the same power to heal and cast out demons as He was to do good! Hence we have reduced Jesus to a powerless puppet of God who cannot even "do good" except by the power of the Spirit. Any contention that proves too much proves nothing. A sound approach to this passage is that Jesus was anointed by the Spirit to "set Him apart" for the work of His ministry, to fulfill the word of prophecy, and to crown Him with the insignia of the Messiah/Mediator office (cf. Luke 4:18-21; Isa. 35:5, 6; etc.). Bible anointing conveyed the idea of being *set apart* for a specific work. Kings were anointed to rule (1 Kin. 19:15, 16). Saul was anointed to be king (1 Sam. 10:1). When he was disobedient, God took His Spirit from him (1 Sam. 16:14). When God anointed David, His Spirit came upon him, "Then Samuel took the horn of oil and anointed him in the midst of his brothers; and the Spirit of the Lord came upon David from that day forward . . ." (1 Sam. 16:13). When men were anointed as such, they were considered the Lord's anointed (see Cyrus, Isa. 45:1). For this reason, Jesus was called the "Christ" which meant "anointed." Jesus was anointed by the Spirit for the work of God in redemption and the apostle wanted Cornelius to know that Jesus is the Messiah. He is not speaking of Jesus being granted super powers derived by another member of the Godhead, but rather, that the dynamite power that Christ displayed were the works that God had *set Him apart to do*!

### Other Arguments for the Immutability of Christ

The immutability of Christ is in reference to His essence and being. He as God does not change. "Jesus Christ is the same yesterday, today, and forever" (Heb. 13:8). He is true to His promises. This does not mean that Jesus could not experience the change of being clothed in a body of flesh, experience the appetite of the flesh, and display sorrow with saline tears from human eyes. Still, Jesus is the same in the fact that He is still God; He is still holy and works what is righteous. The arguments that may be used to prove the immutability of Christ as God are as follows:

1. The prophecies about the Messiah-Child are forceful.
    - "But you, Bethlehem Ephrathah, Though you are little among the thousands of Judah, Yet out of you shall come forth to Me The One to be Ruler in Israel, Whose goings forth are from of old, from everlasting" (Mic. 5:2). It was Jesus as a baby that came out of Bethlehem (Matt. 2:1). Yet, Micah not only affirms His place of birth, but His endless life, *from everlasting.*
    - "Therefore the Lord Himself will give you a sign: Behold, the virgin shall conceive and bear a Son, and shall call His name Immanuel" (Isa. 7:14). Who was called Immanuel? The baby, born of a virgin was *Immanuel* (God with us). Jesus was God while a baby and called "mighty God" in prophecy (Isa. 9:6). Isaiah shows us His unique entrance into the world and Micah defines His place of birth and eternality.

2. Statements about the nature of God are relevant.
    - God changes not (Mal. 3:6; cf. Heb. 13:8).
    - God is God from everlasting to everlasting (Ps. 90:2).
    - All the fullness of the Godhead bodily dwelt in Christ (Col. 2:9).
    - His glory was observed, "And the Word became flesh and dwelt among us, and we beheld His glory, the glory as of the only begotten of the Father, full of grace and truth" (John 1:14). This was not another's glory. It was the Son's glory united with the flesh. Hence they saw "His" glory when He taught with astonishing authority, when He worked miracles, and observed Him at the transfiguration.
    - He must have God's nature to be God (Gal. 4:8). The reasonable conclusion is then that all of the attributes of God were in Jesus while on earth. Because He displayed emotions of anger and

sorrow or because He was tempted does not change that fact. Because He allowed man to crucify Him does not mean that He was not 100 percent God in 100 percent flesh. He had the totality of being God in the flesh. He was *God with us.*

3. Statements about the knowledge of Jesus are useful. He:
   - knew where He came from (John 6:38; 8:42; 7:29; 13:3).
   - knew what was in heaven (John 1:18; 14:2).
   - knew why He came to earth (John 6:38; 12:49, 50; 18:4; Luke 19:10; Heb. 10:8, 9).
   - knew thoughts of others (Luke 5:22; 6:8; Matt. 9:4; 12:25; John 16:19).
   - knew how He would die (John 3:14; 12:32, 33; 18:4).
   - knew when He would die (John 12:23; 13:1; 17:1).
   - knew who would betray Him (John 6:64).
   - knew when all He came to do was finished (John 19:28; Luke 24:44).
4. Clarifying what Jesus took on to become man is important.
   - This involves the question of what did God have to take on to become man? Jesus did not have to deny being spirit; He had to take on the flesh.
   - Jesus Christ on earth = God (Word) + body.

**Conclusion**

The world needs to know the case for Jesus as the Christ, the Son of the living God. Without such, no one can ever have a hope of life eternal. We ourselves need to be convinced that Jesus is the "I AM," and we need to be bold and faithfully persuasive in presenting the true Christ of the Scriptures to the world. Speaking of things and majoring in areas that reside primarily in the realm of speculation will not aid in fulfilling the commission that Christ gave to preach the gospel to a lost and dying world. Neither will it promote peace within the brotherhood. The *church* will be fragmented, the *cause* will be lost, and the *lost* themselves will not be convinced to reach that grand conclusion preserved for us in the sacred text which flowed out of the Eunuch's mouth, "I believe that Jesus Christ is the Son of God" (Acts 8:37).

# We Cannot Deny It

**Danny McKibben**

"Expect a Miracle tonight." "We are Having a Miracle Crusade this week." "A Daily Guide to Miracles." "Jesus Came to Bring Life and Health to People." "Be Baptized in the Holy Ghost and Begin Speaking in Tongues." On and on it goes in many human denominational pulpits across the land. On the radio waves, on television, through the Internet, in books and by word of mouth these messages are taught and propagated. The charismatic movement has grown to a slew of followers in many of the denominations in the modern era since 1906, with advent of the contemporary Pentecostal doctrine. Even some among us in the body of Christ have gone astray in the movement. But what does the New Testament say about miracles, are they for today? Do people receive the miraculous gifts of the Spirit today? Let's look into the word of God and let God speak through His word and let's let Him be the final authority on the subject.

**Why?**

I think when we can grasp *why* miracles were performed in the Bible

---

**Danny McKibben** was born and raised in Louisville Kentucky. He did not attend church growing up, but was converted to the Lord in the September, 1977. He began preaching every Sunday in Feburary, 1979 at Oak Grove in Louisville, Kentucky. Then he began preaching at Bearwallow in Horse Cave, Kentucky in May of 1979. He married his wife Kathy Reynolds on July 7, 1979. They moved to Campbellsville, Kentucky in 1981. They had four sons: Josh, Luke, Aaron, and Ben. In 1988 the McKibbens moved to work with the Providence church near Mount Vernon, Kentucky where Danny continues to work and worship with the saints. Danny serves as one of the overseers at the Providence congregation. Danny has been traveling to overseas countries in evangelistic efforts since 1998. Areas of work include: the Philippines; Ecuador, Colombia; and Chile, South America.

times, we will go along way in understanding the temporal nature of the miraculous gifts of the first century. In John 3:1-2 we read, "There was a man of the Pharisees, named Nicodemus, a ruler of the Jews: The same came to Jesus by night, and said unto him, Rabbi, we know that thou art a teacher come from God: for no man can do these miracles that thou doest, except God be with him." Nicodemus saw the proof that the miracles gave Jesus as a spokesman for God.

If I come and say I have a message from the President of the United States, what proof or evidence do I have to show the truthfulness of that claim? If I had a letter written on White House stationary that was sealed with a official stamp, that would be good evidence. If a man claimed to have a message from God, what evidence does one have to back up that claim. Miracles would back up that claim, that is what these following texts talks about, signs.

John 20:30-31, "And many other signs truly did Jesus in the presence of his disciples, which are not written in this book: But these are written, that ye might believe that Jesus is the Christ, the Son of God; and that believing ye might have life through his name." In Acts 2:22, Luke wrote, "Ye men of Israel, hear these words; Jesus of Nazareth, a man approved of God among you by miracles and wonders and signs, which God did by him in the midst of you, as ye yourselves also know." In Acts 2:42, "And fear came upon every soul: and many wonders and signs were done by the apostles." In Acts 5:12, "And by the hands of the apostles were many signs and wonders wrought among the people; (and they were all with one accord in Solomon's porch. . . )." Acts 8:13, "Then Simon himself believed also: and when he was baptized, he continued with Philip, and wondered, beholding the miracles and signs which were done." In Acts 14:3, "Long time therefore abode they speaking boldly in the Lord, which gave testimony unto the word of his grace, and granted signs and wonders to be done by their hands." Paul said in 2 Corinthians 12:12, "Truly the signs of an apostle were wrought among you in all patience, in signs, and wonders, and mighty deeds."

What do we see in all these verses? That the miracles were signs, an indication, a mark, a token of miracles and wonders by which God authenticates the men sent by him, or by which men prove that the cause they are pleading is God's. These miracles and spiritual gifts were not to merely accommodate the needs and desires of men (though some did accommodate men). They were given to provide divine credentials, a badge of authority to the men who spake.

The word God gave them was confirmed to be of God. That is what we see in Mark 16:20, "And they went forth, and preached every where, the Lord working with them, and confirming the word with signs following. Amen." The word "confirm" means to make firm, establish, confirm, make sure. The gospel was a new message from God in the first century, how would people know to trust that it was a message for God? He confirmed it with the miracles, signs and wonders. They were called *miracles*, because that shows the divine origin. They are called *signs*, to show the purpose of the miraculous gifts. And they were called *wonders*, because that would be the effect it would have on people who saw them take place. Now since the word of God has been confirmed, we can begin to see the temporal nature of them.

Once the word of the gospel was confirmed, it would not have to be confirmed over and over. For example, when I bought my car many years ago, I got a bill of sale, that was notarized and then the car was registered to me. Once that was recorded and confirmed to be mine, I do *not* have to confirm it to be my automobile every year. I have the title that proves it is mine. Once God established the gospel to be His message for humanity in the first century, it did not have to be confirmed over and over every year. The evidence is sure and steadfast to cause any honest soul to believe. John 20:30-31, "And many other signs truly did Jesus in the presence of his disciples, which are not written in this book: But these are written, that ye might believe that Jesus is the Christ, the Son of God; and that believing ye might have life through his name." Those men were inspired to record the message and it was confirmed by these wonderful miracles. I have no doubt in the message today.

### How The Gifts Were Received?

Let me begin by first affirming that there are only two historical cases of Holy Spirit baptism found in the New Testament: the apostles in Acts 2 and Cornelius and his group in Acts 10. In Acts 2, observe what Jesus promised the apostles in Acts 1:4-5, "And, being assembled together with them, commanded them that they should not depart from Jerusalem, but wait for the promise of the Father, which, saith he, ye have heard of me. For John truly baptized with water; but ye shall be baptized with the Holy Ghost not many days hence." In Acts 2:1-4 we read of the fulfillment of this promise ten days after Jesus spake it (Acts 1), that the apostles were baptized with the Holy Ghost. "And when the day of Pentecost was fully come, they were all with one accord in one place. And suddenly there came a sound from heaven as of a rushing mighty wind, and it filled all the house where they were sitting. And there appeared unto them cloven tongues like as of fire, and it sat upon each of them. And they were all filled with the Holy Ghost, and began to speak with other tongues, as the Spirit gave them utterance." Notice in these verses the pronoun "they." Who are the "they"? The antecedent of "they" is "the apostles" in Acts 1:26. Those who spake were Galileans (Acts 2:7), the apostles were all Galileans (Acts 1:11). "Which also said, Ye men of Galilee, why stand ye gazing up into heaven? This same Jesus, which is taken up from you into heaven, shall so come in like manner as ye have seen him go into heaven." Notice in Acts 2:14, "But Peter, standing up with the eleven, lifted up his voice, and said unto them, Ye men of Judaea, and all ye that dwell at Jerusalem, be this known unto you, and hearken to my words." The passage did not say Peter standing up with the *one hundred and nineteen*, "but Peter, standing up with the *eleven*." Thus we must conclude that only the apostles were baptized with the Holy Ghost on the day of Pentecost.

One more observation, in Acts 2:2 it said of the apostles, "and it filled all the house where they were sitting." You don't read of them seeking, on their knees praying, anointing with oil, going to the altar, agonizing before God, laying on of hands in order to get baptized in the Holy Spirit; but they were sitting when they were baptized with the Holy Spirit. Christ is the one who baptized them in the Holy Spirit.

Now we want to study about Cornelius and his group being baptized in the Holy Spirit in Acts 10 and 11. Cornelius and his group were the first Gentiles converts to Jesus Christ. God sent Peter to preach to Cornelius and his group, the gospel of Jesus Christ. In vv. 34-43 we read Peter's speech to this group. Then something very interesting happened as Peter was speaking. Notice Acts 10:44-45, "While Peter yet spake these words, the Holy Ghost fell on all them which heard the word. And they of the circumcision which believed were astonished, as many as came with Peter, because that on the Gentiles also was poured out the gift of the Holy Ghost." As with the apostles, there was no seeking, kneeling in prayer, anointing with oil, going to the altar, or laying on of hands in order to get baptized in the Holy Spirit. God simply poured out the gift of the Holy Spirit.

In Acts 11 Peter was "called out on the carpet" about what took place with the Gentiles. Peter rehearsed this matter step by step of what took place. Notice in, Acts 11:14-17, ". . . who shall tell thee words, whereby thou and all thy house shall be saved. And as I began to speak, the Holy

Ghost fell on them, as on us at the beginning. Then remembered I the word of the Lord, how that he said, John indeed baptized with water; but ye shall be baptized with the Holy Ghost. Forasmuch then as God gave them the like gift as he did unto us, who believed on the Lord Jesus Christ; what was I, that I could withstand God?" Observe that Peter calls this a baptism of the Holy Spirit, and notice also, that he has to refer all the way back to Acts 2, to what happened to the apostles on the day of Pentecost, to find anything like it.

Notice that statement again in verse 15, "And as I began to speak, the Holy Ghost fell on them, *as on us at the beginning*." He did not say, "As I began to speak, the Holy Ghost fell on them, *as on all the churches*." Nor did he say, "As I begin to speak, the Holy Ghost fell on them as on us *since* the beginning," as if this was an everyday occurrence. Beloved, we do not read of these people agonizing, on their knees praying, singing and shouting, seeking, anointing, going to the altar, or laying on of hands, in order to get baptized in the Holy Spirit.

Why were Cornelius and his group baptized in the Holy Spirit? In order to prove to the Jews that the Gentiles can be Christians. "When they heard these things, they held their peace, and glorified God, saying, Then hath God also to the Gentiles granted repentance unto life" (Acts 11:18). Thus Holy Spirit baptism does not take place today!

Others received miraculous gifts by the laying on of the apostles' hands. In Acts 8:14-19 we read, "Now when the apostles which were at Jerusalem heard that Samaria had received the word of God, they sent unto them Peter and John: Who, when they were come down, prayed for them, that they might receive the Holy Ghost: (For as yet he was fallen upon none of them: only they were baptized in the name of the Lord Jesus.) Then laid they their hands on them, and they received the Holy Ghost. And when Simon saw that through laying on of the apostles' hands the Holy Ghost was given, he offered them money, Saying, Give me also this power, that on whomsoever I lay hands, he may receive the Holy Ghost." Even though Phillip could work miracles (v. 7), he could not impart the miraculous powers and gifts to others. It took the apostles to come and impart the gifts of the Spirit.

I would that people could see what Simon saw, "And when Simon saw that through laying on of the apostles' hands the Holy Ghost was given." What did he see? "That through laying on of the apostles' hands the Holy Ghost was given." If people could only see that today.

Other texts show that the apostles imparted the miraculous gifts. In Acts 6:6-8 we read, "Whom they set before the apostles: and when they had prayed, they laid their hands on them. And the word of God increased; and the number of the disciples multiplied in Jerusalem greatly; and a great company of the priests were obedient to the faith. And Stephen, full of faith and power, did great wonders and miracles among the people." Consider Paul imparting these gifts in Acts 19:1-7,

> And it came to pass, that, while Apollos was at Corinth, Paul having passed through the upper coasts came to Ephesus: and finding certain disciples, He said unto them, Have ye received the Holy Ghost since ye believed? And they said unto him, We have not so much as heard whether there be any Holy Ghost. And he said unto them, Unto what then were ye baptized? And they said, Unto John's baptism. Then said Paul, John verily baptized with the baptism of repentance, saying unto the people, that they should believe on him which should come after him, that is, on Christ Jesus. When they heard this, they were baptized in the name of the Lord Jesus. And when Paul had laid his hands upon them, the Holy Ghost came on them; and they spake with tongues, and prophesied. And all the men were about twelve.

Here are twelve more reasons to understand how the Spirit's gifts were given to men in the first century. Paul laid hands on them, to give it to them.

Also look at Romans 1:11, "For I long to see you, that I may impart unto you some spiritual gift, to the end ye may be established." Paul wanted to come and lay hands on the brethren at Rome to impart some spiritual gift upon them. When we see that the miraculous spiritual gifts were given by the laying on of the apostles' hands, we see the temporary nature of these gifts. How many apostles do we have today? None who is living. So we have none to impart the miraculous gifts of the Spirit. Thus the means to impart the gifts of the Spirit was limited to the first century.

### The Duration of the Gifts

In 1 Corinthians 12-14 Paul affirms the duration and regulations of the gifts in the first century. Chapter 12 shows that the gifts came from the one Godhead, and that there should be no division over them. 1 Corinthians 12:4-6, "Now there are diversities of gifts, but the same Spirit. And there are differences of administrations, but the same Lord. And there are diversities of operations, but it is the same God which worketh all in all." Notice Paul says the same Spirit, the same Lord, and the same God, emphasizing the unity in the Godhead and what should have been concerning the gifts.

They had divided over the gifts and missed the point of them. At the end of chapter 12 he said that he was going to show a more excellent way. Chapter 13 gives us the more excellent way, the way of love. The gifts would pass away in a few years from the time of Paul's writing, but the way of love would continue, even into eternity. In Chapter 14 Paul shows us, while the gifts were still in existence, how they were to be used in the assembly. He regulates the use of spiritual gifts.

Notice in chapter 13:8-13,

> Charity never faileth: but whether there be prophecies, they shall fail; whether there be tongues, they shall cease; whether there be knowledge, it shall vanish away. For we know in part, and we prophesy in part. But when that which is perfect is come, then that which is in part shall be done away. When I was a child, I spake as a child, I understood as a child, I thought as a child: but when I became a man, I put away childish things. For now we see through a glass, darkly; but then face to face: now I know in part; but then shall I know even as also I am known. And now abideth faith, hope, charity, these three; but the greatest of these is charity.

The language of verses 8 and 10 says, "they shall fail," "they shall cease," "it shall vanish away," and "shall be done away." Does that sound like these gifts would continue on and on, or does it sound like that they would come to a grinding halt? Sounds to me like the gifts were going to stop. And indeed they did, when the word was fully revealed and confirmed. Paul said, "For we know in part, and we prophesy in part." When one spoke in a tongue (*i.e.,* a language one had never studied and learned), and gave the interpretation of that divine message, that was only a part of the whole of divine truth. Or if one prophesied a lesson (*i.e.,* preached a lesson by inspiration and miraculous means), that was only a part of the whole of divine truth. But when the perfect would come (*i.e.,* the completion of the word of God given by inspiration and confirmed by miraculous signs), then that which is part shall be done away: they would fail, they would cease, they would vanish away.

Paul gives two illustrations of the temporary nature of the gifts. In verse 11 he said, "When I was a child, I spake as a child, I understood as a child, I thought as a child: but when I became a man, I put away childish things." A child plays with toys and games in his youth, but when adulthood comes the childish games are set aside. Even so in the infancy and childhood of the revelation of the gospel, the spiritual gifts were necessary for revelation and confirmation, but when the revelation was fully given and confirmed, the adulthood of God's word, the childish gifts were put away. Then in verse 12 Paul gives another illustration, "For now we see in a mirror, dimly, but then we will see face to face" (NRSV). The word of the Lord is compared to a mirror of the soul. It was a dim and incomplete reflection when only parts of that revelation were given at a time. But when the fullness and completeness of the word was given, we would see into the perfect mirror of God's word.

The word of the Lord is complete as is affirmed by these texts: 2 Timothy 3:16-17, "All scripture is given by inspiration of God, and is profitable for doctrine, for reproof, for correction, for instruction in righteousness: That the man of God may be perfect, thoroughly furnished unto all good works." In Jude 3, "Beloved, when I gave all diligence to write unto you of the common salvation, it was needful for me to write unto you, and exhort you that ye should earnestly contend for the faith which was once delivered unto the saints." And again in 2 Peter 1:3 we read, "According as his divine power hath given unto us all things that pertain unto life and godliness, through the knowledge of him that hath called us to glory and virtue." Jesus had said that the Holy Spirit would come and reveal all truth. "Howbeit when he, the Spirit of truth, is come, he will guide you into all truth: for he shall not speak of himself; but whatsoever he shall hear, that shall he speak: and he will show you things to come" (John 16:13). Did Jesus know what He was talking about? Was the Spirit able to accomplish the work He was sent to do? Did the apostles rebel against what the Spirit came to do? To ask those questions is to answer them! When we have grasped these basic concepts we will not be led down the erroneous path of men's devising. "That we henceforth be no more children, tossed to and fro, and carried about with every wind of doctrine, by the sleight of men, and cunning craftiness, whereby they lie in wait to deceive" (Eph. 4:14).

# No Creed But Christ

**Mark Dunagan**

I'm into tidiness. Several times per year my wife goes through every cabinet, drawer, and closet in our house and performs what has been lovingly dubbed "An Organization Celebration." I'll come home and grab a stack of my clothes to put away, open my armoire, and Bingo. Everything I own is stacked neatly, right where it belongs. Ahh, order. Sweet tidiness.

About every summer, my family out in Beaverton, Oregon has a garage sale. When our kids were littler, this annual event would be a major blowout, and we'd walk away with several hundred dollars. But you know what the best part always was? That moment when the leftovers are either in our garbage can or in the back of my old yellow truck. When the garage sale tables have been folded down, the garage is neatly arranged, we've swept the dust bunnies up and I have new, open space. Glorious, empty space. Sweet!

---

**Mark Dunagan** was born on Thanksgiving Day 1958 in Arlington, Virginia near the end of his father's Navy Career and grew up in Silverton, Oregon. He became a Christian on September 18, 1979. Mark is a self-taught man who began preaching on the weekends at various churches in Oregon between 1981-1985 and began his first full-time work with the church in Forest Grove, Oregon (1986-1992). He has been married to his wife, Cindy, for twenty-nine years. They have three living children whom they have homeschooled: Ashley (Dunagan) Martineau (26), Zachary (19), and Clarissa (Kiki) (18). Mark has been preaching for the church in Beaverton, Oregon for sixteen years where he serves as an elder and since the year 2000 has trained young men dedicated to preaching the gospel in his two-year program. Many of his sermons and commentaries are available on online at www.beavertonchurchofchrist.net. Those interested in the preacher training program, or other inquiries may contact Mark at mdunagan@verizon.net.

Same goes for a congregation. I love to visit a congregation where there's order. You see it when you pull up to their place of worship. Hedges are trimmed, bark dust is down, the building has fresh paint on the outside, and the inside is as fresh and well kept as the outside. Better yet, when the body of Christ is as organized spiritually as the Lord intended, with vigilant elders who lovingly guard and feed the flock among them, and deacons who eagerly carry out their areas of service. I love when everyone seems to have found his talents and is zealously using them in a happy, buzzing congregation.

Order is beautiful. It makes our roadways function. It makes our economy function. It makes our government function. It's no wonder, I suppose, that in one of the most important aspects of our lives, our religious beliefs, that years ago people began to think, "You know, if we write down a streamlined list of 'the important parts' of Scripture, or 'the essentials,' then we'd be able to tell who is a 'true believer,' and who is a heretic." Potential converts could read our list of beliefs and decide whether or not to attach themselves to our organization. It would all be so tidy. So orderly. So *not* a biblical idea. In this lesson I hope you will begin to see why.

It might seem odd to people, both in and out of the religious world, that there are Christians who oppose creeds. Is not the English word "creed" merely a term derived from the Latin *credo* for *I believe* and *credimus* for *we believe*? Does not the Bible itself stress that "belief" or faith is essential to salvation (Heb. 11:6), and that the person who is to be saved is one who believes (Mark 16:15)? We find various places in Scripture where an individual says, "I believe" (Mark 9:24; John 9:38; 11:27; Acts 8:37). Clearly, Christians are enthusiastically in favor of faith in Christ and faith in His will revealed in Scripture. What His followers, those sheep who hear and heed His voice oppose, is the tragic misplacing of one's faith in human writings and uninspired statements of faith.

The Bible time and again confirms that it is indeed the complete and final word of God. Jude says the faith was *once for all* delivered to the saints (Jude 3). Peter says that God *has given* all things that pertain to life and godliness (2 Pet. 1:3), Paul told Timothy that *Scripture* makes the man of God complete for every good work (2 Tim. 3:16-17), and Jesus promised the apostles they would be guided into *all the truth* (John 14:26; 16:13). Obviously then, since *all truth* was to be revealed through the writings of the apostles, everything written after the lifetime of the apostles is not the word of God and is therefore not inspired. This would of course include all creedal statements and confessions of faith. If God has given us all things we need for living a godly life, who would be so bold as to argue "except a simplified list of necessary beliefs, Lord." If God says that Scripture well prepares us for every good work, who would dare claim to be unequipped without his manmade creed? What could possibly make a creed necessary? What tool could possibly accomplish more or be more effective in the souls of His creation, than God's own words?

### The Origins of Creeds

In the New Testament we find people in beautiful simplicity confessing their faith in Christ prior to baptism (Acts 8:37). The practice of putting together an authoritative statement of faith arose from the desire to have candidates for baptism accept a short summary of belief. "By the fourth century A.D. these baptismal confessions had become more universal."[1] The same source also acknowledges, "When a man looks, however, to the Scriptures themselves, he finds no formal creedal statement."[2] Eventually, the *Apostles Creed* in the Western part of the Roman Empire and the *Nicene Creed* in the Eastern have become the accepted baptismal confession.

### The Purpose of Creeds

One common argument on behalf of human creedal statements is that they served an important role in stabilizing the early Christian church. Initially they were used to teach beliefs to new converts, and soon served other purposes, such as showing the boundaries between real believers and those who adhered to false teachings. Questions derived from creeds were used to prepare believers for baptism. In addition, the creeds guarded against heresy by clearly stating the church's beliefs. Thus, formal statements of belief were viewed as being necessary to guard the church against error and preserve unity among believers. McClintock and Strong write, "The first object of creeds was to distinguish the Church from the world. . . .The second object was to distinguish between persons professing the Christian faith; between those who retained the apostolic doctrine, and those who, through unauthorized speculations, had departed from it."[3] It is as sad as it is ironic, however, that while various people were working on authorized creedal statements designed to keep the church pure, the church was *already* in apostasy. As professed Christians were seeking to counter the errors of

---

[1] *The Zondervan Pictorial Encylopedia of the Bible*, "Creed", I: 1025).

[2] *Ibid.,* 1026.

[3] *Cyclopedia of Biblical, Theological, and Ecclesiastical Literature*, II: 559.

Gnosticism by preparing creedal statements regarding the true nature of Christ, they had already departed from the biblical patterns, including the terms "elder" and "bishop" being applied to the same office (Acts 20:17,28; 1 Pet. 5:1-2), and instead created positions of much higher power for the bishop as opposed to the elder. Ignoring 1 Peter 5:2, they extended the authority and jurisdiction of elders or bishops beyond the congregations which they attended, to additional congregations where they were not "among." Those who met to put together such creedal statements were blind to the fact that: (a) The Scriptures alone can completely keep us on the right path (2 Tim. 3:16). (b) There was no Bible authority for them to meet in order to come up with such a statement of faith. (c) Such a statement would have no real and eternal authority, for only Scripture possesses divine authority.

In examining various creeds, especially the early ecumenical creeds, it is clear they have by no means provided a defense against error. For example, the *Apostles Creed* says,

> I believe in God the Father Almighty, Maker of heaven and earth, and in Jesus Christ his only Son our Lord, who was conceived by the Holy Ghost; born of the Virgin Mary; suffered under Pontius Pilate, was crucified, died, and buried; he descended into hell (omitted in other versions); the third day he rose from the dead; he ascended into heaven, and sitteth on the right hand of God and Father Almighty; from thence he shall come to judge the quick and the dead. I believe in the Holy Ghost; the holy Catholic Church, the communion of the saints; the forgiveness of sins; the resurrection of the body; and the life everlasting. Amen.

In addition to the creed mentioning a "holy Catholic Church" a term unknown to Scripture, one could believe everything else in this creed and still be lost, for among other countless teachings, this creed fails to mention, among other things, repentance or baptism being the final step between an individual and his or her salvation (Acts 2:38).

The following are just a few shortcomings and dangers of adhering to such creeds:

- Creeds are not inspired, and are therefore not authored by the Holy Spirit, nor "the power of God unto salvation" (Rom. 1:16). Creeds are the result of fallible men gathering like congressmen to wheel and deal, bending a little here and there, in the attempt to seek to put together a statement *that the majority can vote upon to accept.* How unholy. How carnal. The Bible was by no means put together in such a manner. The Bible is anything but the result of compromise, conferences, politics, or voting. The Bible is the Word of God; it is God telling us, without any input from fallible man, what truth is. Scripture was not intended to find favor with the majority of religious people, and it was not designed to be a document that most religious people would accept. It is simply the truth (John 17:17).

- Creeds make the erroneous assumption that man can sum up into one statement all the "essentials" in Christianity. The essentials of the Christian faith cannot be summed up into any creed or statement of faith, for the essentials include everything found in the word of God. God's word is truth (John 17:17), and one part of God's word is not any more true than any other part. Baptism, which is not mentioned in the above creed, is essential (Eph. 4:4-6), as are prayer, honesty, diligence, self-control, and other qualities.

- Creeds do not weed out false teachers, nor do they protect the church from error. In spite of all the creeds and statements of faith produced by men, apostasy still hit and many fell away (2 Tim. 4:2-4; 1 Tim. 4:1-3). Today, many religious groups have creedal statements and statements of faith which their current membership and leaders do not even accept. Even those who defend creedal statements admit this much,

> A creed is not the solution to doctrinal questions nor does it end theological controversies. A creed does not guarantee orthodoxy in any group; it merely publishes what the organization considers to be of sound doctrine. In fact, some church bodies which today would deny the virgin birth of Christ, the inspiration of the Scriptures, and who classify the Bible story of creation as a myth, have official doctrinal statements which would be acceptable in the most evangelical circles.[4]

- Creeds did not make various controversial issues any clearer than Scripture. The *Nicene Creed* which dealt with the nature of Christ, reads, "One Lord, Jesus Christ . . . very God of very God, begotten not made, consubstantial (*homoousios*) with the Father, by whom all things were made." Does anyone truly find "consubstantial (*ho-*

---

[4] Arnold T. Olson, head of the Evangelical Free Church of America. *This We Believe: The Background and Exposition of the Doctrinal Statement of the Evangelical Free Church of America* (Minneapolis: Free Church Publications, 1961), 42.

*moousios*)" more clear than the simple truths stated so clearly in John 1:1 or Hebrews 1:3?

- If the "list" of all the doctrines a Christian must believe is nothing more or less than the New Testament, the doctrine of Christ (2 John 9), or what the apostles taught (Acts 2:42), then why disobey the prime directive of not adding to or taking away from God's words (Deut. 4:2; Prov. 30; Rev. 22:18-19)? The truth is, these creeds always contain *much less* than the New Testament teachings, and often times, *much more.*
- Creeds give precious souls a false and therefore dangerous sense of security.

### Do Creeds Promote Unity Or Division?

Creeds and the motivation behind them is a good working example of the limitations of human wisdom (Jer. 10:23). Initially men intended that creedal statements would promote unity and protect the church from error, yet in the end they did the exact opposite. "It seems evident, then, that creeds have become both uniting and divisive, bringing together those portions of the Christian community which agree and excluding those who disagree. It is also evident, therefore, that the briefer the creedal statement, the more universal it can become, and the more specific the creedal statement, the more exclusive or divisive it may become."[5] McClintock and Strong add that creeds oblige Christians "differing considerably in non-essentials to form themselves into distinct religious societies."[6] In other words, creeds are used to justify the formation of human denominations. Again, we find that instead of promoting unity and keeping all Christians united, creeds and confessions of faith have actually accomplished the reverse. Some might think it is a good idea for professed Christians to form separate groups if they are disagreeing over non-essentials and that somehow this will promote unity. Yet 1 Corinthians 1:12-14 and Romans 14 indicate the apostles would be horrified by such an idea.

### Do Creeds Promote Truth or Error?

Creeds were initially designed to protect the church from heresy, yet in the end they have promoted it. For example, the *Westminster Confession*, a creedal standard for all Presbyterian churches teaches: Totally depravity,

[5] *Zondervan Pictorial Encyclopedia*, I: 1026

[6] II: 559.

inherited sin (despite Ezek. 18:20), the loss of free will (despite John 3:16), the salvation of only those God predestined for salvation (despite 2 Pet. 3:9), the impossibility of falling from grace (despite Gal. 5:4), The Sunday Sabbath, immersion not being the necessary mode of baptism, and infant baptism (despite Mark 16:16; Acts 8:37-38)—all beliefs that are utterly contrary to the word of God.

Consider as well what the *Standard Manual for Baptist Churches,* published in June 1903, said about the subject of baptism:

> It is most likely that in the Apostolic age when *there was* but "one Lord, one faith, and one baptism", and no different denominations existed, the baptism of a convert by that very act constituted him a member of the church, and at once endowed him with all the rights and privileges of full membership. In that sense, "baptism **was** the door into the church."

Of course, this is true (Acts 2:41,47). Yet notice what the manual says next:

> *Now, it is different*; and while the churches are desirous of receiving members, they are wary and cautious that they do not receive unworthy persons. The churches therefore have candidates come before them, make their statement, give their 'experience,' and then their reception is decided by a vote of the members. And while they cannot become members without baptism, yet ***it is the vote of the body which admits them to its fellowship*** on receiving baptism.[7]

These erroneous statements prove once and for all that such creeds truly do promote error and endanger the very souls that would come to God.

### Restoration Attitudes Toward Creeds

**"Speak Where the Bible Speaks" (1 Pet. 4:11).** It was in the house of Abraham Altars, between Mt. Pleasant and Washington, Pennsylvania that one of the most famous meetings of the restoration was held. Thomas Campbell's speech closed with the famous motto: "Where the Bible speaks; we speak; where the Bible is silent, we are silent."

> The idea which Campbell embodied in this motto was not new. Many years before, in 1659, Edward Stillingfleet, who later became Bishop of Worchester, had said: "For the church to require more than Christ Himself did, or make the condition of her communion more than our Saviour did for discipleship, is wholly unwarranted." His conclusion, "The Bible, I say, the Bible only, is the religion of Protestants" purported to be the claim

[7] *The Standard Manual for Baptist Churches*, Edward T. Hiscox, 22.

> of all Protestant bodies. Yet notwithstanding the idea Campbell presented in his motto was not new, it nevertheless was revolutionary in one phase: a few people now applied it to Protestant creeds and confessions of faith whereas, the Protestant bodies had almost exclusively applied it to Roman Catholic traditions. For the first time there were some who realized that the motto struck with equal force against human creeds as it did against Catholic traditions (West, I: 47).

There was a solemn hush in the assembly after Campbell had made this statement. Andrew Munro, was the first to respond, he said, "Mr. Campbell, if we adopt that as a basis, then there is an end of infant baptism." Thomas replied, "Of course, if infant baptism be not found in the Scriptures, we can have nothing to do with it." Thomas Acheson then arose and said, "I hope I may never see the day when my heart will renounce that blessed saying of the Scripture, 'Suffer little children to come unto me and forbid them not, for of such is the kingdom of heaven.'" Then he burst into tears. James Foster then cried out, "Mr. Acheson, I would remark that in the portion of Scripture you have quoted, there is no reference whatever to infant baptism" (see Robertson Richardson, *Memoirs of Alexander Campbell* (Cincinnati: Standard Publishing Co., 1897), I: 238).

A man by the name of James O'Kelley often listened to sermons written by John Wesley, and was struck by the fact that the sermons viewed the Bible as being all sufficient. O'Kelley wrote, "They (certain ministers) come to us under the direction of John Wesley. . . .His writings magnified the Bible, and gave it preference and honor; he declared he regarded the authority of no writings but the inspired. He urged the sufficiency of the Scriptures for faith and practice, saying, 'We will be downright Bible Christians'" *(J. Pressley Barrett, The Centennial of Religious Journalism* [Dayton, Ohio: Christian Publishing Association, 1908], 19). O'Kelley later became dissatisfied with the Methodist Church and on August 4, 1794, during a meeting at Old Lebanon in Surry County, Virginia, O'Kelley and others, after laying aside all other books and turning only to the Bible willing embraced no creed but Christ, understanding:

- The Bible should be the only creed and the only sufficient rule for faith and practice
- The Lord Jesus is the sole head of the church
- The Lord is honored in the wearing of the name Christian to the exclusion of all other party and denominational names
- Christian character should be the only test for church membership

- God has given the right of private judgment and a liberty of conscience to all

### Living in a Society of Unwritten Creeds

Today, members of denominations often neither know, nor care what their church's creeds may teach. The leaders of denominational churches have varying reactions to such apathy. Olson argues,

> Through the centuries the very idea of a creed has been under attack. This is an age of emphasis on freedom and freedom from conscience. It is a time when strong convictions are considered reactionary. Theology is taught on a cafeteria basis. "Here it is, take what you like, leave the rest." It is a period when men refuse to commit themselves. The example set by the teachers of our universities in refusing to commit themselves through the loyalty oaths is reflected more and more by the graduates in refusing to commit themselves positively to a statement of faith.[8]

First, in one sense he is right. Ours is an age in which people want the freedom to, with a clear conscience, pick and choose what to believe in the Bible, yet human creeds are still not the answer to this problem. In fact, human creeds themselves are the original "picking and choosing" or "cafeteria approach" to Christianity, for all creeds are an attempt to pick the "essentials" from the Scriptures. Yet considering that the ". . . the sum of (God's) word is truth" (Psa. 119:160), the writings of the apostles constitute "all truth" (John 16:13), and every command is essential (Jas. 2:10), nothing of God's word should be tossed aside as not essential.

### Unbelieving "Born-Agains"

Various polls and surveys conducted in this country reveal a definite theological collapse among professing Christians. In 2003 researcher George Barna discovered that among those who claim to be "born again," 26 percent believe all religions are essentially the same, 35 percent do not believe Jesus rose physically from the dead, 52 percent do not believe the Holy Spirit is a living entity, 45 percent do not believe Satan exists, 29 percent believe it is possible to communicate with the dead, 33 percent accept same-sex unions, and 39 percent believe it is morally acceptable for couples to have a sexual relationship before marriage. Gene Edward Veith observes that these polls are "strong evidence of how American Christianity is conforming to the dominant secular culture. It is all right to be religious, according to the dictates of postmodernism, as long as your faith exists just in your head.

---

[8] Olson, 17.

If you start claiming that your beliefs are more than just a private mental state that makes you feel good, asserting instead that what you believe is objectively real and valid for everybody, then you are an intolerant menace to society."[9] Such prevalent religious error can only be remedied by an authentic great awakening and willing embrace of all that has been told us in the imperishable, living, and enduring Word of God. Only the truth will set us free from these lies and the incalculable consequences they breed.

## Unbelieving Religious Leaders

As one would expect, religious error is not isolated to just the laity of the denominational world. The Barna Research Group also polled the leaders of various denominations. To do so, George Barna compiled a list of biblical teachings he assumed leaders of every denomination would accept. This list included such basic concepts as: the existence of absolute moral truth based on the Bible, the accuracy of biblical teaching, Jesus being without sin, Satan literally existing, God's omnipotent and omniscient nature, and the Christian's personal responsibility to evangelize. Southern Baptists (71 percent) had the most leaders who agreed with the list, while Methodists (27 percent) had the least. Mr. Barna who discusses his results in his book *Think Like Jesus*, says that if these numbers are bad among church leaders, they are even worse for church members. He found that just 7 percent of American Protestants agreed with these very basic biblical teachings.

These results are discouraging, yet people among the denominations are not the only ones who are confused in this country. "Atheists are just as confused about their theology. 'Half of all atheists and agnostics say that every person has a soul, that heaven and hell exist, and that there is life after death,' reports Mr. Barna."[10] Go figure.

## Part-Time Calvinists and Full-time New Agers

The religious landscape in our country is ever changing, and the people we encounter are often changing accordingly in these belief patterns. We will find ourselves encountering people more varied in their beliefs than ever before. They, for example, may only subscribe to part of Calvinism (as illogical as that may be). As Olson earlier noted, we are living in a world where denominations are filled with members (and leaders) who are completely ignoring the doctrinal foundations of that particular denomina-

---

[9] "Unbelieving 'born-agains,'" Gene Edward Veith, *World Magazine* (12-6-2003), 33.

[10] *Ibid.*, 33

tion. So we can no longer assume that a Presbyterian believes Presbyterian doctrine. Relativism and Humanism rule the day, thanks to such influential people as Oprah Winfrey. "Winfrey was called 'arguably the world's most powerful woman' by CNN and Time.com, 'arguably the most influential woman in the world' by the *American Spectator*, 'one of the 100 people who most influenced the 20th Century' and 'one of the most influential people' of 2004, 2005, 2006, 2007, and 2008 by *Time*. Winfrey is the only person in the world to have made all six lists." *Wikipedia* further states

> Credited with creating a more intimate confessional form of media communication, she is thought to have popularized and revolutionized the tabloid talk show genre pioneered by Phil Donahue, which a Yale study claimed broke 20th century taboos and allowed gays, transsexuals, and transgender people to enter the mainstream. By the mid 1990s she had reinvented her show with a focus on literature, self-improvement, and spirituality. Though criticized for . . . promoting controversial self-help fads, she is generally admired for overcoming adversity to become a benefactor to others. In 2006 she became an early supporter of Barack Obama and is credited with delivering over a million votes in the close 2008 Democratic primary race.[11]
>
> "*Christianity Today* writer LaTonya Taylor said: 'To her audience of more than 22 million mostly female viewers, she has become a postmodern priestess—an icon of church-free spirituality.' Oprah speaks less about salvation through Christ than she does Christ-consciousness. Likewise, she describes heaven not as an eternal destination but an inner realm of consciousness. And she dismisses the idea that there is "one way" to God, when she says, "There couldn't possibly be just one way." "One of the mistakes that human beings make is believing that there is only one way to live," she said. Instead, "there are many paths to what you call God."

### Unwritten Creeds and Pop Culture Creeds

Within the last few years, Oprah has used her this immense influence to direct her audience toward three books, books that probably more than any others, are influencing the minds everywhere around us. There are today many unwritten human creeds adhered to by the masses, or books such as Eckhart Tolle's *A New Earth* which may not call itself a creed, yet is forming the thinking of the next generation by repackaging and remarketing tired 1960s Relativism and Humanism. New Earth Web Event, one of the largest single online events in the history of the Internet, was participated in my

[11] http://en.wikipedia.org/wiki/Oprah_Winfery#Rankings_as_world.27s_most_influential_woman

more than a half million people. Every Monday night for 10 weeks more than a half million online members continued to join in this live interactive webcast, led by Oprah Winfrey and Eckhart Tolle, which included "audio meditations" and "awakening exercises." In chapter one of his book *The New Earth*, Mr. Tolle audaciously declares, "Man made God in his own image, the eternal, the infinite, and unnamable was reduced to a mental idol that you had to believe in and worship as my god or your god."

The twenty million viewers who tune in daily to "The Oprah Winfrey Show" have been introduced to other influential books including Marianne Williams' teachings of *A Course in Miracles. A Course In Miracles* describes itself as

> . . . a direct communication from God through Jesus Christ indicating the apparent conditional situation between God and man, which is one of false separation, and to the manner in which that apparent schism is and was repaired. The *Course* does not aim at teaching the meaning of Love, for that is beyond what can be taught. It does aim, however, at removing the blocks to the awareness of Love's Presence, which is your natural inheritance. The sole purpose of *A Course In Miracles* is to bring Enlightenment through the transformation of your mind.

The *Course In Miracles* warns its students to "…not make the pathetic error of clinging to the old, rugged cross" and asserts, "The only message of the crucifixion is that you can overcome the cross." Meditations in this course begin, "Nothing I see in this room means anything," and then move to such mantras as, "These thoughts do not mean anything. They are like the things I see in this room."[12] "My thoughts do not mean anything." "My holiness is my salvation." "My salvation comes from me." "I am entitled to miracles." "All things are echoes of the Voice of God." "I am the holy Son of God Himself." "Whatever suffers is not part of me." "My Self is ruler of the universe." "Let me remember that there is no sin." "The Holy Spirit speaks through me today." "My sinlessness protects me from all harm."

Another modern "creed book" of sorts also promoted by Oprah was written by Rhonda Byrne's and is entitled *The Secret*. The synopsis given online at http://en.wikipedia.org/wiki/The_Secret_(2006_film) states,

> *The Secret*, described as a self-help film, uses a documentary format to present the *Law of Attraction*. This law is the 'secret' that, according to the tagline, 'has traveled through centuries to reach you.' The film features

[12] www.**miraclescenter.us**/The Complete ACIM/Urtext/**Urtext Workbook**.doc

> the short dramatized experiences and interviews of a team called personal transformation specialists, spiritual messengers, feng shui masters, and other experts. As described in the film, the "Law of Attraction" principle posits that feelings and thoughts can attract events, from the workings of the cosmos to interactions among individuals in their physical, emotional, and professional affairs. The film also suggests that there has been a strong tendency by those in positions of power to keep this central principle hidden from the public.

The previews or "clues" to the film, show men who "uncovered the Secret." Those who promote this false teaching include a three part process: (1) Ask: Know what you want and ask the universe for it. This is where you need to get clear on what it is you want to create and visualize what you want as being as "real" as possible. (2) Believe: Feel and behave as if the object of your desire is on its way. Focus your thoughts and your language on what it is you want to attract. You want to feel the feeling of really "knowing" that what you desire is on its way to you, even if you have to trick yourself into believing it – do it. (3) Receive: Be open to receiving it. Pay attention to your intuitive messages, synchronicities, signs from the Universe to help you along the way as assurance you are on the "right" path. As you align yourself with the Universe and open yourself up to receiving, the very thing you are wanting to manifest will show up.

The Baptist Press was right in calling "The Secret" "another narcissistic, self-centered lie that denies the sovereign, all-powerful creator God."

> Larry Eskredge, associate director of the Institute for the Study of American Evangelicals at Wheaton College in Illinois, said, "Oprah's theology seems to be a version of America's secular theology of self-improvement, doing good to others, and the prosperity gospel. She is also able to foster a tremendous sense of community around her TV show. People who watch feel they are involved in a great quest to improve society and improve themselves."[13]

These are the unwritten creeds, and creeds that do not call themselves creeds that explain the mindsets of those in our country with the most influence: You will find its influence in all forms of media, in universities, in your children's classrooms, and beyond. Let's be prepared to give a persuasive answer (1 Pet. 3:15) to the dear souls entangled in the following old lies wrapped in pretty new paper.

---

[13] *Christian Examiner*, Web site: www.christianexaminer.com

## Preparing To Give An Answer That Debunks Today's Cultural Creeds (1 Pet. 3:15)

In Colossians 4:6 the Holy Spirit exhorts Christians to have speech seasoned with salt, "so that you may know how you should respond to each person" (Col. 4:6). How can you prepare you to reach out to the priceless souls within your influence?

1. **God's existence** is, for many, the foundation we need to establish and build upon. On the one hand, His existence is so clear that all men are without excuse for not acknowledging or obeying Him (Rom. 1:20). In fact, we see the clear evidence for His existence every day and night (Psa. 19:1-2). God is our designer; therefore, we will never live up to our true potential if we ignore Him. He is the fuel on which we were designed to run. For those who seek more detailed evidence, I recommend books such as *Investigating Christian Evidences: A Study Course* by Bert Thompson and Brad Harrub and *Mere Christianity* by C.S. Lewis

2. **The Bible as God's word.** The next logical question that a good and honest heart must confront after acknowledging God's existence is "What has God said?" (Heb. 1:1-2). Building faith in *the Bible as God's word* is the second foundation that must be established. We must make ourselves familiar with the prescientific foreknowledge, fulfilled prophecies about nations, individuals and the Messiah, historical and geographical accuracy, in order to prove this book is God's written will for mankind. I recommend books such as Josh McDowell's *Evidence That Demands a Verdict* or *When Skeptics Ask: A Handbook on Christian Evidences* by Norman L. Geisler. The Bible must be seen for what it is: the "owner's manual" for life, not written to deprive us of happiness, but to prevent us from ruining our chances for happiness (1 Pet. 3:10-11). His communication is not only understandable to all (Eph. 3:4), it is accessible to all (Mark 16:15), and all are able to obey it (1 Tim. 2:4).

3. To reach those who believe the Bible is God's infallible word, yet have embraced religious error, there is no better way to prepare yourself to reach them than by knowing what the Bible teaches by diligently reading it.

4. Once the authority of God's word has been deemed faith-worthy by the good and honest heart, it becomes quite easy to show that while

often those in the New Age Movement claim it is compatible with any religion, the slogans of the New Age Moment are simply not compatible with the truth as God has revealed. For example, in answering some of the exercises in *A Course in Miracles* the following thoughts and Scriptures may be helpful:

- *"Nothing I see in this room means anything" (1):* Does this include the *Course of Miracles Workbook*?
- *"My thoughts do not mean anything" (10):* My thoughts are very meaningful, for God will judge the thoughts of the heart (Heb. 4:12).
- *"My holiness is my salvation" (39):* My salvation is the blood of Christ (Rom. 5:9).
- *"My salvation comes from me" (70):* "God is my salvation" (Isa. 12:2).
- *"I am entitled to miracles" (77):* Salvation is by God's unmerited favor—that means I am entitled to nothing, much less miracles (Eph. 2:8-9). All the miracles I need are already found in the Scriptures (John 20:30-31) and have established as true all that Jesus taught.
- *"All things are echoes of the Voice of God" (151):* "All *Scripture* is inspired of God" (2 Tim. 3:16).
- *"I am the holy Son of God Himself" (191):* John 20:31 says that "Jesus is the Son of God."
- *"Whatever suffers is not part of me" (248):* Romans 8:17 asserts, "We suffer with Him."
- *"My Self is ruler of the universe" (253):* "We do not know what to do, but our eyes are upon thee" (2 Chron. 20:12). One can hardly rule oneself (1 Cor. 9:27), much less the universe.
- *"Let me remember that there is no sin" (259):* All have sinned (Rom. 3:23); Jesus did not die to remove something that never existed.
- *"My sinlessness protects me from all harm" (337):* To claim to be sinless is a lie (1 John 1:8-10).
- *"Do not make the pathetic error of clinging to the old, rugged cross"* (text, p. 47; T-4.in.3: 1-3, 7- 10): Jesus Himself instructed us to treasure His death by remembering it (1 Cor. 11:23-26); every day

we are not only to cling to the cross, but bear our own cross (Luke 9:23). ". . . everything that you enjoy in Christ—as a Christian, as a person who trusts Christ—is owing to the death of Christ. And all your rejoicing in all things should therefore be a rejoicing in the cross where all your blessings were purchased for you at the cost of the death of the Son of God, Jesus Christ."[14]

- *"The only message of the crucifixion is that you can overcome the cross"* (text, p.47; T-4.in.3: 1-3, 7- 10): The message of the crucifixion is that God loved the world (John 3:16), all men have sinned (Rom. 3:23), and sin is so horrific and real that it could only be removed by a beautiful and glorious God giving His life.
- *"Ask the universe for it" (The Law of Attraction/The Secret):* "Every good thing given and every perfect gift is from above, coming down from the Father" (Jas. 1:17).

In addition to the dangerous slogans in *The Course on Miracles*, Christians will also encounter the following popular cultural creeds:

- *"There is no absolute truth. What is true for you may not be true for me."* There is absolute truth, in fact, any attempt to deny the existence of absolute truth only results in an absolute statement or denial, as in the dogmatic response, "There is no absolute truth." Whatever people may think about Jesus, He did teach absolute truths (Matt. 7:13-14, 21-23; John 8:24; 12:48; 14:6; 17:17). Truth never contradicts truth. Seeing that there is a Creator, who made all things and all men (Acts 17:24-26), all truths are His truths. He is the author of mathematics and biology as well as theology. Therefore, the truths in the realm of science and the truths revealed in the Scriptures will never be in conflict, because God is both the author of the universe as well as the author of Scripture (2 Tim. 3:16).
- *"We do not need authority for everything we do":* "Nadab and Abihu, however, fell dead before the Lord when they made an offering with unauthorized fire before Him in the Desert of Sinai (Num. 3:4, NIV).
- *"There couldn't possibly be just one way":* "Jesus said to him, 'I am the way, and the truth, and the life; no one comes to the Father but

[14] John Piper, *Don't Waste Your Life*, 51.

through Me'" (John 14:6). "And there is salvation in no one else; for there is no other name under heaven that has been given among men by which we must be saved" (Acts 4:12).

- *"There are many paths to what you call God":* "Enter through the narrow gate; for the gate is wide and the way is broad that leads to destruction, and there are many who enter through it. For the gate is small and the way is narrow that leads to life, and there are few who find it" (Matt 7:13-14).
- *"Follow Your Heart":* Our feelings are great liars (Prov. 16:25). Maturity means thinking first with your head and not your heart (Prov. 28:26). God is God and we are not, and the sooner we admit that, the sooner we will grow up. All human philosophies and religions are only "kids toys." If you desire to think maturely and independently (1 Cor. 14:20), you must admit the obvious and bow the knee to Christ. The decision to follow Christ is a decision to grow up (Phil. 3:15-17).
- *"Heaven is not an eternal destination but an inner realm of consciousness":* "Blessed be the God and Father of our Lord Jesus Christ, who according to His great mercy has caused us to be born again to a living hope through the resurrection of Jesus Christ from the dead to obtain an inheritance which is imperishable and undefiled and will not fade away, reserved in heaven for you" (1 Pet 1:3-4).
- *"Something is only sinful if is hurts someone":* ". . . your iniquities have made a separation between you and your God, and your sins have hidden His face from you so that He does not hear" (Isa. 59:2). Even when no one else is involved, sin hurts not only the sinner, but God Himself.
- *"Any sexual relationship is right as long as it is mutually fulfilling. Love trumps Law":* "Or do you not know that the unrighteous will not inherit the kingdom of God? Do not be deceived; neither fornicators, nor idolaters, nor adulterers, nor effeminate, nor homosexuals . . . will inherit the kingdom of God." (1 Cor. 6:9-10). The "How can two homosexuals marrying hurt you?" argument is often used as justification and even legalization of homosexual marriages. I found it interesting that C.S. Lewis had actually dwelt with this type of argument back in the 1940s in England. In his book *Mere Christianity,* he writes,

Morality, then, seems to be concerned with three things. Firstly, with fair play and harmony between individuals. Secondly, with what might be called tidying up or harmonizing the things inside each individual. Thirdly, with the general purpose of human life as a whole: what man was made for. . . . You may have noticed that modern people are nearly always thinking about the first thing and forgetting the other two. . . . When a man says about something he wants to do, 'It can't be wrong because it doesn't do anyone else any harm,' he is thinking only of the first thing. He is thinking it does not matter what his ship is like inside provided that he does not run into the next ship. . . . Almost all people at all times have agreed (in theory) that human beings ought to be honest and kind and helpful to one another. But though it is natural to begin with all that, if our thinking about morality stops there, we might just as well not have thought at all. Unless we go on to the second thing—the tidying up inside each human being—we are only deceiving ourselves" (72-73).

- *"God would not want me to be unhappy":* ". . . we also exult in our tribulations, knowing that tribulation brings about perseverance; and perseverance, proven character; and proven character, hope; and hope does not disappoint" (Rom. 5:3-5).
- *"Grace will just cover me":* "What shall we say then? Are we to continue in sin so that grace may increase? May it never be!" (Rom. 6:1-2). "You have been severed from Christ, you who are seeking to be justified by law; you have fallen from grace" (Gal. 5:4).
- *"I could never believe in a God that would send people to hell":* "The Lord is not slow about His promise, as some count slowness, but is patient toward you, not wishing for any to perish but for all to come to repentance" (2 Pet. 3:9). ". . . you repudiate it and judge yourselves unworthy of eternal life" (Acts 13:46).

### Taking Every thought Captive

"We are destroying speculations and every lofty thing raised up against the knowledge of God, and we are taking every thought captive to the obedience of Christ" (2 Cor. 10:5).

Regardless of the numbers that stand against us, let's spend our lives in fruitful labor (Phil. 1:21, 23). Let us be active in the work of saving ourselves and others (1 Tim. 4:16). Let's fulfill our commission of being the pillar for the truth (1 Tim. 3:15), and light and salt to the world (Matt. 5:13-16). In the spirit of those who have waged spiritual warfare before us, let's work toward the emancipation from old creeds and new creeds.

- "No creed by Christ, no law but the Lord's, no book but the Bible, no name but the Master's."
- "Where the Bible speaks, we speak. Where the Bible is silent, we're silent."
- Let's "call Bible things by Bible names; do Bible things in Bible ways."
- "In matters of faith, unity; in matters of opinion, liberty; in all matters, charity."

# Part Four
# Ladies Classes

# The God of All Comfort

**Sue Cooper**

Human beings have an inborn need for both physical and emotional comfort. From the moment a baby is born, he makes it clear that he needs to be comforted. Screaming from the arduous task of being born, he wants to be touched, held, wrapped and soothed. As that child grows, he continues to cry for comfort when he is hungry, when he is in pain, or when he is lonely. As he gets older, he expresses the need for comfort when he scrapes his knee, cuts his finger or gets his feelings hurt. The child's loving parents (or other caregivers) try to give their child the comfort he needs when he needs it. We have all heard about babies who grow up in certain orphanages where their needs for comfort are not met. These children often develop severe psychological and physical disorders. Psychologists have found that young children in orphanages who were fed, bathed, and diapered regularly nevertheless developed severe problems when they had no comfort or affection from a regular caregiver. Not only was their psychological health compromised, but their physical health suffered as well. Often such children are diagnosed with "failure to thrive" and sometimes even die as a result of lack of attention, affection, and comfort from their caregiver(s).

One of my favorite passages in Scripture is found in 2 Corinthians 1:3-4. It says:

---

**Sue Cooper** was born in Danville, KY to Kelly and Claudia Ellis. Her father was a well-known preacher and teacher and served as an elder for many years. She married Dickie Cooper in 1964 and they have two daughters, a son, and a daughter-in-law. Their only grandchild, Adam, was born in July 2007. Sue graduated from Centre College in 1966 with a teaching certificate, but instead of teaching she and Dickie worked in their own insurance agency for over forty years. They retired from the insurance business at the end of 2007. Sue and Dickie live on their farm in Lincoln County, KY and work and worship with the Fort Logan church of Christ in Stanford.

> Blessed be the God of our Lord Jesus Christ, the Father of mercies and God of all comfort; who comforts us in all our affliction so that we may be able to comfort those who are in any affliction with the comfort with which we ourselves are comforted by God.

What a beautiful passage! Our Creator knows our need for comfort because He created us with this need and He is eager and able to fulfill that need. To know that our great and powerful God cares enough about us to be ready to comfort us in our affliction is a true blessing. But with that blessing comes a responsibility – the responsibility to comfort others as we have been comforted. As we look into this passage in depth, there are four questions I would like to consider:

1. What does the word "comfort" mean?
2. How, specifically, does God comfort His children?
3. How do we comfort others?
4. *Must* we comfort others?

### What Does the Word "Comfort" Mean?

"Comfort," as a verb, is defined in the *World Book Encyclopedia Dictionary* as (1) to ease the grief or sorrow of; to cheer; (2) to give ease to; make comfortable; (3) to help; support. As a noun, it is defined as (1) anything that makes life easier to bear; (2) anything that makes life easier or takes away hardship; (3) a cause or matter of satisfaction; something reassuring; (4) freedom from pain or hardship; (5) help; support. *Vine's Expository Dictionary of Old and New Testament Words* says the Greek word *paraklesis*, from which the word "comfort" is translated in the first chapter of 2 Corinthians means "called to one's side" for the purpose of consolation, exhortation, encouragement, or to give aid, to succor, to soothe or to support. In *Truth Commentaries, The Book of 2 Corinthians* (57-58), Melvin Curry says:

> Behind the English word "comfort," which derives, in part, from the Latin *fortis*, "strong," "brave," stands the Greek verb *parakaleo*. This term pictures God calling his children to his side to assist and to strengthen them. Therefore, Paul speaks here not of "soothing sympathy" but of "the comfort which brings courage," or "the comfort which enables a man to cope with all that life can do to it," writes Barclay (190).

The true meaning of the word "comfort" can be better understood by looking to Jesus as our perfect example. In John 14:16-17, Jesus tells His apostles that He "will ask the Father and He will give you another Helper, that He may be with you forever; that is the Spirit of truth." In this passage, the word "Helper" is often translated "Comforter," and by saying He will send *another* Helper or Comforter, Jesus is indicating that *He* was, at that time, the apostles' Comforter. Our Perfect Example literally called these men to His side and consoled, exhorted, encouraged, aided, supported, soothed, helped and assisted them in order to give them the strength and courage to do the job they would have to do as His apostles, especially after Jesus ascended back to the Father. Shortly after Jesus promises to send the Holy Spirit to be their Comforter when He is gone, He prays the beautiful prayer recorded in John 17. In that prayer, He prays for the apostles and asks God to "keep them in Thy name" (v. 11), to help them "have My joy made full in themselves" (v. 13), to "sanctify them in the truth" (v. 17), and to "keep them from the evil one" (v. 15). In the prayer Jesus also says that He "guarded them" (v. 12) in such a way that not one of them perished except for Judas "that the Scripture might be fulfilled." Jesus was a true Comforter to His apostles.

Jesus' example as a Comforter extends not only to His apostles but to others as well. Consider the parable of the Good Samaritan in Luke 10: 30-37. That parable teaches us, among other things, that we should have compassion and extend mercy and comfort to our fellow man. Consider the widow whose only son had died, as recorded in John 7:11-15. Verse 13 says the Lord "felt compassion for her and said to her 'Do not weep.'" He then brought her son back to life. Consider Luke 14:1-6, where Jesus, on the Sabbath, healed the man with dropsy. He said, in verse 6, to the Jews who were present at that healing: "Which one of you shall have a son or an ox fall into a well, and will not immediately pull him out on a Sabbath day?" This healing, although a lesson to the Pharisees, was also an act of comfort and compassion. Consider Matthew 5:32 when Jesus fed the five thousand because He felt "compassion for the multitude" because they were hungry. Consider Matthew 9:36 in which Matthew says of Jesus: "And seeing the multitude, He felt compassion for them, because they were distressed and downcast like sheep without a shepherd." Because of His compassion, He said to the apostles in verses 37 and 38, "The harvest is plentiful, but the workers are few. Therefore beseech the Lord of the harvest to send out workers into His harvest." Since He had compassion on the multitudes, He wanted to send them workers to help them. Consider the comfort He showed to Mary and Martha at the time of their brother Lazarus' death (John 11). Consider the comfort He showed to Mary, His mother, and the concern He had for her well-being even as He hung on the cross. In John 19:26-27 John says, "When Jesus therefore saw His mother, and the disciple whom He loved standing nearby, He said to His mother 'Woman behold your son!'

Then He said to the disciple, 'Behold, your mother!' And from that hour the disciple took her into his own household." Mary was comforted by Jesus, even in the worst hour of His life. Finally, consider Jesus' ultimate act of comfort, consolation, aid, and compassion. He died on the cross willingly for each of us. I believe that with these definitions and with Jesus' perfect example, we can know exactly what the word "comfort" means. It is evident that it means a great deal more than just extending sympathy with a brief "I'm sorry" or a mere pat on the back. Perhaps we need to remember what has been called the "Golden Rule" which teaches us to treat others as we want to be treated. (Luke 6:31).

**How Does God Comfort His Children?**

Before we attempt to answer the second question, "How does God comfort us?" we need to look at few passages of Scripture which talk about comfort. As we do so, we learn that God promises comfort to those who mourn (Matt. 5:4), to the afflicted (2 Cor. 1:4), to the depressed (2 Cor. 7:6), to the fearful (Heb. 13:6), and to those who are tempted (Heb. 2:18). These passages assure us that for whatever reasons we might mourn, be afflicted, depressed, fearful, or tempted, we have the assurance that God is there to comfort us through it all. When we mourn because of a terrible illness, our own or that of someone we love; when we mourn as we face death, our own or that of a loved one; when we are afflicted with temptations or with mistreatment or persecutions; when we are depressed because of family problems, abuse, sinful behavior, loneliness, or regret; when we are fearful for economic reasons or for some harm that might befall us; through these things and all others, God comforts us. But how, exactly, does He do this?

Romans 15:4 says: "For whatever was written in earlier times was written for our instruction, that through perseverance and the encouragement of the Scriptures we night have hope." In 2 Thessalonians 2:13-17 we learn that through the Scriptures we can have comfort, hope, and strengthened hearts and in 1 Thessalonians 5:18, we are told to wear the helmet which is "the hope of salvation." Titus 3:7 tells believers that they are "made heirs according to the hope of eternal life." 1 John 5:11 proclaims that "God has given us eternal life and this life is in His Son," and following in verse 13 John says, "These things I have written you who believe in the name of the Son of God, in order that you may know that you have eternal life." The hope that we learn about in Scripture, the hope of eternal life, obviously gives comfort and consolation to the believer. The believer knows that there is something better waiting after this life is over. In 1 Thessalonians 4:18, after Paul explains to the Corinthians that believers who have already died when Christ returns will be raised, he says, "Therefore comfort one another with these *words*." The comfort that believers receive through the *words* of Scripture is tremendous! Hebrews 10:22-23 tells believers that since they can have a "sincere heart in full assurance of faith," they should "hold fast the confession of our hope without wavering." Finally, 1 Peter 3:15 tells believers to "sanctify Christ as Lord in your hearts, always being ready to make a defense to everyone who asks you to give an account for the hope that is in you, yet with gentleness and reverence." Hope and comfort stream forth from God's holy word in countless ways.

As we consider this long list of passages, what do we learn that helps explain how God comforts us? As we come to a better understanding of the great God that we serve, the Christ who died for us, the hope of eternal salvation we have through Him, and the promises we have as God's heirs, we are comforted by Him as we learn about Him through His word. As the word "dwells in us richly," we come to understand that God is in control, that He keeps His promises, and that there is a reward for the faithful. Through His word, we realize who we are, where we came from, where we are going, and what our purpose is while we live in this world. As we encounter problems and trials, it is easier for the faithful to put them into their proper perspective. "This, too, shall pass"; "God knows what is best"; "We'll understand it, all 'bye and bye'" may all be overused sentiments, but they are nevertheless very true for believers. The hope that we have through our God and His loving Son helps us to persevere through all that life can send our way.

If we lived in a perfect world in which there were no trials, no temptations, no problems, no heartache or pain, there would be no reason to look forward to what God has prepared for His children when we die. We would be more attached to this world more than we already are. His promises would not mean nearly as much to us. God reveals Himself to us so that when we are in pain we can look through that pain and still see Him. He wants us to remember that, even in great pain and heartache, we still enjoy His wonderful blessings. In a book called *The Shack* by William P. Young, the author reminds us "that in the midst of all your pain and heartache, you are surrounded by beauty, the wonder of Creation, art, your music and culture, the sounds of laughter and love, of whispered hopes and celebrations, of new life and transformations, of reconciliation and forgiveness."

All of these things are blessings from the good God revealed in Scripture. Galatians 6:9 says: "And let us not lose heart in doing good, for in due time we shall reap if we do not grow weary." (Verse 8 says that what we shall reap is eternal life.) Hebrews 12: 2-3 asks us to fix "our eyes on Jesus, the author and perfector of faith, who for the joy set before Him endured the cross, despising the shame, and sat down at the right hand of the throne of God. For consider Him who has endured such hostility by sinners against Himself, so that you may not grow weary and lose heart." Jesus Himself is our example for enduring trials because of the joy that God has prepared for those who do not lose heart. Hebrews 4:16 tells believers: "Let us therefore draw near with confidence to the throne of grace, that we may receive mercy and may find grace to help in time of need." How wonderful to know that God will give help to us in our time of need! How wonderful to know that our great God of all comfort has given us the blessed assurance that He loves us, that we have the hope of eternal life and that He keeps His promises to us.

I asked a good friend of mine if she could tell me a specific time when God had comforted her. She immediately said that God had comforted her through a dream. She then told this story:

> My father died on Christmas Day. It was also my thirtieth birthday. My mom was a young 52 and Daddy was the love of her life. I was married with two small children who would now have to grow up without their grandfather. I was a mess! By the next summer, I was not any better. That summer I had "The Dream."
>
> When Daddy was alive, he loved to get all dressed up. He had a white suit, and when he put it on, he used to joke, "When I get to heaven, I'm going to wear this suit and drive around the streets of gold in a big Cadillac." In my dream, I was vacuuming and I looked out the window to see a Cadillac parked in my driveway. I did not know anyone who drove such a car and I wondered whose it was. Then, there was a knock on my door. When I went to the door, there stood Daddy in his white suit and that big shiny Cadillac behind him. When I started to open the door, he would not let me. He said I could not touch him but that he just wanted me to know that everything was alright. When the dream was over, I woke up crying but after that, I began to heal. I just know it was God's way of giving me the comfort I needed.

Do I think that God sent this dream directly to her in order to comfort her? No, I don't. But because the word of God dwells in her, because she believes God's promises, because she knows about the hope of eternal life to those who are faithful, I think during her dream she was reminded of what she already knew and was comforted through that knowledge. God comforted her and He comforts us through His word as we come to know Him and understand the promises He has made to us.

While it is evident and absolutely true that God comforts us through His word, I believe that God, in His infinite wisdom, has another way in which He comforts us. He comforts us by and through His children. It is God's plan that His children should comfort, encourage, console, uplift, succor, aid, help, and soothe one another. This is God's plan – another way He has chosen to comfort us. Romans 15:1-2 says: "Now we who are strong ought to bear the weaknesses of those without strength and not just please ourselves. Let each of us please his neighbor for his good, to his edification." Galatians 6:2 says: "Bear one another's burdens, and thus fulfill the law of Christ." Philippians 2:3-4 encourages us to be humble so that we will regard others as more important than ourselves and "do not merely look out for your own personal interests, but also for the interests of others." Romans 12:10 says that we should "be devoted to one another in brotherly love; give preference to one another in honor." Now, remember the main text, 2 Corinthians 1: 3-4. It says that God comforts us "so that we may be able to comfort those who are in any affliction." Again, looking to Jesus, the Perfect Example, He said in Matthew 20:28 that He "did not come to be served, but to serve." If Jesus came to serve others, how can we not do the same?

### How Do We Comfort Others?

The observation, that God wants us to comfort others, leads to our next question: "*How* do we comfort others?" 2 Corinthians 1:4 indicates that if we have been comforted by God, we should be able to comfort others. Have you ever mourned? Perhaps you have suffered loss through the death of a spouse, a child, another family member or close friend. Perhaps you have struggled through a serious illness or the illness of a loved one. If you have, you should be able to help someone who is dealing with a similar situation. You know what they are enduring. You can have true empathy, not just sympathy for, that person. If you were comforted when you mourned, you are better able to comfort others who mourn. Have you ever been depressed, afflicted, or fearful? Have you ever had a serious family crisis, problems with a child, difficulties in your marriage, or had a loved one to fall away from the Lord? Have you ever struggled with an addiction (of any kind), had a family member in jail, a child or grandchild with a birth defect, suffered through an abusive relationship? If you have, who better to offer comfort and aid to someone else suffering in the same way? If you were comforted at such a time, you are better able to comfort those who are depressed, afflicted, or fearful. Have you ever been lonely? We live in a world full of people and yet so many are lonely. Comforting the lonely might be as simple as a visit or a phone call to let the lonely person know that someone cares. If you have ever been lonely, you may understand better than someone who has never experienced loneliness just how important that visit or call means. Have you ever been lost, needing to find the Lord? If so, can you help others to find Him? Have you ever fallen away from the Lord and found your way back? Have you ever wavered in your unbelief? If you have, you can help the person who is struggling spiritually in a gentle and understanding way.

It is God's plan for us to help and comfort others, especially our brothers and sisters in Christ. As we have already seen, Romans 15:1-2 tells those who are strong to bear the weaknesses of those without strength. If you have been through any of these adversities (and who hasn't?), you have been made stronger by them. James 1: 2-3 tells us that various trials test our faith in order to produce endurance. Hebrews 12:11 tells us that God's discipline "yields the peaceful fruit of righteousness." As disciplined children of God who have been made stronger by our various trials, we should remember 1 Thessalonians 5:14 when Paul says to "encourage the fainthearted, help the weak." I have a friend, a woman whom I have known for nearly fifty years. She has to be stronger than anyone I know because of the trials she has endured. She has lost a three-year-old son to leukemia, she has a son who suffers from cystic fibrosis (he is thirty-seven years old and has suffered more than we can imagine for all these years), she has a daughter who has a drug addiction, she has another daughter who has fallen away from the Lord, and she is a widow having lost her husband many years ago. Yet through it all, she has remained faithful to the Lord, never wavering at all! She is a marvelous example of strength and courage, and because of her faith she is able to comfort others in ways that most of us could not.

### Must We Comfort Others?

Finally, we need to consider the last question: "*Must* we comfort others?" As human beings, it is easy to make excuses for not doing what we should do. You might say that you can't be of comfort to anyone because "I'm not good with people," or "I don't know what to say," or "This is not one of my talents, so God doesn't expect me to do this," or "He/she needs professional help and I'm not a professional," or "I don't know him/her well enough to be of comfort," or "It makes me really nervous," or "I'm afraid he/she might think I'm being nosy," or "I'm just not comfortable talking to other people about their problems." And the list goes on and on! Have you ever used any of these excuses? I am ashamed to say that I have. Have you ever heard about someone who needs comfort (perhaps an announcement you heard at church services), and intended to do something, at least send a card or make a phone call, and then just forgot? I have done that very thing way too often and then hoped that person would "understand" because after all, look how busy I am! We are so eager to make excuses for ourselves and so reluctant to do what we know we should do. Look again at the main text. What does it say? "Blessed be the God and Father of our Lord Jesus Christ, the Father of mercies and God of all comfort; who comforts us in all our affliction *so that we may be able to comfort those who are in any affliction with the comfort with which we ourselves are comforted by God."* So, *must* we comfort others? As children of a loving God, it is a question we should not even need to ask. Of course it is our responsibility to comfort others. But as children of God, we should look at it as a privilege because of the comfort we have already received from our great, loving, kind, and compassionate God.

Sometimes, I think, we are comforted when we see our own efforts and prayers on behalf of others rewarded. My husband and I have dear friends, a husband and wife, who are wonderful people but are not members of the church. They are members of a denomination. Several years ago the woman developed breast cancer and while she was receiving chemotherapy for the cancer, her husband had a severe heart attack. He was in a coma for weeks and the prognosis was so poor that she quit her chemo sessions so she would not be too sick to attend his funeral. He pulled through the crisis, but soon after, she was diagnosed with kidney cancer and had to have a kidney removed. Before she recovered, he then began to have severe hip and leg problems, stemming from a birth defect in one of his legs, and had to have surgery. After the surgery, he got a resistant staph infection and was at death's door again. Again, he recovered. Once, I remember an occasion when my husband was in a board meeting and got a call from this man. He was so ill that he was sure he was dying. He had called to ask my husband to pray for him right then and of, course, he did so. Through it all, my husband and I were there. We prayed for them privately and we prayed with them when we visited. We visited often. We helped in whatever way we could. We believe that the comfort we were able to give and the prayers we offered to God made it possible for them to get through a situation that at times seemed impossible. They give us credit for their recoveries. We give God the credit. Were we comforted as much as they were? Of course we were!

We all know that, as God's children, we are to have a genuine love and concern for others, especially our brethren – God's children. There is simply no question about this. Much of 1 John is devoted to this very subject. "If God loved us we ought to love one another" (1 John 4:11). "We love because He first loved us. If someone says 'I love God' and hates his brother, he is a liar; for the one who does not love his brother whom he has seen, cannot love God whom he has not seen. And this commandment we have from Him, that the one who loves God should love his brother also" (1 John 4: 19-21). If we love our brothers and sisters, we will be moved to encourage, help, comfort, console, aid, succor, or assist them in any way we can! If we love them, we should be eager to literally "call them to our side" to help them bear their burdens. Here, it is necessary to mention that we cannot help bear the burdens of others if we do not know what those burdens are. Too often we are embarrassed by or ashamed of our burdens. We do not want to appear to be weak, so we try to carry all of our own burdens. If I do not know that you have a burden or know what that burden is, how can I help you carry it? We have a responsibility to ask for help as well as the responsibility to help when asked!

In 2 Peter 1:5-7, Peter tells us to add (or supply) to our faith seven qualities or virtues: moral excellence, knowledge, self-control, perseverance, godliness, brotherly kindness, and love. I have heard sermons and been a student in classes in which each of these qualities has been examined and dissected so that we can know what they are and learn how to add them to our faith. The last two qualities listed are *brotherly kindness* and *love*. It seems evident to me that we need these two qualities in order to be able to comfort others with the same comfort with which we ourselves have been comforted by God.

Now, look at the next few verses in 2 Peter 1. Verses 8-11 say:

> For if these qualities are yours and are increasing, they render you neither useless nor unfruitful in the true knowledge of our Lord Jesus Christ. For he who lacks these qualities is blind or shortsighted, having forgotten his purification from his former sins. Therefore, brethren, be all the more diligent to make certain about His calling and choosing you; for as long as you practice these things, you will never stumble; for in this way the

> entrance into the eternal kingdom of our Lord and savior Jesus Christ will be abundantly supplied to you.

This passage clearly states that if we do not add brotherly kindness and love to our faith, we have forgotten our purification from our former sins. Can we therefore say that, if we fail to comfort one another (a commanded exhibition of our love for each other), it also means that we have forgotten our purification from our sins? Can we even remain a faithful child of God if we forget what Jesus has done for us? I do not think we can. We must always remember and be thankful for what Christ has done for us! Part of the proof that we have *not* forgotten what Christ has done for us is that we love our brothers and sisters. We must love them enough to call them to our side to comfort them. Our willing assistance is a reflection of the love that we have for Christ. Our reward for that love, as Peter tells us in verse 11, is "entrance into the eternal kingdom."

## Conclusion

Our comfort comes from God. It comes to us through the truths found in Scripture and from His plan for His children to comfort one another. We should always be thankful for the "God of all comforts" who always comforts us. In the last chapter of 2 Corinthians (13:11), Paul says: "Finally, brethren, rejoice, be made complete, *be comforted*, be like-minded, live in peace; and the God of love and peace shall be with you." "Be comforted." How wonderful that God's children, living in a sinful, chaotic world, can be comforted and live in peace. What a blessing that our God is the God of all comfort!

# How Feminism Affects Women in the Church

**Lorie Baker**

## Why I Chose This Topic

The word "feminism" can be difficult to define because it has different meanings to different people. For some feminism is a war cry, a call to arms for all women to end oppression. It promotes dignity and fairness for women, lifts them from being second-class citizens, and puts them on the same level as men. For others it brings a feeling of pride and patriotism, a sense of accomplishment for young and old. They see feminism as a measurement of all of the contributions of women throughout the ages. Still for others, feminism is a radical term that conjures images of burning bras and unladylike behavior, a symbol of rebellion against traditional roles and stereotypes. Whichever view you take, I think that it is fair to say that feminism has had an effect on women and has changed our perception of what it means to be successful and fulfilled in today's world.

As I've grown older, one of my favorite things to do is talk with my par-

---

**Lorie Baker** was born on July 18, 1972 to her parents, Benson and Martha Needham in Memphis, TN. Lorie attended Florida College from 1990 to 1992, where she received a Liberal Arts degree. She met Rich Baker at Florida College and they were married in August of 1992. They spent the first ten years of their marriage in Ohio and then relocated to Bowling Green, KY in 2003. Once they settled in Bowling Green they began worshiping and working with the Eastside Church of Christ. One of the great blessings of living in Bowling Green is that they have been able to reconnect with friends that they met while at Florida College. In April of 2007, they were blessed with the adoption of their daughter Natalee. Lorie has enjoyed being a stay-at-home mom since they brought Natalee home from the hospital.

ents about how things were when they were kids. I love to hear the stories of family meals, how they walked to the one room schoolhouse, worked with the mules to plow the fields, and rode in the wagon on Sunday morning to go to church. As I listen to their stories, I often marvel how much has changed over the past seventy years. So many things have changed for the better: indoor plumbing, cleaner water, medical breakthroughs, cars, planes etc. Sadly, things have also changed for the worse: lack of family values, moral and spiritual decline, the breakup of the family, single parent homes or non-parenting parents, and God banished from our daily lives. Far be it from me to lay the root of these changes at the feet of feminism, but in many ways I think that the feminist movement in America is at odds with God's plan for women and the family.

Since becoming a parent last year, I have lost many hours of sleep wondering how on earth I am going to make sure that I teach my daughter that success is not defined by earthly values, but godly values. It is such a challenge today to raise a young woman who has the ambition to be a wife and mother. For the most part, the pattern set forth for young women today has more to do with being a successful businesswoman than being a godly woman. You hear stories about waiting lists and testing to get into the proper pre-school, advanced testing for academics as young as first and second grade, middle school and high school kids taking advanced classes to get a head start for college, and college students with double majors and academic plans for careers that will take years and years to complete. Please understand, I think that education is extremely important and have no problem with educating children. What I do have a problem with is that we are giving our children worldly educations, but not spiritual ones. We are training them to put their education and their careers before God. We are taking God's plan for women and their roles in the home and family and making them second class, changing such a noble and important job into something that is considered by the world to be a waste. I hope that by carefully considering what God's Word has to say about women and the role that He intended for us will help us to change our mindset and embrace the role that God intended for us.

### Feminism in America

In order to understand how feminism has affected women and their role in God's plan I think that it is important to understand some of the background of the movement. Feminist scholars have divided the feminist movement into three distinct waves.

> According to feminist.com, the First Wave of feminism is the time of the abolitionists and suffragettes. These women fought for the abolition of slavery and the right for women to vote. They also won women the right to own and inherit property, the right to divorce and to joint custody. The Second Wave came alive in the mid-1960s and its most obvious rallying point was an Equal Rights Amendment. These women also helped to legalize birth control pills, the right to have an abortion and equal pay. They also brought attention to sexual harassment and domestic violence. The Third Wave has come about mostly because young women who grew up in the Second Wave wanted a voice of their own. It is really meant to put the second wave along toward its goal of full-equality. While we have seen more women take on careers, responsibilities that have been labeled "masculine," hopefully, we will have more men take on things that have been labeled "feminine," this will lead us to a place of not having our qualities defined or limited by our gender (www.feminist.com/askamy/feminism/fem; accessed on December 8, 2008).

In her book *The Feminine Mystique*, Betty Freidan outlined the sense of dissatisfaction felt by many housewives. She contends that women have been spoon fed an idea, a belief that femininity has been mystified and manipulated. This distortion of what women should be as defined by society has really caused emotional problems, marital tension, and general unhappiness. This was a groundbreaking text in the 1960s. Alvin Toffler said that it was "the book that pulled the trigger on history." This type of text fueled women to believe that they could not find fulfillment in being a wife, keeping a home, and being a mother. This social ideology took root and turned into a poisonous plant that began working to systematically destroy our homes and families.

### Affirmation or Contradiction?

The most basic premise of feminism is that a woman should be allowed the right to choose. She should be able to choose what she does with her body, she should be able to choose whatever career she wants, and she should be able to choose to do whatever a man can do if she wants. What I find ironic is that feminists support this wholeheartedly unless a woman chooses to be a stay at home mom or put her family above her career. The recent presidential election exposed the flaws of the feminist movement more than any other event in our lifetime. We had Sarah Palin on the Presidential ticket, a woman as the second-in-command, a heartbeat away from the most powerful position in America and what happened? Feminists should have been sounding the rally cry, shouting Sarah Palin's virtues from the rooftops. Instead they set about to sully her reputation and discredit her accomplishments because of her conservative beliefs. How dare a woman stand up in front of America and refuse to have an abortion when she knows that her unborn child has Down's Syndrome? How dare a woman support her daughter's decision to go through with a teenage pregnancy rather than have an abortion? If the feminist movement were truly for the advancement of women and seeking equality for women, they would have been thrilled by the choice of Sarah Palin for Vice-President. On the contrary, the showed their true colors in support of the far left, liberal agenda that is prevalent in our nation's government. The feminist movement is no longer about equality for women; it is about abortion, lesbian rights, and same sex marriage. Again, this is as far away from God's plan as you can get.

### God's Plan for Women

So, what is God's plan for women? What specific roles or tasks has God outlined for women? You don't have to look very far in the Bible to see that God had a specific plan in mind when he created woman. In the book of Genesis He tells us that man needed a "helper comparable to him" (Gen. 2:18) and created woman to be that helper. It is telling that the word "helper" was used, not "servant," "slave," "subordinate," or "inferior being." God described woman as a "helper." *Webster's Dictionary* defines "helper" as, "a person that helps or gives assistance, support." This is where the feminist has it wrong, being a helper does not imply inferiority, and it describes functionality rather than worth. God intended for woman to be a vital part in man's life, essential to populating the earth, and someone to share in his daily life and responsibilities to God.

God clearly had a plan for women in the first century church. We are told in Paul's letter to the saints at Galatia, "There is neither Jew nor Greek, there is neither slave nor free, there is neither male nor female; for you are all one in Christ Jesus" (Gal. 3:28). In the book of Acts, when Peter was speaking to the household of Cornelius he said, "In truth I perceive that God is no respecter of persons; but in every nation he that feareth Him, and worketh righteousness, is acceptable to Him" (Acts 10:34-35, KJV). Paul also makes reference to Euodia and Syntyche saying that they "labored with me in the gospel" (Phil 4:3). David Thomley summed these thoughts very well in his class book, *Exalting Woman to Her Rightful Place*. He states,

> If we are to understand the biblical teaching on woman in Christ, it is essential that we grasp the ***difference*** between ***persons*** on the one hand, and their ***roles*** on the other hand! Husbands and wives, parents and children, masters and servants have ***equal dignity*** as creatures made in the image of

> God; yet they have ***different God-appointed roles!*** It is disturbing when Christians stumble over the woman's role in the church, suggesting that the woman is inferior, of less value than someone else. This suggests an attitude which carries over into every other relationship in the body of Christ (Thomley, 1989).

During the course of this study, we are going to delve into the Scriptures and outline the roles that God intended for women as she took on the mantle of being man's helper. Specifically, we will look at the role of women as wives, mothers, and keepers of the home. We will look at what the Bible tells us and refute the assertion of the feminist that the roles outlined for women in the Bible are archaic and old fashioned.

### Role 1: Wife

A few years ago, I was watching Oprah on television and she had a guest named Ayelet Waldman on her show. The title of the show was "A Mother's Controversial Confession." Mrs. Waldman had written an article that had really shaken things up. In her article she confessed that she loved her husband more than she loved her children. She went on to say that her children are not the center of her universe and thus, she and her husband have a very good relationship and a very happy marriage. She contended that in today's society, mothers tend to focus all of the energy, attention, and love on their children and their husbands get moved to the back burner. What struck me about this topic was that it had a very biblical premise. God outlined the marriage covenant shortly after woman was created, "Therefore a man shall leave his father and mother and be joined to his wife, and they shall become one flesh" (Gen. 2:24). Here we see that the marriage covenant had three distinct parts:

1. Leaving father and mother – a reference to the public ceremony or commitment
2. To be "joined" – suggesting affection and faithful commitment in a permanent relationship of growing love
3. To "become one flesh" – a physical union, which notes the deepest and most exclusive intimacy

This is a covenant relationship, not only with one's spouse, but with God. Furthermore, we are told by Jesus in the Matthew 19:6, "So then, they are no longer two, but one flesh. Therefore what God has joined together, let not man separate." This is a relationship that is ordained by God and should be treated as such. It is not disposable and should not be taken lightly.

That being said, what then are my responsibilities as a wife? Paul outlines them quite clearly for us, "admonish the young women to love their husbands, to love their children, to be discreet, chaste, homemakers, good, obedient to their own husbands, that the word of God may not be blasphemed" (Tit. 2:4-5). Some may scoff at the idea that young women are to be admonished to love their husbands; after all, you wouldn't get married to someone unless you loved him, right? I don't think that love in this context is the typical love that we think of, holding hands and thinking of someone all the time. This love is a respect and admiration for one's husband, not loving with feeling, but behaving in a way that is consistent with love.

The first aspect of this type of love is affection. It is essential in a marriage that you show one another affection. The apostle Paul told the Corinthians:

> Let the husband render to his wife the affection due to her and likewise also the wife to her husband. The wife does not have authority over her own body, but the husband does. And likewise the husband does not have authority over his own body, but the wife does. Do not deprive one another except with consent for a time, that you may give yourselves to fasting and prayer, and come together again so that Satan does not tempt you because of your lack of self-control (1 Cor. 7:3-5).

Here we are told that our bodies do not belong to us, they belong to our mate. Affection is a basic need of humankind and the expression of affection through sexual intimacy is the highest form of the communication of love.

The second aspect of this type of love is submission. This word alone will raise the hackles on any self-respecting feminist, but God's plan dictates that the woman is to be in submission to her husband. I admit this is an aspect of the marriage relationship that gave me a hard time when I was a younger woman. I thought that submission meant that I had no voice, that I had nothing to offer. As I grew older and became more knowledgeable in Christ, I came to understand that a wife's deference to her husband is a duty given by the Lord. Paul wrote in his letter to the Ephesians, "Wives, submit to your own husbands, as to the Lord. For the husband is head of the wife, as also Christ is head of the church; and He is the Savior of the body. Therefore just as the church is subject to Christ, so let the wives be to their own husbands in everything" (Eph. 5:22-24). Submission is not so much to her husband as it is to God and His plan for marriage. Being submissive does not mean that I have no voice; it means that I share my voice with my husband and then defer to him as the leader in our household. Being submissive does not mean that I have nothing to offer; it means that I offer my opinions and thoughts to my husband and then defer to him when he makes a decision. This concept is completely foreign to those in the world. In today's culture of selfishness, all that one can think about is doing things "my way." There is not a lot of thought given to being selfless and doing things God's way.

It must also be said that part of being submissive is being respectful. It is not uncommon to hear wives speak to their husbands in a way that is completely inappropriate. Unkindness, rudeness, and arrogance towards one's husband have no place in the marriage relationship and do not relate the proper attitude that a wife should have towards her husband. A passage of Scripture that is often quoted at weddings is 1 Corinthians 13. Sadly, in many instances it is never put into practice. Here is a reminder of what God says that love is:

> Though I speak with the tongues of men and of angels, but have not love, I have become the sounding brass or a clanging cymbal. And though I have the gift of prophecy, and understand all mysteries and all knowledge, and though I have all faith, so that I could remove mountains, but have not love, I am nothing. And though I bestow all my goods to feed the poor, and though I give my body to be burned, but have not love, it profits me nothing. Love suffers long and is kind; love does not envy; love does not parade itself, is not puffed up; does not behave rudely, does not seek its own, is not provoked, thinks no evil; does not rejoice in iniquity, but rejoices in the truth; bears all things, believes all things, hopes all things, endures all things. Love never fails (1 Cor. 13:1-8).

### Role 2: Mother

This role is still new to me. I've only been a mother for nineteen months, but I can tell you, it is the hardest job I've ever had. There are no 8-to-5 days in motherhood, no lunch breaks or coffee breaks, and you can forget having a sick day or a vacation day. All jokes aside, it is so rewarding to be a stay-at-home mom and get to see my child grow and develop right before my very eyes. Sadly, in our society, women have traded this glorious and fulfilling job to be career women, working out of the house in secular jobs for a paycheck. Let me clarify that I am not saying that women cannot work outside of the home, nor am I saying that it is sinful to leave your children with a day care provider. I understand that there are situations that make working outside of the home a necessity and depending on outside child care a necessity. What I am saying is that this is a decision that must be made with much prayer and thought. We need to start teaching our daughters at a very young age that it is acceptable to aspire to grow up to be a wife and a mother. We need to teach our sons that it is their job to grow up to be providers so that their wives can stay at home and raise their children. We need to go back to biblical principles and teach our children their roles according to God's plan and not the world's.

Let's take a moment to look at God's plan for women and see what His intentions are with regards to children. God's functional arrangement for the family has been laid out for us in the New Testament. Men are told to be providers for their family, "But if anyone does not provide for his own, and especially for those of his household, he has denied the faith and is worse than an unbeliever" (1 Tim. 5:8). Women are told, "Admonish the young women to love their husbands, love their children, to be discreet, chaste, homemakers, good obedient to their own husbands, that the word of God may not be blasphemed" (Tit. 2:4-5). We have already discussed our role as wives and our responsibility to love our husbands, let's now discuss our role as mothers and loving our children.

By the standards of the world, loving your children means giving them everything that their heart desires, making sure that they have food, clothing, and every electronic device available, and providing them with a good education before turning them out into the world to fend for themselves. I present to you that God's plan for raising children has a different theme all together. After the children of Israel had fled from Egypt and were wandering in the wilderness, God presented them with a list of commandments that must be followed. He gave them what he called the greatest commandment, "Hear O Israel: The Lord our God, the Lord is one! You shall love the Lord your God with all your heart, with all your soul, and with all your strength" (Deut. 6:4). What has always been interesting to me is that God did not stop there, he went on to tell the Israelites, "And these words which I command you today shall be in your heart. You shall teach them diligently to your children, and shall talk of them when you sit in your house, when you walk by the way, when you lie down, and when you rise up" (Deut. 6:6-7). These are my favorite verses in the Bible. They are my favorite because they teach us what our relationship to God must be, but they also let us know how important it is for us to teach this relationship to our children and to show it by being an example to our children in our homes. That being said, one of our greatest responsibilities in loving our children is to teach them to love God. In Proverbs we are told, "Train up a child in the way he should go, and when he is old he will not depart from it" (Prov. 22:6). This is not absolute as children are still free moral agents, but the premise is that, if you give a child a good foundation, he will have a better chance at becoming a good and moral person than if you don't. In order to provide this good foundation, we must give our children a good example to follow. As mothers we must lead our children by example. In the Sermon on the Mount, Jesus said, "Blessed are those who hunger and thirst for righteousness, for they shall be filled" (Matt. 5:6). It is our responsibility to teach our children to hunger and thirst for God. We must take an active role in teaching our children on a daily basis and not just leave it up to their Sunday school teachers. It is our responsibility as mothers to read Bible stories, talk about moral character, teach right from wrong, and instill in our children a love for God above all else.

Another aspect of loving our children is providing discipline. There is nothing more disturbing to me than to be out somewhere and see children running around wildly, blatantly disobeying their parents, and then seeing parents ignore the situation completely or throwing up their hands in disgust. I can tell you one thing that I have definitely learned in my nineteen months as a parent, my daughter has a strong will. My will is stronger and more often than not, I win in any contest of wills. I win because I am the adult and she is the child. It hasn't always been an easy road, but little by little she is coming to understand that what Mommy or Daddy says is the way to go, because if she just goes ahead and does what she wants there are not-so-good consequences. I've learned first hand that discipline is not easy. It's not easy always to be consistent, it's not easy to know that what you are about to do is going to make your little one cry, and it's not always easy to sacrifice the things that you want to do because your child's behavior warrants discipline. Once again, we must come back to God's plan for our children and rely on His wisdom in dealing with situations that involve discipline. Solomon gives us several insights about discipline in the book of Proverbs: "The rod and rebuke give wisdom, but a child left to himself brings shame to his mother" (Prov. 29:15). "Correct your son and he will give you rest; yes, he will give delight to your soul" (Prov. 29:17). "He who spares his rod hates his son, but he who loves him disciplines him promptly" (Prov. 13:24). The ultimate outcome of parental discipline is to teach children to be self-controlled, to be independent decision makers and eventually to live a lifestyle where he is under God's control and follows God's laws. The Hebrews writer tells us about how God disciplines His children,

> Furthermore, we have had human fathers who corrected us, and we paid

> them respect. Shall we not much more readily be in subjection to the Father of spirits and live? For they indeed for a few days chastened us as seemed best to them, but He for our profit, that we may be partakers of His holiness. Now no chastening seems to be joyful for the present, but painful; nevertheless, afterward it yields the peaceable fruit of righteousness to those who have been trained by it (Heb. 12:9-11).

While the world may view discipline as barbaric and unjust, we are told in the pages of the Bible that it is necessary.

Finally, in fulfilling our roles as mothers, we must pray for our children. I remember when my husband and I were waiting to adopt our daughter I prayed constantly that things would go well. I prayed that our birth mother wouldn't change her mind, I prayed that the baby would be healthy, and I prayed that we were ready to be parents, I prayed that God would help me to be a good mother, I prayed that we would always look to Him for guidance as our daughter grew. Since I was a first-time mother, I felt that I lacked wisdom. James tells us, "If any of you lacks wisdom, let him ask of God, who gives to all liberally and without reproach, and it will be given to him" (James 1:5). In her book, *That They May Train the Young Women*, Ruth Thompson says, "I think the rearing of children requires the greatest amount of wisdom of any responsibility we face in life. Pray everyday about it. Ask God to continually guide you through life to the end that your child will be properly reared by you" (Thompson, 1980). We can also see this example from Jesus. He did not have physical children, but spiritual children in His disciples. In John we see Jesus' prayer for His children, "I have given them Your word; and the world has hated them because they are not of the world, just as I am not of the world. I do not pray that You should take them out of the world, but that You should keep them from the evil one" (John 17:14-15). Here again we see an area that is foreign to the world, asking God for help.

In today's culture parents often look to whatever child psychologist is popular and making the talk show circuit for guidance. These scholars peddle their theories about child rearing and many Americans take their advice, only to find out later that it does not work. One of the reasons that we have a generation of undisciplined children running amok is because someone, somewhere decided that it was cruel to spank children. As Christians, we should always look to God for our advice, especially when it comes to our responsibilities as parents. On her website, *Mothering from the Heart*, Audrey Broggi wrote a list of things that we should pray for our children:

1. That they will know Christ early in life. 2 Timothy 3:15
2. That they will hate sin. Psalm 97:10
3. That they will be caught when guilty. Psalm 119:71
4. That they will be protected from the evil one in each area of their lives; spiritual, emotions, physical. John 17:15
5. That they have a responsible attitude in all their personal relationships. Daniel 6:3
6. That they will respect those in authority over them. Romans 13:1
7. That they will desire the right kind of friends and be protected from the wrong friends. Proverbs 1:10-11
8. That they will be kept from the wrong mate and saved for the right one. 2 Corinthians 6:14-17
9. That they, as well as those they marry, will be kept pure. 1 Corinthians 6:18-20
10. That they will learn to totally submit to God and actively resist Satan in all circumstances. James 4:7
11. That they will be single-hearted, willing to be sold out to Jesus Christ. Romans 12:1-2
12. That they will be hedged in so they cannot find their way to wrong people or wrong places and that the wrong people cannot find their way to them. Hosea 2:6

She also states, "You can see that there are 12; one for each month. Within a year, you will have consistently prayed this entire list" (www.mfth.org, accessed 12/15/2008).

It bears mentioning that the role of the father in the home is just as important as the role of the mother. In the book of Ephesians Paul writes, "And you, fathers, do not provoke your children to wrath, but bring them up in the training and admonition of the Lord" (Eph. 6:4). He specifically gives fathers the responsibility of "bringing them up." In some cases women today have decided that they don't even need husbands to have children, instead they visit a fertility clinic so that they can have their children via donor conception. This is another breakdown of God's plan for families as it completely takes the father out of the picture. A father must play an active role in the education and training of his children in order to be in accordance with God's will. All you have to do is turn on the television and watch any sitcom to see that the role of man in the family has been minimized in today's culture. It doesn't seem to matter what show you are watching they all follow the same plot lines. Husbands and fathers are the jokes of the show, their wives mock them, their children blatantly disobey and disrespect them; even the dog ignores them! Most men are shown in as bad a light as possible; they are depicted as lazy, egotistical, self-absorbed men who would rather do anything in the world than spend quality time with their families. It is a sad commentary on our times that there are homes out in the world that mimic these types of television shows, but there are. The only way that we can keep it from happening in our Christian homes is to follow the instructions that God has provided for us. Children are a wonderful blessing from God and they must be treated as such. The Psalmist tells us, "Behold, children are a heritage from the Lord, the fruit of the womb is a reward. Like arrows in the hand of a warrior, so are the children of one's youth. Happy is the man that has a quiver full of them" (Psa. 127:3-5). It is up to fathers and mothers to treat their children as if they are blessing from the Lord and teach them to love the Lord above all else, if we do this, we can keep worldly influences at bay and preserve our families.

### Role 3: Keeper of the Home

You'll remember from earlier in our text that the second wave of the feminist movement was born from housewives who felt like there had to be something better out there for them than keeping a home. The magazines and literature of the late 1950s and 1960s were full of articles that expounded on the sense of dissatisfaction plaguing housewives. This only fed the notion that being a housewife was somehow demeaning. I've been in a room of women and overhead conversations about what each one does. Many times there will be someone who says, "I'm a homemaker," this is usually followed by a tense silence and finally the question, "What do you do all day?" I'm here to tell you, there is always something to do, especially if you have children at home, but there is still plenty to occupy you if you don't. I never stayed at home before we adopted our daughter, but I knew several women who did and I was always a little envious of their clean house, freshly baked goods, and empty laundry baskets. These women devoted themselves not only to making a home, but visiting the sick and caring for the needy. God gives us an example of a virtuous woman in Proverbs. The acrostic poem in Proverbs 31:10-31 describes what kind of woman every man should look for and what kind of wife every woman should want to be. She ran her household efficiently and effectively, "She also rises while it is yet night, and provides food for her household" (Prov. 31:15) while making sure that her husband was honored, "The heart of her husband safely trusts her; so he will have no lack of gain. She does him good and not evil all the days of her life" (Prov. 31: 11-12). Her children were loved. "Her children rise up and call her blessed; her husband also, and he praises her" (Prov. 31:28). Her attributes are laid out for all to see and we should try to live up to her example.

One other lesson that we can take from the virtuous woman is the foundation that she supplied for her husband and children. Her home was their safe haven, their rock. It reminds me of the parable of the wise man that was recorded for us in the book of Matthew. The wise man built his house upon the rock and it stood firm when the rains and floods came. For our purposes, a wise woman, keeper of her home, builds the foundation of that home on The Rock, our Lord and Savior, Jesus Christ. She does this by abiding in His word and fulfilling the duties that He requires of her. If she does this, her home will withstand the floods of the world and will stand firm in the face of evil.

## Conclusion

Throughout this study, we have learned about the feminist movement in America and seen the effects that this movement has had on women in the church today. The family as outlined by God has decayed in American culture over the last fifty years and will undoubtedly continue to crumble if we as Christians don't uphold it. We may not be able to change what the nation as a whole chooses to do and what laws are enacted that desecrate the family unit, but as women, we can influence what is taught, said, and exemplified in our own homes. David Thomley stated in his workbook, "The world will give standing ovations and plenty of positive reinforcement to the woman who succeeds out in the world" (Thomley, 1989). Older women in Christ also have a role (Tit. 2) in influencing other family units by teaching the younger wives. Thomley went on to say,

> Somebody needs to be telling the young wives and mothers that their success before God will be measured by their homes – the relationship they sustain there as wives and mothers, and the training of children which goes on there! Young Christian women need their self-esteem boosted and reinforced on occasion, and the world is not going to provide it! It is right and honorable for a woman to choose to devote herself fully to the

> tasks of being a wife, mother and homemaker. Christians, of all people, ought to be shouting the message.

After all, Paul tells us in Romans, "Do not be conformed to this world, but be transformed by the renewing of your mind, that you may prove what is that good and acceptable and perfect will of God" (Rom. 12:2). This should be the Christian woman's war cry as she makes her way in the feminist world, we should stand up and be counted for what we are, women who are willing to serve God and follow His will in all that we do.

### Bibliography

David Thomley, *Exalting Woman To Her Rightful Place.* Bowling Green: Eastside Church of Christ, 1989.

Ruth Thompson, *That They May Train the Young Women.* La Mesa: B & D Enterprises, 1980.

All Scripture quotations are cited from the New King James Version.

# "Be of the Same Mind in the Lord"

**Lydia H. Casey**

Throughout our lives as Christians, we may find ourselves joining different congregations as, for example, we move from one state to another. Thinking back on where you've been, does one group of Christians stand out in your mind as having been particularly strong, active, and faithful? Do you remember your time with that congregation as an enjoyable and productive period?

On the other hand, have there been times when it's been a challenge to be part of a congregation? Have there been conflicts, disagreements, and perhaps incorrect attitudes displayed by one Christian toward another?

Congregations can be joyful bands of committed Christians who, as true friends, genuinely love each other. Unfortunately, a congregation can also be a collection of cliques, with little being accomplished toward the collective goals of serving God and winning souls with the gospel.

On the night of His betrayal, Jesus told His apostles that they would be known as His followers because of the love that was apparent among them (John 13:35). Can gossip, impolite or argumentative speech, or an unfriendly attitude by one group toward another group within the congregation possibly be a part of this picture of "love" that Christ wants? God's word informs us otherwise, in many places (e.g., Rom. 12). In fact, we know that these

---

**Lydia Casey** lives in Salem, Indiana, with her husband, Evan, an evangelist. Before her marriage in 1997, she worked in radio broadcasting and teaching, both in the U.S. and abroad. She graduated from Western Kentucky University with a B.A. in English and Allied Language Arts. Evan and Lydia lived in Budapest, Hungary, for two years (1999-2001) while he was preaching and teaching the gospel there. They have three daughters, Rachel, Julia, and Carolyn.

wrong actions and ways of thinking are destructive to the work of the church and have an undeniably dissuasive effect on young people who may be considering becoming Christians.

Paul commanded the Ephesian saints, "Let all bitterness, wrath, anger, clamor, and evil speaking be put away from you, with all malice. And be kind to one another, tenderhearted, forgiving one another, even as God in Christ forgave you" (4:31-32). An inspired apostle, Paul knew that keeping a spirit of humble, loving unity within a congregation was essential for the group to function as it should. Of course, we all make mistakes and at times fail miserably in this regard, but we must not stop "endeavoring to keep the unity of the Spirit in the bond of peace," as Paul instructed the Ephesians (4:1-3). By doing so, we give ourselves the best chance of making it to heaven and bringing others – perhaps our own children – there with us.

### "Forgive, and You Will Be Forgiven"

Elementary school teachers warn their students not to pass out birthday party invitations at school, so as not to hurt the feelings of a child who has not been included. This is a valuable life lesson for school-aged children to learn, and I hope that it stays with them throughout their lives. Kindness and thoughtfulness should be second nature to us as Christian women, but sometimes they aren't – perhaps not out of a deliberate desire to wound another person, but only because we don't stop and think about what the other person might be thinking or feeling. We must *resolve* to be kind and thoughtful toward each other, not just be that way when it's convenient or when we happen to think of it as we rush headlong through our days (Rom. 12:10).

When we do hurt each other, either by design or by neglect, our response to the situation says a lot about how seriously we take our responsibilities as Christians. If I have caused a problem, I need to fix it as quickly and painlessly as possible. To do less is to invite a buildup of resentment in the heart of the person I hurt, and that certainly will not promote a peaceful, unified environment within the church.

If I just shrug off the problem lightly, thinking, "Oh, she'll get over it eventually" or "She's just too sensitive," how helpful is that? How can we "dwell together in unity" with unpleasant, unresolved issues coming between us (Ps. 133:1)? Or, not wishing to accept full responsibility, I might decide that the other person had a hand in the situation, and that *she* should apologize, also. But if I waited until the other person made the first move, I would be violating numerous passages that teach us to extend love, generosity, and kindness, even if they are not offered to me (Matt. 5:38-41).

What are my responsibilities as a Christian if I am the one who has been hurt? First, I should control my irritation and not spread the news of my injured feelings around to anyone who'll listen (Jas. 1:19). In this situation, I have a choice to make in what to do next. I can choose to calm down and remember that sometimes we all slip up and do things without regard for the other person's feelings, without meaning to hurt each other. Even if I have not been asked to, I can decide to forgive that person and not harbor a grudge against her (Matt. 18:21-22; Luke 6:37; Col. 3:12-13). I can conquer the temptation to fight it out to the bitter end while forever after harboring resentment toward the one who wronged me.

However, if the matter is sufficiently important to address with the person who has done me harm, the Scriptures clearly outline the procedure I must follow (Matt.18:15-17). This kind of conversation can be tricky: both sides need to come together in a spirit of love and meekness, not with spears at the ready and combat boots on. I can't blast away in an accusing tone at someone and expect a good result. I need to approach cautiously and maturely, making sure there hasn't simply been a misunderstanding. We must not let our egos get in the way of our friendships and undermine the spiritual unity that we sisters in Christ should be upholding (Prov. 17:17).

### "Be Swift to Hear, Slow to Speak"

Much of what goes wrong within a congregation can be attributed to the sins of the tongue. An obvious but sometimes overlooked means of avoiding saying something wrong is to stop and think before we speak. James tells us to "be swift to hear, slow to speak, slow to wrath" (1:19). Before we blurt out the latest news about someone, give an opinion about something, or just vent about what's bothering us, we might benefit by asking ourselves some questions. Is this a productive thing that I'm about to say? Is it going to help the situation, or will it make it worse?

Even if my comments are crying out to be made and I might have every right to be angry, I must consider the well-being of everyone concerned, especially if those involved are other Christians (Gal. 6:10; Rom. 12:18-19). Verbally ambushing a sister in Christ in front of others or otherwise embarrassing her is not in keeping with passages like Romans 12:10, which exhorts us to be "kindly affectionate to one another with brotherly love."

Another question we might ask ourselves before speaking is whether or not what we want to say is absolutely true. Even if a statement *is* true, it can still be gossip, and we surely want to stay away from committing that sin. Is the moment of questionable pleasure in sharing a piece of gossip worth the price I would pay for all eternity (Matt. 12:36-37)?

Even if we don't go through the whole process of thinking through these types of questions before going ahead with something we wanted to say, maybe the fact that we just stopped to *ask* ourselves those questions will buy us some time. Maybe we just need a few minutes sometimes to allow that heated moment to pass, to let tempers cool, to let the topic of conversation be changed, and to be distracted from a difficult subject. This practice of stopping to think before we speak can buy us some valuable time during which we can extinguish that little fire that's starting to burn within and realize that we don't need to say anything, after all.

However, when we do blunder and say something we shouldn't have, is the best tactic to follow the maxim, "Least said, soonest mended"? Perhaps not. If I have created a wrong impression in someone's mind or been guilty of slander or idle gossip, is it necessary for me to go to the one(s) who heard me and set the record straight? Considering the wealth of passages in the Bible dealing with the subject of honesty (e.g., Prov. 6:16-17; Col. 3:9), I believe the sincere Christian's answer to that question is "yes." I've got to swallow a humility pill, apologize, and clear things up. The woman who does this consistently can be an example to those around her and set the proper spiritual tone for the behavior of all the women within a group. We need to be ready and willing to say those underused, all-important words, "I made a mistake. I'm sorry."

Just imagine what it would be like if the women of an entire congregation were careful in how they spoke to each other, and, if by chance a problem developed, it was cleared up immediately, with humble and loving attitudes displayed by all. As mentioned earlier, this – *and only this* – is the atmosphere Christ envisioned for His disciples (John 13:34-35). In Proverbs 31, we are given the great example of the worthy woman, who "opens her mouth with wisdom, and on her tongue is the law of kindness" (v. 26).

Instead of harsh criticism or unkind gossip, let's look for ways to extend compassion and give loving encouragement to one another. For example, consider the plight of young mothers, who are often self-conscious about their parenting skills or their children's behavior. A supportive word from an older woman who has found something to admire in that young woman's efforts will go a long way toward making her feel better. Similarly, a young woman can make an older woman's day if she will compliment her on the way she led a class or extended hospitality. I have seen a woman's face light up when she is given an unexpected pat on the back. It's so easy to be generous with praise and appreciation if we will just take the time to do it.

### "The Genuine Faith That Is in You"

For a moment, put yourself in the place of a ten-year-old son or daughter of Christians. You have been a student in Bible classes for years and are at the time of life when some consider becoming a Christian. But there's a problem: the congregation to which your parents belong is constantly embroiled in controversies of one kind or another. There has been harsh, rude speech, and people have been gossiping about each other. Feelings have been wounded, yet no forgiveness has been asked for or given. Kindness, gentleness, and humility have all been in short supply. You are at the point at which you aren't sure the grownups in your congregation even *like* each other.

Sometimes when we adults are in the middle of a difficult situation with other Christians, we are so upset that we can't see past the noses on our faces. We might not be able to see how deeply our differences with each other are affecting our children. We may not understand that our children are seeing, hearing, and perceiving much more than we realize. They may not show by their words or behavior that they are picking up on our messages, but we are sending them, just the same. What are the messages that we are sending our children about Christianity and the New Testament church?

While there are no worldwide church of Christ records that give statistics on members' children who never obeyed the gospel or who have become unfaithful, several congregations have kept records on the young people within their own groups who have grown up. Some congregations report that they have lost more than half of their young people to the world.

But it doesn't have to be this way. Just as Lois and Eunice gave young Timothy a firm foundation in "genuine faith" (2 Tim. 1:5), we women can have a powerful, uplifting influence on our children. Grandmothers and mothers can teach and correct their grandchildren and children. Aunts and older cousins can be good examples in faith and action. Before I married and had my own children, I did my best to be a good influence on the Bible class students I was entrusted with teaching. The bottom line is that all of the adults within a congregation need to acknowledge the very real impact that their words and behavior have – for better or for worse – on the young of that number. We are *all* teachers, whether we realize it or not.

### "Remove the Plank from Your Own Eye"

We who are parents must never forget that, as they grow, our children are watching us all the time. They are learning from us how to speak and act. Do we want our sons and daughters to observe in us signs of spiritual weakness, superficiality, or pretense? Or do we want to show our children true commitment to the church and genuine love for God? We should strive to live the life of a Christian that we want our children to live. Some young people who choose not to become Christians or who become unfaithful after conversion cite the hypocrisy they have observed among church members as a spiritual turn-off. Don't let it be you to whom they're referring!

Do we gossip about, criticize, or belittle other Christians in the car on the way home from worship services or do we speak kindly and lovingly, even when we're concerned or disturbed about something? Our children are listening. Do we participate enthusiastically when we worship? Or do we sing halfheartedly, not bothering to open our Bibles during the sermon? Our children are watching us carefully. Very likely, they will grow up imitating our model of Christianity. How Christlike will they be?

When our sons and daughters notice inconsistencies or failings among some Christians, we can remind them that "all have sinned and fall short of the glory of God" (Rom. 3:23). A huge favor we can do for our children is to teach them to be patient with another's faults and frailties and to realize with humility the extent of their own (Matt. 7:4-5; Luke 6:42). Cultivating the development of "longsuffering" (Eph. 4:2) will pay dividends in future years, when the young people growing up now become the men and women of the church.

### "Be of the Same Mind in the Lord"

Congregations exist all over the world. Whatever their size and wherever they are, they will all confront the same issues from time to time. It is *how* those issues are handled that, in part, determines to what degree the congregation may be affected by them. When we face differences that stem from our personalities and preferences, our God-given watchword ought to be "humility" (1 Pet. 5:5; Rom. 12:3, 16).

We cannot control what others may do that is wrong, but we always have a choice as to how we respond. We can react angrily and cause an even greater problem by spitting out curt words, or we can exercise patience and forbearance, taking the time to find a solution together. While our tongues can be a monstrous hindrance to reconciliation, they can also be a source of assistance in the process of resolving problems.

Which way is pleasing to God? Which scenario is more likely to cause impressionable young people to admire the sincerity of mature, loving Christians and perhaps consider becoming Christians themselves?

Certainly, there are many factors that influence a young person's decision of whether or not to be baptized, and we are given no guarantee that our children will follow our lead in joining the church. We can't afford to assume that the youth in our congregation will obey the gospel right on cue. However, as in every situation in life, God has offered us help and hope through the Scriptures, which teach that each one of us is obligated to try hard to preserve the "bond of peace" within the congregation (Eph. 4:1-3; Rom. 12:18). Common sense tells us that loving cooperation, rather than ill-tempered bickering, will encourage interest and dedication in the hearts of the young people among us. In this way, we as Christians – whether we have children or not – are all responsible for the growth and future well-being of the Lord's body.

Toward the close of his letter to the church at Philippi, Paul earnestly addresses two women specifically: "I implore Euodia and I implore Syntyche to be of the same mind in the Lord" (4:2). Presumably, the pair were having a disagreement that was of sufficient severity that it came to the attention of Paul, imprisoned far away in Rome. Isn't that sad? We don't know what the nature of their problem was; all we know is that these women went down in history as two people who caused discord within the Philippian church. And isn't that the way it often is – we disagree, we fuss, we fall apart – and in the end, we sometimes can't remember exactly what caused the friction to begin with?

As the psalmist David wrote so eloquently, "How good and how pleasant it is for brethren to dwell together in unity" (133:1)!